CURRICULUM PRACTICE: SOME SOCIOLOGICAL CASE STUDIES

Canavy

CURRICULUM PRACTICE: SOME SOCIOLOGICAL CASE STUDIES

*Martyn Hammersley &
Andy Hargreaves*

 **The Falmer Press**

A member of the Taylor and Francis Group
London and New York

© This selection and editorial matter copyright M. HAMMERSLEY and
A. HARGREAVES 1983.
All rights reserved. No part of this publication may be reproduced, stored in a retrieval system, or transmitted in any form or by any means, electronic, mechanical, photocopying, recording or otherwise, without permission in writing from the Publisher.

First published 1983

ISBN   limp   0 905273 49 4
       cased 0 905273 50 8

Typeset by
Imago/Graphicraft Typesetters Limited, Hong Kong

Jacket design by Leonard Williams

Printed by Taylor and Francis (Printers) Ltd
Basingstoke, England
for
The Falmer Press
Falmer House
Barcombe
Lewes, Sussex
BN8 5DL

Contents

Introduction ... 1

Section 1. School Subjects

1. Preparing to Write in Further Education
   Douglas and Dorothy Barnes ... 17

2. English: A Curriculum for Personal Development?
   Caroline St. John-Brooks ... 37

3. A Subject of Privilege: English and the School Curriculum 1906–35
   Stephen J. Ball ... 61

4. Defining and Defending the Subject: Geography versus Environmental Studies
   Ivor Goodson ... 89

5. One Spell of Ten Minutes or Five Spells of Two ... ? Teacher-Pupil Encounters in Art and Design Education
   Les Tickle ... 107

6. The Teaching of Art and the Art of Teaching: Towards an Alternative View of Aesthetic Learning
   David H. Hargreaves ... 127

Section 2. Gender and the Curriculum

7. Gender and Curriculum Choice: A Case Study
   Teresa Grafton, Henry Miller, Lesley Smith, Martin Vegoda and Richard Whitfield ... 151

8. Gender and the Sciences: Pupil's Gender-Based Conceptions of School Subjects
   Lynda Measor ... 171

Section 3. Examinations, Accountability and Assessment

9. The Hidden Curriculum of Examinations
   Glenn Turner ... 195

10. Teachers' School-Based Experiences of Examining
    John Scarth ... 207

Contents

11 A Question of Content and Control: Recent Conflicts over the
    Nature of School Examinations at 16+
    Richard Bowe and Geoff Whitty   229

12 Assessment Constraints on Curriculum Practice: A Comparative
    Study
    Patricia Broadfoot   251

Contributors   271
Index   273

Introduction

There is a point about education and schooling that is so glaringly obvious that it hardly seems worth mentioning. The point is this: in order to understand any system or pattern of education it is important to know just *what* is taught within that system; to know exactly what *kinds* of knowledge are deemed to be valid, important and worthwhile. Self-evident as this statement may seem, we do, as Williams (1961, p. 145) points out, nonetheless have a tendency to

> speak sometimes as if education were a fixed abstraction, a settled body of teaching and learning, and as if the only problem it presents to us is that of distribution: this amount, for this period of time, to this or that group.

Indeed, until the last decade or so, such problems of distribution and availability, of who gets an education and in what kind of institution, were the ones that dominated educational debate and research, with questions about the *content* of education receiving very little attention. Moreover, even on those occasions when questions *were* asked about the school curriculum, they did not usually address the prestigious curriculum of the 'academic' minority. That such a curriculum offered a passport to success was self-evident: its availability, not its validity, was the point at issue.

All this began to change in the mid-1960s, however. Various attempts were made to restructure school subjects to bring them into line with university practices – notably the Nuffield Science Project and the 'new maths'. In addition, comprehensivization of the secondary school system raised important questions about what was to be, and indeed what could be, taught to whom, and for what purposes. Comprehensive school teachers had to face the problem of what to offer the large numbers of potentially disaffected pupils who lay outside the net of examinations, a problem later exacerbated by the raising of the school leaving age.

One of the solutions adopted was to extend the number of pupils entered for examinations, in part by making use of the Mode 3 regulations offered by CSE and some GCE Boards. Another was to replace streaming and banding by mixed ability grouping (Ball, 1981). However, these adjustments created new problems of their own: often teachers had to devise materials which not only motivated the 'less able' and staved off their disaffection, but which did this *in the very same classes* where 'high ability' academically inclined and university aspiring pupils were also being taught. In a comprehensive system the merits of the grammar school curriculum could no longer be assumed, for reasons of professional survival if nothing else. The curriculum as a whole had to be subjected to the most serious re-examination.

Over the course of the 1960s and 1970s the Schools Council played a key role in this process of curriculum re-evaluation. It mounted a large number of curriculum development projects covering a wide range of subject areas, and also made a number of ambitious attempts to integrate previously distinct subjects, the Humanities Curriculum Project and the Keele Integrated Studies Project being perhaps the best known examples. While their direct influence was limited, these projects served to increase further the pressure on teachers for curriculum change. Teachers in many schools felt the pressure for curriculum change from this direction too.

In the 1960s and 1970s, then, the curriculum became a central issue for teachers where before its nature, particularly at secondary level, had been largely taken for granted. Moreover, towards the end of the period, the curriculum was placed firmly on the agenda of public educational debate; a shift first marked by the appearance of the ominously titled *Black Papers* (Cox and Dyson, 1969, 1970a, 1970b; Cox and Boyson, 1975). These challenged much that had previously been taken as given. The authors of the *Black Papers* claimed that, as a result of rampant egalitarianism and naive progressivism, standards were declining and schools were failing to serve society, and in particular the needs of industry. While initially such views seemed to be cries in the wilderness, by the mid-1970s many of them were beginning to form the basis of a new consensus in what came to be known as the Great Debate (Callaghan, 1976; for a commentary see CCCS, 1981).

From this point on, the small chink that the Great Debate had opened in the wall surrounding the 'secret garden' of the curriculum was rapidly widened into a yawning gap through which policy-makers at the highest levels entered with little hesitation, armed with their plans for remodelling the educational landscape. From both DES and HMI, a string of documents has appeared in recent years questioning some of the central assumptions on which the secondary school curriculum is currently based (DES, 1979, 1980 and 1981). Less dramatically, but no less significantly, LEAs have been encouraged to undertake large-scale reviews of the curricula in their schools. In the field of assessment, too, there has been a flurry of proposals for changing the pattern of examining at 16+, as well as the development of procedures for assessing pupil performance in a more regular and routine manner (in particular, the work of the Assessment of Performance Unit.) More recently, the Schools Council has been abolished and a new Examinations Council set up whose members will be nominated by central government. Such moves in the direction of centralized control of the school curriculum have added a new dimension to the debate about what should be taught in schools and why.

With the emergence of curriculum as a practical and public issue, 'curriculum studies' began to develop as a new area of specialization within institutes, departments and faculties of education. Simultaneously, curriculum theory and methodology became growth areas in educational publishing. The large North American literature on curriculum design and evaluation was quickly absorbed and applied by British curriculum theorists. Later, indigenous approaches to curriculum studies developed, such as Hirst's (1975) attempt to identify basic forms of knowledge, Stenhouse's action research approach to curriculum change (Stenhouse, 1980) and Lawton's work on the 'politics of the school curriculum' (Lawton, 1980). Methodological issues also attracted attention in the context of attempts to evaluate the effectiveness of curriculum projects. Here, too, there was a gradual shift away from the positivistic approach characteristic of North American work to the use of qualitative case-study methods such as 'illuminative evaluation' (Hamilton *et al.*, 1978). More recently, with the progressive move away from national curriculum projects towards school-based and school-focused curriculum innovation (for a commentary see Hargreaves, 1982b) the concept of 'teachers as researchers' has become central to discussions about curriculum innovation and school self-evaluation (Nixon, 1981). The Ford Teaching Project and SAFARI have been particularly influential here.

But despite all these important changes and developments, the contribution of empirical research to curriculum studies has been surprisingly small, with a primary emphasis on to the evaluation of curriculum projects. There has been much speculation about the nature of what is taught in schools on a day-to-day basis, away from the glare of curriculum evaluation, and about its effects on pupils. However, very little systematic empirical research on this has been carried out. One might have expected such research to be taken up by sociologists of education. But for most of the 1960s, with one or two exceptions (Bernstein, 1975; Musgrove, 1968), they took little interest in the curriculum, continuing to be concerned primarily with issues of access and performance. It was not until the end of the decade that the curriculum began to attract the attention it deserved amongst sociologists.

The 'New Sociology of Education'

This shift in focus was symbolized by the publication in 1971 of *Knowledge and Control: New Directions for the Sociology of Education*, edited by Michael F.D. Young (Young, 1971). *Knowledge and Control* captured the imagination of many people by directing attention to aspects of education, and especially the curriculum, which had previously been neglected. Equally important, it broadened the focus of the sociology of education to include what went on in classrooms. This made the subject especially attractive to teachers and to teacher trainers. For, despite the recommendation of the Newsom Report in 1963 that sociology of education should be made a part of all courses of teacher training so as to help intending teachers understand the plight and deprivations of less able children, that discipline had had disappointingly little to say about the things which mattered most to teachers: pedagogy and curriculum. This deficiency, so it seemed, could now be set right.

Introduction

As well as offering a professionally relevant application of sociological perspectives to teaching, the new sociology of education, as the new directions proposed by the authors of *Knowledge and Control* came to be called (Gorbutt, 1972; Karabel and Halsey, 1977), also promised a more practical and realistic appraisal of the school curriculum than was available in curriculum studies. It gave a keen sense of the 'is' rather than the 'oughts' of curriculum practice – warts and all! This stood in sharp contrast to the kind of curriculum theories then in vogue, theories which were largely speculative and prescriptive in character, often far removed from the problems which teachers encountered daily within their own classrooms. Compared with the philosophical arguments of writers such as Phenix (1964) and Hirst (1975) which asserted the independent existence of definite 'areas of knowledge' or 'realms of meaning' irrespective of how the weak or the powerful defined them, or with the 'behavioural objectives' school with its elaborate taxonomies of curricular possibilities (Bloom *et al.*, 1956) and its appeal to cool-headed rational planning (Tyler, 1971), the new sociology of education seemed a little more in touch with the realities and the unavoidable daily 'messiness' of teaching.

However, the new sociology of education appealed not only to hard-nosed practicality, but also to the sentiments of idealism and radicalism which were widespread amongst young teachers at the time. These sentiments were fuelled by the general cultural radicalism of the late 1960s among university students, with its emphasis on the reassessment and transformation of personal and interpersonal experience. This attitude was enhanced by the exciting rapidity of change within education itself as comprehensive schools began to establish new curricula and as more and more curriculum projects were set up. Furthermore, the brand of radicalism contained in the new sociology of education was particularly attractive to classroom teachers. It did not ask them to become revolutionary Marxists, to engage in class struggle and political action and transform the capitalist system. Rather, it suggested to teachers that since the conceptions of worthwhile knowledge they held and the categories they used to distinguish academic from non-academic, bright from dull, able from stupid were, in Young's (1971, pp. 2–3) words, not absolutes but 'socially constructed', then teachers could presumably choose to *redefine* what counted as worthwhile knowledge and avoid labelling working-class pupils as thick or dull. Without ever having to join a union or participate in staffroom politics, new teachers could, so it seemed, be world-changers within the protected confines of their own separate classrooms. They could have a central role in the business of educational and social change while retaining their professional autonomy: their right to teach as they wished in the security of their own classrooms free from political and other kinds of interference. This kind of radicalism, cultural rather than political in character, left the insulated classroom, and not the staffroom, the community or the union branch, reassuringly at the centre of the teacher's job.

In addition to this individualistic strain in the 'new sociology of education', which credited teachers with great power to define and redefine classroom realities as they wished, there was an equally strong social theme too. Here the content and process of schooling was seen to be inextricably connected to structures of power and control in the wider society. The curriculum, Basil Bernstein and Pierre Bourdieu argued in their contributions to *Knowledge and Control* (Young, 1971), reflected and was determined by the dominant structures of power and control in society which it in turn helped to reproduce. Within the English education system, Bernstein argued, much of this process was achieved through a curriculum whose contents were strongly separated from one another – a subject specialist curriculum in which the inner mysteries and uncertainties of the subject were only revealed to those whose subject loyalty had already been secured (usually at the university stage), and which left the unsuccessful with a 'conservative' sense of the naturalness of this curriculum and of their own failure. School subjects, that is, were regarded as being not just intellectual but also social systems. The new sociology of education asked us to view

> subjects both within the school and in the nation at large as social systems sustained by communication networks, material endowments and ideologies. Within school and within the wider society subjects are communities of people, communicating and collaborating with one another, defining and defending their boundaries, demanding allegiances from their members and conferring a sense of identity upon them. They are bureaucracies, hierarchically organized, determining conditions of senior membership establishing criteria for recruitment to different levels.... (Musgrove, 1968, p. 101)

The new sociology of education opened up three main areas for research on the curriculum. One was the history of school subjects. Young (1971) argued that subjects must not be viewed simply as reflections of basic forms of knowledge given for all time, as philosophers of education had proposed. Rather, what currently passes for history, geography, physics, English, etc. must be treated as socio-historical products resulting from past conflicts between contending groups who sought to define those subjects in different ways. Moreover, this was a process where dominant groups within society were in a particularly strong position to impose their own definitions. These conflicts, Young went on, were by no means concluded but were continuing as strongly as ever in attempts to integrate previously distinct subjects – to combine history, geography and social studies into humanities, for example. Even more recent examples could be added here – integrated science, social education, environmental studies, technology, and so on. The point is that such attempts at integration provide living examples of the continuing conflicts between different groups to establish their own definition of what counts as valid and worthwhile school knowledge.

A second major aspect of the curriculum which the new sociology of education highlighted was the nature of curricular knowledge in the classroom, as it is organized and reorganized in the moment-by-moment process of

Introduction

teacher-pupil interaction. In his influential article, 'Teaching and learning as the organization of knowledge', which appeared in *Knowledge and Control*, Esland commented:

> We know little of how knowledge comes to be organized within educational institutions. This applies not merely to the ways in which its institutionalized forms regulate the structures of 'worthwhile' educational experience, but much more so to the realizations of these forms in the realities of individual pupils and teachers. (Esland, 1971, p. 70)

In another article in the same volume, Keddie examined how an integrated humanities programme was in practice taught very differently to different groups of pupils depending on the stream they were in. Thus, despite the egalitarian rhetoric of the teachers, the educational experiences of top and bottom stream pupils remained sharply different, just as they had done under previous forms of teaching. Innovation, it seemed, was not always what it appeared.

The failure of various attempts at innovation such as this soon came to be a central focus for the 'new sociology of education' and this opened up a third aspect of the curriculum for research: the constraints, material and ideological, which blocked curriculum innovation. Whitty (1976 and 1978), for example, pointed to the way in which examination boards, through their control over syllabi and assessment procedures, placed restrictions on teachers who wished to adopt more radical forms of curriculum and pedagogy. Indeed, he argued that even mode 3 examination procedures represented a serious constraint in this respect.

However, while the 'new sociology of education' placed the curriculum firmly on the agenda for research, the 'new sociologists' produced very little systematic empirical research. It is perhaps unfair to criticize Young and his colleagues too harshly for this. New ventures are often by necessity exploratory. Indeed, it was Young's own stated hope that his book would stimulate the kind of empirical research which would develop and modify his thesis to give it more substance and validity. It remains a real problem from the point of view of the sociology of the curriculum, though, that empirical research in this area has been sparse and disappointing.

At the *macro*-level, the level of curriculum and society, the work has been predominantly theoretical and speculative, exploring the connections between ideology and curriculum practice, outlining the process by which success in certain high status areas of the liberal arts curriculum depends on the students possessing what Bourdieu (1973) calls cultural capital, and so on. These assertions, interesting as they are, have made little reference to students' experiences of school knowledge and the ideological components supposedly contained within it, to the way teachers actually *use* curriculum materials, or to the ways in which cultural capital is actually displayed and evaluated in students' classroom talk and in their writing. Even where empirical data of this kind have been drawn on, as, for example, in the work of Apple (1979 and 1982), Anyon (1979) and Giroux (1981), the analysis has been far from rigorous (McNeil, 1981; Hargreaves, 1982a).

At the *micro*-level, many classroom researchers have followed Keddie's lead and studied the knowledge teachers have of pupils, the criteria by which they define pupils' ability and so on (for a review see Hammersley, 1980). However, while they have carefully examined those aspects of classroom interaction which have come to be known as the *hidden curriculum* of schooling, they have badly neglected those other equally important aspects of what pupils learn in school: the official curriculum itself. Moreover, empirical studies of teaching styles, pupil deviance, patterns of teacher-pupil interaction and so on have been handled as if they somehow transcended this second set of concerns, as if they were peculiarly subject-free. Consequently, we know disappointingly little about the standards which different subject teachers set down for pupil behaviour and achievement, or about how the pupils themselves respond to different subjects in terms of their perceived relevance to later life. We know quite a lot, that is, about classroom relations *in general* but very little about the varying nature of curriculum practice *in particular*.

In between these two levels, at the middle or '*meso*'-level of organizational processes concerned with relations among subject associations, different departments within schools, examination boards and the like, our knowledge of curriculum practice rests on a somewhat firmer empirical base. It includes insights into the perspectives that are embraced by different subject communities and the consequences these perspectives have for classroom practice in each case (Barnes, 1976; Ball, 1981). We also know a little about the degree of ideological unity or disunity that can be found in different subject traditions (Ball and Lacey, 1980). Nevertheless, even here, our knowledge of the historical development of different subject communities is still rather thin and, despite the work of Whitty (1976 and 1978), our understanding of the activities and effects of examination bodies on the school curriculum is very limited. Clearly, there is much work still to be done here too.

Together, the papers in this book make contributions to all three aspects of the curriculum opened up for research by the 'new sociology of education'. Most of them were presented at a conference on the Sociology of Curriculum Practice held at St Hilda's College, Oxford, in September 1981, though they have been extensively revised for publication. We have grouped them into three general sections: School Subjects, Gender and the Curriculum, and Examinations, Accountability and Assessment.

School Subjects

This first section deals with a small selection of school subjects, looking either at their historical development or at the forms they take in the classroom. (Only in the fortunate case of English do we have papers dealing with both

Introduction

these aspects.) Clearly, there are important differences between subjects in how knowledge is selected, reconstructed and transmitted in schools, and the contrasts provided here between English, geography/environmental studies and art/design fully attest to this.

We begin with three papers looking at various aspects of English teaching. In an analysis deriving from their SSRC-sponsored research project, Versions of English, Douglas and Dorothy Barnes look at the different forms English may take in further education. All differ markedly from the kind of English teaching typically to be found in secondary schools (which is documented in the paper by Caroline St John-Brooks). While, as the St John-Brooks' study illustrates, school English is often centred on the study of literature and is aimed at encouraging self-expression, further education English courses vary from those closely linked to the preparation of students for work in industrial and business contexts to those which survive from the older liberal studies tradition and are devoted to consciousness-raising. There is also a third version of English sometimes to be found in this context, one geared to training in 'life skills'. Barnes and Barnes describe these different versions of English and suggest some of the factors which may determine their incidence and character.

St John-Brooks, meanwhile, examines school English through a case study of an English department in a large comprehensive school. But the conflict she identifies between the romantic ideology embodied in the English department and the rationalistic ideology which dominated the rest of the school parallels the contrasting approaches found within English at the further education level by Barnes and Barnes. She documents the variation in teaching style between two members of the English staff and the effects of each on different kinds of pupils, some being left bewildered or bored but others initiated into a new 'form of life'. She notes in particular how, despite their commitment to egalitarianism, the English teachers in effect traded upon, rather than disseminating, cultural capital. Ironically, as a result, the differentiation of pupils along social class lines occurred in their classes just as it did in the rest of the school.

The third article, by Stephen Ball, provides an historical context for the first two papers by tracing the fortunes of competing conceptions of school English during a formative period of its development as a subject. He adopts a conflict or social interaction model, looking at the struggle among different individuals and groups to gain control of the subject. At the same time, and complementing this internal history, he tries to identify some of the factors external to English which seem to have influenced the success or otherwise of these competing definitions of the subject.

Ball's historical analysis of English has close affinities with Ivor Goodson's account of how geographers have successfully defended their subject against the challenge from various integrationist movements, particularly that from environmental studies. The irony of this, as Goodson points out, is that geography itself began as a subject by integrating elements from both sciences and humanities. In defending itself, therefore, geography has had to deny its own origins and character, substituting for these mythical claims about subject 'purity'.

The last two papers in this section look at art and design education. Les Tickle investigates how teachers of this subject at middle school level try to resolve the dilemma between teaching pupils craft skills on the one hand and allowing them free expression for their creativity on the other. The solution to this problem adopted by the teachers Tickle studied involved establishing a differentiated curriculum. The more 'able' pupils were given infrequent but protracted spells of teacher attention where aesthetic ideas were explored, while the 'less able' children received short but frequent bursts of teacher attention in which they were taught basic skills in a highly directive manner. In practice, therefore, Tickle concludes, art and design teachers tend to frustrate the creativity of many of their pupils and in the process contribute to that social class stratification of pupils within the classroom which other commentators, notably Sharp and Green (1976), have identified.

David Hargreaves adopts a strikingly different perspective on art teaching. He considers why it is that art has come to be taught almost entirely through practical activity. This overwhelming emphasis on art *production*, he argues, effectively wastes a key opportunity for schools to engage in the dissemination of cultural capital through the teaching and enhancement of art *appreciation*. However, for this to occur, Hargreaves suggests, it is necessary to move away from a transmission model of art appreciation, where the teacher organizes and supervises a public discussion, to a model based on a 'traumatic' theory of learning, where art products can be responded to in a quiet, unspoken private way before these responses are shared with others. The redistribution of cultural capital, that is, is dependent on radical changes in pedagogy. It is interesting to reflect back on St John-Brooks' paper here and speculate whether English teaching might equally be transformed through similar changes.

Gender and the Curriculum

The second section of the book continues the study of school subjects, but examines these from the particular viewpoint of their differential effects on boys and girls. One of the most striking developments in sociology over the last ten years has been the impact of feminism. Prior to this, very little attention had been given to gender as a form of social division. Class was the category that held the stage. In retrospect, this seems quite extraordinary. The consequences of this neglect have been serious since the predominant tendency to focus on men and boys (Acker, 1981) has led to serious distortions of our understanding of educational processes. Fortunately this defect has begun to be corrected in recent years, though there is still some way to go. One place where these developments are beginning to make an impact is in the study of the relationship between gender and the school curriculum. Two of the papers in this volume look at aspects of this issue.

Introduction

Teresa Grafton and her colleagues focus on the process of subject choice in secondary school. They look first at the extent to which a course on child care is made available to boys and girls respectively. Despite the operation of a subject choice scheme in the third year, Grafton *et al.* note how girls and boys are effectively channelled into different patterns of option choice, both by curriculum differentiation in the craft area in the first three years of secondary schooling and by the way in which the family and child course is inserted into the option scheme, in competition with science and with those craft subjects which are traditionally the preserve of boys. At the same time, the authors recognize that the fact that the subject is taken almost entirely by girls does not just reflect the way in which the school curriculum is organized. Indeed, they speculate that even if the curriculum were organized in a way which directly challenged the conventional stereotypes of what are boys' and girls' subjects, that challenge might still be ineffective. This, they claim, is because gender-based patterns of subject choice in school in large part reflect the sexual division of labour in society at large.

Similar themes run through Lynda Measor's article which looks at an area of the curriculum where the low levels of participation by girls have been the subject of considerable debate: science. The basis of her case study is an examination of girls responses to a Nuffield science course in a large East Midlands comprehensive school. Measor notes how even before they arrive at the school, while they are still at middle school, girls and boys have very different orientations to science. The girls' initial reaction, that physical science is in various ways 'unfeminine', is simply confirmed by their subsequent experience of the subject in lessons. Moreover, Measor argues that the girls actively use science lessons, with all their masculine connotations, as an occasion where they can actively demonstrate their own femininity: for example, by refusing to wear inelegant safety goggles and displaying their revulsion for messy experiments. She compares the reaction of boys in domestic science lessons, where a similar process of laying down markers of gender identity can be discerned; though Measor notes that the ways in which girls and boys demonstrate their rejection of 'gender-inappropriate' subjects are different and themselves carry messages about sexual identity. What is particularly disconcerting, Measor concludes, is that while the school seems to expend considerable effort in attracting boys to domestic science by developing projects with 'masculine' interest, little attempt is made to make physics, chemistry and biology more attractive to girls.

Examinations, Accountability and Assessment

In the final section of the book we examine one of the major influences on the school curriculum: external assessment. Throughout this century there has been repeated criticism of the impact of public examinations on the character of secondary schooling (Board of Education, 1911; Norwood Report, 1943;

Introduction

Schools Council, 1975; DES, 1979; Mortimore, 1980). Examinations, perhaps more than any other single factor in the schooling process, are widely regarded as having an educationally undesirable effect on schools and as representing a significant constraint on curriculum innovation. Despite the importance and persistence of such claims, however, there has been little empirical investigation of this issue. The four articles in this section begin to address this question.

Glenn Turner looks at the 'hidden curriculum' of examinations, and in particular its effects on the orientations of a group of top band pupils in a large comprehensive school. Whereas the school emphasized social values, these pupils were primarily committed to examination success, and in a highly instrumental fashion. As a result, whenever teachers were judged to be engaged in anything other than preparation for examinations, these pupils tended to engage in various forms of classroom deviance. Turner concludes by pointing up the paradox that not only are these able, academic pupils not simply conformists, as some previous models of pupil adaptation to school might have led us to expect, but they come into conflict with the school even in the area where one might have expected consensus: examination work.

As a complement to Turner's focus on pupils, John Scarth investigates the orientations of teachers to external and internal examinations. He argues that, at least in the case of the comprehensive secondary school staff he studied, examinations are not experienced by teachers as an external constraint on their teaching. The teachers viewed examinations as performing a variety of functions, both for pupils and for themselves. For most of these teachers exams formed a normal and natural part of their teaching. Even among those few teachers in the school who had developed major innovations in examining practice, such as Mode 3 courses, preparation of pupils for external assessment was still regarded as an important and legitimate component of their teaching. Scarth rejects the conclusion that these teachers' views are merely the product of ideology. Indeed, he challenges that form of theory, by no means uncommon in the sociology of education, where views with which the researcher disagrees are dismissed as social products, while those which match the researcher's own beliefs are treated as not in need of explanation, as 'natural' or intrinsically rational.

In contrast to the micro-focus of the papers by Turner and Scarth, the remaining two papers in this section provide more macro-level analyses. Bowe and Whitty report the findings to date of the research on examination boards initiated by Whitty in 1973. The original focus was on the extent to which GCE and CSE examination procedures constrained teachers, and in particular the degree to which Mode 3 assessment increased teacher autonomy. The authors argue that Mode 3 enlarged the scope for innovation on the part of teachers in only a very limited way. Moreover, they detect, from the late 1970s onwards, an increasing tendency for examination boards to tighten up Mode 3 regulations and to move back towards more traditional forms of examining. Bowe and Whitty conclude that none of the available macro-theories is able to account satisfactorily for the way in which public policy in this area is

Introduction

currently changing; and they stress the political importance of developing a more adequate theory.

The most significant feature of Mode 3 is the direct involvement of teachers in the assessment process. In one respect the trend that Bowe and Whitty identify reflects a move back towards a more centralized control of education in Britain. However, the issue of trends towards centralization or decentralization is a complex one, as Broadfoot shows in the final article of this volume. She compares France and England as classic cases of centralized and decentralized education systems respectively. But she argues that while the ways in which control is exerted are different, in fact the degree of control over teachers' activities is similar in both systems. Moreover, while each system is currently changing, the overall effect is to make the form that central control over curriculum and pedagogy takes in each society increasingly similar.

Conclusion

This book is not meant to be, nor could it be, a comprehensive account of curriculum practice in schools and the factors which shape it. We are still a long way from having the knowledge base necessary to construct such an account. Research in the area is still at an early stage of development. But the articles here do shed some important light on many aspects of what is taught in schools and its effects. They do this on the basis of a firm grounding in the actualities and day-to-day realities of curriculum practice. Hopefully, this kind of sociologically informed empirical work on curriculum at the level of the classroom, the subject department or the examining body will enable us to test and develop the rather more speculative explanations of curriculum practice that sociologists have advanced to date which are epitomized in concepts like ideology, hegemony and cultural capital. At the same time, it might give curriculum theorists and curriculum planners a fuller and more realistic sense of the problems they are likely to encounter when they seek to implement their ambitiously prescriptive models of curriculum change.

References

ACKER, S. (1981) 'No-woman's-land, British sociology of education 1960–79', in *Sociological Review*, 29, 1, pp. 77–104.
ANYON, J. (1979) 'Ideology and United States history textbooks,' in *Harvard Educational Review*, 49.3.
APPLE, M. (1979) *Ideology and Curriculum*, London, Routledge and Kegan Paul.
APPLE, M (1982) *Knowledge and Power*, London, Routledge and Kegan Paul.
BALL, S.J. (1981) *Beachside Comprehensive*, Cambridge, Cambridge University Press.
BALL, S.J. and LACEY, C. (1980) 'Subject disciplines as the opportunity for group action: A measured critique of subject sub-cultures', in WOODS, P. (Ed.) *Teacher Strategies*, London, Croom Helm.

BARNES, D. (1976) *From Communication to Curriculum*, Harmondsworth, Penguin.
BERNSTEIN, B. (1975) *Class, Codes and Control*, Vol. 3, London, Routledge and Kegan Paul.
BLOOM, B.S. et al. (1956) *Taxonomy of Educational Objectives: 1 Cognitive Domain*, London, Longmans.
BOARD OF EDUCATION (1911) *Report of the Consultative Committee on the Secondary School*, London, HMSO.
BOURDIEU, P. (1973) 'Cultural reproduction and social reproduction', in BROWN, R. (Ed.) *Knowledge, Education and Cultural Change*, London, Tavistock.
CALLAGHAN, J. (1976) 'Towards a national debate', in *Education*, 22, October.
CENTRE FOR CONTEMPORARY CULTURAL STUDIES (1981) *Unpopular Education*, Hutchinson.
COX, C.B. and DYSON, A.E. (Eds) (1969) *Fight for Education: A Black Paper*, London, Critical Quarterly Society.
COX, C.B. and DYSON, A.E. (Eds) (1970a) *Black Paper 2: The Crisis in Education*, London, Critical Quarterly Society.
COX, C.B. and DYSON, A.E. (Eds) (1970b) *Black Paper 3: Goodbye Mr. Short*, London, Critical Quarterly Society.
COX, C.B. and BOYSON, R. (Eds) (1975) *Black Paper 5: The Fight for Education*, London, Dent.
DEPARTMENT OF EDUCATION AND SCIENCE (1979) *Aspects of Secondary Education in England*, London, HMSO.
DEPARTMENT OF EDUCATION AND SCIENCE (1979) *A View of the Curriculum*, London, HMSO.
DEPARTMENT OF EDUCATION AND SCIENCE (1980) *Curriculum 11–16*, London, HMSO.
DEPARTMENT OF EDUCATION AND SCIENCE (1981) *The School Curriculum*, London, HMSO.
ESLAND, G. (1971) 'Teaching and learning as the organization of knowledge', in Young (Ed.) 1971.
GIROUX, H. (1981) *Ideology, Culture and the Process of Schooling* Lewes, Falmer Press.
GORBUTT, D. (1972) 'The new sociology of education', in *Education for Teaching*, 89.
HAMILTON, D. et al. (Eds) (1977) *Beyond the Numbers Game*, London, Macmillan.
HAMMERSLEY, M. (1980) 'Classroom ethnography', in *Educational Analysis*, 2, 2.
HARGREAVES, A. (1982a) 'Resistance and relative autonomy theories. Problems of distortion and incoherence in recent Marxist analyses of education', in *British Journal of the Sociology of Education*, 3, 2.
HARGREAVES, A. (1982b) 'The rhetoric of school-centred innovation', in *Journal of Curriculum Studies*, 14, 3.
HIRST, P. (1975) *Knowledge and the Curriculum*, London, Routledge and Kegan Paul.
KARABEL, J. and HALSEY, A.H. (1977) *Power and Ideology in Education*, Oxford, Oxford University Press.
LAWTON, D. (1980) *The Politics of the School Curriculum*, London, Routledge and Kegan Paul.
MCNEIL, L. (1981) 'Response to Henry Giroux's "Pedagogy, Pessimism, and the Politics of Conformity",' in *Curriculum Inquiry*, 11, 4.
MORTIMORE, P. (1980) 'Time to re-examine the system', in *The Guardian*, 24 June.
MUSGROVE, F. (1968) 'The contribution of sociology to the study of the curriculum', in KERR, J.F. (Ed.) *Changing the Curriculum*, London, University of London Press.
(NEWSOM REPORT) CENTRAL ADVISORY COUNCIL FOR EDUCATION (1963), *Half Our Future*, London, HMSO.
NIXON, J. (Ed.) (1981) *Teachers' Guide to Action Research: Evaluation, Inquiry and Development in the Classroom*, London, Grant McIntyre.

Introduction

(NORWOOD REPORT) BOARD OF EDUCATION (1943) *Report of the Committee of the Secondary Schools Examination Council Appointed by the President of the Board of Education in 1941, Curriculum and Examinations in Secondary Schools.*
PHENIX, P.H. (1964) *Realms of Meaning*, New York, McGraw Hill.
SCHOOLS COUNCIL (1975) *The Whole Curriculum 13–16*, Working Paper, Evans/Methuen.
SHARP, R. and GREEN, A. (1976) *Education and Social Control*, London, Routledge and Kegan Paul.
STENHOUSE, L. (1980) *Curriculum Research and Development in Action*, London, Heinemann.
TYLER, R.W. (1971) *Basic Principles of Curriculum and Instruction*, Chicago, University of Chicago Press.
WHITTY, G. (1976) 'Teachers and examiners', in WHITTY, G. and YOUNG, M.F.D. (Eds) *Explorations in the Politics of School Knowledge*, Driffield, Nafferton Books.
WHITTY G. (1978) 'School examinations and the politics of school knowledge', in BARTON, L. and MEIGHAN, R. (Eds) *Sociological Interpretations of Schooling and Classrooms*, Driffield, Nafferton.
WILLIAMS, R. (1961) *The Long Revolution*, Chatto and Windus.
YOUNG, M.F.D. (1971) *Knowledge and Control: New Directions for the Sociology of Education*, London, Collier-Macmillan.

I
School Subjects

1   Preparing to Write in Further Education

Douglas and Dorothy Barnes

The material on which this paper is based derives from the Versions of English Project,[1] a study of English and Communications curricula in the upper forms of schools and in colleges of further education. The purpose of the study was, in the first instance, to provide as full a description as possible of the different English courses taught in a number of schools and colleges. These descriptions, though centred upon classroom observation, would also take account of teachers' purposes and their students' perceptions of the courses. We expected that various versions of English, once identified, would prove not to be randomly distributed, and hoped to be able to relate them to the contexts in which they occurred, by reference both to institutional structures and to teachers' and students' attempts to pursue goals within these structures. We therefore designed the research so as to enable comparisons such as:

 school with college courses;
 English with Communications;
 courses in business departments with those in technical departments;
 courses for students of higher with those for students of lower academic status (for example, different 'streams' or 'sets' in schools.)

In carrying out this design we chose a representative range of examinations, in order to make further comparisons. In colleges of further education we saw courses leading to the following examinations: GCE O-level, Royal Society of Arts (two levels), Business Education Council (two levels), Technician Education Council, City and Guilds (two levels) and others. The choice of these contextual variables represented a multiple hypothesis that we would find different versions of English to be related to them; that is, that different versions are offered to different groups of students. Besides testing this hypothesis, we hoped to throw light upon two other matters. We wanted to know along what dimensions the versions differed from one another – and indeed the research has given unexpected information about this. Furthermore, we hoped to indicate some of the processes by which a particular version is generated and sustained in its typical context, though no more than an indication of these processes can be expected from a study such as this which lacks a historical dimension.

In this paper we focus on only part of the material we collected: twenty-two hours of observation data from nine courses in four colleges of further education.[2] This sub-sample is defined by the fact that all of the sessions used were concerned with preparing the students to do written work; in this paper only restricted use is made of the interview and other data.

We looked at English and communications courses in college against the background of the more familiar case of school English. English teachers in schools turn towards university English courses dominated by the study of literature for their ethos and values, though there are competing traditions here (Ball and Lacey, 1980; Ball, 1983). Literature plays an ethical role linked with teachers' pastoral responsibilities. Writing has to be an act of self-realization subordinating skills to intention, and is addressed to the undefined general audience to which literature is itself addressed. Spoken language can find little place except as a means to some other end. English must be 'committed' – but committed to the values of the private domain not to public political values (Barnes, 1983).

College lecturers are necessarily more dependent on values deriving from the commercial/industrial contexts from which their students come. Further education colleges have to persuade their students – and often their students' employers – that the courses are relevant to their needs at work. One result of this is that the college view of their relationship with students is often quasi-contractual: the college courses are to satisfy students' requirements for knowledge and skills seen as public and external to students. For this reason it is external conformity that is pursued, not a change of values or personality.

Even so, a close inspection of college English and Communications courses shows that they are far from homogeneous, nor is commitment-based teaching entirely absent, though it takes a rather different form to that found in schools. Indeed, there is a conflict between 'complementary' and 'contrasting' perspectives. They differ because they derive from two different sources. The complementary studies perspective derives from views mediated by technical departments in further education colleges and attributed to employers. This perspective points toward a concentration on language activities which are related to simulated commercial and industrial contexts, from which they derive their criteria. Conformity and efficiency are central values, while personal experience is treated as irrelevant. The contrasting studies version of English is probably derived from the academic social sciences and is linked to the older 'liberal studies' tradition. It points towards attempts to raise students' consciousness of public issues, political, economic and social; although not concerned with personal experience in private contexts, its aim is to change the student's view of the world. In addition, as we shall see, there is a third variant found in courses dealing with groups of low status students and concerned with communication in everyday life; 'everyday life' is here, however, treated as a public domain with a focus upon social competence rather than on self-exploration. Which of these versions of college English particular students experience depends partly on the vocational courses they are following, and partly upon their qualifications, since these determine what examination they are being prepared for. We must therefore distinguish business from industrial courses, and high status (post-O-level) from low status courses.

The teaching of writing in colleges, then, differs markedly from that in schools, but also varies across different courses. Some courses emphasize surface characteristics such as spelling and punctuation; others concern themselves primarily with content. Some writing, although in fact read only by the lecturer, is apparently addressed to the unknown and potentially wide audience that fiction is addressed to; other writing is designed for an imaginary situation that defines a precise audience and purpose. The situation may be taken from the world of business, or from industry and craft, or may refer to private and leisure activities. What is written about also varies considerably, and may carry values and preferred pictures of the world. These differences imply that what students are likely to learn from written tasks will be different in different courses: writing is not a simple skill that can be abstracted from content and situation.

Part of our intention is to search for relationships between the characteristics of courses and the contexts in which they appear (which includes the identity of the students to whom they are offered). We begin with English language courses in general departments and in those concerned with vocational preparation for business, and later turn to Communications courses, first in business departments and then in departments concerned with industry and craft.

English for O-level and RSA

Mrs Sands was teaching a course for would-be shorthand typists who were to sit an examination in English at RSA Stage One. Her attention was primarily directed to surface criteria for acceptable writing – length, presentation, paragraphs, spelling and punctuation. Perhaps unintentionally, she communicated her lack of interest in the subject matter of the writing when, talking to her class about the importance of 'a telling last sentence' she said in passing: 'for example if there's an essay on ... "My Hobbies" or something equally scintillating like that, after they've battled on loyally for about a page....' When she approached deep criteria – 'interest' and 'the ordering of ideas' was how she labelled them – like other teachers she found it difficult to say anything likely to be of value to the students. Mrs Sands says of 'interest', for example: 'Some essays about boring subjects can be very interesting.... Can't think of one. I'm always ... expecting an essay to be interesting.' Length – the surface criterion *par excellence* – for Mrs Sands is an important matter: not only should the overall length of an essay be 300 to 350 words, but length also provides the criteria for paragraphing: '... Do try and write paragraphs that are longer than one sentence,' she urged, and in reply to a student who asked, 'What happens if it's a really long sentence?' she continued: 'Well, in that case I'd either write a shorter sentence or.... It's difficult ... to have a hard and fast rule. If it's a really very long sentence, well all right.' The topics which Mrs Sands eventually set in this session were typically 'private' ones of the type common in schools. (For example, one was: 'A word picture of yourself, including outward appearance and personality'.) She introduced them, however, with the dismissive 'We'll just look at the choice of essays – a bit boring.' Although this is consonant with Mrs Sands' usual strategy as a youthful lecturer of allying herself with student values, it also matches her emphasis throughout this session on surface ('skills and conventions') criteria at the expense of content.

We will now turn to another lecturer teaching for a different examination. This is Mr Pattison who was preparing a class for O-level English language. Amongst our data are three sessions in which he prepared his group for writing, one a personal essay, one a piece of writing about a work of literature, and one an essay on a general 'public' topic.

The first of these was on the topic 'The First Driving Lesson'. Mr Pattison indicated what he wanted: '... where you were all clumsy and inexperienced, you didn't know the driving instructor, it's the first time that you've met him, you're doing most things wrong or most things clumsily at any rate.' He continued, 'We're talking about a description of what you do and how it affects you, how the circumstances make you nervous and how perhaps you do things you ought not to have done.' And later he suggested that they should jot down two lists of notes, 'the sequence of events' and alongside them 'something about what you felt, what you thought'. Although this introductory lesson thus contained one of the indicators of personal treatment (the reference to feelings) Mr Pattison tended to leave the subjective aspect of the experience to his students: he certainly showed no sign of wishing to transmit to them a set of attitudes and values. The essence of his purpose seemed to be to fulfil the requirements for various kinds of writing demanded of the students by this mode of examining. In this sense the examination, and its requirements as interpreted by Mr Pattison and his colleagues, was offering him a set of goals, so that he did not need to look beyond them for purposes that might be drawn from elsewhere.

Under the rubric of an 'Argumentative Essay' another assignment was presented to Mr Pattison's students in the form of a duplicated sheet. This contained essay topics which concerned television, happiness, smoking, full-time education after sixteen, the 1970s, manners. Listed like this, the titles look like a typical list from a GCE O-level paper of some years ago. But they were not presented merely as titles: most offered eight or ten lines of guidance to the candidate. This one can serve as example:

> In order to attract more young people to stay in full-time education after the age of sixteen, particularly those people who find it difficult to do so, it is proposed to offer grants to all students over sixteen. The level of grant will depend on the parents' income. What are your views on this proposal? How will it affect future careers? Will it persuade more people to continue in education? What does attract them to stay at school or college?

Preparing to Write in Further Education

This task deserves our attention. It gives those students who find it difficult to know what to write some starting-points for their thinking by indicating the kinds of issues to be discussed, giving them more access to the examiners' deep criteria than the mere title 'Education after Sixteen' would have done. On the other hand, there is no indication of the audience to whom the writing is to be addressed or the purpose it is to serve. There is no attempt to disguise what it is, a writing exercise to satisfy examination requirements, without any context except that provided by the assessment.

Mr Pattison's treatment of the 'Argumentative Essay' topics was different from his treatment of the private topics. He chose television as his examplar and took his group through it step by step, indicating what they could write. He began with 'the proposition that television broadens the mind', and asked for 'positive examples of the way in which that may be so'. Students suggested various documentary programmes which he then listed on the blackboard. The mention of a *Horizon* programme on acupuncture led Mr Pattison to ask: 'Now in what particular way does that help to broaden your mind?' and by persistent questioning drew from one of the students that acupuncture implied sticking needles into somebody in order to 'overcome some injury, some stress'. Something of the flavour of Mr Pattison's teaching can be gathered from the following summary which closed this part of the lesson:

> They are the same all over the world; our different cultures have tried to deal with those problems in a radically different way. There are other ways of thinking about things, there are other ways of looking at things, other than the ways in which most of European – English – people do. You can say that that was one example of this: you get to know how other people live and think.

In this way Mr Pattison took his students step by step through one of the topics modelling how such 'argumentative essays' can be constructed. At the same time he provided abundant content that could be used by any student who wished to do so, and also illustrated an appropriate style of writing. The appropriateness of Mr Pattison's spoken style to this last purpose is apparent in phrases such as: 'the proposition that', 'the way in which this may be so', 'informed you about a different culture from your own', 'a subject of conversation that people have in common'. What he illustrated for his students was not merely an appropriate content but a linguistic style drawn from certain kinds of books and journals.

Although this procedure included many references by students to aspects of their lives outside the college – watching television, particularly – Mr Pattison's interest seemed to be directed entirely towards the requirements of the examination. This sense of detachment from reality partly arose from the list of topics, which could be said to ask for uncontroversial controversy, since none – except possibly the one about continued education – would be likely to generate much concern. But Mr Pattison's approach was consonant with this. When he interacted with his students – and once or twice he seemed hardly to be listening – his attention seemed to be upon preparing them for writing, and not at all upon influencing their views, as we might have expected in many of the school lessons we have observed. Since the students were to be examined in the same way and for the same award as many of our school classes, we have here an undeniable difference of values between college and school; Mr Pattison's approach is consonant with the approach in other college courses, and not with O-level courses in schools.

Thus the writing in 'English' courses, whether GCE or RSA, usually approximated to the 'general' essay, removed from any naturalistic audience or purpose other than to impress an examiner. If the topic was private it was left to the students; there was a sharply drawn distinction between the students' private worlds and the purposes of the courses. (In most school English the distinction is weak.) When the task required the expression of opinion or analysis of a topic (the so-called 'discursive' or 'argumentative' essay), or the writing of a report or formal letter, the lecturers tended to lay down the content clearly. They thus kept tight control of the content, rather than seeking to communicate deep criteria that would enable students to select, arrange and present material in a suitable manner.

Some English courses however did have an implied audience and 'real world' context of business. In another RSA English class, also related to a shorthand typing course, the lecturer, Mr Peel, required his students to draft a letter, in order to apologize for being unable to attend an interview for a job, and to ask for an interview at another time. He made lengthy references to the importance of letter writing in business contexts, but particularly its relevance to obtaining interviews for jobs, 'because that is what interviews are all about, is selling yourself....' The students had already attempted to draft such a letter; Mr Peel, rather than asking for their versions and commenting on them, chose to provide them with a version he had himself drafted. After some comments about lay-out he dictated this version to the students:

Dear Sir,
    Thank you for your invitation for (to) an interview. I was more than delighted (thrilled) that you should consider (deem) me a suitable candidate.

    Since receiving your letter I have been informed that the time of the examination I was to take on the morning of that day has now been changed to the afternoon. It is a three hour examination and does not start (begin) until 2.30 p.m. This has placed me in a very difficult position as *both* are extremely important to me. At the risk of offending you, for the sake of my long-term future I have decided to take the examination.

    The post for which I was to be interviewed is one which I would dearly love (to have), and I am wondering if under the circumstances it would be possible for the time or day of my interview to be changed.

                                                      Yours faithfully,

When Mr Peel asked the students to discuss the alternative wording, their *sotto voce* comments included 'soppy', 'lovesick' and 'overdone' to characterize the style he had adopted. He responded by saying:

> Put yourself into that position. We really wanted that job. We've built ourselves up to the idea of going for an interview; we've decided what colour eye shadow to put on, what make-up to put on; we've even got as far as pressing the dresses you're going to wear....

He went on to admit: 'You have in fact got to creep a little bit.' Later he added: '... if you look at it from (the other?) person's point of view, that they've been invited to an interview and yet you're going to do something in preference. You see they might take this as an affront.' The clash of perspectives between lecturer and students was recorded in fieldnotes at the time: Mr Peel was speaking from the perspective of the employer, and attempting to demonstrate to future employees their relative powerlessness in such a situation. The writing task, because of its supposed reference to the real world, was transmitting messages about that world.

It has not been possible to test systematically the impact of Mr Peel's advice on the letter-writing style of the students. However, inspection of four letters written soon after this session and supposed to be addressed to prospective employers – though not necessarily in response to the same task – show some attempt to converge upon the recommended style. A few sentences drawn from some of them will illustrate this.

(i) After great consideration to the above post and taking into acount all you have to offer, I am very sorry to say ... etc.
(ii) Having received your reply to my application, I was pleased to find ... etc.
I must stress my dissapointment and apology that [sic.] ... etc.
I regret my grief very much ... etc.
(iii) In consideration with the two firms I had to take in all possibilities...
(iv) I was very delighted when I received this invertation [sic.]....

It seemed that these four students (at least) had received the message about the necessity for a 'high', that is, formal, style, even if they had some difficulty in sustaining it. However, there was no comparable evidence that the message about subservience had been received and acted upon.

Before leaving this session, we must note the influence of examination requirements on Mr Peel's teaching. One student said that rather than writing a letter she would telephone, and Mr Peel replied:

> Well, of course, as we've always said, when we're dealing with an examination situation we're dealing with a situation which is unique for an examination. In practice probably 90 per cent of the letters that we write in class are things where we would use the telephone in an ordinary business situation.

In a previous session he had made a very similar point about using a different lay-out for letters in English examinations, instead of the conventions taught in typewriting classes, so that the examiner may 'know whether you are really following a rule as far as typewriting goes or whether you've forgotten there's a paragraph.' These examples illustrate admirably that there are two competing sources of criteria at work in Mr Peel's lessons, one drawn from examinations and one from the world of business. Certain courses, such as these RSA classes, are beset by this ambiguity, which in effect pulls them in two directions, towards assumptions about the world of business and towards the criteria of the examination, both of which have a life of their own irrespective of their truth to experience. Our data would suggest that English courses in further education tend to maintain a barrier[3] – higher in some cases than others – between the meanings legitimated in the courses and life outside, private or public: the examination supplied purposes and criteria that were interposed between the students and any values and skills that might be derived from outside contexts.

To sum up, if the English courses we saw were typical – and we have no reason to think they were not – it is possible to assert, first, that English Language courses in further education are likely to be concerned with surface conformity rather than attempting to engage with the personal perspectives and values of students. This showed itself in three ways, through the primary concern with surface criteria for writing, through a parallel lack of concern with content, which was either dictated or left to the student, and through the transmission of style as an aspect of the typist's external role, that is, symbolic subservience to an employer. The students who followed these courses were almost entirely young women. Another conclusion we can draw about these courses is that while informed by assumptions about the business world the major influence upon them is the requirements of the examinations. To a considerable degree these undercut the transmission and reception of business values.

Communications Courses in Business and Technical Departments

We now turn to a course in communications taught in a business department to a group of young people, male and female, of higher academic status since they were required to hold four O-level passes. The teaching of writing in this course differed substantially from that in English courses, particularly in that the writing was related closely to business contexts, which in our view were somewhat idealized.

During recent years, lecturers teaching Communications courses in colleges of further education have developed a kind of assignment that is set in an explicit context, which is often but not always commercial or industrial; it will be convenient to refer to it as a 'situated assignment'.[4] For example, the preamble to the assignment may be concerned with a small firm which has to make a decision about moving to a new site, and gives details about organizational and financial aspects of the move, and about some of the personnel involved in the decision. The assignment is likely to contain several parts. For each part the student will be required to assume the role of one of the persons involved in the decision, perhaps a managerial assistant reporting on an imaginary interview with members of the workforce or summarizing relevant legal information (from a document provided). It is essential to this kind of assignment that the social and organizational context – especially roles and relationships – is highly defined, so that each part of the assignment provides an explicit audience and purpose for writing (or in some cases for speech). These assignments contrast sharply with the writing that we have been considering, which has been the basis for testing writing ability for more than a generation. Situated assignments are used as the basis for teaching in many communications courses in further education, while at the same time providing material for assessment.

Situated assignments can be exemplified from courses directed towards People and Communications for the Business Education Council (BEC); others occurred in courses for the Technician Education Council (TEC) and for City and Guilds awards. When we made our third visit to one BEC course the students had already embarked on what was called 'The Recruitment Project', the first stage of which involved the preparation of a job description and a 'Successful Applicant Profile' for the post to be filled, and the design and costing of an advertisement for the post. Mr Davidson's style of teaching was unlike what we had seen in schools, and for that matter in the further education courses so far mentioned. It can be characterized as deductive rather than inductive. For example, Mr Davidson began by showing on the overhead projector a list of the elements of a Successful Applicant Profile:

Age
Sex
Education, qualifications, experience
Character, temperament, demeanour
Any special skills or qualities
Career interests and ambitions

Those ready-made categories were presented to the students for them to use, so that discussion centred on how to interpret concepts such as 'temperament' and 'demeanour'. The categories were authoritative; it was for students to apply them. In this sense they were deductive, in comparison with teaching methods in which a teacher begins with descriptive categories suggested by students, and works inductively with them to refine and sharpen the categories. During the first hour it was a typical communications exercise, a group of spoken and written activities set in an imaginary business context, and mainly shaped by the requirement of writing assignments for the BEC examination. The spirit of this first part can be gathered from this summary which came at the end of the hour:

> OK. Your organization has created the job. You know the kind of person you want. The next stage is to go ahead and advertize it, which is what you in fact do if you're doing it in real life.... You've also got to have a good mental picture of the sort of person that you want, otherwise you won't know what you're doing in trying to make the decision. So all this preparatory work is important....

So far Mr Davidson's presentation was typical of the communications assignment, in that the nature of the task and the criteria governing its success or failure were firmly contextualized in the world of business. Indeed the lecturer easily carried his students with him, since he could so readily demonstrate that the tasks he had set – job description and successful applicant profile – related closely to practical considerations in the commercial world. However, in the very next sentence he moved on to something which was slightly but crucially different.

> ... Now we'll find that lots of organizations don't do this appointing very scientifically; a lot of it's very ... rule of thumb. But I think you'll generally find that the bigger the organization, the more scientifically it goes about appointing its staff.

At this point Mr Davidson was no longer merely defining and justifying his assignment by reference to the world of business, but was presenting a value-laden account of the world, which became most visible in the concepts of 'scientific', 'modern' and 'efficient'. The succeeding part of this long session was devoted to an extended presentation of advertizing, which, though superficially justified by the assignment, went far beyond the knowledge and understanding required to carry out the task of drafting an advertisement (a task in any case sharply bounded by the well-known conventions of the 'classified' columns). The students were in effect receiving a view of the world, or at least of the business world.

Before the students began work in groups designing and costing an advertisement, Mr Davidson analyzed advertizing according to a communications model which represented it as a technical problem of conveying a message from an advertizer through a medium to a target group.

> ... All sorts of ways in which he can do it but he *has to* use one language or another. But also very importantly he has to define the precise nature of his target group. Because ... he wants maximum contact at minimum cost.

The tendency of communications models of this kind is to reduce all communication to neutral techniques, ignoring both aesthetic and politico-moral issues, since considerations of power and access to media, and of the eventual value of the messages, are normally excluded from the analysis. The world is as it is: the student's task is to learn to operate efficiently in this world. Such a view of the world is not really neutral, since under the apparent neutrality lie assumptions about what constitutes efficiency and about what is worth pursuing.

Mr Davidson went on to discuss how advertizers choose appropriate target groups for their advertisements, and to describe different kinds of newspapers and why they charge different fees for advertisements; the discussion of the readerships of different papers led into disquisitions on social class and on how newspapers are financed. It seemed that inherent in his deductive method of teaching was the practice of a particular kind of rationality that showed itself in tightly defined categories. (It is tempting to relate it also to his use of 'scientific' and 'efficient': the concepts and the methods seem to belong together.)

Mr Davidson was an experienced and successful lecturer; his lectures were admirably planned, ran smoothly and undoubtedly carried the students with them. They contained valuable information about the world, and involved the students in analytical thinking of a relatively demanding kind. The main points to be made about this lecture are (i) that it was skill-oriented, that is, concerned with the mastery of communication techniques seen as neutral methodology; (ii) that integral to it was a form of rationality characterized by deductive processes based on authoritative category systems; (iii) that it projected a persuasive account of the world, without appearing to do so, an account dominated by certain unexamined assumptions about the social and economic contexts in which we live. In discussion Mr Davidson and his colleagues were asked whether their courses were likely to produce submissive employees (Lander, 1980). Although this appeared to be an unfamiliar way of looking at it, Mr Davidson was able to reply confidently: '... One of our aims is to get students to think for themselves, to discover evidence, to weigh up evidence, to make decisions and the way to proceed rationally, to do as the evidence appears to indicate, rather than do as somebody tells them to do.' There seemed to be a good deal of truth in this account, in that Mr Davidson's sessions included opportunities for the students to apply, individually and in groups, the productive and analytical techniques he taught; certainly he did not suppress their opinions. What would have most struck a school teacher of English were not only the 'public' topics, and their treatment as subjects for 'public' detached analysis, but Mr Davidson's clear withdrawal from value judgements, apart from those based upon ideas of effectiveness. In the case of advertisements what was noticeably lacking were responses to the aesthetics of advertizing language – of the kind once common in English lessons – and any ethical criticism of a consumer society large parts of whose expenditure are manipulated by industrial producers. The critical training offered by Mr Davidson – and we do not wish to question its existence – appeared to stop short of these aspects of the world.

It is instructive to compare Mr Davidson's teaching with a session taught as part of a General and Communications studies course for a TEC examination. The lecturer, Mr Turner, was teaching *about* economics and power at world level; he was transmitting the truth about the world as he and his colleagues saw it. Thus it would be misleading to suggest that it was 'situated' in the sense that Mr Davidson's work drew its purposes and criteria from the world of commerce. The topic Mr Turner gave to his students was 'Commodities and World Food Resources'. This was based on materials provided by the department; it seemed as if authority lay with the materials rather than with the lecturer. After mentioning the topic, the lecturer showed a series of transparencies drawn from the radical journal *The New Internationalist* which discussed in strip cartoon form various explanations for food shortages in Third World countries. Successively the cartoons gave evidence that shortages are not caused by under-production, or by over-population, and presented the view that colonization had changed the pattern of agriculture in the Third World, forcing farmers to grow cash crops that place them at the mercy of world markets, instead of food crops which would feed them and their fellows. Mr Turner took his students through these cartoons commenting on them and receiving a few responses. Although his presentation lacked emphasis, he clearly approved of the radical message:

> We tend to get the impression that we brought Africa and India out of the dark ages, out of the primitive period in their history, but the more you actually look at it you can see we only developed these countries for our own interests rather than in the interests of the people that lived there. In fact, if this (as it's called) 'colonization' . . . if they went into Africa today, the headlines in . . . *The Times* would talk about 'invasion'. . . . It depends how you're manipulating words.

Here we have an approach to General and Communications studies that sharply contrasts with Mr Davidson's. It is explicitly concerned with transmitting a view of the world: he wishes his students to grasp the injustice to Third World countries of the impact on their economies of capitalism generally, and of the control of the markets by wealthier states. His emphasis falls on content, whereas Mr Davidson's fell on skills, not only communication skills but certain kinds of rationality, treated as detachable from particular content. In his teaching the writing falls into the background. This seems very like what has been called 'raising consciousness', which amounts to directing young workers' attention to social and political aspects of the world about them.

This older interpretation of general (liberal) studies is under attack from the communication studies movement which tends to accept the task of giving young workers skills they may one day use in their work, and appropriate attitudes and values too. Both approaches involved a view of the world: Mr Davidson presented the assumptions of capitalist commerce, and seemed unaware of doing so; Mr Turner presented a case against capitalist economics, and was highly aware of doing so. On the other hand, whereas Mr Davidson's students took a lively part, making suggestions and disagreeing, Mr Turner's manner of exposition did not invite participation: the content of Mr Turner's talk may have been critical of the politico-economic *status quo*, but it was Mr Davidson's students who were learning to enact a critical role. In other respects too the two approaches were in contrast: Mr Davidson saw his task as the teaching of situated communication skills, whereas the written assignment that Mr Turner mentioned briefly seemed little more than an excuse for studying a topic that he felt to be important. From a school point of view, this last is hardly 'English', yet it is relevant to our study in that it is one of the options that parallels Communication Studies on the one hand and decontextualized English on the other.

It is now time to turn to those sessions in which writing was dealt with in an industrial context, rather than a commercial one. Only one course amongst the writing data fulfilled this account: it was directed towards an examination set by City and Guilds for the Construction Industries Training Board (CITB). Each of the two sessions observed lasted about seventy minutes. The first followed closely the expected communication studies pattern, in that the writing task was explicitly contextualized in the world of work. The students were provided with a map of a small estate of semi-detached houses, accompanied by these instructions:

> Your employer has asked you to visit the estate and report back on what facilities (e.g. foreman's office, mess hut, lock-up store, toilet and wash-room, etc.) will be needed, and where best to position them. He has also asked you to contact the Clerk of Works to the Council and obtain his permission for siting the huts.

The tasks included listing the necessary facilities, consideration of the criteria for siting them, writing a letter to the Clerk of Works, and writing a report for the employer. The lecturer, Mr Wilkinson, led off with:

> What we're going to look at today is [the] question of site security and job organization. Really when we're talking about site security what we're talking about is storing materials on site, and this exercise is about what you'd need to do a job ...

The observer's first impression was of Mr Wilkinson's confident first-hand knowledge of the practical considerations relevant to decisions about a work site of this kind. Students were not learning to discuss and write in general terms – in a decontextualized fashion, that is – but to discuss and write about the specific concerns of a precisely defined context. They were led to consider such relevant criteria as the number of workmen on site, the requirements of the Health and Safety at Work Act, the likely duration of the task, communication and access, visibility as a protection against vandalism, and nearness to drains. When the lecturer told an anecdote it was not in order to personalize the discussion – as it always was in our school data – but to contextualize the issues more firmly in real life.

The class had previously done work on letters, and were given a format for the 'short report'. While they wrote, the lecturer walked round giving individual advice, about inventing names, about using a sketch map and about what should go under 'Terms of Reference'. He told one student, 'I think you've got to do a bit more explaining to Clerk of Works than you would to employer', and told another about a student in another group who placed the hut in a garden because 'Mrs So-and-So made good tea' and who 'added to the sketch map the cigarette shop, fish and chip shop and pub'.

We have described this session in order to illustrate what is meant by saying that the writing task is integrated in the world of work. It is not merely that a work site provides the subject matter; it also provides the criteria for evaluating the writing, including criteria of relevance and irrelevance (the fish and chip shop) and stylistically acceptable formats for letters and reports. Thus, preparation for writing involved students in thinking about the considerations relevant to practical action as well as inferring from the practical context those criteria relevant to an effective piece of writing. It would be a mistake, however, to assume that Mr Wilkinson was training his students in skills directly relevant to their present work: in the real world apprentices are not required to write reports for management. A proportion of them might eventually move up to positions such as foreman, but this would be some years away. So what is the function of such contextualized work? It certainly aided control in the classroom by providing tasks perceived as realistic, relevant to the world where men make real decisions. Mr Wilkinson could see another function, however: after another session concerned with progress charts (not included in this data) when he was asked whether this would be useful to the students in their jobs, he said that he had only ever used progress charts when he had been made charge hand. He added that courses of this kind seemed 'to presume a more tolerant workforce if they understood the problems of management', which in his view had political implications. If this interpretation is valid, it may apply also to the courses contextualized in the commercial world, where future (or present) clerks are required to simulate the decision-making of lower management.

Mr Wilkinson's other writing session was different, though taught to the same group. Its purpose was to prepare for writing to be done the following week by considering where in England to site power stations using different fuels. Like Mr Davidson when he talked about advertizing, Mr Wilkinson offered the students an induction into the technical and economic criteria relevant to large-scale industrial decisions; like Mr Turner on food production in the Third World he was far from uncritical of the *status quo*, for example, discussing the social implications of choosing to develop American pressurized-water nuclear reactors 'which personally I would say are unsafe compared with ours but ... cheaper to build'. There were critical elements in Mr Wilkinson's teaching that seemed partly to subvert the rigid structure of the course.

Communication for Everyday Life

Finally we turn to courses which drew their criteria not from business or industry but from everyday life, or at least from those areas of everyday life in which the lecturers felt the students lacked some enabling competences. Mrs Brindley was teaching a group of male students whose previous experience of schooling had not been a great success; some of them would be entered for the Level One Communications examination of the City and Guilds of London Institute. In one session she asked the students to work in groups on a task in which they were required to simulate a dispute between a bus conductor and a female passenger in which an older male passenger also becomes involved. Each group discussed what might be said, and then wrote down a possible dialogue. Then one by one they read what they had written to the rest of the class, thus enabling some discussion of arrogance, swearing, politeness, aggressiveness, and the effect of uniforms. Later the lecturer asked the students each to write two parallel exchanges imagined to take place in a bus, exemplifying respectively aggressive and conciliatory strategies being adopted by the conductor, and the results of each of them. In effect the writing was a device to encourage not very reflective young men to reflect on the likely result of their actions. Its purpose seemed to be to help them to be more effective communicators, which in this case would mean helping them to be more aware of the impact on other people of their behaviour. We are treating this as a use of language contextualized in the concerns of everyday life, yet since this is a course for young workmen we cannot ignore the social and political implications of teaching them to avoid conflict. Since Mrs Brindley clearly intended to communicate values that would change students' behaviour, her concerns were like those we observed in many English lessons in schools. Unlike some other lecturers she did not communicate values unintentionally as a by-product of some other activity. Nevertheless, although the topic, personal interaction in an everyday context, was at the private end of the scale, it was dealt with in a detached way that did not require anecdote, reflective introspection or the expression of feeling. In this way the students' privacy was protected, so that they could take part in the session while remaining detached from the experience and interpretation offered. In this kind of communications work the attitudes and values carry more weight than the skills. Mrs Brindley was communicating 'deep' criteria – she also spent a minute on surface criteria (the spelling of 'they're' and 'their') – but these were deep criteria for living, not for writing. The writing done seemed only a means to advance introspection into behaviour and values. This session was the closest that our further education data comes to the cluster of characteristics most common in school lessons – private topics, personal treatment, moral intentions and emphasis on certain kinds of rationality – yet it was very different, because of the relatively impersonal treatment and the marginal importance of writing.

In two other sessions the preparation for writing also drew its criteria from people's private lives. One was taught by Mrs Brindley and approached quite close to the familiar pattern of the situated assignment. Students were required to plan a holiday trip by car to the south of France. They were given background information, and were required (i) to work out distances and calculate the amount likely to be spent on petrol, (ii) to write a letter to the

French Tourist Office in London, (iii) to tape record an oral message to a firm hiring out camping equipment, (iv) to answer some questions testing comprehension of a document about the hire of such equipment, and (v) to complete an application form for a British Visitor's Passport. Mrs Brindley's teaching on this occasion was mainly directed to ensuring that her students had read the information and instructions with enough care to notice and interpret appropriately the information relevant to carrying out the tasks. She also explained what was implicitly required in form-filling, the layout of a formal letter, reading a ferry timetable, and recording a message on a telephone fitted with an automatic answering system. These were indeed 'social and life skills', the implicit know-how needed to participate fully in our society. Although the form of this situated assignment was very like those we have already considered, it drew its rationale from a version of everyday life; whether it was a likely everyday life for the young workers in this group is another question, though it could be seen as preparing them to be consumers of such a holiday.

Conclusion

The sources of legitimation available to teachers of English or communications to justify the content of their courses vary according to the contexts in which they teach. School teachers, relatively protected from outside influences, turn mainly towards the literary studies in which they were trained. College lecturers teaching English depend upon examination requirements, with occasional reference to the business world. Mr Davidson's BEC communications course turned solely towards business and its values. The courses in technical/industrial departments appeared to have two points of reference, one in the world of work and the other in academic social studies. Although we have represented these last two through Mr Wilkinson and Mr Turner respectively this is a convenient simplification; most lecturers are likely to experience both influences. Many lecturers teaching communications linked to technical courses hold qualifications in social sciences, and all are aware of the liberal studies tradition of consciousness raising. On the other hand, their very employment depends on persuading students and their prospective employers that the courses are relevant to work. Because of this, many lecturers experience the kind of role-conflict that became momentarily visible in Mr Wilkinson's remark about a 'tolerant workforce'. Communication studies in technical contexts are often perceived as a powerful threat to an older and less instrumental set of values associated with the name 'Liberal Studies'. Mrs Brindley's course illustrates yet another pattern which is quite unlike the other strands in further education. Government policy in offering greatly increased opportunities for further education to the young unemployed has led to an increase in lower level courses, which, though nominally linked to some area of vocational training, in effect amount to general education at a very modest level. Such courses – in this case directed towards a City and Guilds Communications examination – take a 'social and life skills' perspective which attributes to students general social deficits and sets out to remedy them. The courses cannot be referred to any clear cut reference group, but draw their legitimation from the lecturers' commonsense' view of what constitutes normal everyday social competences. As we have seen, this led to attempts to influence students' values and behaviour which would have been more characteristic of school than of other further education courses.

How far then do the characteristics of these courses match with the institutional structures with which this paper began? A profound difference between schools and most college courses is visible. English teachers in schools, with a captive audience of pupils and a relatively high boundary screening them from outside influences, take a paternalistic view of their responsibilities, seeking to change at some depth the values of their students. Most courses in further education take a more external view of their responsibilities: the students' relationship with the college and its staff is perceived as nearer to a contractual one, so that courses focus upon qualifications and skills rather than values and perspectives. This statement has to be qualified however: several of the Communications courses seem likely to transmit managerial perspectives on work, and the social and life skills orientation of some City and Guilds courses brought them close to English in schools. Mr Turner's Third World lesson was also intended to transmit values, though the liberal studies tradition of 'raising consciousness' must be seen as no more than a strand running through courses which are predominantly different in nature. These qualifications suggest that the contractual element in students' status will go only part of the way towards accounting for course characteristics, so that we must also look elsewhere.

Next to be considered are the differences between business and technical departments. Within business departments there is a sharp contrast between English and BEC Communications. The former emphasizes surface conformity: it seems probable that this conformity is as important as the knowledge of written conventions in preparing typists for their future roles. In contrast, the Communications courses transmit not only the ability to carry out relatively independent acts of communication, but also the perspectives and values of business management. It is not possible to link this contrast directly to students' qualifications: although many of the least qualified young women follow typing courses so do some of the best qualified (in terms of O-levels). It would be tempting too to link the difference with the establishment of gender roles for women in business, but this explanation in marred by the presence of a substantial number of women students on BEC courses. At this point, students' aspirations play an active part in determining the kind of curriculum they experience, whether they choose a typing course or aspire through BEC qualifications to a career in management.

Technical departments are different in this respect. Here we found no 'English' courses whatsoever, and the Communications courses proved to be more diverse than those in business departments. In contrast too, students' qualifications played a more important part in determining the curriculum: the 'social and life skills' courses we saw were clearly intended for the least able and there was little attempt to relate them to work. Examination demands played a part here. The Technician Education Council requires each college to submit course outlines for validation, and this appears to allow for substantial variation between different TEC courses, and for the continued expression of the 'consciousness raising' purposes of liberal studies though on a relatively small scale. As we have seen, the CITB requirements were much tighter, giving Mr Wilkinson little opportunity to turn away from activities closely linked to work and to managerial priorities.

To account for what curriculum a particular student experiences it is not enough to look solely to the organizational structure in which the course occurs. In the preceding paragraphs we have referred to the effects of compulsory and voluntary attendance, the difference between business and technical departments, the effects of the students' existing qualifications, and the tightness or looseness of examination requirements. But for a full account it is necessary to mention the actors within these structures, the students' career aspirations and consequent choices of course, the lecturers' sources of legitimation in university subjects or in business and industry, and the continued existence of the liberal studies tradition. To this must be added the need to co-opt students' commitment to courses, the so-called 'control' issue. Further education students take seriously those courses which lead to high status qualifications and those courses which appear to be closely related to present or future employment. The sharpest problem faces lecturers who teach courses that are both low in status and not closely related to work; in the 'social and life skills' courses this led to a high sensitivity to students' concerns in everyday life. Lecturers attempted to capture students' interest by responding quickly to their expressed needs. Bowles and Gintis (1976) have proposed a correspondence between modes of control in education and modes of control at work. Business courses might seem to exemplify this: close external control for aspiring typists, but more open tasks requiring students to internalize values for BEC students aiming at the lower rungs of management. But the technical departments showed no such pattern: City and Guilds and TEC alike required active participation by students, while it was the CITB course for future craftsmen that provided the tightest structure.

The processes by which curriculum is created and maintained are not simple or homogeneous. The different versions of the curriculum, mediated by examination requirements, play a role in social control in both college and workplace by encouraging students to accept particular purposes and criteria as valid. The process is reciprocal: the values of the workplace are reflected in college curricula, which in turn reinforce those values in the students' perceptions of work.[5] But this is not the whole story. Lecturers, like students, pursue their own purposes, sometimes in order to advance their careers but sometimes because of commitment to values. The students pursue qualifications, but also want to understand the world and to enjoy classes, and these aspirations too become part of the context within which the lecturers carry out their teaching. Thus there is no simple transmission of the values of business and industry, but a complex interplay of actions and motives within an institutional structure which is itself undergoing piecemeal change.

Notes

1 The Versions of English Project is based at the University of Leeds and is supported by a grant from the Social Science Research Council. It is a study of the variety of English and Communications curricula experienced by different groups of students in the last year of compulsory education in schools and in the following year in schools and further education colleges. The data collected include interviews with teachers and students, classroom observation, written work and documents. The purpose of the project is to describe different versions of English and to investigate how each is related to its institutional context, what justifications were offered by lecturers and teachers and how each was experienced by students.
2 The following table summarizes the material used in preparing this paper; it is no more than a sub-sample of the material gathered from these courses and from further education generally.

	Teaching time observed (minutes)
1 GCE O-level English Language course	312
2 RSA Stage I English courses	154 and 94
1 RSA Stage III English course	50
2 City and Guilds Level 1 course + 1 equivalent college course (Communications)	234 and 160
1 Construction Industries Training Board course (City and Guilds 236)	138
1 BEC (National) People and Communications course	125
1 TEC General and Communication Studies course	85
9 courses	Total: 21 hours 54 minutes

These figures refer to the actual teaching time represented by our observations and not to timetabled time.
3 This is 'strong framing' in the terminology used by Bernstein (1971).
4 Situated Assignments: most writing can be said to have two 'contexts' or 'situations', that in which it is written, and that in which it is likely (or intended) to be read. In schools and colleges the latter context is frequently simulated: a report may be supposed to be read by an employer but will in fact be read only by the lecturer or examiner. The intended or simulated context involves a purpose, a conception of audience, and, based upon these, some ('deep') criteria for choosing content, format and style. When in this paper the term 'situated' or 'contextualized' is used, it refers to the explicitness with which the intended context and its accompanying criteria have been formulated. When a piece of school writing is not 'contextualized', the teacher

who reads it will tacitly assign it to a context, but will not have made that context and criteria explicit to the writer.

5 Gleeson and Mardle (1980) suggest that lecturers in technical departments tend to import into colleges hierarchical relationships drawn from industry and commerce. They also produce evidence that technical departments have exerted pressure to turn liberal studies away from its traditional concern with consciousness raising towards communications studies – that is, towards courses contextualized in the workplace. Thus there is pressure to reproduce not only the relationships but also the ideologies seen by management to be appropriate.

References

BALL, S.J. 'A subject of privilege: English and the school curriculum 1906–35' (in this volume).

BALL, S.J. and LACEY, C. (1980) 'Subject disciplines as the opportunity for group action: A measured critique of subject sub-cultures' in WOODS, P., *Teacher Strategies*, London, Croom Helm.

BARNES, D. and D. (1983) 'Cherishing private souls: Writing in fifth year English classes' in ARNOLD, R. (Ed.) *Timely Voices: English Teaching in the Eighties*, Oxford University Press.

BARNES, D. and D. (Forthcoming) *Versions of English*, London, Heinemann.

BOWLES, S. and GINTIS, H. (1976) *Schooling in Capitalist America*, London, Routledge and Kegan Paul.

GLEESON, D. and MARDLE, G. (1980) *Further Education or Training?*, London, Routledge and Kegan Paul.

LANDER, G. (1980) 'The language of BEC', in *The Social Science Teacher*, 10.

2   English: A Curriculum for Personal Development?

Caroline St John-Brooks

I am not worried they'll be sold a duff car. I am worried that they'll be sold a duff life.

(Mr Davies, English teacher)

Introduction: The Two Cultures of Schooling

How does the social structure reproduce itself, and what is the role of schooling in this process? A likely place to look for some answers is the school curriculum, in the structuring of school knowledge and its effects on the consciousness of the young (Bernstein, 1971; Young, 1971).

In this chapter I consider the teacher's role in first selecting and then transmitting one aspect of the curriculum and its associated values. The analysis is based on observations of the life and work of an English department in a comprehensive school between 1976 and 1977 (St John-Brooks, 1980). The school, which I shall call Crossley Hill, was a mixed school with about 1300 pupils, on the edge of a fair-sized city. The first- and second-year pupils attended a lower school on a separate site; the older pupils attended the upper school. Most of the classroom observation was carried out in the upper school and concentrated, though not exclusively, on years four and five.

The school curriculum structures knowledge according to assumptions embedded in the wider society and passes that knowledge on to the young. However, as Bourdieu (1974) has argued, the young do not themselves arrive at school with the same experience and resources. 'Each family', he says, 'transmits to its children, indirectly rather than directly, a certain *cultural capital* and a certain *ethos*' (Bourdieu, 1974, p. 32). The possession of such cultural capital offers a child the possibility of an unproblematic and familiar relationship to the school curriculum: the assumptions underlying its selection are already the assumptions of the child.

The school curriculum is not all of a piece, though. In the secondary sector it is normally organized into separate subjects which represent a division not only between contents but between sub-cultures: competing subject sub-cultures within the overall culture of the school (Esland, 1971; Ball and Lacey, 1980). Where such subject identities are firm and strongly demarcated, secondary schools operate what Bernstein (1971) calls a 'collection code'.

The strict segregation between individual subjects that characterizes the 'collection code' curriculum can strongly affect pupils' experience of schooling, particularly after subject options are chosen at the end of the third year (Woods, 1979; Ball, 1981). But although this system of subject fragmentation leads to a channelling of differentiation of many parts of pupils' experience at 14+, English is one of the few subjects currently studied by all pupils up to the sixth form. Only then does it become optional – at this point often acting as a major differentiating subject in separating science from arts courses.

But while the compulsory nature of English up until the sixth form suggests that there is a consensus as to its nature and importance, this is far from the truth. As Ball points out (see Chapter 3), the subject itself is, and has historically been, at the centre of immense ideological controversy. At the heart of this controversy is one of the major value tensions in Western society: that between rationalism and romanticism.[1] From the rationalist perspective, education is training for work, and schools are responsible for equipping children with skills to sell in the market place. Romanticism, on the other hand, sees education as personal development. So far as English is concerned, conflict can arise between those who see the subject in terms of the acquisition of literacy skills (spelling, grammar, letter-writing) which are needed to pass examinations and get a job, and those English teachers committed to what they see as the nurturing of human qualities vital to personal and expressive development.

The skills-oriented rationalist approach is that of many teachers – and pupils – as well as parents and employers (Schools Council, 1968). And most, though not all, of the teachers at Crossley Hill regarded training in literacy skills as the overriding task of the English department. Teachers whom I interviewed criticized the English department almost entirely from the point of view of their own department's needs: they saw it as a servicing department. In answer to the question, 'What do you consider to be the role of English in the curriculum?', the typing teacher complained that she had to teach syllabification and hyphens. The careers teacher stressed the need to be able to write a good letter of application for a job, and the modern languages teacher bewailed the fact that children did not know the parts of speech. The car-maintenance teacher described indignantly how 'his lads' could not put down on paper what they knew, and were thus barred from gaining their precious qualifications. And a French teacher suggested that, since schools are not very good at providing opportunities for personal enrichment, perhaps they ought not to try. Survival is what schools are about, he suggested, and more realism is needed. 'The English department lives in a dream world,' he said, 'where everyone suddenly goes from E to A. It's not going to happen.'

In part, this emphasis on skills and qualifications results from the increasing bureaucratization of society discussed by Weber (1947) and explored more recently by Dore (1976) and Collins (1979). Collins notes that paper qualifications are often not actually in the subjects which employers need, but function rather as passports into status groups which are closed to those without the passport. As Dore points out:

Weber made insistence on qualifications part of his classic definition of bureaucracy as an ideal type – and for very good reasons; certificates are objective; governments need, among other things, standards of impersonal judgement which protect them against corrupt favouritism. (p. 74)

Weber suggested that increasing rationalization and bureaucratic domination have far-reaching cultural effects. Schools are increasingly dominated by the need for a training which produces the experts necessary for running modern bureaucratic institutes and understanding modern technology. But this kind of rationalist organization is not without its costs, particularly to individual freedom (Marcuse, 1972). In educational terms, that is, personal development is often subordinated to conformity in the name of examination results.

Credentialism and rationalism do act as powerful forces in education. But along with this emphasis on examinations there runs, too, a much older but equally influential tradition which goes back to the elementary school and, before that, to the dame school. English, for instance, has been taught for generations in terms of basic reading and writing skills, with the stress on spelling, punctuation and some grammar, together with comprehension, composition, and letter writing (see Chapter 3). This is 'common-sense' English, still taught in many schools, often by non-specialists.

James Callaghan's Ruskin College speech of 1976, and the so-called 'Great Debate' which it initiated, reasserted this common-sense tradition of skills as preparation for work. And today, we see fresh attempts to tie schooling ever more closely to the needs of employers and to the improvement of the economic performance of the country as a whole, through the activities of the Department of Education and Science and the Manpower Services Commission.

While the everyday culture of rationalism pervaded the thinking of most teachers at Crossley Hill, it was resisted by the English department. The English teachers were deeply committed to the personal development of their pupils. Accordingly, they placed much emphasis on discussion, writing and literature. In this they were typical of many English teachers in schools. The skills to which the other teachers attached so much importance were seen by the English staff merely as a means to this end. A quotation from Mr Davies probably puts the English teachers' position fairly: 'You will end up banging your head against the examination very severely unless you pay attention to such trivial concerns [as spelling and punctuation],' he told one class, ' – and they are trivial.' The department took up a dissident stance towards the culture of the school, a stance of which many other teachers were aware.[2]

The English teachers held strong ideological commitments and beliefs, central to which were a number of truths which were taken to be self-evident,[3] but which were essentially unprovable. They held that pupils could and would enter a fuller, freer life through writing, discussing their own and other people's writing, and by the act of making the kind of judgments which are made by the writers of fiction, plays and poetry. These truths were the badges of the faithful, and though the English teachers' philosophy was egalitarian when it came to teaching the children, the majority of people in school and in life generally who did not accept their beliefs were thought of as being distinctly less worthy than they, as at best undeveloped in their thinking.

The English Department: The Culture of a Subject

Bernstein (1971) notes that when school subjects are sharply divided from each other, a strong sense of subject identity is created in each group of teachers. This English department certainly saw itself as being very different from the rest of the school. Their 'special identity' was partly related to their common frame of reference, or 'intersubjective meanings' (Taylor, 1971), one which was not shared by most of the other teachers. They rejected the rationalistic model of life which they saw in the school. Good English teaching, they believed, should work *against* such a model, and so they resisted the conception of English as a service subject for other parts of the curriculum. Mr Anderson, the head of the English department, even defined the department's aims to me by setting them against the integrated humanities curriculum of the lower school, where English, history, geography and religious studies were combined. He believed that this latter approach debased English to a mere matter of literacy skills.

During the research period, the English department at Crossley Hill consisted of seven teachers, of whom four could be defined as the core of the department, who shared most strongly a sense of subject identity. Despite the fact that two other key members including the Head of Department, Mr Anderson, had left the previous year, the strong sense of unity built up over several years persisted. Each teacher, of course, interpreted his or her relationship to the department, the pupils and the task rather differently, but the four core members, all men, had enough in common to form a distinct group. And their beliefs as to the nature of English teaching informed their professional identity as English teachers. Their subject identity served to distinguish them not only from the teachers of other subjects, but from other ideologies of English teaching, too.

How was this subject identity expressed in the cultural life of the department? Even patterns of association within the staffroom revealed the English department's separate identity. At break and in the lunch hours, members of the department gathered in a different staffroom from the other teachers – in the 'quiet room', nominally set aside for marking books. Only a few other teachers ever spent much time there: the atmosphere was not particularly welcoming. Reasons given to me by English teachers for this separation included: 'The English department does more marking than other departments;' 'the head of department felt we should be able to discuss our work at any time and not have to call special meetings;' 'I like to read without being disturbed;' and an uncomplimentary remark to the effect that surely the reason was obvious when one listened to the general level of conversation in the main staffroom.[4]

All these reasons served to define the English teachers' commitment vis-à-vis the rest of the staff. They suggested that they marked more, were more interested in their work and wanted to discuss it any time, really *wanted* to read, and only enjoyed serious conversation. They had low opinions of the attitude of most other teachers to their jobs. For instance, one of the English teachers, Mr Rogers, said of some of his colleagues: 'All they're using school for is the furtherance of their own career and after a while it becomes the most blatant and conscious exploitation for their own development. And their excuse is – my wife and family have to live.'

This exclusiveness did not go unnoticed among the rest of the staff. Whereas the Head of Department, Mr Anderson, had described his job to me as 'patrolling the boundaries' so that his staff could get on with their jobs without interference from the headmaster or other staff, his successor was specifically invited by the headmaster to 'try and get the English department out of the quiet room.'

However, by resisting the culture of the school in this way, and retreating from its public life, the department was unable to influence the school as a whole, unlike the English department at Beachside comprehensive (Ball, 1981), which was in the vanguard of the change to mixed ability teaching. Moreover, Ball and Lacey (1980) noted in their study of four English departments that support from the headteacher was crucially important where the standing of the department in the rest of the school was concerned.

At Crossley Hill the English department was engaged in a long war of attrition with the headmaster. This both complicated and intensified its subject identity, for while on the one hand the head did not always offer his support, he was an English specialist. He, however, was a 'rationalistic' grammarian of the kind discussed earlier, who disapproved of the mixed ability classes run by the English (and the mathematics) departments. He had instituted his own 'express groups' for children he identified as 'bright', and ran these in the lunch hour since the English department under Mr Anderson had refused to cooperate. The head, unsurprisingly, saw the department as a dissident cell within the school. He was suspicious, too, of their politics. After one interview, when the tape-recorder had been turned off, he asked me if I had heard any English teacher 'twist' the meaning of a book to make a political point in class.

Furthermore, the headmaster's suspicions were fed by the fact that all four 'core' English teachers demonstrated their resistance to social pieties beyond the classroom. They dressed as students rather than as conventional teachers – jumpers and jeans, long scarves, sometimes Dr Marten boots. Most had longish hair at the time. Not one had a car: two took the bus to work, one rode a bicycle, one walked. Mr Anderson had had a car but could not drive it: his wife did. He once expressed amazement that people bothered to wash their cars: What was the point of spending two hours pouring water over a lump of metal? While prepared to work hard at their own jobs, the English staff opposed a generalized work ethic, offering a strong but slightly self-mocking resistance to the conventions of bourgeois life.

Such a sub-culture gains strength from its isolation and introversion, in that its members offer each other confirmation of the rightness of their beliefs which is denied them by the institution itself. But this English department sacrificed the chance to influence the rest of the school – even sympathetic staff found them unwilling to explain their ideas to those outside their circle. And their failure to convince the headmaster of the value of their approach had important effects. Though they did not respect his views, his institutional power was real: he could, and did, appoint a new head of department whose views were in line with his, not theirs.

In the staffroom, then, the English teachers' ideology was overtly established as being in opposition to most teachers' cultural norms. How was such an ideology embodied in classroom practice?

The Practice of English: Constructing a Curriculum

The ideology of the core English group was expressed both in the curriculum choices that they made, and in the way that these were transmitted in the classroom. The department was in favour of the mixed ability grouping which had operated in third-year English and maths since before the present headmaster had been appointed. In the fourth and fifth years, these classes were banded.[5] But even here, O-level and CSE candidates were not separated: the department taught Mode 3 language and literature courses for both examinations because this gave maximum scope to teachers to choose their own syllabus.[6]

The English syllabus consisted of set books, chosen by individual teachers within a framework of departmental assumptions as to which books offered valuable insights for pupils of different ages.[7] Such assumptions were rarely made explicit, but ideas were circulated through the medium of the chosen books. As Ball (1981) notes:

> The concept of subject sub-cultures is less concerned with subject-content *per se* and the explanatory methodology and epistemology of disciplines than with the organization and selection of subject-knowledge for teaching purposes and the maintenance of collectively-approved subject pedagogies. (p. 185)

All teaching took place through literature – the separation or 'classification' between language and literature was weak (Bernstein, 1971) – and texts which teachers had found fruitful with particular classes were discussed and recommended, building up a core of works over the years.

In the third year, the department liked to use myths, legends and folktales, as well as books by children's authors such as Roald Dahl and the American Betsy Byars. In the fourth and fifth years, though, they were more uncompromising. D.H. Lawrence's stories, plays and essays were often used, as were Arthur Miller's *The Crucible*, Dickens' *Hard Times*, Sophocles' *Oedipus Rex*, George Eliot's *Silas Marner*, Mark Twain's *Pudd'nhead Wilson*, and the poetry and plays of Berthold Brecht. Individual teachers drew from the canon according to taste. One, for instance, said he liked teaching Shaw's *Arms and the Man* because 'the values were so clear.' 'Not to say cardboard,' said one of his colleagues, who had used it only once. But the books, taken together, did form something of a 'selective tradition' of the kind described by Williams (1965).

The nature of this consensus as to why some works were more valuable than others was not usually articulated. Mr Rogers, a probationer in the English department, observed that the established teachers 'played their cards very close to their chests.' Asking for clarification would have revealed that all was not as obvious to him as it was to them, and could perhaps have damaged his credibility as a fully committed member of the group. Mr Anderson told me that he chose books intuitively, according to whether he thought a particular class was intellectually and emotionally ready for them or not.

But intuition is, of course, not free-floating, but grounded in a particular set of ideological and cultural assumptions. In fact, the Crossley Hill English department stood squarely in the literary tradition of Arnold and Leavis which has emanated from the English school at Cambridge University. Three of the original department did their degrees there, including Mr Anderson, the founder of the present department. But this tradition, with its emphasis on literature and individual judgment, was combined with other, newer approaches, particularly those drawn from what Ball and Lacey (1981) call the creative/expressive paradigm.

Literature was important to these teachers not as a means of passing on a fixed cultural heritage, but as offering pupils particular ways of understanding their own experiences – a development from the creative, personal writing which had been stressed during their first three years in the school. It was in this spirit that Mr Davies described Shakespeare, Brecht and Lawrence to his fourth-year class as 'people like you, who thought a great deal about existence, and attempted to put it into words.' By emphasizing that the words on the page came from the mind of a human being like them, he hoped to increase the 'space' in the children's minds where they feel in control and can calmly consider their experience. Lower-band children in particular, he suggested, have low expectations and do not value themselves or their lives.

Mr Davies recalled watching these children doing examinations: fidgeting, dropping things, doing anything rather than try and come to grips with the paper and fail. In class, he asserted, teachers can draw such children in, make them part of the lesson, create a joint enterprise where none stands alone. In an examination, each individual is exposed. Invigilating 'makes one very aware of one's ... yes ... failure,' he said.

Mr Rogers, another member of the core group, stressed common understanding, too. 'The class is involved in a group exercise, not in a number of individual performances,' he said. All the 'core' English teachers saw themselves as working *against* the individualistic, competitive ethic. They quite specifically tried to avoid 'sponsoring' bright children in the way that teachers of mixed ability groups often do. And they also endeavoured to avoid labelling individual children according to their intellectual abilities. Children who had not grasped what was going on were never called 'dim' or 'thick' by these teachers, even in the staffroom. Labels were, instead, behavioural: 'intractable', or 'scatty', or 'all over the place'. Lack of achievement was thus conceptualized as a result of too little effort of self-discipline, not lack of ability. And, while stressing the importance of personal qualities, such labels were non-deterministic. Change was always seen to be possible. Similarly, successful children were not called 'bright', but 'shrewd', that is knowing what was wanted, or just 'all right', independent and autonomous – going ahead with the minimum of help.

Such a value system places a premium on participation in class – 'lively' was always a complimentary term, 'timid' a condemnatory one.[8] Mr Davies once complained that a class on its best behaviour because a visitor was there was 'unteachable'. He offered to me a description of teaching by Gilson (1957) as being closest to what he wanted to achieve: 'The fundamental fact of nature is that no man can understand anything for another one. No master can take his own knowledge out of his own mind and put it in the heads of his pupils. The only thing he can do is help them put it themselves into their own minds.' Mr Davies wanted to keep his pupils' minds in a state of what Gilson, borrowing from Thomas Aquinas, calls 'active potentiality'. He chose books which he hoped would foster this sense of receptiveness, and startle his pupils out of their fixed views of life. In the words of Hodgson (1974), he was trying to communicate a way of knowing, rather than a state of knowledge.

But in refusing to categorize their pupils in cognitive terms – such concepts as 'reading ages' were referred to with scorn – the English teachers ran the risk of ignoring very real difficulties some children had with the books. Because they lacked reading skills and vocabulary, some found it hard even to follow the basic plot of a play or novel. Some were prepared to enter class discussion and struggle for meaning that way, but others were left bewildered on the outside. Too few – even if they enjoyed the books – saw 'the point' of what they were doing. As I will show in the following section, such an approach made relating to the material in the manner required by the teacher very difficult for children who did not already possess the background and experience – the cultural capital, in fact – to intuit what kind of response was being implicitly demanded.

The English teachers were resisting the common-sense assumption that children go to school to have facts and skills put into their heads by teachers. But interviews with pupils revealed that many lower-band children, who were nearly all working-class, thought the English teachers should spend more time on teaching them basic skills, though several of them recognized that a good deal of teaching time had already been spent on such skills, to little avail. The

English: A Curriculum for Personal Development?

English teachers, therefore, were reinterpreting both the teacher's and the pupil's role in a way which some children found deeply problematic. For without carefully constructed bridges between pupils' everyday lives and the world of the English lesson, such teaching is most likely to find a worthwhile response only in those pupils who are already confident in their judgments, who are used to seeing their personal experience as significant: in short, to those from the middle class.

Variations in English Practice: A Study of Two Teachers

Having outlined the general orientation to English teaching and learning within the department, I shall now focus on two individual teachers, both members of the 'core' of the department. While the aims of all 'core' teachers were broadly similar – encouraging pupils to incorporate literature into the conscious experience of their lives – their methods of trying to achieve these were different, according to their convictions, their perceptions of the pupils they taught and their own biographies.[9] The teachers I shall focus on, Mr Rogers and Mr Davies, were strongly committed to both their subject and their pupils, and opposed to the general ethos of the school. However, they still interpreted their task in rather different ways.

Mr Rogers

Mr Rogers was a 'mature' probationary teacher with a fair amount of life experience behind him. Educated at a local comprehensive school, he had read English at Oxford, worked at skilled and unskilled jobs in America and Europe, and then returned to England to do a PGCE. A Marxist, he was a vivacious and entertaining conversationalist, and openly critical of the school hierarchy (he referred to one senior teacher as 'lobotomized') and of the examination system. But his lack of experience, large classes and a heavy timetable put him at the mercy of the examination syllabus. Towards the end of the year he told me: 'I've had everything I believe in minced up by this crappy exam.'

Mr Rogers' frame of reference – which included film, drama and politics – was in some ways more eclectic than that of three other core teachers, but he shared with them the conviction that English is a subject through which children can come to understand themselves and their society better and that literature is an indispensable part of the process.

His teaching, often but not always successful, was bedevilled by the paradox which exists in so much active teaching by radical teachers. In spite of his wide-ranging ideas, his control over his pupils was tight. By seeking to make clear to his classes the connections and relationships *he had* worked out for himself, he presented to some of his pupils what seemed to be an imposed framework, requiring only passive acceptance. Unless they could accept his hard-won ideas and enter an already-established process, they could play little part in the active making of meaning.

A lesson with a fourth-year examination group, for instance, demonstrates two of Mr Rogers' characteristic modes of exposition: structuring and dramatizing. The class is reading D.H. Lawrence's play, *The Widowing of Mrs Holroyed*.

> *Mr Rogers*: In the third act, there's a big balancing of the scales – in the first two acts we see the scales go up and down, but mostly against Holroyd. In the third act, Lawrence is balancing the scales on Holroyd's side. People come in to give his side of things.

On the blackboard, he begins two columns: Mrs Holroyd *v* Mr Holroyd.

> *Mr Rogers*: Lawrence looks on human relations as a battle, a dialectic if you like, a struggle.

He expands the column on the board to: Mrs Holroyd *v* Mr Holroyd
                                         Blackmore   Minnie
                                         Jack   Grandma

in order to show how the characters line up. 'Who else?' he asks. 'The children,' answer the class. When 'the children' have been duly entered, Mr Rogers invites his pupils to relate this balance of power and sympathy both to their experience of the play, and to their own experience.

> *Mr Rogers*: As we look at this play, the balance gets bigger and bigger and bigger until it's the whole of life.... We're in this balance all the time.... You might find yourself to be at one point completely this way, at another completely that way.

In common with the other English teachers, Mr Rogers stressed that literature is the work of human beings expressing themselves to others, but, in harmony with his political interest in the structure of society, he sought to lay bare the structure of each work, and the way in which the writer achieved a particular response in the reader, rather than asking his pupils to identify and consider their own reactions.

Frequent references to his own life counterbalanced the potential dryness of such an approach, but the voice of the writer, so crucial to Mr Davies' lessons as we shall see, was supplemented and sometimes replaced by the voice of Mr Rogers. In one sense, his approach could be seen as 'demystifying' the writers' skills, and, by de-emphasizing the personal response of his pupils, as creating a genuine circle of shared understanding. He was, after all, particularly concerned that pupils should actually understand what was going on – a consideration sometimes neglected by Mr Davies – but this meant spending some of every lesson reminding the class of the story so far, and clarifying difficult points.

English: A Curriculum for Personal Development?

The consequences of this, as indicated by his pupils' responses to a questionnaire which I administered to sixty-four fourth-year pupils (taught by all the English teachers) were that while Mr Rogers was highly regarded by some, he had succeeded only in boring and alienating others. Most of these were quiet girls, who in class otherwise appeared interested and compliant. Mr Rogers' strong interest in elevating the less able, so it seemed, had carried in its wake an unanticipated and unrecognized sexism, differentiation of response between boys and girls respectively, to the detriment of the latter.

Some pupils did find his explanations helpful. Harriet, from his lower-band group, said:

> The teacher reads us the story, and we listen, then he reads to the end of the chapter and he asks us questions to make it [*sic*] sure that we've been listening and we answer it as best we can, and then he starts telling us, you know, what it means, the whole thing, and the feeling of what's happened.

This experience of reading could hardly be more strongly framed by the teacher (Bernstein, 1971). And while Harriet, elsewhere in her interview, said that she enjoyed English and had learned a lot from Mr Rogers, not everyone agreed. Two girls from his fourth-year upper-band group had switched off entirely:

> *Kumari*: They say, 'Don't you do anything in [English] lessons?' and we say, 'No, we just sit and listen, that's all.' Never done any work in lessons.
>
> *June*: We can't wait to get out of class.

An extract from a lesson with June and Kumari's class illustrates the firm grip that Mr Rogers kept on the progress of his lessons; the mixture of reading and exposition is typical. Mr Rogers begins the lesson on Act 2 of *A Midsummer Night's Dream* by saying 'Just to recap....' 'Oh no,' groans one of the class in mock despair. 'All right, not to recap,' says Mr Rogers good-humouredly, but it is significant that he does anyway. 'We're in the fairy wood,' he says firmly, and is quick to quell giggles over the 'King of the Fairies', telling the worst offender that Oberon was usually played by the best-looking actor in the company. Thus he draws on values (the importance of good looks) which he thinks appeal to the class, and relocates the play clearly in the Elizabethan theatre, where 'fairy' did not suggest effeminacy.

Though Mr Rogers wants to draw the whole class into a circle of intersubjective meanings where the play can be considered on its own terms, in practice he 'sponsors' certain pupils in the class and ignores others. When he asks for a description of Oberon and Titania's relationship, two high-status pupils, on whom he often relies, reply. Tony says, 'Not very good.' And when Mr Rogers asks why not, Tina replies, 'She's got a little changeling boy.' Mr Rogers often uses questions like this to explain the action, rather than to draw out different responses or to stimulate certain pupils. So he tends to ask a small range of pupils who are likely to give the right answers; humming and hawing would hold up the action.

Early in the lesson, Mr Rogers stresses the mundane nature of Oberon and Titania's quarrel: 'They've had a bit of a tiff,' he says. 'They're in the state of a household domestic quarrel.' In this way, he encourages the class to relate the happenings in the play to their own experience, and reduces the distracting 'fairy' element. But as the lesson progresses he expects the class to move further into the circle of shared meanings that the play presupposes.

Speaking of Shakespeare's fitting of language to character, Mr Rogers makes his point by exaggerating the triviality of ordinary conversation. He suggests to the class that Titania would hardly say, 'Oh, hallo, had a hard day at the office?', or Oberon, 'Not too bad, how about you, my dear?'

> You must give glorious and fantastic characters the language of dream, the language of poetry. You go into the mysterious wood, and the law is now of magic, the law of the king and queen of the fairies.... By seeing how they rule, we can see the way the world of man is ruled and make comparisons and criticisms.

Mr Rogers is no longer making concessions – indeed, he has broadened the discussion into general theorizing. Those who have followed him this far are now operating within the framework of the play's values, even if they do not understand them clearly yet. But children who have resisted, got bored or lost the thread, such as June and Kumari, are left outside.

Mr Rogers' essentially didactic style of transmission, stressing the ideas embodied in books rather than the imaginative response of the reader, prevented some pupils from making their own peace with the works at their own rate. But for others – notably the high-status group who were eager to answer his questions – he successfully brought quite difficult works alive. David and Tony, for instance, were enthusiastic about Mr Rogers' treatment of *Oedipus Rex*:

> *David*: He makes it fantastic, he brings it through really well.
>
> *Tony*: 'Cos we couldn't really relate it to today. He helps us.

A rather charming example of relating literature to life came from Malcolm, a working-class boy in Mr Rogers' upper-band fifth-year group, who had been reading *Hard Times*. This book, which itself highlighted much of the English department's ideology, features Mr Gradgrind, who believes that children should be brought up on a diet of Fact, since art and imagination merely develop harmful fantasies. 'I reflected [sic] to a book the other night when gymastics was on telly. It was ... er ... Nadia Comanic on telly, and she's just iron, you know, no emotion at all, and I said 'Nadia Gradgrind' [he laughs].

The alienation of some pupils in the upper-band fourth-year group might lead one to expect disaster with the lower band, but quite the reverse was true. Mr Rogers tempered his insights and enthusiasms with some awareness of his pupils' possible limitations, taking care to relate texts to their own lives. His group was small, with a couple of lively and articulate members willing to interrupt, and Mr Rogers took their contributions seriously, which was appreciated by pupils unused to such consideration.

He begins a lesson on Rosemary Sutcliff's *Tristan and Iseult*, for instance, conventionally enough, asking the class to copy from the blackboard the 'Characteristics of a hero'. As he writes, he explains:

> First: courage. Then he must have athletic ability.... Third, again quite logically, he must be intelligent. And I think this intelligence should be ... should be split up into two. He should have a knowledge of men's minds and a knowledge of men's hearts. We've come across this with Tristan. He must have this special ability to estimate the hearts and minds of men. Four: adventurous spirit. You'll remember me saying that a quality of the hero is that he must always be seeking a new challenge.

Again, the structuring and dramatizing make their appearance, but nearly all the class is involved, as the interviews subsequently confirmed. Johnny, a hefty 15-year-old who other teachers found difficult, told me: 'At the end of each chapter he sort of refreshes your mind, and points out things, important things what's in the book.'

When the reading reaches a combat between the hero, Tristan, and a giant, Mr Rogers asks for a modern version of the heroic duel, and Colin answers at once: 'The Western'. 'People have always been attracted by this idea of two forces colliding and one coming up on top,' says Mr Rogers. 'It's got to be even on both sides,' offers Colin, 'not sort of one-sided.' 'Yes,' says Mr Rogers, 'good, there's got to be a sort of to and fro. You've got to be involved in the combat and the emotions of men taking part.' When Colin describes the author's language as 'sharp', Mr Rogers employs one of his favourite techniques: taking up an answer, then enlarging it and redefining it so that it makes a point for him. 'Good,' he says. '*I'll* put it this way. It's got to evoke, that's call out, physical movement, it's got to capture the sound of combat.... Words are sounds, and if you stick them together in a certain way, you can capture the sound of battle, if you're clever.' After reading the passage aloud, he observes: 'After you've read it, you feel you've been through it yourself.' Colin mutters his assent: 'You get carried away.'

But in this class too, where Mr Rogers even suggests to his pupils how they should feel, there were two or three resentful outsiders to the discussions. Kathy found his explanations too complicated: 'If I asked him what it means, he'd still use big words to explain it ... and I'm none the wiser, am I?' (And the short extract above shows that though Mr Rogers defined 'evoke', he still assumed that the class understood 'physical movement', 'combat' and the metaphorical use of 'capture'.) Kathy also disagreed with members of the class who thought Mr Rogers valued their opinions: 'At the moment it's just him talking, he don't ask our opinions.... If he asked our opinions on a book, I'd

49

tell him straight out I think it's crap. I would, I'd tell him it was crap.' So Mr Rogers' direct approach, lively and stimulating though it was for some pupils, bored and excluded others by over-explication, complicated language, and not leaving enough space for their views. 'His ideas are too fixed,' said one fifth-year girl.

Mr Davies

Unlike Mr Rogers, Mr Davies did not spend much time building bridges for his pupils between their everyday preoccupations and the books he had chosen as significant: he expected the texts themselves to work on their minds. An austere but witty man, he became an English teacher after his Cambridge degree through a conviction that giving detailed attention to literature was the most worthwhile way of spending his life. He believed that the expectations of most teachers are far too limited, and that his pupils should be given the chance of reading complex and demanding material which could enrich their lives and clarify their emotions. His opinion of the school was not high: like the other teachers, he saw his commitment as being to the kids, not the institution, and once jokingly expressed a wish for a tunnel which led directly from his chair in the staffroom to his classroom. When pressed for a comment on the school, he managed: 'It stinks.'

Mr Davies taught his fourth-year lower-band group with the minimun of explanation, rather hoping to explore the books as a joint public activity. In reading Berthold Brecht's *The Caucasian Chalk Circle*, he introduces one of the characters, 'The Singer', and advises the class: 'Stick to what the singer says, and you should know what's going on.' He continues: 'We need two doctors who are always arguing ... an architect ... a showman ... we need the governor's wife who is, to say the least, a bitch.' He *is* trying here to bring the play closer to the children, but uneasily. His use of 'bitch', for instance, is inappropriate. Few of the class would use it in a semi-formal public situation. But there is no lack of interest. There is a buzz of conversation as Mr Davies allocates the parts. 'It's best if you try and imagine what it would look like on the stage,' says Mr Davies, but unlike Mr Rogers he does not help them out. Their imaginations are left to their own devices. Mr Davies reads 'The Singer', to keep control and point up such explanation as appears in the play, and describes him as sitting on the stage watching the action.

But when the reading begins, there is much confusion. Those reading together as the peasants keep losing the place and don't seem to know what's going on. The content of the play is in danger of not emerging at all, so Mr Davies orchestrates them: 'Right, Steven, Robert, Deirdre, one ... two ... three....' The reading gets going, haltingly. There is much giggling at the difficult Russian names, which Mr Davies ignores: to him, this kind of consideration is irrelevant. Yet three boys from this group, when interviewed, said they wanted to read 'proper' stories about 'proper' life: 'Cos I don't

English: A Curriculum for Personal Development?

understand what they're on about,' said Bernard, 'or the countries they're in.' Mr Davies tries to increase the momentum. 'We're going to take till next year if we read at this rate,' he says loudly. An alternative strategy occurs to him. 'Robert! What's a beggar?' While Robert is casting round for an answer, Mr Davies cuts in: 'Someone who wants something. And if you want something you do not hesitate and stumble.' You might, of course, in a feudal despotism, but Mr Davies is trying to make the reading more effective so that the play's meaning comes through. The move from individual to actor is not made without embarrassment, however. There is giggling and moaning at having to read aloud. When 'the governor' is asked to stand up to increase his impact, he soon asks to sit down again. Even so, the reading develops some momentum. When Mr Davies interrupts to ask for some deductions, he uses the questions much as Mr Rogers might – to explain and clarify.

Mr Davies: What sort of city are we in? Robert? (Mr Davies, unlike Mr Rogers, uses questions to pounce on people who look as if they need drawing into the lesson. Robert rises to the occasion.)

Robert: Poor, with beggars and that.

Mr Davies: Who's rich?

Robert: The fat prince.

Satisfied with this minimum response, Mr Davies explains that the fat prince is about to kill the governor, and take over the city. With the prospect of violence, interest rises, and the reading restarts with renewed concentration. At the end of the scene, Mr Davies asks the class to write down in their books:

When the house of a great one collapses
Many little ones are slain.
Those who had no share in the *good* fortunes of the mighty
Often have a share in their *mis*fortunes.
The plunging wagon
Drags the sweating oxen down with it
Into the abyss.

Sitting on a table, swinging his legs, he tells the class: 'The only reason I asked you to write it down is so that we can look fairly carefully at what it says and what it means.' The class is now focused enough to explore some of the issues Brecht has raised. But institutional constraints intervene: the bell goes, and the lesson is over.

Driven along by Mr Davies, the class has achieved a growing sense of group effort. The characteristic atmosphere in this group is a jokey unspoken agreement that the children are all hopeless, an agreement which they enter into eagerly, partly because they can then avoid the world of strenuous self-realization which Mr Davies offers. The joke is that Mr Davies' best efforts can so easily be thwarted, by people not listening, or by just losing the place at a critical moment. Why it all *matters* to him is a mystery to them – but they don't bear him any ill-will. For his part, he expects people to join in, but is resigned to their falling short.

Mr Davies' first task has been to bring the individual pupils into some relationship with the play: to this end he has stressed, and achieved, some measure of joint endeavour. But creating shared meanings exists in uneasy tension with pupils' individual responses.[10] Mr Davies' approach assumes certain cultural competencies in his pupils: if they are lacking, he expects them to develop. He does not rely, though, on competent pupils to carry the lesson but rather tends to leave those who are 'all right' alone while concentrating on those he perceives as being on the fringes. In the following extract, Jane is one of these.

Mr Davies and the fifth-year group about to take O-level are discussing D.H. Lawrence's short story, *The Man Who Loved Islands*:

Mr Davies: What happens to him [the hero] when he is alone? Jane?

Jane: I dunno.

Mr Davies: Yes you do. [Ruminatively] What is it to be alone?

He insists that Jane must know, not just because she has read the story but because she is human. She only needs to pay attention to her own unarticulated experience. But Jane is unsure of the appropriate answer. What's more, she wants the spotlight turned onto someone else until she has felt her way into the lesson. Mr Davies moves on.

Mr Davies: What happens when he's alone?

Sally: He starts to hate....

Mr Davies: Yes, he starts to hate human beings. Why?

Sally: He's frightened, he don't want to communicate.
[She compares his reaction to the instinctive hiding of an animal.]

Jane: He's not conscious of himself.
[Mr Davies, sensing a move towards the sort of response he wants, becomes alert and interested.]

Mr Davies: Not conscious of himself: what does he need to be conscious of himself?

Jane: People.

Mr Davies: Yes, good.

In this way, pushing the discussion in the direction he wants, Mr Davies draws out the theme of Lawrence's story, which at the end of the lesson he restates and asks the class to write down: 'The truth is that without his relations to other lives, the individual is nothing.'

English: A Curriculum for Personal Development?

Often pupils in his classes were casting round for the right answers, just as they probably did in other lessons (Holt, 1969). In looking for an 'individual' response, Mr Davies really required a particular kind of response, an understanding from a story as to what the author is saying about the nature of human life or personal relationships. His reactions to what was said in discussions gave his pupils clues as to what direction to move in, but no more.

Though often confused, this class did eventually develop a sense of what understanding Lawrence entails. As Patricia complained to Mr Davies during the following lesson: 'He [Lawrence] sort of hides so much in the story, you have to dig it out.' 'We've had the idea,' said Mr Davies to the rest of the class, 'of things being hidden. Don't you like this?' 'You can't always find them,' said Patricia. Everyone laughed, Patricia too. She had been able to conceptualize the class's difficulties, and in this case Mr Davies' methods of immersing his pupils in the text to sink or swim had paid off.

By the time the fifth year came round, some pupils had been distinctly emboldened by Mr Davies' insistence that they could cope. Take Pauline:

> Reading books at home, I go through all the books we've got and open the *biggest* book. I started reading Thomas Hardy, and I'm not frightened to pick up a big book, whereas I was before. I'd rush and pick up a comic.

Peter outlines a similar development:

> When I first came to his lessons, I didn't know what he was on about, you know, going on about books and that, you know, because I'd never really looked at books in that way before.... After reading, like, Shakespeare, and I thought: 'Shakespeare! I won't understand the words and all that'.... It was a really good story, you know, I couldn't believe it.

Yet in spite of such successes, some pupils felt that English lessons with Mr Davies were conducted in a code they had not cracked. Some of his fourth-year upper-band group clearly suffered because they lacked explicit guidelines. Martin explains: 'He sort of laughs a lot, if you know what I mean, and the people on our table, er ... when he's gone, still don't understand a lot of it. And you've got to get on and do it.' Annie is from the same class: 'He knows what we should do, so to him we should know without asking, and I think that's how he feels, you know, that we shouldn't sort of ask.' Lower-band pupils, too, sometimes felt lost. One politely described *The Caucasian Chalk Circle* as 'too mature for us lot'. All the same, Mr Davies did believe that the play worked away at the children's minds in a quite unpredictable way, and told me that he was getting parts of it 'hiccupped' back to him for weeks. The processes of learning are not so well understood that we can entirely dismiss Mr Davies' account. Nevertheless, the interviews revealed that over half the fourth-years who thought the English books were too difficult were from Mr Davies' classes, though his pupils made up only about a quarter of the sample.

Caroline St. John-Brooks

Discussion

Both teachers, in their different ways, met the needs of some pupils and not others. And their strengths and weaknesses were almost the obverse of each other. Mr Rogers bored and oppressed some pupils by over-explication, while Mr Davies left others bewildered by not building enough bridges between them and the text. Yet Mr Rogers brought the books alive for some pupils, particularly the lower band, by relating them to the pupils' own experience, and Mr Davies had given some, mostly upper-band, pupils the confidence to make sense of the books for themselves.

It was Mr Davies who best fitted the type described by Bourdieu (1974), the teacher who takes for granted that his pupils possess the cultural capital which makes the appropriate relationship to knowledge possible:

> Moving to and fro between the charismatic use of the word as a lofty incantation whose function is to create in the pupil a suitable receptivity to grace, and a traditional use of university language as the consecrated vehicle of a consecrated culture, teachers assume that they already share a common language and set of values with their pupils, but this is only so when the system is dealing with its heirs. (p. 39)

Mr Davies did not, in fact, assume that he and his pupils already shared a common language, but that his job was to develop the understandings that such a language presupposes. The cultural chasm was to be bridged by the pupils through the text. His method depended on using himself as an example of what it was like on the other side: what it was to be in a particular relationship with the text. All the same his language, while certainly a 'university' language, did not derive from scholasticism, but from a peculiarly intense effort to clarify values and emotions within the tradition of literary criticism. It was the *nature* of the enterprise – the 'way of knowing' (Hodgson, 1974) – which mattered, not the specific judgments. A pupil who was prepared to 'dig out' meaning from a text would be quite at liberty to criticize an author's views or approach. But the freedom to say: 'This is boring/too difficult' was not on offer, and the genuinely personal response thus became problematic. Of course, such responses are often partial and limited, but by endorsing only a very specific way of relating to the material, both these teachers excluded pupils who found it hard to enter the circle of shared meanings in class. Given an opportunity to present and explore their genuine reactions, such pupils might perhaps have come to a more fruitful accommodation with the books and their experience of them.

Fulfilling the needs of every child in a class is, of course, impossible. But the ideology of the English department limited its effectiveness unnecessarily. The teachers saw themselves as being on the children's side, recognizing their 'real' needs which the bureaucracy of the school and the examination system ignored: 'the kids are all right' was virtually an article of faith in the department. Yet they sometimes failed to recognize how far their pupils shared

English: A Curriculum for Personal Development?

the values of the rationalistic common-sense world which they condemned, and that they were offering liberation to only a few.

In ideological terms, the Crossley Hill English department saw itself as acting against the rationalist consensus of the school: as a small group holding out for the things that really matter. But this ideology, though expressing a commitment to comprehensive education, mixed ability teaching and an egalitarian approach, was also deeply penetrated by the assumptions of a meritocratic literary elite. Though they rejected materialism, the promotion ladder, the measure of progress in terms of more money, possessions and status, the English department was nevertheless engaged in a private journey of self-improvement which was quite alien to the consciousness of some of their pupils. For them, each person's life was, as it were, a project: personal development was self-consciously sought and monitored.

But within working-class culture, which is essentially a culture of adaptation to oppression and constraint, the relationship between effort and reward which is implicit in this type of strenuous self-realization is more attenuated. For working-class children, defeat is structurally the more likely outcome. But the absence of just such a structural explanation among working-class people requires that, in the interests of self-respect, expectations be lowered and blame attributed to fate or luck.

Common sense, after all, offers its own rationalizations: life is not fair (which is true), the rich and successful can be unhappy too (which is true as well) and so on. Too much stress on personal responsibility implies personal responsibility for failure too, and the rationale for a reasonably satisfactory life must be constructed somehow. Both Ford (1967) and Willis (1977) suggest that this deep-rooted dislocation between cause and effect reduces working-class individuals' sense of their room for manoeuvre. They have little expectation that their personal decisions will make much difference to their lives.

Of course, notwithstanding the arguments of Bourdieu, class position does not entirely determine the destiny of individuals. Some working-class children clearly did enjoy English at Crossley Hill, and benefitted from the English teachers' approach. Conversely, a few of the baffled and bored were middle-class. But the overall pattern was clear enough. Though the department saw itself as acting in opposition to the hierarchic rationalistic value system of the school as a whole, the experience and achievements of its pupils did tend to divide along class lines. Thus, perhaps, the English department – unintentionally and ironically – still acted to reproduce the class structure.[11]

By denying that such structures exist and penetrate the classroom, by being unwilling to recognize that they are embodied in individuals through their possession or lack of cultural as well as financial capital, the department failed to develop consistently effective strategies for intervening in the process. A laudable refusal to categorize children by ability paradoxically resulted in the real needs of some disinherited individuals remaining unmet.

The department, too, by recognizing only personal, individualized modes of interaction as significant, achieved no grip on the mainstream of school life

(Mr Rogers, indeed, recognized this: he pointed out to me that the English teachers complained about staff meetings, but rarely spoke in them. As a probationer, however, he had no influence.) The department as a whole could not defend their position in a manner comprehensible or acceptable to most of the other teachers, especially the headmaster. By rejecting the bureaucratic world of institutions and the realm of public argument and debate, along with the kind of justification it demands, such romantic individuals or groups are destined to remain forever marginal, even if they do hope for social reform. (Among the core Crossley Hill teachers, in fact, while Mr Davies eschewed all political thought and action, the remaining three were all, broadly speaking, socialist.)

It is clear, too, that when teachers insist on a specific mode of relating to literature and experience, while giving only implicit indications of how it is to be achieved, emphasizing group endeavour in the classroom will not prevent the literary culture from being reproduced only through a few pupils: through Bourdieu's 'heirs to the system'. Such pupils need not *always* be middle-class. The point about cultural capital, like financial capital, is not that it is essential, but that progress is a great deal easier for those who already possess it. And as Bourdieu notes: 'The exceptional success of those few individuals who escape the collective fate of their class apparently justifies educational selection and gives credence to the myth of the school as a liberating force' (1974, p. 42).

British schools and teachers have yet to work out where they stand on the question of equality of treatment versus positive discrimination in response to individual needs. The English department at Crossley Hill demonstrated triumphantly, if sporadically, that complex literature can be meaningful and illuminating to all sorts of young people. But when the teachers assumed shared meanings which were not based on the public, common-sense assumptions by which their pupils interpreted their own lives, and when they stressed individual effort and intense focus at the expense of clarity, style and humour, they limited the range of relationships which their pupils could have developed to the texts, and also limited the number of pupils who could enter the circle of intersubjective meanings which slowly built up in class.

While it is true that many teachers' expectations are too low, teaching strategies do need to incorporate the recognition of cultural gaps, and teachers need to develop techniques for bridging them both through the careful selection of content and through sensitive teaching which allows pupils to appropriate that content. For, as Bourdieu (1974, p. 37) has pointed out:

> To penalize the underprivileged and favour the most privileged, the school has only to neglect, in its teaching methods and techniques and its criteria when making academic judgments, to take into account the cultural inequalities between children of different social classes.

Commitment is evidently not enough.

English: A Curriculum for Personal Development?

Acknowledgement

I should like to thank Roger Hampson, Andy Hargreaves and Martyn Hammersley for help in the preparation of this chapter.

Notes

1 I distinguish here between *rationality*, which represents detachment, clarity of thought and analytic power, and *rationalism*, which is, rather, an uncritical assent to the hierarchic structure and demands of society outside the individual. Rationalism can be seen as a debased form of rationality. *Romanticism* is the less-than-ideal word I have chosen to represent a mixture of individualism and social idealism perhaps best defined by T.E. Hulme, quoted by Williams (1961):

> Here is the root of all romanticism: that man, the individual is an infinite reservoir of possibilities; and if you can so rearrange society by the destruction of oppressive order then those possibilities will have a change and you will get Progress.

The root conflict is, of course, that between the individual and society, which in itself is a Romantic construct.

2 Dissident English departments are not uncommon. Ball (1981) refers to the 'stereotypical radical role attributed to English teachers generally', to which the English department at Beachside conformed. Grace (1978) found that English teachers represented 'a complete spectrum of ideological positions, from the Arnoldian to the Marxist stance', and contained as a group more individuals who exhibited 'radical doubts' than any other subject group.
3 Having a low opinion of sociologists, the Crossley Hill English teachers were not always willing to make their beliefs explicit in order to provide me with data.
4 Cf. Hargreaves (1972), who found that a 'norm of cynicism' operated in the staffroom, and serious discussion was not encouraged.
5 About two-thirds of the pupils in each year went into the 'upper band', and followed a common course. O-level candidates did a couple of extra books after CSE examinations had started. The lower-band classes were small – about sixteen pupils in each – and designed for those who would find exam work difficult, though some sat CSE. Since the school was socially mixed, every upper-band class had a fair proportion of working-class children, but there were hardly any middle-class children in the lower bands.
6 The headmaster's 'express group' sat the Mode 1 o-level English language paper – the traditional essay/précis/comprehension combination.
7 Cf. Barnes (1976), who notes the arbitrary nature of much curriculum construction by teachers.
8 Ball and Lacey (1980) suggest that 'stimulus and excitement' are the key words in the creative/expressive paradigm.
9 Woods (1981) gives an account of the importance of teachers' biographies in their approach to their work.
10 The weak classification between public and private (Bernstein, 1971) can lead to unacknowledged difficulties for some pupils, who are unwilling to give their real opinions for fear of 'showing themselves up'.
11 Johnson (1979) rightly warns against seeing this process as tidily automatic, and stresses the 'massive disjunctions and unevenness' in social and cultural reproduction.

References

BALL, S.J. (1981) *Beachside Comprehensive*, Cambridge, Cambridge University Press.
BALL, S.J. and LACEY, C. (1980) 'Subject disciplines as the opportunity for group action: A measured critique of subject sub-cultures', in WOODS, P.E. (Ed.) *Teacher Strategies*, London, Croom Helm.
BARNES, D. (1976) *From Communication to Curriculum*, Harmondsworth, Penguin Books.
BERNSTEIN, B. (1971) 'On the classification and framing of educational knowledge' in YOUNG, M.F.D. (Ed.) *Knowledge and Control: New Directions for the Sociology of Education*, London, Collier-Macmillan.
BOURDIEU, P. (1974) 'School as a conservative force' in EGGLESTON, S.J. (Ed.) *Contemporary Research in the Sociology of Education*, London, Methuen.
COLLINS, R. (1979) *The Credential Society: An Historical Sociology of Education and Stratification*, New York, Academic Press.
DORE, R. (1976) *The Diploma Disease: Education, Qualification and Development*, London, George Allen and Unwin.
ESLAND, G. (1971) 'Teaching and learning as the organization of knowledge' in YOUNG, M.F.D. (Ed.) *Knowledge and Control: New Directions for the Sociology of Education*, London, Collier-Macmillan.
FORD, J., YOUNG, D. and BOX, S. (1967) 'Functional autonomy, role distance and social class' in COSIN B.R. *et al.* (1971) *School and Society*, London, Routledge and Kegan Paul in association with the Open University Press.
GILSON, E. (1957) 'Learning as actualising', in PEGIS, A. (Ed.) *A Gilson Reader*, New York, Doubleday and Co.
GRACE, G. (1978) *Teachers, Ideology and Control*, London, Routledge and Kegan Paul.
HARGREAVES, D.H. (1972) *Interpersonal Relations and Education*, London, Routledge and Kegan Paul.
HODGSON, J. (1975) *Changes in English Teaching: Institutionalisation, Transmission and Ideology* unpublished PhD thesis, University of London.
HOLT, J. (1969) *How Children Fail*, Harmondsworth, Penguin Books.
JOHNSON, R. (1979) 'Histories of culture theories of ideology' in BARRETT, M. *et al.* (Eds) *Ideology and Cultural Production*, London, Croom Helm.
KEDDIE, N. (1971) 'Classroom knowledge' in YOUNG, M.F.D. (Ed.) *Knowledge and Control: New Directions for the Sociology of Education*, London, Collier-Macmillan.
MARCUSE, H. (1972) *One Dimensional Man*, London, Abacus.
ST JOHN-BROOKS, C. (1980) *The Transmission of Values in English Teaching*, unpublished PhD thesis, University of Bristol.
SCHOOLS COUNCIL (1968) *Enquiry 1: Young School Leavers*, London Her Majesty's Stationery Office.
SCHUTZ, A. (1967) *The Phenomenology of the Social World*, Evanston, Illinois, Northwestern University Press.
SHARP, R. AND GREEN, A. (1975) *Education and Social Control*, London, Routledge and Kegan Paul.
TAYLOR, C. (1971) 'Interpretation and the science of man', in *Review of Metaphysics*, 25, 1 January.
WEBER, M. (1947) *The Theory of Social and Economic Organization*, London, Collier-Macmillan.
WILLIAMS, R. (1961) *Culture and Society 1780–1950*, Harmondsworth, Penguin Books.
WILLIAMS, R. (1965) *The Long Revolution*, Harmondsworth, Penguin Books.
WOODS, P. (1979) *The Divided School*, London, Routledge and Kegan Paul.
WOODS, P. (1981) 'Strategies, commitment and identity: Making and breaking the

teacher', in BARTON, L. and WALKER, S. (Eds) *Schools, Teachers and Teaching*, Lewes, The Falmer Press.

YOUNG, M.F.D. (1971) 'An approach to the study of curricula as socially organized knowledge', in YOUNG, M.F.D. (Ed.) *Knowledge and Control: New Directions for the Sociology of Education*, London, Collier-Macmillan.

3 A Subject of Privilege: English and the School Curriculum 1906–35

Stephen J. Ball

This chapter has two central concerns and objectives which are closely interwoven and interrelated in the text. The first is to provide a substantive, narrative account of the early struggles involved in establishing English as a separate and respectable school subject. The second is to outline and explore, through the narrative, a *social interaction* model of curriculum change. In relation to this a number of relevant concepts are introduced into the analysis of the substantive material. In attempting to do this I have been made very aware of the difficulties involved in combining theoretical discussion with historical exposition and I am only too ready to acknowledge the resulting weaknesses.

In a recently published paper Goodson (1981) has presented a careful critique of the two major perspectives (one sociological and one philosophical) which have underlain many of the recent attempts to theorize and study empirically the processes which define and validate school subject knowledge. The sociological perspective, which is spelt out most clearly in the early papers of Young (1971 and 1972), views school subjects as defined and maintained by unspecified 'dominant interests' who have power in society. This is essentially a top-down, social-structural and relativistic conception of the determination of school knowledge. The philosophical perspective, what Goodson calls the 'Establishment view', is represented in the work of writers such as Hirst, Peters and Phenix. In their work school subjects are analyzed as defined by and derived from certain 'forms of knowledge' and

> What is implied is that the intellectual discipline is created and systematically defined by a community of scholars, normally working in a university department, and is then 'translated' for use as a school subject. (Goodson, 1981, p. 38)

But in common with a number of other contributors and commentators Goodson's presentation of a polar model, with a sociology of knowledge approach on the one hand and a philosophical approach on the other, fails to identify the development of a third, equally coherent, perspective. This third perspective, within which Goodson's own work stands, may be called the Weberian or *social interaction school*. Its premises and orientations have been adumbrated by a number of writers (Musgrove, 1968; Eggleston, 1977; Archer, 1979; and to some extent Esland, 1971).

As Goodson states it the argument behind this perspective is, in simple terms, that 'the study of knowledge in our society should move beyond the ahistorical process of philosophical analysis towards a detailed historical investigation of the motives and actions behind the presentation and promotion of subjects and disciplines' (p. 39). As suggested here, changes in the definition of school knowledge are to be viewed in two dimensions, in one dimension changes over time are envisaged, in the other the changes are related to various social influences. The 'subject' is viewed not as an abstract intellectual conception but as a changing body of knowledge produced by a social collectivity. Musgrove (1968) translates this into a programmatic statement for the researcher, who should, he says:

> Examine subjects both within the school and the nation at large as social systems sustained by communication networks, material endowments and ideologies. Within a school and within a wider society subjects as communities of people ... [are] competing and collaborating with one another, defining and defending their boundaries, demanding allegiance from their members and conferring a sense of identity upon them ... even innovation which appears to be essentially intellectual in character can usefully be examined as the outcome of social interaction. (p. 101)

As Musgrove's prescription indicates, such a conception of subjects necessarily embraces an awareness of competition between opposing groups in the pursuit and defence of perceived vested interests. Eggleston (1977, p. 23) goes on to suggest that the process of social interaction involved here, inevitably perhaps, produces conflict. And it is such conflict that gives 'rise to a range of compromises, adjustments and points of equilibrium of varying degrees of stability. In all these negotiations an underlying concept is that of *power*....' Power here operates in the control of and influence over various strategic arenas by certain dominant groups and the challenges to that control and influence by other assertive groups. There are many arenas at stake: teacher training courses; school examinations; consultation with the educational civil service and state educational agencies; educational conferences; journals and other publications; and memberships and officerships of significant committees. Some of the groups involved are subject and professional associations, teacher trade unions, government officials and HMIs, educational pressure groups, examination boards and consortia, universities, polytechnics and colleges and their representative associations, local authorities and their officers and representative associations and teacher training organizations. The definitions of school subjects occurring within such a kaleidoscopic complex of interacting and negotiating groups are not predetermined by fixed 'forms of knowledge' as Hirst suggests. The identification of the relevant dominant and assertive contenders in any particular case and their versions of the subject are empirical questions. Archer makes this clear:

To say that education derives its characteristic features from the aims of those who control it immediately raises problems concerning identification of controlling groups, the basis and processes upon which control rests, the methods and channels through which it is exerted, the extensiveness of control, the reaction of others to this control, and the educational consequences. Similarly, where change is concerned, it is not explained until an account has been given of why educational goals change, who does the changing and how they impose the changes they seek. To control these problems is to recognize that their solution depends upon analyzing *complex forms of social interaction*. Furthermore, the nature of education is rarely, if ever, the practical realization of an ideal form of instruction as envisaged by a particular group. Instead, most of the time the forms that education takes are the political products of power struggles. They bear the marks of concessions to allies and compromises with opponents. Thus, to understand the nature of education at any one time, we need to know not only who won the struggle for control, but also how, not merely who lost, but also how badly they lost! (p. 23)

The social interaction perspective is given further support by Waring (1979), who employs it in her study of the Nuffield Foundation Science Teaching Project. She writes, referring to the process of curriculum change, that:

Social changes and social pressures are not entities, but the products of the interaction of men and women with distinct and differing attitudes and interests, who perceive and select from the milieu not only what is the case, but what they take to be the case. The motive power of any pressure group lies in a shared belief in their perception of what is wrong or lacking in the current situation, and of what can be done about it, and in the ability of the leadership to canalize the dissatisfaction of the group, and of others, into line with these beliefs, by crystallizing, defining and focusing it in such a way as to create a widely shared frame of reference. (pp. 7-8)

Furthermore, there are distinct parallels between this social interactionist formulation of subject control and subject change and Bucher and Strauss' (1961) account of professions as loose amalgamations of segments with particular 'missions' and interests. Bucher and Strauss use the analogy of 'social movements' to conceptualize the origins, recruitment, leadership, strategies and organization of professions and thus again produce a model based on power and conflict. The segments that constitute a profession involve, they suggest, 'shared identities manifested through circles of colleagueship' and that 'professional identity may be thought of as analogous to the ideology of a political movement; in this sense segments have ideology.' However, Bucher and Strauss clearly recognize the limits of their analogy as an analytical mechanism and some of the differences between political movements and professional life that they identify are of relevance to the descriptions and analyses presented below.

> First of all, professional movements occur within institutional arrangements, and a large part of the activity of segments is a power struggle for the possession of them or of some kind of place within them. Second, the fates of segments are closely intertwined: they are possibly more interdependent and responsive to one another than are other kinds of movements. It is probably impossible to study one segment in movement adequately without taking into account what is happening to others. Third, the leaders are men who recognize status within the field, operate from positions of relative institutional power, and command the sources of institutionalized recruitment. Finally, it must be pointed out that not all segments display the character of a social movement. Some lack organized activities, while others are still so inchoate that they appear more as a kind of backwash of the profession than as true segments. (p. 333)

Thus, English as a professional community may be regarded as made up of an amalgamation of contending segments; the English Association, discussed in detail below, itself contained and represented at least two loosely allied and separately discernible examples of such segments.

In a previous paper I have attempted such an enterprise as that outlined by Archer above in the case of English as a school subject (Ball, 1982). Employing a social interaction perspective, I attempted to plot changes over time between 1900 and 1975 in the definitions of school English; to identify the reasons for change and continuity and thus also the reasons for the demise or unfashionableness of particular definitions. This involved the use of social network analysis and the examination of conflicts over the control of English subject associations. In this chapter I wish to reanalyze in more detail the first period of the historical career of English as a school subject, 1900–35. I believe that such a reanalysis will further illustrate the usefulness of the social interaction perspective in the sociological study of the curriculum *and* that, in particular, changes taking place during this period, with regard to the definition and overall status of English, provide an understanding of the political 'groundrules' within which much subsequent curriculum debate has taken place. That is to say, the examination of the early career of English as a school subject goes some way towards identifying the major and dominant social groups and organizations, political and institutional arenas, strategies and tactics involved in the control of and changes in the curricula of English secondary and elementary schools during this period.

There are also useful parallels to be drawn between changes in the role of the Board of Education during this period and recent changes in the role being played by the DES in attempts to redefine aspects of the contemporary school curriculum.

English Emerges: The Early Struggles

To state the position boldly, before the turn of the century English as a school subject, in the sense that we would understand it today, simply did not exist.

In both the elementary and secondary schools most of the work done in 'English' during this period was based on imitation for composition work and parsing for grammar work. In the case of the former, the ubiquitous 'reader' provided the models which pupils were expected to reproduce in essays on abstract or general subjects. Composition and grammar were taught as separate lessons with composition definitely cast in the role of 'poor relation . . . merely a testing device, proof of the grammar pudding' (Shayer, 1972, p. 22). Indeed we must recognize that composition here does not refer to any sort of creative writing by pupils but rather to the skills of correct expression or manner of presentation. The grammar work, which Shayer describes as 'frankly, nasty', normally employed and relied upon the use of 'grammars', books of exercises containing examples and lessons in the parsing of sentences. Essentially for children of ages 8 and upwards, the learning of English was done through orthography, etymology and syntax aimed solely at the systematic inculcation of the principles of English grammar. The stress was upon 'correct usage'. Lessons were expository, consisting of rote exercises and tests taken from the grammars. In these ways, both grammar and composition, especially in the elementary school, served to impose and maintain the dominance of the patterns, structures and conventions of *Standard English* and received pronunciation.

The dominant conception of English as a school subject both at elementary and secondary level was that which derived from the established methods and approaches of the classics. Language was considered to be 'got' best by parsing, imitation and the writing of compositions on set topics. Literature teaching relied on working through annotated editions of English classics, modelled on classical commentaries, which directed attention to linguistic, archaeological, historical or geographical points. The author's style and methods were not normally matters of concern. The dominance of the classicist approach was maintained indirectly in the elementary schools through the legacies of the revised codes and, with some exceptions, through the work done by the inspectors and through government control of teacher training.

In the secondary sector in the last quarter of the nineteenth century, the classical tradition continued to dominate the public and the endowed grammar schools, despite the various attempts to widen the curriculum,[1] and as Eggleston (1977) notes, 'after 1902, it formed a major component of the model set out by Morant for the new local education authority grammar schools' (p. 26). This classical dominance was both defended in law[2] and firmly maintained by the examining practices and entry requirements of Oxford and Cambridge. The absence of modern 'literary' English studies in the universities at the time directly inhibited the development of English as a separate school subject.[3] Furthermore, the absence of modern 'literary' English courses at university greatly affected the supply of qualified and committed teachers. The notion was already well established that anyone with a 'decent education' could teach English. This was noted in the 1910 Circular 753 issued by the Board of Education.

> The teaching of English in a school is not only being treated as a water tight unit, but is being taught by any member of staff who can be induced to 'take a few periods' to fill in time.

It was against this background that in 1906 the English Association was founded. A late arrival compared with the other major subject associations, over the next twenty-five years the English Association was to play a major role in the making of English as a school subject. Boas later recalled that the Association was founded in response to strong feelings that 'as Classics, History, Modern Languages and other subjects had supporting Associations, one was needed to uphold the claims in education and otherwise of the mother tongue.' The founding and early activities of the Association were clearly based upon the recognition of a need to promote the cause of English in schools. And the underdevelopment of school English was strongly associated in the minds of the early activists with the underdevelopment of English as a university discipline. In 1907 Sir Sidney Lee, who acted as Chairman of the Association's first AGM, pointed in his address to the weak position currently held by English in the curriculum of British schools and universities.

> There is an infinite deal for the Association to do as is obvious to anyone who is acquainted with the strides that English teaching is making through all the grades of the educational system in America, in Germany, and strangest of all, in France. (English Association document, 1907)

The founding of the Association, in terms of recruitment at least, was certainly a success: by 1907 it had 700 members and by 1913 this number had risen to 2000.[4] Fairly early on the Association, through its more prominent members, began to make its presence felt in matters relating to the teaching of English. In 1909 F.S. Boas was appointed Chairman of the Committee set up by the LCC to enquire into 'The Teaching of English in London Elementary Schools', and there were five other English Association representatives among the thirty-two committee members. Later the Newbolt Committee set up in 1919 by the Board of Education to enquire into 'The Teaching of English in England' contained ten English Association members in its full complement of fifteen. The other early work of the Association included the publication of pamphlets on aspects of English teaching (the first three were 'Types of English Curricula in Boys' Secondary Schools'; 'The Teaching of Shakespeare in Secondary Schools'; and 'A Short List of Books on English Literature for the Use of Teachers') and matters of literary criticism and review, and 'various meetings are held during the year at which papers are read in furtherance of the general objects' of the Association (*The Times Educational Supplement*, 1913, p. 4). Rudduck (1979) reports that:

> For several years, the Annual meeting was followed by a one-day conference. In 1912, the topic for the conference was 'The Teaching of English Comprehension in Schools' and papers were read by Dr. Rouse, the Headmaster of Perse School ('The Place of English Composition in the Language Scheme of a Secondary School'); by Miss Ford, from the Clapham Day Training College ('The Teaching of English Composition in Relation to the Teaching of Literature'); and by George Sampson, Headmaster of an Elementary School ('Oral Composition in Upper Classes') ... at the Summer Meeting of 1912, held on Friday June 21 at Kings College, Mr. H.J. Newbolt – later to chair the Newbolt Committee of Enquiry – spoke on 'Poetry and Politics'. (pp. 57–8)

The 'mission', in Bucher and Strauss' terms, of the English Association was clear. The Association strove first to unify the separate elements of English as currently taught in schools – grammar, composition and literature – into a single, recognized school subject with its own specialist teaching force. Second, they intended that literature should become the dominant component of the new discipline. And third, they wished to replace the methods and practices of the classical curriculum with forms of teaching which gave greater emphasis to the literary qualities of their subject matter and, to some extent at least, to the creative expression of the pupils. Formal grammar was no longer to be taught as an isolated subject but only in connection with the skills of composition. The English Association, representing an assertive segment in the general field of English studies, set itself to wrest control of or influence over English teaching from those in the universities and the public and grammar schools who sought to maintain the dominance of grammarian and philological versions of the subject. As Bucher and Strauss suggest:

> The problems for a new speciality are particularly those associated with status and power. New specialist groups are likely to be seeking social accreditation. Deprived as they often are of the full measure of their expected status and function, new groups may take on expansionist policies. Since the expansion of one jurisdiction often means the diminution of another, this method of increasing status produces conflict. (p. 327)

Perhaps with hindsight the most significant of the pre-war activities of the Association in the promotion of English was involvement in the discussions related to the writing of the 1910 Board of Education, Circular 753, *The Teaching of English in Secondary Schools*.

The Circular itself is an important document in the process of establishing English as a permanent and central subject in the secondary school curriculum. But the method of its production is perhaps of greater importance. As to its substance the Circular states that: 'The claim of English to a definite place in the curriculum of every secondary school is admitted.' The condemnation of the use of classical methods in the teaching of English is unequivocal: 'In the past formal teaching of English Grammar was based on Latin Grammar. It is now realized that this was a mistake founded on a whole set of misconceptions.' With regard to the place of grammar generally in English teaching, the Circular suggests: 'Grammar should not bulk largely in the regular school teaching of English, and it should not be isolated from composition and literature.' The Circular draws attention both to the struggle to establish English as a subject in its own right and to the conflicts over what is to count as English in terms of its subject content and its teaching methods.

As to the manner of its production, for the first time the Board of Education in the process of the writing of a document intended for publication saw fit to consult directly and in detail with the relevant subject association, the English Association.

From an examination of internal Board minutes it would seem that the initial impetus for this consultation came from Morant. He drew Assistant Commissioner Bruce's attention to the 'very important Association on the teaching of English which is, I think, under the presidency of Mr Arthur Acland' (26 January 1910). Bruce then passed on the suggestion in more formal terms, and in doing so also drew attention to the general significance of the move. Referring to the Curricular Review Committee he wrote:

> When this committee have got a draft ready, we should, I think, ask the English Association if they would put us in communication with a small committee mainly composed of persons of experience in the teaching of the subject in Secondary Schools, one at least having such experience in Girls' Schools, with a view to discussion of the draft ... but I should point out that it is open to the objection that the consultation of the Association in that way will mean a publication of the fact and will be a precedent for other Associations. I think, however, that we must be prepared sooner or later to recognize these organizations of expert opinion all along the line, and must face the inconvenience of their standard of merit and efficiency being at present very uneven. (15 February 1910)

The English Association was contacted and a committee formed and these representatives met with the Board of Education Curricular Review Committee for the first time on 15 July 1910. The English Association's representatives were Mr Percy Simpson (St Olave's Grammar School, Tower Bridge, London), Miss L.L. Faithfull (Principal, Cheltenham Ladies College), Mr J.H. Fowler (Clifton College) and Miss C.L. Thompson (a writer of school books and books for children). The meetings were, it is apparent from the minutes, busy and detailed but never highly contentious or acrimonious. The Association representatives were mainly concerned with correcting matters of detail in the draft circular. The tone was set before the meetings began when Mr Simpson

English and the School Curriculum 1906-35

submitted a set of written objections by letter on 22 March 1910. He wrote:

> In view of the fact that the points which we submit to you are necessarily a series of objections I am asked to say that we warmly appreciate the whole spirit of the 'outline' and believe that it will have a high educational value ... [and] will have a powerful effect for good upon the schools.

When the process of consultation was completed and the Circular ready for publication Commissioner Bruce commented on the contribution made by the English Association Committee in a memo to Morant (8 December 1910). Interestingly, he refers to the consultation as an experiment.

> The results of this experiment in inviting outside cooperation were very gratifying. No points of difference arose which caused any real difficulty. Several valuable suggestions were made and useful information given, and in sending their final remarks on the draft Circular the representatives said that both they and the Association as a whole had greatly valued the privilege of criticism.

Hodgson (1975), in discussing the Circular, suggests that 'more than any other previous official pronouncement, it was highly representative of the consciousness of English teachers at the time' (p. 98).

However, there are two main respects in which the accuracy of Hodgson's statement may be regarded as dubious. One is related to the extent to which the Circular addressed in any real sense the immediate interests or concerns or commitments of those teachers in secondary schools who were, at this time, charged with the responsibility of teaching English. Hodgson's view was certainly not shared by Commissioner Bruce. In an internal memo to Morant (8 December 1910) defending the length of the Circular, he wrote:

> I think its length is justified in view of the great neglect of the subject hitherto, and the very low standard of the teaching even now that the subject is beginning to get fair treatment in the Timetable. I doubt if there are more than one or two schools to which we should care to send a foreigner to see effective teaching in the mother tongue.

It can be argued that the arena of discussion within which the formulation of the Circular took place is separate and distinct from the everyday world and educational consciousness of the ordinary teacher of English. What is notable about the English Association at this time is its elite nature (both politically and intellectually). The work of defining and promoting English as a school subject, nationally and publicly, was being carried out, literally, in various 'corridors of power', not in school classrooms and staffrooms in discussions between or including teachers. The elite character of this 'definitional work' is marked in a number of ways. For example, in the make up of the English Association 'leadership'. The original concept of the Association came from a school teacher, Mr Valentine, English Master of Dundee High School. With the support of the professors of English in Scottish universities and a teacher in Liverpool, he had contacted the University of Liverpool. It was there that a preliminary meeting was held. For the first AGM a list of supporters was drawn up which included 'most of the Professors of English in the Universities, the Headmasters of Eton, Winchester, Westminster, Dulwich; well known teachers of secondary schools ... representatives of elementary teachers; some officials of the Board of Education; and last but not least, a few representatives of that profession of which I am a humble member – the class of authors – notably Mr Harris and Mr Hardy' (Sir Sidney Lee's Address, AGM, 1907). We may also note the composition of the committee formed to discuss the drafting of the English Circular with the Curricular Review Committee of the Board of Education. Apart from Arthur Simpson, a grammar school master, they were an author; the Principal of Cheltenham Ladies College; and a public school master. And it is probably not insignificant that the original suggestion of contacting the English Association, made by Morant, refers to the President of the Association, Sir Arthur Acland, who had served as vice-president of the Committee of Council for Education 1892–5, with a seat in Cabinet (in effect the Minister of Education). He had worked hard in support of the entry of the County Councils into education and was Chairman of the President of the Board of Education's Consultative Committee from 1907 to 1916. He was, in other words, a close colleague of Morant. The importance of personal contacts of this kind cannot be underestimated when considering the workings of the Board of Education during this period. Many letters and notes appear in the Public Records Office files that amount to personal representations and recommendations, and the officials of the Board regularly made informal personal responses to these representations separate from the formal, public ones.

In 1913 Arthur Balfour was elected president of the Association, and in an article in *The Times Educational Supplement* in that year, headed 'The English Association: A Record of Good Work', it was noted that:

> ... the roll of past presidents, which includes the Master of Trinity College, Cambridge, Lord Morely of Blackburn, and Mr A.C. Bradley, is sufficiently notable in itself. And in addition, Mr Balfour will find amongst the vice-presidents, the general committee and the rest of his fellow-members a further large number of men and women who have rendered distinguished service to the twin causes of English literature and English education. Without in any way attempting to give a complete list of the most eminent, we may note that letters are represented by, among others, Mr Thomas Hardy, Mr J.M. Barrie, Sir Sidney Lee, Mr John Buchan, Professor E. de Selincourt, the Dean of Norwich, Mrs Edith Sichel, the Rev. Stopford Brooke, Mr George Trevelyan, Mr William Watson, Mr Alfred Noyes, and Mr John Bailey, the Chairman of the Association; and the Universities and schools by Lord Curzon, Dr A.W. Ward, Professor Dowden, Sir

Henry Craik, The Bishop of Southwark, the Headmasters of Eton, Harrow, Winchester, Charterhouse, Westminster, Shrewsbury, Tonbridge, Wellington, Durham, the Hackney Downs school, and the Hickley Grammar school, and the Principals of Girton, the Clapham Day Training College, the Godolphin and Latimer Girls School, the Ladies College Cheltenham, the Laxton Street London County Council School, the Girls Grammar School, Bradford.

The English Association, as far as its involvement in the politics of the curriculum is concerned, can hardly be thought of as a grassroots movement.

The strategy of elite sponsorship employed by the English Association to further its 'mission' highlights the class basis of educational change during the late nineteenth and early twentieth centuries. The Association sought to legitimate its aims by identification with the leading public schools and universities (although paradoxically, as already indicated, these institutions were the bastions of the opposition to the Association's version of English) and with eminent writers, politicians and educationalists. These elite sponsors were a major resource in establishing a prestigious public image for the Association, as Bucher and Strauss (1961, p. 334) suggest that 'segments from time to time must engage in tactics to project their own images to the public'. This strategy was acknowledged by the 1942 Chairman Nowell Smith in his Address:

> I do not at all minimize the strictly educational work done by members of the Association in the early days, both individually and in Committee. But what did most to put English on the educational map, was, I cannot doubt, the Annual Meeting in London, and that not because of the business it transacted but because of the distinguished names of the President and the speakers at the banquet which followed the President's address. This and the literary quality of our pamphlets, the literary lectures given up and down the country, the social amenities enjoyed on these occasions – all this gave an effectiveness to our more specific educational propaganda which its own intrinsic worth would not have secured.

There is a second sense in which Hodgson's comment on Circular 753 seems to be over-optimistic. It is not only the case that few teachers of English from the state schools were involved in the 'instrumental activities' (Archer, 1979) of the English Association, but also few such teachers appeared to have been actually influenced by the work of the Association in their conception of English as a set of classroom practices. Indeed, for another forty years the dominant mode of grammar school English was to remain that inherited from the procedures and teaching methods of classics. In the short term some indication of this dominance may be gained from the comments made by R.L. Archer in his survey of the educational scene, published in 1921.

> Much of what is now called English Grammar was taught in the old grammar schools as part of the Latin teaching. Indeed, we are now

becoming conscious that most of what has passed as 'English Grammar' is merely the technology of Latin Grammar transferred to a language which it does not equally fit. Matthew Arnold, who was a firm believer in the 'logical training' afforded by a study of Latin, was very anxious to see English Grammar taught to all pupils who did not learn Latin: Thring too wrote text-books and taught the subject at Uppingham. Modern questionnaires suggest that it is the best hated subject in the curriculum; possibly this confirmed the high opinion formed of it by the old disciplinarian school of thought. Another merit in the eyes of some teachers was that, being entirely formal and standing in no relation to the world outside the classroom, it did not necessitate any fresh reading to keep abreast of the times or to impart freshness of presentation. It has now become the natural target of all enemies of formalism and believers in making school work a live thing.

In the longer term, between 1925 and 1960 the teaching of English in schools changed very little, there was a widespread adherence to traditional practices. The Latin-based norm of 'correct' English remained as the dominant approach to the teaching of the subject, supported to a great extent by the syllabuses of the School Certificate. But whatever gaps may have existed between the rhetoric and the reality of English as a school subject, during the period 1906–13, it is undoubtedly the case that publicly English established a firm claim for a place as a separate subject in the curricula of both elementary and secondary schools.

The interesting question is 'how was this achieved?' The *social interaction* perspective, outlined previously, might be of some assistance here. The 'pressure group politics' of the English Association, and its 'power struggles' with the defenders of the classical tradition, are obviously of importance. The English Association was able to mobilize what Archer (1979) refers to as *bargaining power* and *instrumental activities* in support of its objectives. The former, 'sufficient numerical support and organizational strength to challenge domination' (p. 107), is evident in the rapid rise in membership and the publications and meetings of the Association. The latter, 'devaluing the dominant group's monopoly', can be gauged in terms of headway made in the elementary and the new secondary schools. But I want to stress that these pressure group activities and the other *complex forms of social interaction* involved in the process of changing the structure of educational knowledge must not be viewed as if they emerge and develop with total autonomy. The mobilization of social and political pressure and the demand for change must be set against and understood in the context of the political, social and economic *conditions of change*. For example, in the period 1900–13 a number of significant political and administrative factors – the passing of control over the elementary school curriculum into the hands of teachers (as a result of the 1904 Code of Regulations for elementary schools); the provision for the first time of state secondary schooling; the support of the Board of Education – combined to provide a very appropriate context for the English Association to pursue its objectives. I will discuss further the role of such *conditions of change* below.

Archer (1979) also makes the point that the 'activities' of contesting groups are not in themselves sufficient to provide a basis for opposition to the *status quo:*

> ... diffuse discontent must be consolidated into organized assertion, which recruits further support, if constraints are to be subverted. To this end a counter *ideology* is required, partly to inform the movement of its goals, to recruit participants ... and support from a wider audience, and ultimately to justify using the bargaining power at their disposal. (p. 106)

This counter-ideology was provided, in specific relation to English in the elementary school, by a line of educational thought derived from the work of Herbart, Froebel, Pestalozzi and Montessori, which Abbs (1982) refers to as the 'Progressive Movement'. The main exponents of the movement during this early period were Greening Lamborn, Edmund Holmes, Percy Nunn, W.S. Tomkinson and Caldwell Cook.

> *Self-expression prohibited.* That was the cry and challenge of the Progressive Movement in English. Against the mechanical forms of teaching, the Progressives asserted the need for a freer and more spontaneous approach allowing the child to generate much of the curriculum according to creative needs. (Abbs, 1982 p. 8)

At secondary level another set of influences and vocabulary of motives were at work, that is, the elite cultural tradition of Coleridge and Arnold represented, in particular, by George Sampson (author of *English for the English*) and Arthur Quiller-Couch (first Cambridge Professor of English), which stressed the educational role of the English literary heritage.

English Established: The Struggle of Examinations

In 1917 the Board of Education established the Secondary Schools Examination Council in an effort to coordinate the standards and curtail the influence of the university examination boards. The regulations of the new School Certificate examinations (Circular 1002) probably represents the last attempt of the Board to assert what Stray (1980) calls the principle of 'organic unity', the 'Edwardian concern with generality' (p. 17) in the school curriculum. That is to say, the regulations themselves mark a turning point in Board policy and practice away from this 'Edwardian' to a recognizably modern approach to the management of the curriculum in which the dominant ideological principle was 'the superiority of theory over practice, of academic over practical subjects' (Stray, 1980, p. 17). The report on which these regulations were based, the *Report of the Consultative Committee of the Board of Education on Examinations in*

Secondary Schools (1911) (chaired by A.H.D. Acland), was itself clearly set in the context of the original 1904 Regulations for Secondary Schools. These regulations stated that in secondary schools 'the instruction must be general; i.e. must be such as gives a reasonable degree of exercise and development to the whole of the faculties, and does not confine this development to a particular channel, whether that of pure or applied science, or literary and linguistic study.'

The important point as far as English is concerned is that in the originally published list of the subjects approved for study in *Advanced Courses* for the Higher School Certificate it was listed, apparently, only as a subsidiary subject. Boas summed up the 'outraged' response to this state of affairs in his Presidential address to the 1919 English Association conference:

> In the Regulations for the scholastic year that is now ending there was contained the first provision for 'Advanced Courses' for boys and girls between 16 and 18. This important 'step forward' in education was hailed with unanimous approval, but for those especially concerned with the teaching of English there was one blot on the scheme. In the 'Modern Studies' group opportunity was given for the teaching of History and of the languages and literatures of Western Europe, but English was allotted only a subordinate place. Many of us felt that much of the work of recent years for the development and consolidation of the higher study of English was gravely imperilled.

Ardent representations were made to the Board of Education by the English Association and from several other quarters. As was their wont, the Board were moved to establish the Office Committee on English in Advanced Courses in Secondary Schools (14 May 1918). Part of the brief of the committee was to 'confer on the matter with representatives of the English Association'. But the committee did more than just this, it considered memoranda and resolutions from nine groups and bodies and also interviewed a group of ten specially selected, senior and respected teachers on the matter. According to the committee's report:

> The English Association in their Memorandum and in their interview with us looked at the matter principally from the point of view of the University professor and insisted strongly on the detrimental effect which they held the Regulations would produce on the study of English in the Universities. Pupils would be debarred from taking English up to an honours standard and those desirous of competing for University Scholarships in English would find themselves penalised. This would greatly affect the supply of qualified teachers of English.

But the committee on this occasion seemed more moved by the evidence of the Modern Languages Association and their expert teacher witnesses: '... it is noteworthy that the representatives of the Modern Languages Association

English and the School Curriculum 1906-35

showed themselves no less sensible of its importance than those who held a brief for English in particular' The comments of the expert teachers on the status of English as a subject in their schools appeared to be in total accord:

> The teachers were quite clear that any suggestion, however remote from the intention of the regulations, that English is a subject unworthy to play more than a minor or subsidiary role in any well considered scheme of higher Secondary Education would tend to lower its prestige and injure its teaching all through the School, and its elevation to the rank of a principal subject would immediately effect a marked change of attitude toward it on the part of the whole school, both staff and pupils.

The report also serves to represent the views of those who did consider English to be unworthy of advanced status, although these views are not directly attributed.

> It has been suggested that English does not afford sufficient training in accuracy and definiteness and will involve risk of encouraging mental 'sloppiness' and inexactitude; that such a course as English, French and History will not provide a sufficiently strenuous curriculum, will compete undesirably with better courses of study; and will become a refuge of weaker schools.

Despite the clear recommendation of the committee that English be admitted as an advanced subject and the endorsement of this by the Standing Advisory Committee, the examinations affair may still be regarded realistically as a 'close run thing'. Advanced level teaching was effectively fixed by the 1918 Regulations for the next thirty years up to 1950. Only four more subjects, all practical, were added to the published schedule of courses during this time. Allocation as a subordinate subject could have been disastrous in the ongoing campaign to establish English firmly in the secondary curriculum. As it was, Boas closed his presidential address with the words, 'the field is therefore open to teachers of English, and it behoves them to equip themselves as fully as possible for their increased responsibilities.' Archer (1921, p. 339) underlines the importance of this decision:

> English literature owes its entrance into schools almost entirely to external examinations. The older schools believed that it could not be profitably taught in class, and tried to encourage it by school libraries, by holiday work, and by occasional readings given to a class as a kind of hour's holiday. The need of introducing it seemed axiomatic to opponents of classics. 'Why teach Greek and Latin, even French and German literature, and not teach the incomparable literature of our own tongue?' It was introduced, and taught exactly as Latin and Greek

authors were taught. The teacher was snowed under by the notes.... Rarely has a subject suffered so severely at the hands of its friends!

If it is not examined, while other subjects are, it probably will not be taught at all; if it is examined, it follows that it will be taught badly. Even in the universities, where it now usually forms an honours course by itself, a constant struggle is needed to prevent 'English' from becoming predominantly philological.

While advocates of classical, grammarian English could rely on recruits from the universities who had studied the classics, the literary version of English depended much more for its continued viability and vitality on establishing its own route of subject socialization and accreditation through new advanced courses in schools and new university courses.

The basic program of recruitment probably tends to be laid down by powerful segments of the profession. Yet different segments require different kinds of raw material to work upon, and their survival depends upon an influx of candidates who are potential successors. (Bucher and Strauss, p. 334)

Before leaving the deliberations of the Office Committee, there is one other point of note to be made about their report and their consideration of 'evidence'. I refer to the particular attention given to English teaching for girls and the representations made by three bodies concerned with the education of girls: to wit the conference of London Headmistresses, the Association of Headmistresses, and the Joint Conference between the staffs of Girton and Newnham Colleges and representatives of the Association of Public School Headmistresses. The committee report duly noted that:

... as a constituent subject of Higher Education, English makes a greater appeal in Girls' schools. The commercial value of Advanced English can never be high ... [but in Girls' schools] there will always be a certain number who have no practical pursuits in view and a larger proportion than in Boys' schools of pupils for whom a course in which English forms an important part is indicated as the kind of Advanced work best suited to their aptitudes.

This comment illustrates the considerable unevenness in the spread and acceptance of English in secondary education, an unevenness that was reiterated in the findings of the 1922 Consultative Committee on the Differentiation of the Curriculum for Boys and Girls Respectively in Secondary Schools, which reported that:

The general conclusion expressed by our witnesses and on the whole corroborated by the evidence furnished by examining bodies was that in this subject the average achievement of girls was distinctly superior to that of boys. This result is largely due to the more assured position

> given to the subject in girls' schools, and to the larger proportion of well qualified women teachers and the better teaching which is consequently given. (p. 25)

The evidence submitted to the 1922 Consultative Committee not only marks different levels of performance and provision and quality of teaching but also the different orientation of the teaching and definition of the subject in girls' and boys' schools. It is apparent that in the boys' schools English continued to be cast in the classical mould, while the girls' schools displayed a more considerable investment of time and energy in literature and creative work. Thus the committee recommended:

> That more care and attention should be given (a) in boys' schools to the use and comprehension of English and to the study of English Literature as a means to this end, and (b) in girls' schools to the analysis and understanding of the logical content of works of literature. (p. 26)

It is probably not implausible to suggest that these differences, derived as they were from the contemporary views of differences between the sexes in terms of conceptual abilities (Dyhouse, 1976), would tend to reinforce a low status position for English, and thus also inhibit the dissemination of innovations in English teaching into the boys' schools for similar reasons. Schiff (1977, Preface) underlines this point: 'for men students classics still retained a monopoly of social cachet until well into the 1930's. English being regarded as a soft option for them.'[5]

In the universities a similar bias was evident. Sir Sidney Lee reported in his chairman's address to the English Association AGM in 1907 that at Oxford the pupils of the Professor of English 'are for the most part not undergraduates but women students, who are not allowed by that ancient foundation any status at all, but are yet ahead of their brethren in intelligent zeal for English Study' (quoted in Boas, 1956, p. 45).

As a result of the reorganization of the examination system in 1918, four committees were established by the Board of Education 'to enquire into the position of' those subjects enshrined in the new advanced courses. In the case of English this led to the publication in 1921 of the Newbolt Report, *The Teaching of English in England*. In several respects the Report marks a further step toward the total supercession by English of the role previously held by classics, 'it insists that the classicists bow to the logic of events and yield – what they have already yielded – in practice if not in theory – the centre of the literary stage to English' (Shayer, 1972, p. 67). Even so, the evidence taken by the committee firmly underlined the marginal status still held by English in many schools, a status in the curriculum not unlike that occupied by, say, drama and dance in the contemporary scene.

> From the evidence laid before us it became speedily clear that in many schools of all kinds and grades that part of the teaching which dealt

directly with English was often regarded as being inferior in importance, hardly worthy of any substantial place in the curriculum, and a suitable matter to be entrusted to any member of staff who had some free time at his disposal. (pp. 9–10)

Many of the criticisms noted in English Association papers published between 1908 and 1920 are reiterated in the report. But in another sense the Report represents a compromise of the kind referred to by Eggleston (1977) and Archer (1979). According to Shayer (1972), the Report 'chooses its words a little too scrupulously' (p. 68). For instance, there is very 'wary' support for the use of creative and imaginative work in the secondary school. 'Imaginative subjects, too long neglected, are today sometimes used to excess', the Report suggests. It goes on to recommend the need for hearty doses of practice in the construction, writing and revising of sentences. Neither is the writing of poetry to be given free rein, rather the application and knowledge of prosody is what is recommended. Furthermore, in contrast to the constant protestations of the English Association, the role of examinations is seen to be mainly beneficial.

Here then there would appear to be exactly the sorts of 'concessions to allies and compromise with opponents' described by Archer (1979, p. 23), here too one finds the *complex forms of social interaction* that she identifies with control of and change in educational goals. In sacrificing the creativity advocated by the Progressive Movement, the English Association was able both to underline the centrality of literature in its conception of English and to disarm those critics who spoke of the excesses of imagination in some areas of English teaching. To reiterate Archer's analysis: '. . . to understand the nature of education at any one time, we need to know not only who won the struggle for control, but also how, not merely who lost, but also how badly they lost!' (p. 23). Bucher and Strauss (1961, p. 331) make the point that 'Associations are not everybody's association but represent one segment or a particular alliance of segments.' As it turned out the English Association was not the association of the Progressive Movement, or was at least not strongly committed to the cause of creativity in English.

As far as university English is concerned, apart from some remarks about keeping a sense of proportion, there is support in the Report for the continued importance of Old and Middle English studies. But the major area of equivocation is undoubtedly with respect to that most contentious of issues, what to do about 'grammar'? The witnesses before the committee represented the complete spectrum of opinion from that of P.B. Ballard (an LCC Inspector with psychological training and pioneer of the use of psychological testing in schools) that 'in the elementary school formal grammar (a) fails to provide a general mental training, (b) does not enable teachers to eradicate solecisms, (c) does not aid in composition, and (d) takes up time which could more profitably be devoted to the study of literature'; to that of J.E. Barton, who argued that 'immense harm has been done by the well-meant discouragement of formal grammar in the elementary schools.' The report resolved that 'Grammar of some kind, then, should be taught either in the elementary school or in the secondary school, or both'. As a result of this, which Shayer (p. 70) calls a 'sleight of hand', the existing 'practical classroom status quo' was left 'virtually unchanged', with teachers advised simply to 'go on teaching grammar' (p. 70). Again, this Report highlights the coincident but separate issues of, on the one hand, disputation over the shape and priorities of the whole school curriculum, with the Report strongly defending and advocating the role of English as a separate, coherent and centrally important school subject; and, on the other hand, that of disputation within the English community. The Report opted for a compromise between those advocates of English as essentially creative and literary and those defending it as an analytical and philological discipline, with some ideological support for the former but practical reinforcement for the existing dominance of the latter in schools.

From this point on it is the latter conflict that is central to the changing nature of English as a school subject. This shift of emphasis, if it is to be properly understood, must be seen against a wider backdrop of *conditions of change*. In particular, we must return to the apparent change at this time in the role of the Board of Education as regards the management of school curriculum. Several relevant points can be noted. Following the publication of the reports of the four subject committees, the Board of Education published a circular (No. 1294) presenting the major conclusions. One point noted in the circular is the 'increasingly acute squeeze of subjects' (p. 8) created by the fact that the total of 'claimed' time made in the subject reports exceeded the normally available time in a typical school timetable. This was most acute in the case of girls' schools where shorter hours were worked. The Board's response is an interesting and important one. Indeed, the Circular in some respects anticipates the conflict perspective underlying this paper. It stated that:

> If every subject, as it develops from a subsidiary subject into one regarded by its expert teachers as of the first importance, with a philosophy and technique of its own, claims a larger place in the general curriculum ... there will come to be little variation between the curriculum of one school and another.... The Board believe, therefore, that less insistence should be laid on the general character of the curriculum and that so long as a proper balance of subjects is maintained, more freedom should be exercised in the allocation of time to different subjects, and even omitting some subjects from the curriculum altogether, at least for some pupils, at some stage of the course. (p. 3)

In some respects the first prediction in the extract probably underestimates the extent of curriculum conflict *within* schools (see Ball and Lacey, 1980). Such conflict provides for institutional variations in the curriculum despite changes nationally and ideologically in the nature of the claims made for particular subjects. However, the statement does give a clear indication of what was to be the guiding principle of the Board and its successors from this point until the mid-1970s. As Stray (1980, p. 17) suggests, this amounts to 'abandonment of the role of arbiter in matters of curriculum.... The pressures of the curricular market are to be allowed to operate.'[6] In one particular respect, with Morant having been replaced in 1911 by Selby-Biggs, the Board ceased to give overt support to classics in the secondary curriculum. Oxbridge also abandoned Greek as an entry requirement at approximately this time. As a result, Stray (1980) demonstrates a steady replacement of classics by Latin during the 1920s and 1930s, 'full classics' continuing only in the independent sector and the most prestigious grammar schools. English was thus able to further assert itself under the conditions of curriculum competition created by the Board, and in particular at the expense of classics.

English under Scrutiny: Persistence and Reaction

The whole period from 1920 to 1960 may be analyzed and understood in terms of the conflict within the English subject community, between the advocates of the two major positions identified above, the literary and the grammatical.[7] After 1960 the picture becomes far more complex (see Ball, 1982). However, it is far too easy and too simple to portray this conflict as a steady erosion of the grammatical position by way of a kind of Kuhnian paradigm shift until 'only a few elderly hold-outs remain' (Kuhn, 1969, p. 159). Furthermore, as I have stressed above, the process of curriculum change cannot be isolated from the wider social *conditions of change* in which it is set. Thus as Currie (1973, p. 25) notes:

> There were, of course, progressive measures at work in the thirties in education but the depressed state of the profession, with problems of unemployment of teachers and stagnation of promotion led to a climate in which most teachers were prepared to perpetuate tradition as it was found in the prescribed books of a given department, rather than to experiment and introduce new directions of study.

Also, in some senses the equivocal conclusions of the Newbolt Committee on the matter of the teaching of grammar checked the swing, at the ideological level, away from grammar. Indeed, during the 1920s and early 1930s a number of publications appeared which were critical of the abandonment or subordination of the teaching of grammar in school English, and of the standard of written and spoken English in schools. This period, and 1931–4 in particular, also saw a radical decline in the membership and thence the influence of the English Association, which was virtually moribund between 1935 and 1970.

Prior to the publication of the Newbolt Report it appeared that the anti-grammarians had the upper hand. As early as 1909 the LCC *Report of Conference on the Teaching of English in London Elementary Schools* noted that:

> The tendency today is one of extreme reaction. Some authorities hold and act on the principle that there should be no teaching of grammar apart from the other English lessons. We have devoted considerable attention to this remarkable revolution in opinion and practice, and endeavoured to discover a middle course between such markedly contradictory positions as those we have here indicated. (p. 40)

But then according to Shayer (1976, p. 89):

> ... the period from approximately 1927 to 1932 is marked by a seemingly concerted attempt to starve off creative developments and keep to the straight and narrow of traditional English teaching – and that included a demand for a return to the most formal grammar teaching.

For example, the IAAM (Incorporated Association of Assistant Masters) *Memorandum on the Teaching of English*, first published in 1923 and reissued in 1927, gave primary emphasis to the role of grammar:

> It is unanimously agreed that from the earliest stage of the secondary school course some training in formal grammar is necessary and desirable. Without it, it is hardly possible to promote clear thought about the purpose and study of language or to expect clear expression.

This latter point was taken up by a number of writers who felt that things had already 'gone too far' and that the reaction against the teaching of grammar was responsible for an identifiable decline in standards of written and spoken English in schools, and in the country generally. J.H. Fowler wrote in 1931:

> The outcry of a few years ago against the study of grammar in elementary schools, however reasonable as a protest against the shibboleths of grammatical labels and the wearisome and mechanical practice of parsing and elaborate tabular analyses, had some lamentable results. Sometimes one is tempted to think that the grammatical incoherency of the popular press at the present day may be accounted for by that period of educational history in which grammar was recklessly abandoned. (*The Art of Teaching English*, p. 141)

In the same year *The Times Educational Supplement* carried a number of articles and letters, most of them critical, addressed to the current state of English in schools. On 21 February a front-page article 'From a correspondent' appeared under the heading, 'English Should Be Better Taught'.

> It is a well-worn platitude that children come to school to learn to think; the first duty then is to train them to use the universal instrument of thought, the English Language; and they cannot be trained to use that instrument without understanding its structure....
> To effect this training we must first get into their bones the essential

meanings and the functions of the ordinary British words and the essential structure of the ordinary British sentence.... (p. 65)

This was followed some weeks later by a letter of support from a master of Dulwich College.

> I fancy it is high time that we had the point of view urged by your contributor put against the opinions (and prejudices and lack of grammar) which have so long directed and confused the teaching of English in secondary schools. (*The Times Educational Supplement*, 28 February 1931, p.81)

A small-scale moral panic ensued not unlike that which led up to the setting up of the Bullock Committee in the early 1970s.

In May another front-page article 'From a correspondent' appeared under the heading, 'Why Teach English Grammar'. This again referred to the two schools of thought contending to define what was to count as English in schools, the literary and the grammarian.

> If we are of the literary class, and believe that our way to success in English teaching is through soaking our classes in 'copious examples taken from the great writers of the past and distinguished men of letters of our own time', we get the particular impression of a few even of our better pupils writing very pretty superficial imitations of Lamb or Macaulay or Masefield or de la Mare. If, on the other hand, we belong to the school of grammarians, and hold that 'the teacher's work centres on the analysis and construction of the sentence (and the paragraph) in English', we get orderly internal arrangement of sentences and a logical sequence of ideas; but the resultant compositions do not produce much impression of any sort, unless it be of a catalogue. Faced, as we are, with classes which possess little knowledge that is of value of their own language, it would be safer to assume that they have no knowledge at all, and to start from the very beginning. And that is where the teaching of English grammar must come in. They must learn the structure-habits of their own language, and how to speak in accordance with these. If they do not, their command of that language will be throughout life feeble and confused. (*The Times Educational Supplement*, 9 May 1931, p. 165)

However, on 30 May Sir Philip Hartog[8] replied in a letter, from the literary perspective, reacting against both the idea of a grammar for its own sake and 'correct' English as the aim of English teaching.

> ... the teacher should refrain from turning a composition lesson into a grammar lesson. I know how hard it is to resist the temptation to do so.... A composition containing faults in grammar may be admirable in arrangement and expression generally, and calculated to produce (apart from those faults) exactly the impression desired by its writer.

English and the School Curriculum 1906–35

Again, Bucher and Strauss' (1961) analysis seems appropriate:

> the emergence of new segments takes on a new significance when viewed from the perspective of social movements within a profession. Pockets of resistance and embattled minorities may turn out to be the heirs of former generations, digging in along new battle lines. They may spearhead new movements which sweep back into power. (p. 333)

It was in the 1930s that Percival Gurrey (tutor at the London Day Training College, later Institute of Education) first began to contribute to debates about the role of grammar in English teaching. His work, and to an even greater extent that of this student, James Britton, provided the basis for an alternative linguistic version of English which was to develop through the London Association for the Teaching of English during the 1950s and to make a major national impact through NATE in the 1960s. Britton's grammar book, *English on the Anvil*, was published in 1934.

Conclusions

For me personally, as a sociologist dabbling in history, this exercise serves a number of important functions as regards my grasp of contemporary curriculum policy and curriculum practice. In specific relation to English, much of the contemporary conflict and conceptual precariousness evident involving practitioners of the subject can be understood in terms of the first emergence and early development of the discipline and the strongly 'segmented' nature of its professional community. In more general terms, the case of English illuminates important aspects of the processes of and constraints upon curriculum change.

In this respect it is vital to recognize the social distribution and uneven penetration of the 'literary' version of English represented by the English Association. For example, the elementary-secondary split is important, with the *creativity* emphasis of the progressive movement making little or no headway outside the elementary sector, and within the secondary sector the penetration of literary English being much more thorough-going in the girls high schools and newly founded state grammar schools. The public schools and boys grammar schools tended to resist for much longer the move away from classics and the introduction of specialist English teaching. Thus the 'new' English made most headway in low status areas of schooling – in the education of girls, the children of the working-classes in elementary schools, and the lower middle classes in the new state secondary schools.[9] Finally, the gap between rhetoric and practice, between the 'intended' and 'transacted' curriculum, needs to be stressed. The work of the English Association and the published materials of the Board of Education were clearly far in advance of the classroom practice of the general population of English teachers – insofar as such a population existed. The pace of curriculum change is revealed to be immensely slow, to be understood in terms of several decades rather than shorter periods. In relation to this, the importance of generational shifts in the sort of preparation and training available is clearly indicated, although not dealt with centrally in this chapter.

Conceptually, I hope to have demonstrated the viability and usefulness of the *social interaction perspective* in the study of the curriculum, with school subjects seen as the 'political products of power struggles' between social groups with differing and competing vested interests and differing resources and status (Cooper, 1982). But I would want to reiterate the necessity of setting these *relations of change*[10] within the educational community against the *conditions of change* provided specifically by the existing political and economic context and, more generally, by the concomitant ebb and flow of the climate of public opinion.[11] In the case of English (and quite possibly other subjects), the periods 1904–11 and 1918–21 provided moments or 'gaps' wherein, by virtue of policy changes and economic and political circumstance, curriculum change was possible. In the same way, in the period 1928–33 it could be said that general financial cutbacks in educational provision, the stagnation of the teaching profession and the changed climate of opinion about 'progressive' teaching severely reduced the possibilites of further development and allowed the 'grammarians' in the English community to mount a counter-attack upon 'literary English'.

Such a two-component model, of the *relations and conditions of change*, tempers the analysis of curriculum innovation in two ways and in two directions. First, in stressing the importance of context and constraint it draws attention to the limits of the autonomy of the education system. Second, it works the other way in inhibiting the drift into what Mansell and Silver (1979) call 'innocent functionalism', that is, attempting to explain educational change solely in terms of 'dominant social and economic *needs* and pressures'. The model draws attention to the 'uncertainties and conflicts involved in interpreting pressures on the curriculum'. It is often within these uncertainties and conflicts that the 'mission' of a new segment or specialism is lodged – 'the contribution that the speciality, and it alone, can make in a total scheme of values' (Bucher and Strauss, 1961, p. 326).

The arenas in which English as a school subject was established – the Board of Education, the English Association conferences, the Newbolt Committee – and the interest groups involved – the universities and public schools, politicians and educational civil servants, and eminent writers and educationalists – clearly define curriculum change in terms of the influence and decision-making of and conflicts of interest among a number of overlapping educational elites. There is no single interest represented by these groups and there is no formal resolution. The struggles and competition between segments described here remain embedded in the English subject community, and indeed, more recently, new segments with new and different 'missions' have emerged to join the fray.

Finally, in the light of recent actions by the Secretary of State for Education with regard to the Schools Council, the publication of a number of surveys and discussion papers by Her Majesty's Inspectorate and the setting up of the Assessment of Performance Unit, it is worth reiterating the important changes which occurred in the role of the Board of Education in the period 1902–25. The beginning and end of this period are marked by Board of Education activities and general stances towards the curriculum which represent the opposite extremes of intervention and non-intervention. At the beginning under Morant the Board stood for and instrumentally supported a particular view of the curriculum based on the nineteenth-century principles of a 'rounded education'. The advocacy of the Board was critical in the recognition and legitimation of English as a separate and coherent school subject, and the English Association as its professional representative. Between 1911 and 1918 the introduction of school examination regulations systematized – a 'prussianization', one contemporary commentator called it – the structure and provision of public examinations, severely curtailing the market freedom of university boards and secondary schools in doing so. By 1925 the Board, under Selby-Biggs, having established a framework of indirect control over the curriculum through the examination system, virtually abdicated any direct control over curricular provision in schools and the classroom work of teachers. White (1975) hypothesizes that this abdication, in the elementary sector at least, was a deliberate political act orchestrated by the President of the Board, Lord Eustace Percy, and that it was considered that the responsibility for the continuing stability of curricular provision in schools could be safely left in the inherently conservative hands of the school teachers (see note 8). Indeed, what is notable about the school curriculum in the period 1930–60 is the virtual absence of significant changes in the range of subjects available.

The off-stage, administrative role of the Board of Education, then Ministry of Education, then Department of Education and Science has only begun to change again since the mid-1970s. We now see the DES engaged on a number of fronts in an attempt to recover its position as arbiter of the school curriculum.

Acknowledgement

I am indebted to Peter Abbs, Barry Cooper, Ivor Goodson, Martyn Hammersley, Carole Kay and Colin Lacey for their insightful comments on a previous draft of this chapter.

Notes

1 Several attempts were made in the second half of the nineteenth century to update the curricula of the public and endowed schools; the Clarendon Commission of 1864 which examined the nine great public schools and the Taunton Report of 1868 which looked at the endowed schools, both recommended expansion. The Clarendon

Commission suggested that some time should be devoted to the teaching of mathematics, modern languages, some science, drawing or music, a general knowledge of geography and English history and 'grammatical' English, but the Commission accepted that Latin and Greek should remain as the principal subjects for study. The Royal Commissions of 1872 and 1895 made further pleas for the inclusion of science teaching. The university curricula were also beginning to change; the founding of new provincial universities and the availability of external London degrees made a much wider range of subjects available. The London matriculation examinations demanded passes in a range of prescribed courses which meant that school curricula had to be broadened to prepare candidates in the required subjects. The importance of Latin and Greek was diminished in that they carried no more weight than other subjects.

2 The 1904 secondary school regulations defined a secondary school as 'offering to each of its scholars up to and beyond the age of sixteen, a general education, physical, mental and moral ...' and went on to say, 'where two languages other than English are taken, and Latin is not one of them, the Board will require to be satisfied that the omission of Latin is for the advantage of the school.'

3 At Cambridge the conflict between the literary and philological versions of English began before the First World War around the planning of an English tripos based upon the critical study of literature as defined by Matthew Arnold. The early 'missionary' activity of H.M. Chadwick, H.F. Stewart and A. Quiller-Couch was taken up in the 1920s by F.R. Leavis and the new English tripos finally became independent of the Modern Language Board in 1926. But it was to be many years before the epithet 'Novel-reading tripos' was finally laid to rest. At Oxford English continued to be taught as a linguistic discipline much influenced by German linguists.

4 The membership was 300 by 1907; 2000 by 1913 (declining to about 1700 during the war); 5000 by 1922; and 7000 by 1927, but by 1936 'membership was falling and money was short' (Ruddock, 1979). In the 1970s the Association again began organizing conferences, for sixth-form students, and in 1978 the membership was 1400.

5 The status of English as a 'girls subject' is still evident at a number of levels in the education system. At the end of compulsory schooling more girls than boys take English examinations and girls are markedly more successful than those boys who do take English examinations. For example, in 1979, according to DES, *Statistics of Education, School Leavers CSE and GCE*, 85.5 per cent of girl school leavers attempted O-level or CSE examinations in English compared with 80.6 per cent of boy school leavers and 44.8 per cent of marks received by girl candidates were CSE grade 1s and O-level grades A-C compared with 36.1 per cent of marks received by boys. Also at university level English remains among the minority of subjects where girls outnumber boys.

6 White (1975) has hypothesized that the Board of Education's abandonment of direct supervision of the elementary school curriculum, as a result of the omission of curricular recommendations from the 1926 Regulations, can be understood as a strategy to ensure that any subsequently elected socialist government would not have direct control of the curriculum of the elementary schools. Apart from the rational arguments presented by the Board in Circular 1294, there is no reason to believe that the same thinking did not lie behind the decision to relinquish direct supervision of the secondary school curriculum. The newly created examination system effectively provided a rigid check upon the range of subjects available in the secondary school until the introduction of the CSE in the 1960s.

7 After 1933 approximately, the cudgels were taken up on behalf of the literary version of English by the advocates of the Cambridge School of English, primarily F.R. Leavis and Denys Thompson (for details see Ball, 1982).

8 Sir Philip Hartog was an educationalist, Academic Registrar of the University of London, 1903-20, author of *The Writing of English* (1907), Vice-Chancellor of the University of Dacca, 1920-7, Chairman of the Committee on Indian Education, 1928-9. *The Dictionary of National Biography* notes 'Apart from Hartog's academic activities his studies on educational systems had a marked influence on contemporary thought and practice.'
9 The opponents of literary English both at school and university levels certainly attempted to stigmatize it as low status, as merely a matter of reading novels rather than a rigorous academic discipline.
10 The analysis of a complex network of social interaction referred to by this term can equally well explain the absense of change.
11 One might want to be more specific in the use of this term and talk about 'informed' or influential opinion.

References

ABBS, P. (1982) *English within the Arts*, Sevenoaks, Hodder and Stoughton.
ARCHER, M.S. (1979) *The Social Origins of Education Systems*, London, Sage.
ARCHER, R.L. (1921) *Secondary Education in the Nineteenth Century*, Cambridge, Cambridge University Press.
BALL, S.J. (1982) 'Competition and conflict in the teaching of English: A socio-historical analysis', in *Journal of Curriculum Studies*, 15, 1, pp. 1-28.
BALL, S.J. and LACEY, C. (1980) 'Subject disciplines as the opportunity for group action: A measured critique of subject sub-cultures', in WOODS, P.E. (Ed.) *Teacher Strategies*, London, Croom Helm.
BOISSEVAIN, J. (1974) *Friends of Friends: Networks, Manipulators and Coalitions*, Oxford, Basil Blackwell.
BUCHER, R. and STRAUSS, A. (1961) 'Professions in process' *American Journal of Sociology*, 66, January, pp. 325-34.
COOPER, B. (1982) *Innovation in English Secondary School Mathematics: A Sociological Account with Special Reference to the Origins of the School Mathematics Project and the Midlands Mathematical Experiment*, unpublished DPhil thesis, University of Sussex.
CURRIE, W.B. (1973) *New Directions in Teaching English Language*, London, Longman.
DYHOUSE, C. (1976) 'Social-Darwinistic ideas and the development of women's education in England 1880-1920', in *History of Education*, 5, 1, pp. 41-58.
EGGLESTON, J. (1977) *The Sociology of the School Curriculum*, London, Routledge and Kegan Paul.
ESLAND, G. (1971) 'Teaching and learning as the organization of knowledge', in YOUNG, M.F.D. (Ed.) *Knowledge and Control*, London, Collier-Macmillan.
GOODSON, I. (1981) 'Becoming an academic subject: Patterns of explanation and evolution', in *British Journal of Sociology of Education*, 2, 2, pp. 35-52.
GREAT BRITAIN BOARD OF EDUCATION (1910) *The Teaching of English in Secondary Schools*, Circular 753, HMSO.
GRIFFITHS, B.C. and MULLINS, N.C. (1972) 'Coherent social groups in scientific change' in *Science* 15 September, pp. 959-64.
HIRST, P.H. (1974) *Knowledge and the Curriculum*, London, Routledge and Kegan Paul.
HODGSON, J.D. (1975) *Changes in English Teaching: Institutionalization, Transmission and Ideology*, unpublished PhD thesis, University of London.

KUHN, T.S. (1969) *The Structure of Scientific Revolutions*, Chicago, University of Chicago Press.
MANSELL, T. and SILVER, H. (1979) 'Themes in higher education in America and Europe', in *Post-War Curriculum Development*, History of Education Society.
MILLS, C.W. (1956) *The Power Elite*, London, Oxford University Press.
MILROY, L. (1980) *Language and Social Networks*, Oxford, Basil Blackwell.
MUSGROVE, F. (1965) 'The contribution of sociology to the study of the curriculum', in KERR, J.F. (Ed.) *Changing the Curriculum*, London, University of London Press.
RUDDOCK, J. (1979) *Notes on the English Association and National Association for the Teaching of English*, unpublished.
SCHIFF, H. (Ed.) (1977) *Contemporary Approaches to English Studies*, London, Heinemann for the English Association.
SHAYER, D. (1970) *The Teaching of English in Schools*, London, Routledge and Kegan Paul.
SMITH, L.E.W. (1973) *Towards a New English Curriculum*, London, Dent.
STRAY, C. (1980) 'The crisis in classics teaching: Towards a historical sociology of English cultural tranmission', unpublished paper.
WARING, M. (1979) *Social Process and Curriculum Innovation*, London, Methuen.
WHITE, J. (1975) 'The end of the compulsory curriculum', in HIRST, P. (Ed.) *Studies in Education (2), The Curriculum, The Doris Lee Lectures*, University of London, Institute of Education.
YOUNG, M.F.D. (1971) 'An approach to the study of the curriculum as socially organized knowledge', in YOUNG, M.F.D. (Ed.) *Knowledge and Control*, London, Collier-Macmillan.
YOUNG, M.F.D. (1972) 'On the politics of educational knowledge', *Economy and Society*, 1, 2, pp. 194–215.

4   Defining and Defending the Subject: Geography versus Environmental Studies

Ivor Goodson

From its position as a low status integrated school subject in the early twentieth century, geography has progressed to broad acceptance as a high status university 'discipline'. The story behind this remarkable progress has been told elsewhere (Goodson, 1981 and 1983), but the implications for new contenders for subject status need to be carefully explored. Basically, geography, particularly through the activities of the Geographical Association, has followed the four-point strategy recommended by one of the leading activists, H.J. MacKinder, in 1903:

> Firstly, we should encourage University Schools of Geography, where Geographers can be made.... Secondly, we must persuade at any rate some secondary schools to place the geographical teaching of the whole school in the hands of one geographically trained teacher.... Thirdly, we must thrash out by discussion and experimentation what is the best progressive method for common acceptance and upon that method we must base our scheme of examination. Lastly, the examination papers must be set by practical geography teachers. (MacKinder, 1903)

Above all, in the galaxy of geographers' priorities, was the overwhelming concern for academic status and subject control, rather than, for instance, considerations of pupil interest or motivation. Exams were chosen as part of the pursuit of the 'common acceptance' of the subject.

The implications of such subject priorities for curriculum practice have been hinted at in a short article written by David Layton and no doubt partially derived from his studies of the history of science education. Layton (1972) suggests that there is a tentative model for the evolution of school subjects in the secondary curriculum. The model has three stages:

In the first stage:

> the callow intruder stakes a place in the time-table, justifying its presence on grounds such as pertinence and utility. During this stage learners are attracted to the subject because of its bearing on matters of concern to them. The teachers are rarely trained specialists, but bring the missionary enthusiasm of pioneers to their task. The dominant criterion is relevance to the needs and interests of the learners.

Ivor Goodson

In the interim second stage:

> a tradition of scholarly work in the subject is emerging along with a corps of trained specialists from which teachers may be recruited. Students are still attracted to the study, but as much by its reputation and growing academic status as by its relevance to their own problems and concerns. The internal logic and discipline of the subject is becoming increasingly influential on the selection and organization of subject matter.

In the final stage:

> the teachers now constitute a professional body with established rules and values. The selection of subject matter is determined in large measure by the judgments and practices of the specialist scholars who lead inquiries in the field. Students are initiated into a tradition, their attitudes approaching passivity and resignation, a prelude to disenchantment. (p. 11)

Layton's model has some relevance for geography for progressively the subject came to be 'made' in the universities as MacKinder's strategy had proposed. The existence of a base in schools as an integrated subject taught by non-specialists was used to call for the setting up of university geography departments. Thereafter the definition of geography through the universities instead of the schools confirmed the replacement of utilitarian or pedagogic rhetoric common in the early stages by arguments in favour of purer, more theoretical, academic 'rigour'. As early as 1927, for instance, Hadow had contended that 'the main objective in good geographical teaching is to develop as in the case of history, an attitude of mind and mode of thought characteristic of the subject.'

However, for several decades, even though university departments were being established, the subject was plagued by its image as essentially for school children and by the idiosyncratic interpretations of the subject emanating from the universities, particularly in respect to fieldwork. The major period of advance in the universities came after 1945 when many new departments of geography opened. However, while establishment in the universities solved the status problems of the subject in the schools by confirming the claims for academic rigour, within the universities themselves the subject's status still remained low.

The launching in the 1960s of 'new geography' as a rigorous quantitative subject has to be viewed in this context. The subject was promoted with full aspirations to the scientific or social scientific character which would finally establish its status at a higher level. In this respect the current position of the subject in universities bears elegant testimony to the success of 'new geography' in establishing parity of esteem with other university disciplines.

In effect the push towards academic establishment for geography, how it was 'rendered a discipline', was a process of promotion from the base in schools to bring about a discipline base in the universities. An interesting aspect of this process was the way it defended itself against the threat of new contenders for subject status in its area, especially those promoting the concept of 'integrated studies'.

Geography and 'Integrated Studies': Historical Background

Since its early beginnings in the nineteenth century, geographers in England have been preoccupied with finding an answer to MacKinder's (1887) question, 'can Geography be rendered a discipline?' The quest has been continuous, and more recently Honeybone (1954, p. 70) has noted: 'The question of internal balance in geography is ... one which must, of necessity, be always with us. A discipline which recruits its students from the sciences and the humanities alike has continually to keep its synthesis under review.' This continuing identity crisis at the heart of geography is accentuated by the relationship between university geography and 'school geography', and most of all by the relationship between geography and other subjects. As Williams (1976) has noted, these problems are interlinked for, 'if geographers divide over definitions of "geography" and "school geography", it is not surprising that when geography is allied with other subjects the problem of definition of terms is almost insoluble" (p. 8).

The relationship between geography and integrated studies has been historically difficult, notably because 'complication arises from the nature of geography itself' (Williams, 1976, p. 8). But the fears relating to geography's identity which integrated studies evoke have been compounded by the complex historical relationship between geography and other subjects. Crucially, geography itself was created by specialists from other disciplines whose studies were integrated by concentration on problems perceived as geographical. As Kirk (1963) has stated, 'modern geography was created by scholars, trained in other disciplines, asking themselves, geographical questions' (p. 357). At the level of scholarship, therefore, geography was one of the earlier 'integrated studies', but this was also true in schools. To tentatively establish a position in schools, geography was initially presented as an ingredient of integrated courses, as Williams (1976, p. 8) has noted: 'The early attempts at introducing integrated courses stemmed from the struggle to introduce geography into secondary schools ... often as an ingredient of courses integrated with history but also sometimes with the sciences, notably physics.

As a result, any new versions of 'integrated studies' stand as a dual reminder to geographers of the prolonged and continuing quest for a stable subject identity through a process of internal 'integration' and of the early days when the subject itself was a low status ingredient of integrated courses. Once geography was established as a separate subject in its own right in the early years of the twentieth century, geographers began to obsessively patrol their subject borders. They sought to ensure that no other integrated subjects could follow their route to separate subject status.

The first opportunity to scrutinize this symbiotic relationship is in the period before the First World War for 'no sooner had geography taken its place as an accepted part of school curricula than it was subjected to pressure to relate more closely to other subjects' (Williams, 1976, p. 8). The main pressure group at this time was concerned with 'Education for Citizenship' and, as a result, attempts were made to link history and geography. One of the leading protagonists was H.J. MacKinder, who advocated 'a combined subject' in 1913 in an address to the Geographical Association (MacKinder, 1913). He was mindful of the vested interests of those who taught history (by then a well-established school subject) and recalled the fears of geologists twenty years before that geographers would 'make inroads upon their classes' and that their careers would thus be limited as less posts became available. He added: 'Well, even scientific folk are human, and such ideas must be taken into account.' Thus he assured historians: 'There need be no question of vested interests in connection with the two subjects.... There is no idea of attacking the teaching of history as such in training colleges and in similar institutions.' He was concerned only with the 'upper half of elementary education and the lower tiers of secondary education': 'There what I suggest is the teaching of a single subject, geography and history. In those stages of education, let us have one subject, but let that subject be taught by a teacher who has learnt both geography and history, and learnt them separately.' MacKinder's arguments in favour of integration were clearly linked to a view about geography's aspirations as a school 'subject':

> How are children going to use their curiosity? By taking up a 'subject'? That is an academic idea. A special subject will be taken up by a few scattered people as a hobby, but the vast majority will increase their knowledge not by the study of any definite subject, but by reading this and that cheap book, by reading the newspapers, by talking with friends and by seeing what they can when travelling.

This leads MacKinder to argue that for the vast majority

> ... what is important is not to send them out with the rudiments of history as such and the rudiments of geography as such in their minds, but to send them out with some sort of orderly conception of the world around them. Whether a fact is historical or whether it is geographical matters not one straw to them.

Significantly, MacKinder adds that:

> It does, perhaps matter to those who are going to increase the knowledge of history or the knowledge of geography, or who are to be specialized teachers of those subjects, and who are going to prepare for examinations in those subjects. (MacKinder, 1913 in Williams, 1976, p. 5–6)

In fact, the specialist teachers of geography reacted to MacKinder's suggestions in a manner which confirmed his last point. Thus, in the discussions which followed MacKinder's address a school teacher, Miss Spalding, argued that the most effective way of achieving the better citizenship desired by MacKinder was to train pupils 'to love one or two subjects so much that they really go on and study them by themselves' (MacKinder, 1913, p. 10). Dr J.F. Unstead, a university geographer and textbook author, agreed and offered an alternative view of geography as a school subject:

> What is a subject? It is an organized body of knowledge, the different parts of which naturally hang together, and I think in practical teaching it is well to develop it as a whole ..., in geography, the facts do hang together; children can see relations, they may get the sense of proportion if they have the thing treated as a whole.... (Unstead, 1913, p. 10)

A few years later the Council of the Geographical Association issued a statement since 'the question of the position of geography in the curricula of schools and universities is a fundamental one at the present time':

> It is first necessary to understand what is meant by geography and the reasons why it is studied. Among many of those who have not followed closely the recent development of geographical study, an impression prevails that there are important divergences of opinion on these points, that different authorities hold different and conflicting conceptions even of the subject. But a more careful scrutiny reveals the fact that a close agreement is being steadily reached. (Council of the Geographical Association, 1919, in Williams, 1976 p. 15–16)

The statement then refers to the growth of the Geographical Association and to a recent manifesto on the subject 'which has met with practically universal acceptance'. Geography, they argue, is a unique combination, 'a balanced subject with a unity of its own', and may claim '... to contribute in a unique fashion to an education which aims at the appreciative interpretation of the modern world' (*ibid.*, p. 18).

Alongside the group pursuing a combined subject of history and geography was another group which felt that geography was 'rapidly taking its place as a definite science'. The dangers of scientific aspiration were that taken to its logical conclusion it presented 'a very strong argument in favour of geography being taught by the chemistry or physics master' (Carey, 1913).

In the inter-war period, geography was confronted with a new integrationist initiative in the form of the growing social studies movement. Thus in 1935 Happold argued for a reconstructed curriculum to take account of the fact that 'a boy comes to school not to learn geography or history or English, but to be trained how to live'. With a sexism characteristic of the period, he replaced these subject divisions by social studies, '... a unified course designed to give the boy a knowledge and understanding of his own age, considered not in isolation, but in relation to its origin – that is, a picture both of his environment and his heritage' (Happold, 1935, p. 67).

After the war the moves towards social studies continued to be linked with the Association for Education in Citizenship and were seen primarily as courses in civic education. In 1949 the Ministry of Education, reporting on 'Citizens Growing Up', saw geography and history as the most relevant of the traditional subjects:

> The question which teachers of these subjects have to ask themselves today is how far they will make this civic value their sole value and criterion in their syllabus and presentation. Many history and geography teachers have taken up advanced positions in this respect, and the older subject names have sometimes in such cases given place to 'social studies' – an indication of the change in point of view. But others are reluctant to allow the illumination of the contemporary scene to become the sole purpose in this range of work, and hold to the more traditional approach which proceeds historically through the centuries and geographically through the regions of the world. (Ministry of Education, 1949, in Williams, 1976, p. 62–3)

The position of these traditional geographers who were reluctant to embrace social studies was eloquently summarized in a memorandum prepared in 1950 by the Royal Geographical Society's Education Committee. The committee stated frankly that social studies would 'destroy the value of geography as an important medium of education' and hence was 'concerned at its spread in the schools' (Royal Geographical Society, 1950, in Williams p. 81). The comments of the committee indicate considerable fear that geography might be replaced by social studies especially, it was noted, in secondary modern schools:

> 'It is difficult to estimate precisely how far this elimination of geography as an ordered study has proceeded. There is, however, much evidence of a strong tendency to 'break down the barriers between subjects' (an explanation given for the change) and to teach an amorphous hotch-potch of geography, history and civics under the heading of social studies. (in Williams p. 110)

The report conceded that the nature of these amorphous hotch-potches varied considerably between schools, and that most contained some geography 'but in a disjointed and attenuated form, insufficient to preserve the characteristic outlook and discipline of the subject' (p. 81). Above all, the report sees any integration of subjects as likely to impair 'standards of instruction' in geography.

> An attempt to study a group of subjects together introduces such complexity that children cannot see any general pattern or gain a clear and memorable educational experience. The geographer is well aware that knowledge is whole, but makes no apology for dividing it into

> separate subjects for the purpose of learning. History and geography, for example, are distinct branches of study, and each is recognized as having a unique contribution to make to the intellectual equipment of the educated citizen of today. But these contributions are different and cannot be made unless the recognized content and characteristic method of presentation of each subject are preserved. (*ibid.*, p. 82)

Thus the integrationist perspective of social studies is presented as wholly undesirable: 'The result is exactly what happens when the lemon is squeezed: the juice is removed, and only the useless rind and fibres remain' (*ibid.*, p. 80–1).

The report of the Royal Geographical Society engendered considerable discussion at the time, and Ernest Fereday summarized some of the main objections to the views presented. He concentrated on the two most emotive phrases in the report: firstly, the dismissal of social studies as an 'amorphous hotch-potch'. Fereday argued that geography itself could easily be presented in this light:

> Any highly regarded textbook of geography affords ample evidence that school geography is a brilliant reconciliation of the carefully selected essentials of several specialized sciences. Most of us owe so much to those clear-thinking teachers of geography in the last generation who patiently and purposefully expounded such well-ordered symposia to us that we should at once condemn as unkind any one who could characterise such work as an 'amorphous hotch-potch'. (Fereday, 1950, in Williams, p. 66)

Secondly, Fereday argues that the 'most ardent advocate of social studies could hardly better their image of the squeezed lemon.' Thus in selecting the materials of study from a widely increased range of possibilities it would appear, he argues, sensible to 'retain the nourishing and necessary while rejecting the noxious, the nebulous and the nugatory' (*ibid.*, p. 67).

In spite of the arguments of Fereday and other supporters of social studies, by the mid-1950s it was quite clear that the opposition to the new approach was succeeding. Channon (1964, in Williams p. 110) reported that for social studies: 'The period of post-war experiment had faded by the mid-1950's, by which time many schools appear to have returned to a traditional curriculum.' She adds that one of the main reasons was the criticism of geographers (and also historians) 'who saw the new proposals as a threat to the integrity and status of their own subjects.' (*ibid*, p. 112)

From the geographers' point of view the result of the opposition to social studies was presented differently. In 1954 Honeybone summarized the developments which followed:

> If the Social Studies controversy has no other effect than that of making us put our house in order, then it will have made a very important contribution to the development of geography teaching in school. It is a pity that by reason of its brevity, the Royal Geographical

> Society's pamphlet does not develop the case for geography at greater length. We have a very strong and positive case, and ... the present time is particularly hopeful for a wide-spread advance in the teaching of geography in school. (Honeybone, 1954, in Williams p. 89–90)

This 'widespread advance' was linked with the advance of geography at university level. This advance transformed the prospects for school geography and culminated in the opening of many university departments in the 1950s and in the launching of 'new geography' in the 1960s. In future conflict with any 'integrated studies' school geographers were able to call in very strong allies.

Geography versus Environmental Studies

The geographers, ever alert to the threat from integrated studies, first formally discussed the 'problem of environmental studies' in 1969. The worry was that the pressures exerted by headteachers on specialist teachers of geography to teach environmental studies, often in place of pure geography, would reduce demand for geographers and weaken the subject position. As a result it was thought that

> the Geographical Association should involve itself in a dialogue with practitioners of environmental studies, to discover the geographical content in such studies and to ensure that, if such studies continue to proliferate, geographers will be included in the appropriate teaching teams and will be able to contribute their distinctive concepts, skills and techniques.

However, it was moved that 'some members felt that to do so would be tantamount to admitting the validity of environmental studies or would indicate a measure of approval' (Geographical Association Executive Minutes).

In addition to the legacy of geographers' responses to the 'threat' of integrated studies stretching back half a century, the reaction to environmental studies was complicated by internal dissent among geographers with reference to the growth of the 'new geography' in the 1960s. In large measure the opposition came from those with a 'regional' or 'fieldwork' orientation in their training and practice. The close relationship between regional geography and the fieldwork tradition was reflected in the work of Professor S.W. Wooldridge. He argued that the aim of geographical fieldwork is 'regional synthesis' (Wooldridge and Hotchings, 1957, p. xi) and in his obituary in *Geography* it was recorded by M.J. Wise, later an advocate of close links with environmental studies, that: 'Above all, geography was for him regional geography' (Wise, 1963, p. 330).

In 1966 Professor C.A. Fisher read a paper to the Research Committee of the Royal Geographical Society – it was later published in extended form under the title 'Whither Regional Geography?'. Fisher argued that geographical research was in serious danger of 'over-extending its periphery at the expense of neglecting its base' (Fisher, 1979, p. 374). For Fisher, the 'traditional core of geography' was regional study as against the 'new', systematic geography, but he noted: 'While systematic geography now flourishes like the Biblical bay tree, regional geography (however defined) appears to be declining and even withering away' (*ibid.*, p. 315–6). Fisher added some details of this decline of regional geography:

> ... not only has there been a noticeable decrease in the importance attached to it in the university syllabus, but this process is apparently also spreading to the schools, and it has been announced that the Southern Universities Joint Board 'O' level Geography examination for 1970 would include no paper in regional geography. (*ibid.*, p. 376)

The increasingly threatened supporters of regional geography were faced with the pervasive challenge of new geography and the traditional challenge of integrated studies epitomized by environmental studies. For once the internal threat seems to have been deemed greater than the external dangers represented by the emergence of environmental studies. The obituary of Professor P.W. Bryan, an eminent regionalist, records that in 1967:

> Only twelve months before his death, and already a sick man, Pat Bryan attended a strenuous full-day conference at Leicester University on Environmental Studies. He probably felt that this term expressed more clearly his own life's work and ambitions as a geographer. (Millward, 1969, p. 93)

Similarly, in 1970 P.R. Thomas asserted in *Geography* that:

> The tendency towards an environmentalist approach to explanation in school geography is at least partly due to the survival of the regional concept as the basis for syllabus construction, despite the progressive decline in the importance of regional geography at most universities and its virtual disappearance from some. (Thomas, 1970, p. 274–5)

But the alliance between regional geography and environmental studies was not to last, partly because after 1970 the 'new geography' tradition began to lose impetus and became increasingly assimilated into traditional patterns of geography. As one college geography lecturer noted: 'The new geographers became less violent ... they flushed regions out but then accepted regionalism back in not as facts ... but as a spirit and concept'. He also identified another reason for the alliance ending:

> The crisis in Geography caused traditional regional geographers to flee into Environmental Studies ... they wanted a refuge to go on teaching as they were teaching ... but they were overtaken by the Environmental crisis and the rapid growth in Environmental Studies that followed it.... The threat to all Geographers from this new subject

became much greater than any internal disagreements. (interview, 14 December 1976)

The increasing convergence of new, systematic geography and regional and field geography, together with the rapid growth of environmental studies, once again helped unite geographers in their opposition to the perceived external challenge.

The challenge came quite rapidly as large numbers of newly reorganized comprehensive schools began drawing up environmental studies courses; in addition, several new universities set up courses with this title. Most notable were the initiatives from Hertfordshire, led by rural studies teachers, to promote environmental studies as a new school subject and 'scholarly discipline' which culminated in the Offley Conference of 1971. This led to a working party being set up to submit an A-level syllabus in environmental studies. The spokesmen for geography at the conference reflected the growing concern. Dr. Douglas, for instance, sought to define environmental studies in a way that would not 'overlap too much' with geography. Indeed, commenting on the claims the geographers made, Mr Hartrop, in a manner reminiscent of the Norwood Report's complaints at the 'expansiveness of geography' nearly thirty years before, commented that 'parts of geography could be expanded to consume almost everything.' The reasons for the geographers' reaction can be partially deduced from the evidence of a sample survey of secondary schools carried out by HM Inspectors in 1971/72. They found that whilst in grammar schools only one 'combined studies' course had replaced geography (one out of forty-four schools), in secondary modern schools forty schools out of 104 had replaced geography by such courses and in comprehensive schools twenty out of fifty-nine schools (DES, 1974, p. 6).

That the geographers were intensely worried by the threat of Hertfordshire teachers developing an 'A'-level in environmental studies was illustrated when Sean Carson, the leading advocate of the 'A'-level, went to speak to them at this time. Interviewed recently about this he recalled:

> I was invited to go and speak on environmental studies.... The Royal Institution was probably where it was held ... [laughter]. There was a really good start when the chairman said 'I'm Chairman of this meeting but I can't adopt a neutral attitude on something I feel so strongly about....'
>
> Then I made my spiel about Geography not being God-given religion, but a range of knowledge we had assembled to our convenience and there was no reason why we shouldn't reassemble it in any other form. This [Environmental Studies] was another form in which it might be reassembled and just because one had learnt things in a different tradition, there's no reason why you should go on repeating so other people repeat it after you....

After his speech:

S.C.: There broke out shouting and rude remarks and the Chairman was not willing ... made very little effort to control it....

I.G.: Were you nervous?

S.C.: I wasn't nervous at all.... I'm not nervous in that sense.... On this occasion I was frankly amused and amazed! It was so irrational.

I.G.: What kind of things did they say?

S.C.: Well, I can remember one chap who stood up and said, 'I'm a professor of geography and I turn out 60 honours graduates every year.' So I said, 'Well, what do they do? Do they produce more students for you to turn out honours graduates every year? What's the end of that?'... There were things like that being said.

I.G: Did they take the line that they were doing it anyway?

S.C.: Yes, and that I was out to destroy Geography.... Rural Studies was a hotch-potch of various subjects being out together for no particular purpose, it had no respectability.... I remember thinking, 'This is what it must be like, facing a Congressional meeting in America.' It was quite an experience – a lot of people afterwards apologised to me ... I think, pretty ashamed of it. I got a letter of thanks from the Conference not mentioning it at all! I did think of writing a sarcastic reply, but I didn't.

The geographers' official reaction to environmental studies was summarized in a presidential address to the Geographical Association on 1 January 1973 by Mr A.D. Nicholls. His speech began by asserting, somewhat wishfully: 'It is not surprising that in the minds of most teachers environmental studies should be associated with geography rather than with the numerous subjects which, in greater or lesser degree, are considered to be constituent parts of this educational field.' Having hinted at the thrust of his argument, he later stated: 'The definitions given by well-known geographers to provide answers to the question "What is geography" might equally well be used to answer the question "What are environmental studies?".' And similarly: 'In the first decade of this century the founding fathers of the then "new" geography came from many and varied disciplines. Their original choice of discipline would make an admirable list of environmental studies' (Nicholls, 1973, p. 197). Nicholls' views were undoubtedly shared by most geographers. One college of education lecturer remembers that at this time: 'At an early Environmental Studies meeting we felt that geography had been doing it for years and we said so ...' (Interview, 14 December 1976). Tony Fyson also claimed that:

> On a pragmatic level a new subject dealing with the environment is still going to leave a lot of geography teachers claiming that their traditional fare is the true way to approach the topic; on an academic level it is

> possible to argue that geography ... can develop to include the aims of the environmental studies lobby. (Ward and Fyson, 1973, p. 106)

Nicholls' second argument turned on the need for 'a subject'; again he drew on a long tradition. In 1913 Dr J.F. Unstead had argued against MacKinder's advocacy of a combined subject, saying that a subject is an organized body of knowledge and that: 'in geography, the facts do hang together' (Unstead, 1913, p. 10). Unstead's argument was again used in the 1960s when there were fears about school geography: 'No subject can claim a place on the school curriculum unless it has a clear structure, a precise theme and a worthwhile purpose ... if geography is to survive in school, it, too, must be a scholarly discipline with a clearly defined purpose and a carefully organized structure' (Scarfe, 1965, p. 24).

Nicholls began by conceding that environmental studies were generally accepted as useful in teaching 'young children' but then argued that:

> As the width and depth of knowledge acquired increases so does the need to specialize, subject divisions appear and the need for subject disciplines arises. These codes of study are the framework or basic principles which are necessary for specialized learning and understanding. Indeed, without them we tend to accumulate only encyclopaedic, unrelated facts. (Nicholls, 1973, p. 200)

The role of geography as a subject discipline ordering and unifying the 'unrelated facts' of environmental studies was widely promoted by geographers at this time.

> Geography because it is an integrated discipline at the heart of Environmental Studies is better placed than any of the other constituent nuclei to co-ordinate and unify the larger body of studies of which it is the core. To adapt a well-known analogy, it may well be the leaven which will make the loaf palatable. (Thomas, 1969, p. 12)

The implicit hierarchy contained in this statement is clarified by another geographer exploring the same relationship: 'To put it in terms of a model, geography may be likened to a pyramid the base of which is environmental studies, but the apex is the sharp intellectual discipline fashioned in the university.' (Wheeler, 1971, p. 87). A university professor confirmed this view, and explained the implications for school geography: 'You need high level theoretical development first of all ... then you break it down to digestible level in school' (Interview, 14 December 1976).

The third strand of Nicholls' argument, undoubtedly the most convincing aspect for the many teachers in the audience, dealt with the 'practical realities' for 'practising teachers'. Crucial to this argument was the recognition that:

> It is likely, but by no means certain, that if environmental studies or environmental education is considered as a subject in its own right, some, but not all, of the time previously devoted to constituent

subjects will be made available to the new omnibus subject. With constant pressure on teaching time, headmasters are ever searching for new space into which additional prestige subjects can be fitted, and the total loss of teaching time to environmental subjects may be considerable. Nor, in my experience, have I found departments very eager to surrender precious teaching time, particularly with the more able classes, to make good other departments' losses.

Nicholls stressed a further practicality:

> Next, as a practising teacher, I must refer to what is an all-important consideration in every type of school – the teaching staff available. Many among you will think I should have referred to the staff before considering the timetable. If undifferentiated environmental studies of an omnibus nature are to be introduced into a school curriculum which of the academic disciplines is going to cater for suitably qualified men and women to take charge of them? Or instead of using one suitable member of the staff to cover all aspects of the studies is team work by a mixed group drawn from the allied disciplines to share the work? Can you imagine the wrangling over the relative importance of their particular shares which might go on? (Nicholls, 1973, p. 200)

A publication prepared by the Environmental Education Standing Committee of the Geographical Association (1972), which included Mr Nicholls, clarifies the nature of the fears over such 'wrangling'. They assert: 'The concerns of Environmental Education render the presence of a person with geographical training in each team quite essential.' Similarly, '... a team with [a geography specialist] would have a wider range of possible activities'.

Nicholls explored this theme in considerable detail in his address:

> Qualified men and women of academic stature have selected their subjects because of their interest in them and the importance they consider them to have. They also like to see the inspiration of their teaching reflected in their pupils 'advancement': indeed, this is one of the rewards for those who engage in a profession which has been described as richly rewarding but badly paid....

The relationship between subject expertise and pupil advancement is later elucidated:

> A shallow approach to any subject inevitably becomes less satisfying, and finally utterly boring both to teacher and class. Not every question from a class calls for an immediate answer in depth, but when the teacher's ignorance of the subject becomes evident to the class and pupils lose confidence in their teacher, and more pitifully, the teacher loses confidence in himself, and confusion becomes chaos. The teacher must know his subject.... (Nicholls, 1973, pp. 200–201)

The relationship between the status of a 'subject' and the pupils which traditional subjects attract is alluded to by Nicholls in discussing a DES survey's findings with regard to environmental studies:

> Four varieties were distinguished:
> (a) one comprehensive school used environmental studies for all first year pupils and thereafter separate subjects were taught.
> (b) two schools gave environmental studies for slow learners in year 1, 2 and 3 only. The average and able pupils did ordinary subjects.
> (c) two schools gave environmental studies in year 4 only for fourth-year leavers. These were non-examination pupils. The rest did ordinary subjects.
> (d) one school gave environmental studies for able fifth year pupils for O-level as an option against other subjects.

From these findings Nicholls concludes:

> First, average and above average pupils are considered to be able to cope with ordinary subjects, though it might be unsafe to assume they enjoy these subjects more or that they would rather not spread their abilities. Secondly, environmental studies are thought to be easier or can be made more attractive to less able scholars. Thirdly, separate subjects may be easier to teach successfully. Cynics might suggest that combined studies provide a more successful opiate to potentially rowdy classes. You as teachers, may reach other equally valid conclusions. (Nicholls, 1973, p. 205)

The last sentence confirms that the message, despite its philosophical and logical shortcomings, aims to focus on the teachers' perception of the practical realities of their work.

The final strand of Nicholls' argument concentrates on the need to keep geography as a unified discipline. An earlier President had touched on the socializing role of the universities:

> University departments have a duty to ensure that, at least at the first degree level, the core of our subject is neither forgotten nor neglected and that the synthesis of the specialist fields and their relevance to that core are clearly appreciated by our undergraduate students. (Garnett, 1969 p. 389)

Garnett also noted the symbiotic relationship between university geography and school geography:

> There is now an intake from sixth forms, into our university departments of at least one thousand students each year to read geography. The recognition of our subject's status among university disciplines which this gives, together with the now costly provision made available for its study, could never have been achieved without this

remarkable stimulus and demand injected from our schools. This is a matter that university teachers must not forget; we have a duty at all times and in every way possible to return help to our colleagues in schools and colleges and to forge closer links between school and university teachers.

Nicholls argued from a similar position about what is required of geography as a subject:

> At sixth form level it must ... provide a challenge to the young men and women who may have ambitions for the future and wish to carry their studies further and go to a university. They will become, in the best sense, students. Some of these will furnish the university schools of geography with young men and women who will expect to have some knowledge with sound and deep foundations so that understanding between them and their lecturers, readers and professors is mutual. We should be wise not to stray too far from the recognized routes – the frontiers of the subject are alluring, but not all are worth extending, at least not in school. If we provide the universities with undergraduates who have a wide but shallow acquaintance with many subjects, will they prefer these students before those with a sound foundation in fewer relevant subjects? (Nicholls, 1973, p. 201)

Nicholls' conclusion stressed the need for staying within 'the recognized routes':

> Ten years ago, almost to the day and from this platform, Professor Kirk said 'Modern geography was created by scholars, trained in other disciplines, asking themselves geographical questions and moving inwards in a community of problems; it could die by a reversal of the process whereby trained geographers moved outwards in a fragmentation of interests seeking solutions to non-geographical problems'. Might not this be prophetic for us today? Could it not all too soon prove disastrous if the trained teachers of geography moved outwards as teachers of environmental studies seeking solutions to non-geographical problems? (Nicholls, 1973, p. 206)

Nicholls' conclusion is as explicit a statement of the geographers' 'party line' as it is possible to make: in effect he is saying that they must not allow the process which created geography to be repeated.

That Nicholls' view was predominant among geographers was confirmed by events. In the negotiations over the environmental studies A-level in the Schools Council the geography sub-committee was consistently unhelpful. As a result the A-level was delayed for more than a year and when finally accepted it was only as an experimental syllabus. More important was the ruling noted 'with approval' by the geography sub-committee chairman, that candidates could not take the examination with geography. The geographers filibustering tactics, together with the insistence on this qualification, proved sufficient of a barrier to ensure environmental studies was not taken up widely. Carson noted at the time, 'candidates may not take geography at the same examination.... Some of our teachers particularly wanted to take the subject with geography but the decision was a "political one" by a group of geographers (who gave me a rough reception at the G.A. annual conference)' (Carson, 1973). In 1975 a Schools Council working party on environmental studies confirmed this view, whilst phrasing the matter more diplomatically:

> At present students taking Environmental Studies at G.C.E. A-level are not allowed to combine this choice with geography. Subject compatability is frequently a source of discord but it is important to prevent the prefectly legitimate misgivings of academics about subject demarcations being turned into obstacles unfairly placed in the path of students....

Conclusion

In the conflict between geography and environmental studies, groups defending an established academic subject confronted those promoting an aspiring subject. As Nicholls (1967) states, the threat of losing able students, departmental resources and, by implication, career prospects would have been made real if academic parity were to have been conceded to environmental studies. By placing this threat to material self-interest and conditions of classroom practice at the centre of the debate over the definition and defence of geography, the implicit exhortation was to subjugate the claims of pupil interest, subject content, pedagogic orientation and intellectual scholarship to those of individual and subject *self-interest*.

The reasons for 'defending' the status of the subject as an academic discipline are of course identical with the reasons behind the promotion of a university base for the subject. Within school subjects there is a clear hierarchy of status which is based upon assumptions that certain subjects, the so-called 'academic' subjects, are suitable for 'able' students while other subjects are not. In her study of resource allocation in schools, Byrne has shown that educational planning unquestioningly assumed that able students should have *more* resources and finance, 'that they need more staff, more highly paid staff and more money for equipment and books' (Byrne, 1974, p. 29). Hence the appeal of being viewed as an 'academic discipline' for subject teachers. Once an A-level base is legitimized through status passage at the university level, the school subject is able to claim the status, resources and territory that are preferentially reserved for the 'able students'. 'The conflict over the status of examinable knowledge is therefore partly a battle over the material resources and career prospects available to each subject community' (Goodson, 1983, p. 000).

Having a university base from which scholars can define and refine the subject allows the school subject advocates to present their subject as an unchallengeable 'discipline'. In the face of claims from 'integrated studies' (with no scholars to define their discipline) the conflict between geography and new integrated contenders became increasingly one-sided. For geography, of course, the irony was that they had themselves travelled the route from low status integrated school subject to 'discipline'. Clearly they did not wish for a return journey.

References

BOARD OF EDUCATION (1927) Report of the Consultative Committee: The Education of the Adolescent, *Hadow Report*, HMSO.
BYRNE, E.M. (1974) *Planning and Educational Inequality,* Windsor, NFER.
CAREY, W. MACLEAN (1913) 'The correlation of instruction in physics and geography', in *The Geographical Teacher*, 5.
CHANNON, C. (1964) 'Social studies in secondary school', in *Educational Review*, 17, 1, January.
COUNCIL OF THE GEOGRAPHICAL ASSOCIATION (1919) 'The position of geography', in *The Geographical Teacher*, 10.
DEPARTMENT OF EDUCATION AND SCIENCE (1974) *Education Survey 19, School Geography in the Changing Curriculum*, London, HMSO.
FEREDAY, E.L. (1950) 'Social studies in the secondary modern school,' in *Journal of Education*, November.
FISHER, C.A. (1979) 'Whither regional geography'?, in *Geography*, 55, 4.
GARNETT, J. (1969) 'Teaching geography: Some reflections', in *Geography*, 54, 4, November.
GEOGRAPHICAL ASSOCIATION. ENVIRONMENTAL EDUCATION STANDING COMMITTEE (1972) *Environmental Studies*, a discussion paper for teachers and lecturers, draft ed., January.
GOODSON, I.F. (1981) Becoming a subject: Patterns of evolution and explanation', in *British Journal of Sociology of Education*, 2, 2, summer.
GOODSON, I.F (1983) *School Subjects and Curriculum Change: Case Studies in the Social History of Curriculum*, London, Croom Helm.
HAPPOLD, F.C. (1935) *Citizens in the Making*, London, Christophers.
HONEYBONE, R.C. (1954) 'Balance in geography and education', in *Geography*, 34, 184.
KIRK, W. (1963) 'Problems of geography', in *Geography*, 48.
LAYTON, D. (1972) 'Science as general education', in *Trends in Education*, January.
MACKINDER, H.J. (1903) Report of the discussion on Geographical Education at the British Association meeting, September.
MACKINDER, H.J. (1887) 'On the scope and methods of geography', in *Proceedings of the Royal Geographical Society*, 9.
MACKINDER, H.J. (1913) 'The teaching of geography and history as a combined subject', in *The Geographical Teacher*, 7.
MILLWARD, R. (1969) 'Obituary: Patrick Walter Bryan', in *Geography*, 54, 1, January.
MINISTRY OF EDUCATION (1949) 'Citizens growing up', Pamphlet No. 16, HMSO.
NICHOLLS, A.D. (1973) 'Environmental studies in schools', in *Geography*, 58, 3, July.
ROYAL GEOGRAPHICAL SOCIETY (1950) 'Geography and social studies in school', memo prepared by the Education Committee.

SCARFE, N.V. (1965) 'Depth and breadth in school geography', in *Journal of Geography*, 24, 4, April.
THOMAS, I. (1969) 'Rural studies and environmental studies', in *Society of Environmental Education Journal*, 2, 1, autumn.
THOMAS, P.R. (1970) 'Education and the new geography', in *Geography*, 55, 4.
UNIVERSITY OF LONDON (1975) 'GCE A-level environmental studies', paper presented to Schools Council Working Party on Environmental Education.
UNSTEAD, J. (1913) 'Discussion of MacKinder's paper' *The Geographical Teacher*, 7.
WARD, C. and FYSON, A. (1973) *Streetwork – The Exploding School*, London, Routledge and Kegan Paul.
WHEELER, K.S. (1971) 'Review of D.G. Watts' *Environmental Studies*' in *Journal of Curriculum Studies*, 3, 1, May.
WILLIAMS, M. (1976) (Ed.) *Geography and the Integrated Curriculum*, London, Heinemann.
WISE, M.J. (1963) 'Obituary: Prof. S.W. WOOLDRIDGE' in *Geography*, 48, 3.
WOOLDRIDGE, S.W. and HUTCHINGS, G.E. (1957) *London's Countryside: Geographical Field Work for Students and Teachers of Geography*, London, Methuen.

5   One Spell of Ten Minutes or Five Spells of Two...? Teacher-Pupil Encounters in Art and Design Education

Les Tickle

The charge of Pink Floyd that pupils are regarded as no more than bricks in a wall and that teachers are engaged in a process of mind control over their pupils may be written off as extreme adolescent-like protest. Yet the charge echoes much earlier ones which are illustrated by the work of many distinguished educationists. One, Krishnamurti (1953), claimed that the system of education, whilst perhaps doing something to awaken the intellect, also makes people subservient, mechanical and deeply thoughtless, and leaves the individual incomplete, stultified and uncreative. Furthermore, Torrance (1962) argued that teachers are actually punitive towards pupils who show creative potential. And from a Marxist perspective Bowles and Gintis (1976) have asserted that by serving the needs of capitalism for a stratified, compliant workforce, schools inhibit and distort personal development and prevent the achievement of that very social equality which they purport to serve. Thus, while the relationship between schooling and personal development has usually been associated with an optimistic public view that education is concerned with maximizing that development in intellectual, physical and social/emotional terms, the arguments of critical educationists and some sociologists have run counter to that view: for them contemporary schooling is essentially anti-creative and inegalitarian in nature.

Despite the strength of these claims and counter-claims, however, little evidence about the nature of schooling has been produced which would allow us to arbitrate between them. The production of such evidence is an important priority for in their different ways the two perspectives – one of teaching as a controlling mechanism which tends to stunt growth through punitive action; the other of education which by its very nature develops the creative potential of individuals – highlight a major conflict for teachers. That conflict is especially acute at the very centre of the classroom enterprise where teachers and pupils are involved in interactional and curricular processes; particularly so in those parts of the curriculum – art, design, English, etc. – which are explicitly concerned with creativity and personal growth. This chapter focuses on one such area of the curriculum – art and design – and is derived from my analysis of classroom processes in that subject in two middle schools. In art and design the relationship between 'greater control and rigour' by teachers and 'freedom for children to do things their own way' is a contentious one which has been widely voiced and recorded (Schools Council, 1974). In addition to offering insights into art and design teaching *per se*, therefore, this study also provides an important testing ground for the examination of wider pedagogical and curricular issues concerning the effects of curriculum practice on personal development.

The view that schooling essentially inhibits development and stunts personal growth might be expected to induce particularly grave concern among teachers of art and design. For some, these subjects provide the key to the whole span of education, being the means by which individual potential can be fulfilled (Read, 1934), even if in practice they have more often been simply interludes in the school curriculum during which pupils can indulge the luxury of pursuing 'creative expression'. In either case, though, artistic work in schools has come to be seen as intrinsically, essentially and necessarily 'creative', providing a vehicle for the fostering of personal growth in children. Most teachers of art and design intend that pupils should engage in some form of creative activity, and recent curriculum development projects (Schools Council, 1974 and 1975), as well as other publications in this area (Field, 1970; Shaw and Reeve, 1978), explicitly demand that children should be involved in problem-solving processes and creative experience.

Assertions about schooling's restricting effects on creativity and personal development offer a devastating blow to teachers who subscribe to a more optimistic view of education, where children are seen as exploratory, creative, problem-solving beings who engage actively in learning. While existing evidence suggests that teachers of this kind may be thin on the ground (Bennett, 1976; Galton *et al.*, 1981; Boydell, 1981), they are probably more concentrated in art and design teaching than almost anywhere else. Also, arguments that schooling is inimical to personal development and creativity either because of the institutional character of schooling (Illich, 1971) or through its relation to the needs of capitalism (Bowles and Gintis, 1976; Sharp and Green, 1975) run counter to the assumptions of art and design educators about creativity and personal growth. Those optimistic assumptions (particularly at points in the school system far removed from formal selection and examinations) and their more critical counter-arguments pinpoint the need for a study of art and design education as a test case for these claims. In this study I will examine some of the effects of schooling on personal development, creativity and the equality of pupil treatment in an area of the curriculum and at a point in the school system where one might reasonably expect to find individual potential being fulfilled. This will be achieved by studying how teachers allocate their time among pupils, and by examining the kinds of educational content and experience that are offered to different pupils within this time.

The research on which the chapter is based (Tickle, 1979) examined aspects of classroom practice in art and design, involving four teachers[1] with third- and fourth-year pupils in two 9–13 middle schools. The study focused on teaching strategies; the teachers' perspectives relating to classroom practices; and the outcome of these perspectives and strategies for the pupils' experience in art and design subjects. Data were collected by observing how teachers interacted with their pupils (recorded in field notes and on tape) and by formal and informal interviews with the teachers. The data used here relate to practical sessions which took place after lesson introductions with whole classes.

The 'main dilemma' of art and design teachers identified by the Schools Council (1974) – between imposing 'skills' on pupils yet granting freedom for children to do things their own way – is one which reflects conflicting pressures in creative activities not only in schools but in the social production of art generally (Wolff, 1981). In classrooms the conflicts and dilemmas impinge everywhere, not only on the content of learning but also on the form of its transmission and on the criteria by which learning products are judged; on curriculum, pedagogy and evaluation, that is. In the case study each of the teachers was concerned with the didactic teaching of 'basic skills' while also fostering (in varying degrees) creativity, problem-solving and individuality in the pupils' expression of personal ideas. They identified basic skills as manipulative craft skills; knowledge of tools, equipment and craft processes; kinaesthetic experience in the use and control of a variety of materials; and aesthetic skills and modes of visual representation. At the same time, expectations for creativity, problem-solving and use of personal ideas played an important part. These involved the use of 'design ideas' which incorporated individual decision-making; problem-solving in open choice situations; kinaesthetic exploration of materials; and the expression of personal ideas and image-making.

The conflicting demands of imposing 'basic skills' in which all pupils are expected to succeed on the one hand while valuing personal growth and fulfilment for individual children on the other has been discussed by Berlak and Berlak (1981) in the context of the primary school curriculum. These demands, they point out, are part of a wide variety of influences acting on teachers, who respond to the dilemmas these influences present in different ways. In this case study the conflicting demands of imposing basic skills in art and design on the one hand and fostering creativity and individuality on the other were reconciled through similar strategies by each teacher. These strategies ensured that pupils received instruction in manipulative and technical skills while incorporating some, albeit limited, elements of freedom for children to express ideas and make choices.

The balance between the opposing principles did not occur equally for all pupils, however. Some were granted greater opportunity to pursue individual ideas and engage in problem-solving while others' learning experiences were more closely controlled and restricted. Those deemed to be 'more able' were engaged increasingly in the 'creative' elements while others continued to work under pressure to perform in 'basic skills'. Moreover, these different categories of pupil received different allocations of teacher time, not only in quantity but in quality too.

I shall now examine in detail the classroom practices of the three teachers – Mr Penketh, Mr Tansley and Mr Sankey – to show how the dilemmas were experienced and resolved in each case.

Les Tickle

Mr Penketh

Mr Penketh can be typified as being a 'discipline-based' teacher (Hammersley, 1977). The traditional craft teacher element was dominant within his professional identity yet he had also been influenced by a number of different orientations to teaching since working within the middle school. These included the organizational demands of mixed ability teaching; the headteacher's perspectives on individualized teaching and the integration of subjects; and the views of two LEA advisers who shared a 'progressive' view of education (Hammersley, 1977) and who had close contact with the school and with the art and design department in particular.

Mr Penketh's strategies centred on notions of *limited choice* and *choice of jobs*. At the beginning of their course every pupil did the same job – a model railway engine or similar toy. Later, different jobs were available, in the form of models made by the teacher, the patterns of which could be copied. As pupils progressed through the course more open choice was offered, without models to be copied. During the first year of the course pupils who were perceived by the teacher as 'less able', 'average', or 'more able' respectively in terms of performance in basic skills were then 'turned' towards 'appropriate' tasks, with increased 'choice' over time. As Mr Penketh himself put it: 'I think in the fourth year you've to give them some choice of jobs. By the fourth year I think you've got to, I think they need it. It's not complete choice, they've got limitations.' It is the ways in which 'choice' and 'limitations' were applied by Mr Penketh in relation to pupils' perceived abilities in basic skills which will be considered.

Choice of jobs was implemented by producing models on a simple-to-difficult scale, whereas 'limited choice' allowed pupils only to make simple modifications to the job set for the whole class. Mr Penketh explained the choice of jobs: 'I've done three carts, one's a tip cart, one's called a Devon Wain which is a haycart, and one is ... just a cart. That one is quite a difficult one, it's the most difficult of them all, the tip cart is a bit easier, the Devon Wain is much easier....' The range of jobs from which pupils could 'choose' was extended further into allowing the pupils to design their own jobs, as illustrated in the case of a class doing metal/forge work:

> I'm going to explain to you what jobs you are going to do next week when you come to Design. I'm going to show you various processes in metal and you're going to design certain jobs.... So between now and next week you can think of the type of work you would like to do. You can bend it round, you can twist it, you can shape it, you can make sculptures....

Within both frameworks – a range of set jobs or the opportunity to design jobs – Mr Penketh incorporated the option of *changing the job* which a pupil chose. For instance, when we discussed a group of 'less able' boys in the fourth year who were making the less difficult of two types of marionette, and I asked what would happen if they chose the more difficult one, Mr Penketh replied: 'They wanted to make the puppet so I suggested that they try the simpler one, otherwise they'd get frustrated.... Well if they chose that [the difficult one] I'd have to change the job.' An example of how this operated when pupils designed their own jobs occurred when the class doing metal/forge work presented ideas for the type of work they 'would like to do'. Each pupil in turn showed the design to Mr Penketh for approval. Some were given the 'OK' with little more than a nod of approval; some received brief comment regarding dimensions or similar detail; others were scrutinized more closely:

> *Mr Penketh to Janice:* I don't like your 3. Do you? [Mr P. hands a book of lettering to the pupil.] Take that away, see if you can find a large 3 in there, OK. You might, have a look. Can you improve your 3 and then we can get to work.
>
> *Mr Penketh to Melanie*: How many of those [supports on a plant stand] are you going to make?
>
> *Pupil*: Two
> [Pause]
>
> *Mr Penketh*: Are you only having two? Are you sure? Are you positive you only want two? Are you sure?

(This was said in a pleasant joking manner, reciprocated by the pupil.)

> *Mr Penketh*: Watch

Mr Penketh turned to another pupil in the class, standing nearby, to illustrate the point he wanted to make:
Open your legs, stand with your feet wide apart, right.

He then turned to the girl again.

> Now look. He's difficult to push over there isn't he? [pushes boy gently] He's difficult to push over there [pushes other side of boy gently] but he's easy to push that way isn't he? [pushes boy from front and he begins to fall backwards] It's the basic principle of Judo that is [joking again] How many are you having?
>
> *Pupil*: Four.

Like Janice who was now redesigning her figure 3, Melanie left to redesign the supports. The next pupil in line was Russell. Russell had been pointed out to me as a boy with learning difficulties. He was also new to the school. He offered his design for approval:

> *Mr Penketh*: You want to do that, do you? Can you wait a moment and I'll see you last Russell. Don't go away.
> [Later, at a time when the queue had disappeared and more time could be devoted to Russell.]

> I think I'll find you a slightly different job Russell. Unless you specially want to do that one, do you?
>
> *Russell*: Yes
>
> *Mr Penketh*: OK, Russell, I'll let you have a go at it but don't be disappointed if you have trouble will you? [undistinguishable....] to give me trouble if you have trouble with your job. Good, but we'll see what we can work out for you, OK?

Russell was seen the following week doing a different job, one which Mr Penketh had given him to do.

I asked if it was necessary to sort out which children would want to do a particular kind of job. Mr Penketh replied:

> Yes. At the moment I'm giving them limited choice, so it sorts itself out, and guiding certain children where I can. But of course within this guidance you're going to have a certain amount of ... [pause] ... what you might call slack. You know, one or two children that's ... it's like the 11+, isn't it, you have fifteen per cent that you're sort of going to lose if you're not careful....

The notion of limited choice and a choice of jobs amounted to no choice at all for pupils like Russell and the boys working on the less difficult marionette. But changing the job as a mechanism for fitting pupils to appropriate tasks could also apply upwards in the hierarchy of difficulty where differentiated models were involved. If 'more able' pupils chose a simple job they could be guided to more difficult ones. Where jobs were not of the set kind and pupils were asked to design their own jobs, the possibility of using design ideas incorporating individual decision-making was available to some pupils, while others were prevented from pursuing their own ideas and were given jobs set by Mr Penketh.

From classroom observation it became clear that limited choice within a set job, some choice of different jobs, and in the case of some pupils freedom to design jobs, all operated within the same classes. Some pupils were granted greater freedom to make major design decisions, and were expected to do so, while others, like Russell, were given jobs which they could attempt to copy as a means of developing (or *not* developing!) basic skills. With pupils like Russell, proof of their incompetence in and lack of opportunity to develop basic skills was confirmed in teacher-pupil interaction, where the teacher often took over the pupil's work, effectively doing the job for him or her.

With 'more able' pupils who exercised a wider range of choice, teacher intervention of a quite different kind was provided. This difference is well illustrated in the case of two boys (as recorded in field notes):

> *Boy 1*
> trying to make wire 'eyes' for the joints of the limbs of a marionette; having obvious difficulties. Mr Penketh arrived at the workbench.

Mr Penketh: How many do you need?

Boy: Lots.

Mr Penketh proceeded to make 'lots' with the boy looking on. Some minutes passed.

Mr Penketh: Hey, it's like going into production, this. There you are then, you can get on with those, you should be alright now.

The boy had not been shown explicitly how to make the loops, the teacher making them as quickly as possible while other pupils waited for attention.

Boy 2
making a stool, asked Mr Penketh for some plywood and was given a large sheet of it. He proceeded to clamp the plywood to a sawing bench, measured and marked a required piece, using rule, tri-square and T-square as needed, selected a saw and began to cut it, though apparently not accurately. I held the wood for him and commented, 'are you supposed to cut to the line?' He replied that he did not want to make the piece too small. He completed cutting, thanked me, and took the tools and remaining plywood away. Taking his own piece to the bench it was checked, planed, sanded, and checked for 'fit' on the stool.

I later established that Boy 1 was regarded as 'less able' and Boy 2 as 'more able' by Mr Penketh. While both boys were offered guidance from time to time, the exact nature and amount of contact over time differed between the two, even though the classroom circumstances were similar. In the case of Boy 1 intervention by Mr Penketh was characterized by frequent, short periods of contact during which the teacher gave specific instructions, solved problems for the pupil, or actually did the work. With Boy 2 the pupil worked for long periods without contact with Mr Penketh. When it did occur contact was of a 'servicing' kind when the boy asked for and was granted the use of tools and materials, or it involved discussion of design ideas being incorporated into the job.

Sharp and Green (1975) have argued that one reason for the existence of inequalities in achievement among pupils is that they receive different amounts of teacher time, the more able being more favourably treated. They claimed, in other words, that teachers in the progressive infant school they studied interacted more frequently with those pupils they construed as being more successful. In addition, the attention these pupils received, along with the way their learning was structured and directed, was different from that of pupils who were viewed less favourably (Sharp and Green, 1975, p. 115). However, evidence to support these assertions is rather thin (D. Hargreaves, 1978; Boydell, 1981). The data from the present case study, interestingly, cast further doubt on the details of Sharp's and Green's claims, for Mr Penketh seemed much more concerned with and aware of the dealings with the less able than Sharp's and Green's teachers were alleged to be. Moreover, although Mr Penketh did give pupils unequal slices of his time, more of these interactions were with the less able.

Mr Penketh recognized clearly the problem of the unequal allocation of his time to different pupils – a problem which he had to overcome in order to achieve success in learning for *all* his pupils. It was the greater allocation of time to the 'less able' which he saw as the major problem area.

> theoretically, educationally, that [different approaches to match different rates of progress] shouldn't happen, but it doesn't work like that in practice. I've got two choices. I could give them [the less able] all my attention and ignore the others, but then the others would miss out.... One answer would be to make the work so they could cope, but then you'd have the problem at the other end [the more able] with the others getting frustrated.

Solving the less able's problems for them went some way towards a solution:

> There's a new lad, Russell, who's got very low ability, cannot concentrate, cannot hold on to anything for any length of time, so I gave him a little job. He chose a giraffe, and he made a sketch and it was a mess, so I sent him away. Remember I had a whole class with me. He came back and it was not much better but we improved it together.

But an alternative solution also emerged in the shape of offering a 'choice' of jobs, or 'changing the job'. The solution in these cases was to provide a limited choice of projects which allowed the more able to progress (within limits) while the less able could be controlled and 'helped' more closely.

> This is the crux of the whole matter, in that, do I develop them up in skills slowly to a point where I can say the whole class can handle that job, or do I go along as I am, trying to keep my eye on those who are lagging a bit, or those who are struggling, or even those who are a bit lazy, don't want to make that extra effort. It's difficult to assess on that one.

Crucial to Mr Penketh's problem was the difficulty of reconciling the didactic teaching of craft skills with the encouragement of individuality, the expression of personal ideas, and problem-solving. These two aspects of curriculum content related closely to the difficulty of reconciling intentions for equal treatment and success for all pupils in a given curriculum, with the provision of opportunities for the personal development of individual pupils through creative activities. The strategies of offering pupils limited choice in modifying the end product, of offering a choice of jobs and of providing the opportunity to design their own jobs were seen as different ways of reconciling the problem of *what* was done. Changing the job was an attempt to control *when* pupils should be exposed to basic skills or allowed to engage in design/problem-solving experiences. The nature and amount of teacher attention allocated to particular pupils demonstrates one of the mechanisms of *how* these strategies were used between different groups.

In this latter sense the strategies adopted by Mr Penketh varied depending on the pupil. With some – the less able – acts of imposition and close structuring of jobs along with much 'helping' and 'improving it together' were invoked in attempts to develop competence in manipulative skills. The 'more able' pupils, on the other hand, experienced less imposition over time, and were presented with work which involved decision-making, problem-solving and the use of design ideas. These differences became acute in mixed ability classes where, because of the large numbers, Mr Penketh had yet further difficulties in providing for individual pupils' personal development, particularly in the management, allocation and use of his time. When a class worked on the same job, the management of time was relatively easy. But when work was differentiated, Mr Penketh's concern for those 'lagging a bit' or 'struggling' led to further acts of imposition on his part, with continued stress upon skills and a consequent restriction of personal development. Thus, while, in contrast to Sharp's and Green's teachers, Mr Penketh allocated the greater part of his time to less able pupils, the way he *used* that time confirmed the two curricula for less able and more able pupils respectively: a curriculum of imposition for 'the less able' and one of opportunities to engage in creative work for 'the more able'.

Mr Tansley

Unlike Mr Penketh, Mr Tansley did not identify himself with traditional craft teachers. He had made a number of changes in his teaching since working in a middle school, and his current ideas reflected an amalgam of traditional and progressive views. Despite these differences, however, the pattern of events in Mr Tansley's classroom closely paralleled that in Mr Penketh's. When pupils started the course in 'technical studies' – at the beginning of their third year – they were all presented with exactly the same tasks: to make a pencil box using the same materials, tools and skills, and at approximately the same pace. From this kind of activity Mr Tansley claimed to be able to identify which pupils were the more or less creative ones. This indicated who could be guided towards different kinds of learning, who could be given greater degress of freedom, choice, decision-making and problem-solving, and who needed more careful guidance in manipulative craft skills. Controlling who did what and guiding individual pupils was achieved by similar means to Mr Penketh's, as illustrated in Mr Tansley's explanation of his strategies and tactics. He felt that the kind of work provided in the early stages formed a base upon which later learning was built, but that elements of both 'skills' and 'creativity' were important in all work:

> In both [skills/creativity] you build on what's gone before and you deviate from it in some particular direction. The creative aspect in the very first instance with the eleven year olds is as simple as giving them the opportunity to govern the basic shape and then a few trimmings added on ... from that you go to things where the choice is greater.

> I do set out to allow for both. A good many teachers don't, but I think it's much more worthwhile to put them side by side. If you separate them then you've got to start with skills and then follow up with perhaps the design aspect, but to take away all creativity and to lay it straight down the line for a child exactly what he's got to do defeats a lot of the aims of my teaching ... you've got to pre-determine to some extent what skills are involved, and teach the necessary ones ... and at the same time allow the child some freedom as to what the final result is.

When I discussed with Mr Tansley those pupils who had been granted more choice, he pointed out that choice and freedom for these pupils operated 'within your direction': 'to give them complete choice of ideas for half of them is a formula for disaster in the size of group I get. If you'd got, say, nine children of varying ability a choice of ideas might be on.' The curriculum was 'set for them, but, of course, the choice comes in exactly what they produce within that framework.' The framework itself and the degree of choice within it varied from pupils being given no choice at all, as in the pencil box job which they all did, to subtle expectations for 'design considerations' to be included in closely restricted jobs, to a choice of different jobs or to granting approval for some pupils to deviate from an 'expected course'.

As pupils gained experience in the manipulative skills, knowledge of tools and materials and understanding of processes, Mr Tansley viewed increased freedom in decision-making and the development of personal ideas in pupils as both necessary and desirable:

> Initially the amount of freedom has got to be very constrained, but gradually the brakes can come off and with each child it's a matter of releasing the brakes at a slightly different rate, and certainly by the time the child leaves the middle school, the more advanced children at least, the brakes can be ... not removed entirely, you've still got to direct their operations but, emmm ... you don't need to stamp on every little deviation from the expected course. You can allow them not to go almost exactly as they want, but within your direction....

This led to a strategy of *directing pupils towards appropriate tasks* and of *turning them in the direction you want them to go in*. Such guidance and direction was closely related to Mr Tansley's perception of pupils as 'bright' or 'backward'. These two types of pupils were consequently offered quite different curricular experiences, not only in what was done, but in the allocation of teacher time and in the nature of the teacher-pupil interaction which filled that time.

> Occasionally the bright child gets a poorer deal, and as he's not coming to see me every five minutes there are occasions when he gets left out altogether. He feels that he can get on on his own.... The backward child falls into a pattern of rushing to me more frequently than even they need, and perhaps I tend to get too involved with them, and perhaps tend to solve too many problems for them. I'm not saying that they get a very good deal, but, emm ... I find myself involving myself a little too much with them at the expense of the brighter ones.

The brighter ones had certain compensations. They were not totally 'ditched' by the teacher but gained their 'independence':

> ... You've got to give them that independence, but even with them there has got to be limits, because if you don't impose some limits on them at some stage even they are capable of hanging themselves. And there's got to be a success factor with them just as much as the others, probably equally important. In fact I don't always set the same work for the whole class.

The relationship between the different degrees of freedom intended by Mr Tansley and the ways in which the 'real guidance' occurred was critical to the experiences of the pupils. Central to that relationship was the frequency and nature of contact with the teacher.

> What I like to feel happens is that the less able need me at very regular intervals, usually very short intervals, but their problems can often be solved very quickly because there's no great depth to them. The brighter child doesn't need me anywhere near as often but when they do need me I like to think that I go into things in some depth, I should have one spell of say ten minutes with a bright child or several bright children who are doing similar things. And then with the less able probably five spells of two minutes. The rest will fall between these two extremes, they need me less frequently than the less able child and probably for a little longer.

Mr Tansley recognized the difficulty of achieving such an accurate share-out of time, and he recognized that he became 'too involved' with the pupils deemed less able: '[that's] ... what I like to feel happens, although I know it doesn't always.'

To sum up, Mr Tansley's notion of giving 'more able' pupils greater independence to pursue design ideas and engage in individual problem-solving activities was realized through less frequent but longer encounters during which problems were considered in depth. When Mr Tansley attempted to achieve a balance in the management of classroom time, he was conscious that the demands of the 'less able' predominated. But this did not mean that the 'more able' were neglected. Rather, in the extended periods when they were left to their own devices, and in their less frequent but more sustained interactions with the teacher, they enjoyed greater opportunity for the development of their own personal ideas. In Mr Tansley's classes, therefore, while the less able get more of his time the fact that the time is used up in frequent short bursts of routine managerial activity actually seems to reinforce the differentiation between pupils in their experience of design activities. In effect, it confirms restrictions upon and opportunities for personal development for 'less able' and 'more able' pupils respectively.

Mr Sankey

Mr Sankey regarded himself as a 'progressive' teacher adopting a child-centred approach to teaching and learning (Hammersley, 1977). The development of the creative process was central to his aims, as was his desire to extend to the child as much autonomy as was consistent with the development of 'personal ideas' in a 'free' environment. On the face of it both the perspectives and the classroom activities of Mr Sankey offered a dramatic contrast to those of his colleague, Mr Penketh. Mr Sankey's views of teaching and learning were radically progressive. His actual practice, however, shares many similarities with Mr Penketh's, indicating major discrepancies between intention and action. Stimulating children to develop and express ideas of their own, through exploration of their environment, was central to his teaching perspective. His ideal was for each individual to have personal ideas which they wanted to express and for the teacher to facilitate such expression. This ideal was not matched in practice because of various influences, not least the activities of the pupils themselves: 'If I give them too many alternatives I find they can't cope and in the end they come back and ask me to tell them what to do...!' These influences resulted in his adopting a strategy of using a *'common starting-point'* for all pupils, in the form of visual stimuli to generate ideas.

Following the common starting-point with the whole class, individual pupils were then expected to *'develop an idea'* – an individual, personal idea. In practice, this use of ideas, along with the promotion of personal expression in pupils' work, was followed by teacher sanctions upon the art products and the ideas that pupils represented in them, particularly with regard to aesthetic composition and modes of visual representation.

> One girl's produced a super piece of work. She put this hand in up here, so I had to explain to her that it was a still life and you don't have living things in it. She made the whole thing up though, it's come from us doing pencil shading and she did it all on her own at lunchtime.

Such inconsistencies between Mr Sankey's stated intentions and his classroom practice were particularly noticeable in his concerns for developing skills in the control and knowledge of materials. In this respect he adopted a strategy of *'experimenting with skills'* at the beginning of each session. This, in sharp contrast to his stated aims, led to identical class exercises in pencil shading and colour mixing, using the same sized paper, the same tones and colours, organized in exactly the same way on the paper. In this way all pupils were expected to learn the same skills, at the same time, under close direction from the teacher. Mr Sankey also wanted children to understand the creative process, and to engage in qualitative problem-solving. The responsibility for generating problems was vested in the pupils. It was Mr Sankey's hope that over time the visual forms used – paintings, collages, ceramics, etc. – would develop through different aesthetic 'styles' or modes of representation as the pupils became accustomed to and ready for their use. Thus, for example, he would not 'teach perspective', but would encourage its use in drawing and painting if an individual pupil 'needed it' or was 'ready for it'. He did not want to set the same work for all pupils, though he hoped that they would all encounter the same range of experiences over the duration of the course. For example, Mr Sankey hoped that pupils would choose to work in a range of media. If they did not, he would implement a strategy of *'guiding them in that direction'*: 'If that happened [pupils chose a range of media] it would be ideal, but I don't think it will happen, it would be nice if it did. If it didn't then I'll suggest it, guide them in that direction.' What varied for different pupils was the form of guidance. Pupils who 'tuned in', who 'understand what I want' and who gave Mr Sankey the feeling that he had 'projected myself very well in the first place', were permitted to proceed 'independently'.

> If I can get them to understand then in any new piece of work there shouldn't be any reason why they can't come up with a statement that's fair for that individual child. I'm taking individuals you know ... and then from that understanding they can develop their own work, if they've got the inclination.

Some pupils, however, did not 'tune in'. They did not achieve the prescribed learning which underlay much of the work Mr Sankey set (as distinct from his ideals). As I have already indicated, allowing pupils to express individual ideas was difficult enough in itself. Discussing individual pupils' ideas with them proved even more problematic.

> Well, I'm trying to. I can do it more simply if I tune all the kids in to the same piece of work ... I know there are kids who need attention and the ones who can't quite tune in are demanding more attention. I think this is the mixed ability thing coming into the class, there's such a diverse ability range.

Some pupils, on the other hand, 'work so well you hardly need to bother them at all.'

The difference between those pupils demanding more attention and those hardly needing any at all is paralleled by differences in the amount and kind of attention Mr Sankey gave to different pupils. There were those 'like that girl last week, the still life... I want to let her get on with that', and those like 'that lad who did that bizarre landscape. I've made him go back and back to that.... I'm going to make sure he sticks with it.' Pupils of the first kind who were left to 'get on with it' were usually identified as 'more able', 'tuned in' and of 'innate ability'. The second group, identified as 'less able' (or even 'remedial' or 'dyslexic'), received or demanded more frequent 'help' or intervention from the teacher. Such attention was also qualitatively different from that devoted to the 'more able', and usually involved closer control and explicit, specific directives about the requirements of work. Pupils' freedom to make decisions was contained within limits of particular aesthetic values, as illustrated in the following incident (as recorded in field notes):

> A girl was working on a large painting of a landscape which was mainly tones of blue, green and yellow. In the lower right hand corner she had put a large crimson shape.
>
> *Mr S*: You'll have to be careful there ... that colour's very strong.
>
> He took the painting and stood a short distance from her, holding it for her to see.
>
> *Mr S*: Look [he covered the red shape, then uncovered it]. Your eye goes through it. Before your eye went up here, now it goes straight to that shape because it's so strong. You'll have to be careful with the colours.
>
> At the end of the lesson Mr Sankey spoke to the class: OK, next lesson we'll look at some of the problems some of you are having and talk about them. One girl was putting....' [He described the problem of the red shape.]

Mr Sankey was unhappy about pupils 'like that girl there, she'll ask me if it's the right blue!' In his ideal teacher perspective Mr Sankey related success to individual pupils' own ideas, and measured achievement against criteria which were related to each pupil's development. In practice, however, the achievement of success also required pupils to satisfy certain implicit criteria which Mr Sankey applied. These criteria differed sharply between 'problem' and 'ideal' pupils. Such differences were reflected in the nature and amount of teacher interaction each received:

> *Group work*
> A group who had 'performed disastrously' when asked to present ideas without directives were addressed by Mr Sankey: 'Look at this one of Sandra's. Now try to do one like that.' After the pupils began work, individuals approached Mr Sankey to ask if their work was 'alright'. This pattern was common in several groups observed. One boy had

Teacher-Pupil Encounters in Art and Design Education

made a painting of a section of rose tree. He approached Mr Sankey for 'approval' and was told that the spikes were not pointed enough – the wrong shapes had been used. Most noticeable was the number of children who came to Mr Sankey for approval. He discussed the work and gave explicit directions about what they could or should do. A girl had made pencil sketches of a cluster of Scots Pine needles. She was told to choose the centre detail of one drawing and to enlarge it, using pastel, on a sheet of paper approximately 30 × 50 cm. She did an enlarged drawing of the centre point or bud and approached the teacher. He said she had not done the needles and demonstrated how this should be done. She followed instructions, for *one* needle and returned. Mr Sankey said: 'But now you've got to darken them down on one side, haven't you?' She went to a table and did so, and soon returned. Mr Sankey told her to include the other needles in the drawing in the same way, and similar interaction continued for most of the lesson with the girl doing one part and returning for further instructions at each stage. (Field notes)

In instances of this kind Mr Sankey repeatedly issued directives on technique in the application of media and on composition. Type and size of paper, media to be used, colours allowed, ideas to be incorporated and length of time to be devoted were all included in the decisions that Mr Sankey took for such pupils. At times it seemed that he even tried to enjoy the work for them:

Joanne, looking unhappy, approached, handed over a drawing of a teasel and stood silently. Mr Sankey enquired what she wanted. She shrugged. Others approached and he attended to them, then turned to Joanne and asked what she wanted. She didn't answer. He was distracted by further demands and whilst attending to another pupil, Joanne was approached by a friend:

Friend: [showing Joanne her work] I did this in one lesson.

Joanne: Yeh, but did you like doing it?

Friend: No.

Joanne: I hate it, I'm bored.

Mr Sankey returned. Joanne told him she was bored. He took her to the display boards and showed her some examples of work she could do if she wished. He suggested she use an object: 'to take out simple shapes, limited colours, and so on', and tried to stimulate her ideas. Fully aware of Joanne's lack of involvement, he was trying, he said, to get her to involve herself with her own ideas but was finding it very difficult. (Field notes)

Mr Sankey was aware of some of the differences that occurred in the kind and amount of his interactions with different pupils. This presented him with a major dilemma which was most acute in his imposition of aesthetic standards with 'problem' pupils. As Mr Sankey put it when asked how he conveyed appropriate standards: 'On a personal ... yeh ... I think ... I put it across ... [long pause] ... it might be a personal thing of my own ... yeh ... it could be indoctrination.'

'Indoctrination' – the imposition of particular aesthetic standards and modes of image-making – was not a problem with those pupils who 'tuned in'. These pupils, ones who were seen as having 'innate ability' in the subject, were Mr Sankey's ideal. Such was the case of a boy I observed painting a landscape, meticulously mixing tones of colour in small quantities, quite dry, applying it by a stipple technique. The boy had worked quietly at this on one side of the room, with no intervention, for most of the lesson. I saw Mr Sankey watching the boy but not intervening; then he came to speak to me: 'Have you seen his tree over there, it's beautiful.' This kind of interaction was emphasized further in the case of a girl making design decisions:

> *Melanie*
> After an introductory session when pupils had been asked to 'develop ideas' from stimuli, Melanie approached Mr Sankey with her idea. She had drawn a small triangle on a piece of paper and tried to explain her intentions. The explanation was incomprehensible. Mr Sankey suggested she should sketch her ideas more fully: 'Can you put them down on paper, whatever ideas you want to use?' He was distracted by other pupils. Melanie started to section off the paper in triangular shapes, and showed that each was to be enlarged on to a triangle of cardboard, with folded edges which would cause the triangle to stand in relief (a double fold) to give a deep section and allow for fixing onto a base. The sections would be mounted with small spaces between each, so that each contained an independent section of a larger whole picture. The idea was communicated to me without interjection. It was very carefully thought out and had not come from the teacher, with whom I discussed the incident later. It was 'far better' that that idea had come from the girl. He was very aware that in 'telling them what to do' he was not fulfilling his intentions with some pupils. (Field notes)

The success of such pupils was measured by implicit criteria linked to displayed achievement in 'adult' modes of image-making. Because they satisfied such criteria these pupils were presented with opportunities to engage in qualitative problem-solving and to express personal ideas through the use of a particular sequence of experiences with media.

Imposition of aesthetic standards and tight control over pupil time ran counter to Mr Sankey's ideal of encouraging pupils' personal development. Yet 'problem' pupils were expected to 'stick with it' and experienced more frequent contact during which standards in aesthetic qualities and the requirements of particular modes of image-making were consistently and explicitly imposed.

On the other hand, pupils who 'tuned in' satisfied Mr Sankey's criteria and were able to pursue his ideal of using personal ideas, exploring media and engaging in problem-solving. The differentiation among pupils in the amounts of time allocated, and their different experiences within that distribution of time, confirmed the restrictions upon and opportunities for personal development for 'problem' and 'ideal' pupils respectively. In both cases the teacher imposed standards which were derived from models of 'adult' aesthetic competence. This occurred through interactions which were qualitatively different for each 'type' of pupil, giving some support to the assertions of Sharp and Green in their study of infant classrooms. But, in contrast to Sharp and Green's findings, it was those pupils seen in favourable terms by the teacher who received *less* interaction, and engaged in more exploratory learning, while those seen in less favourable terms experienced frequent, brief and closely directed interactions with Mr Sankey.

Conclusion

What, then, do the perspectives and practices of these three idealistically inclined art and design teachers reveal about the effects of teaching on creativity and personal development? And do these effects vary for different kinds of pupils? Each of the teachers held different pedagogical perspectives. Yet the patterns of interaction and the distribution and nature of teacher-pupil contact time were similar in each classroom. Although there were differences in perspectives about how learning should occur, each teacher intended that creativity should play an important part in pupils' development, and that it should be encouraged and fostered through clearly established expectations about the kinds of creative experiences which pupils should engage in – including the establishment of their own expressive, aesthetic or design problems. Yet in the classroom these intentions were continually frustrated, acutely so in relation to the 'less able' pupils. I have shown that from the two main strands of curricular intention – basic skills and creativity – there evolved two curricula, one which involved the imposition of basic skills for pupils seen as 'less able', the other involving opportunities to engage in creative work for those seen as 'more able'. I have also shown how these different curricular experiences became predominant for each group, and how this occurred through the unequal distribution of teacher-pupil contact and differential treatment of pupils during interaction with the teachers. Pupils seen unfavourably in terms of a perceived lack of success in basic skills received greater amounts of attention and closer structuring of their experiences than those seen more favourably by the teachers. What is more, each of the teachers was conscious of these differences in treatment even though it was their intention to treat pupils equally. Thus with these teachers of art and design in these two middle schools creativity and personal development of many pupils were persistently inhibited, despite intentions to the contrary.

Ironically, it was the closer structuring of skills teaching with the 'less able', arising out of teacher concern for those pupils' success, which enhanced opportunities for others to engage in creative dimensions of experience. Restricted chances for some ran side by side with afforded opportunities for others to fulfil creative potential. Within that divisive curriculum the teachers' management of classroom time mirrors a major dilemma of art and design education and opposing views about the nature of schooling in general. Conflicting views about whether art and design curricula are concerned with imposing control through the rigorous teaching of predetermined practical skills, or with fostering personal growth through problem-solving processes and creative experience met head-on in these classrooms. Furthermore, more general images of education concerned with maximizing personal development and creative potential came face to face with ones in which schooling is anti-creative, inegalitarian and stultifying to the individual.

Given the variable experiences of these pupils in art and design within the same classrooms – indeed, within the same curricular intentions – to assume that art and design education necessarily or even usually offers the chance for individual potential to be fulfilled would be to dismiss the perspectives and practices of these teachers and the experiences of their 'less able' pupils in particular. But if the optimistic assumptions about education are clearly problematic, so too are the charges that education is essentially controlling in nature. These are not equally applicable to all pupils – pupils' experiences of art and design are, in this sense clearly variable, but systematically so.

What assumptions are highlighted in these experiences of art and design? That skills of a specific kind precede and are a prerequisite to creative, problem-solving learning experiences was a predominant feature. That success in the former signals ability and likely success in the latter was a view which had a strong influence on the way classroom time was managed. Further, that more 'help' with skills would enhance individual, creative development was assumed. If change in classroom practice is to be effected these assumptions deserve and require reappraisal.

What are the implications for art and design education policy? If policy is not to be unrealistic and unrealizable, further and more extensive scrutiny of the classroom experiences of teachers and pupils is obviously needed. In this way informed understanding rather than trendy slogans about creative development might lead the way for teachers and pupils. In particular, the demands of curriculum projects (Schools Council, 1974 and 1975) as well as art and design educators (Read, 1943; Field, 1970; Shaw and Reeve, 1980) need to take full account of classroom experiences and the perspectives of teachers and pupils, such that any statements about the importance of creative activities in school experience are made with pupils like Russell in view. And what of schooling in general? This case study suggests that even where optimistic public and professional assumptions about the nature of education are strong – as with these middle school teachers of art and design – their picture of aesthetic experience at the point of classroom interaction is often out of focus with those assumptions. For some pupils at least the messages of increasing failure and increasing control, in the face of assertive attempts to raise success, are painted both clearly and early on the walls.

Note

1 For reasons of brevity, data relating to only three of them will be used here.

References

BENNETT, N. (1976) *Teaching Styles and Pupil Progress*, Open Books.
BERLAK, A. and BERLAK, H. (1981) *The Dilemmas of Schooling*, Methuen.
BOWLES, S. and GINTIS, H. (1975) *Schooling in Capitalist America*, Routledge and Kegan Paul.
BOYDELL, D. (1981) 'Classroom organization 1970–7', *in* SIMON, B. and WILLCOCKS, J. (Eds) *Research and Practice in the Primary Classroom*, Routledge and Kegan Paul.
FIELD, D. (1970) *Change in Art Education*, Routledge and Kegan Paul.
GALTON, M., SIMON, B. and CROLL, P. (1980) *Inside the Primary Classroom*, Routledge and Kegan Paul.
HAMMERSLEY, M. (1977) *Teacher Perspectives*, Course E202, Units 9 and 10, Open University.
HARGREAVES, A. (1978) 'The significance of classroom coping strategies', *in* BARTON, L. and MEIGHAN, R. (Eds) *Sociological Interpretations of Schooling and Classrooms: A Reappraisal*, Nafferton.
HARGREAVES, D. (1978) 'Whatever happened to symbolic interactionism', *in* BARTON, L. and MEIGHAN, R. (Eds) *op. cit.*
ILLICH, I. (1971) *Deschooling Society*, Penguin.
KRISHNAMURTI (1953) *Education and the Significance of Life*, Harper and Row.
POLLARD, A. (1982) 'A model of classroom coping strategies', in *British Journal of Sociology of Education*, 3, 1.
READ, H. (1943) *Education through Art*, Faber.
SHAW, D.M. and REEVE, J.M. (1978) *Design Education for the Middle Years*, Hodder and Stoughton.
SCHOOLS COUNCIL (1974) *Children's Growth through Creative Experience, Art and Craft Education 8–13*, Van Nostrand Reinhold.
SCHOOLS COUNCIL (1975) *Education through Design and Craft*, Edward Arnold.
SHARP, R. and GREEN, A. (1975) *Education and Social Control*, Routledge and Kegan Paul.
TICKLE, L. (1979) A Sociological Analysis and Case Study of the Organization and Evaluation of Art and Design Subjects for Third and Fourth Year Pupils in a 9–13 Middle School, unpublished MA thesis, University of Keele.
TORRANCE, P. (1962) *Guiding Creative Talent*, Prentice Hall.
WOLFF, J. (1981) *The Social Production of Art*, Macmillan.

6 The Teaching of Art and the Art of Teaching: Towards an Alternative View of Aesthetic Learning

David H. Hargreaves

Ethnographic researchers are usually open-minded people. Rarely do they seem to begin their fieldwork with a clear set of research intentions, a neat set of hypotheses they want to test, or even with a definite problem they want to clarify. Certainly they have their own vague ideas and preferences, but for the most part they display the optimism of nineteenth-century explorers, contentedly anticipating that something interesting and, with luck, important will simply turn up. Of course, their personal values and commitments may influence their later selection of specific problems and shape subsequent interpretation; but only in exceptional cases do passionate commitments seem to precede, or are overtly acknowledged to precede, the fieldwork itself. The present study is such an exception. In a book I wrote on the future of the comprehensive school,[1] I proposed that the creative and expressive arts ought to be part of a compulsory core curriculum. This proposal sprang from my firm conviction that *all* pupils are potentially capable of deriving great pleasure from the arts, both as producers and consumers, and if more status and time were accorded to the teaching and learning of the arts, then this potential in pupils could be realized.

I soon discovered that very little research had been done on the teaching of the arts, at least in comparison with the resources devoted to science and mathematics; and I sensed that the teaching of art, where I decided to begin my research, had changed substantially since my own schooldays. I expected that art teachers would now assign more importance to art appreciation than in the past and I hoped to find more lessons in art appreciation. These hopes were, as we shall see, to be dashed. By chance I was then invited to talk to some art teachers and during this talk I suggested that too few pupils derived from their education either (at best) an abiding interest in art or (at least) an open-mindedness about art. If, I continued, by the age of 16, any comprehensive school pupils passed by an art gallery and said to themselves, 'Such places are not for the likes of us' or 'We'd be bored in there' then in some very real sense their art education had been a partial failure. I was surprised by the amount of dissent this comment provoked among the art teachers. Visiting an art gallery was, some of them vehemently protested, an inadequate, irrelevant or even improper measure of the effectiveness of their teaching. Some even denied that the enjoyment by pupils of any of the 'high art' of the kind to be found in galleries was something they should strive to achieve.

David H. Hargreaves

One teacher invoked the work of Bourdieu[2] to support his argument against me. According to his interpretation of Bourdieu, the teaching of 'high art' in the school would be an unwarranted *imposition* of the *arbitrary* tastes of the upper classes on (mainly) working-class pupils who would thereby be led to disvalue their own cultural forms. Bourdieu's work, he said, had fully convinced him that middle-class pupils achieve well in school because they possess what Bourdieu calls 'cultural capital' (of which familiarity with the 'high arts' is a central component), which is largely inherited or transmitted through the family. The educational system acts as if it is fair to pupils with different social origins, but in practice only rewards those middle- and upper-class pupils who have acquired their cultural capital from home. The greater the loading of the 'high arts' in the school curriculum, the greater will be the advantage that accrues to middle-class pupils and the more the working-class pupil will be destined to fail. He concluded – and in so doing went beyond what Bourdieu says – that an art teacher should, in the interests of justice and equality of opportunity, exclude as far as possible 'high art' from the curriculum. By this method he hoped to undermine the present functions of the school, which, according to Bourdieu and others, serve to reproduce the class structure.

I could readily follow the lines of argument and see how this teacher had drawn these implications for his practice. Yet precisely the opposite conclusion can be drawn from Bourdieu's work, without much damage to the general validity of his arguments. I argued that Bourdieu greatly underestimates the extent to which educational institutions (at least in Britain if not in France) can actively disseminate to working-class pupils the cultural capital they cannot obtain from home. Both Halsey and his associates and Musgrove have shown that in this country substantial numbers of working-class pupils passed through the grammar school and many of them entered higher education, where they do at least as well as their middle-class peers.[3] In Britain working-class pupils at university are not the very rare exceptions that Bourdieu's thesis both suggests and demands. Musgrove has rightly pointed out that some of Bourdieu's own evidence is hardly in support of his thesis. It is true that as one's length of formal education increases, so does the likelihood that one will be a regular consumer of the arts. But Bourdieu's evidence shows that the greatest readers of books and the most regular visitors to theatres, museums, exhibitions and art galleries are not the upper classes – heads of industry and commerce, managers, engineers, professionals and public administrators – but *school teachers*. And it is well known that school teachers tend not to be drawn from the upper classes.

Now if we take this evidence seriously, we can interpret the educational task to be this: that the teachers, who are the major consumers of the arts, should transmit their own capacities to appreciate the arts to more and more pupils. The school should, in short, increase its power to disseminate cultural capital. If this task of greater dissemination is to be accomplished, then initiation in the 'high arts' must be given more, not less, importance in school.

Art is now a low status subject and as pupils get older it becomes an optional subject that 'gifted' pupils are encouraged to drop. Inevitably the aspects of cultural capital that relate to art become progressively less available to pupils, and those who already derive pleasure from 'high art' and visit galleries because of their home environment lose little or nothing by its exclusion from the curriculum. As long as art is an optional and low status subject, it is working-class pupils who will be denied opportunities for the acquisition of the appropriate cultural capital.

Bourdieu shows that those who have received higher education are greater consumers of the arts than those who have not. Precisely how such people, when they are working-class in origin, come to be consumers of 'high art' is obscure, and it may well be related to peer group activities rather than to the formal curriculum of higher education. I am just such a person; there was nothing in my working-class origins to endow me with this aspect of cultural capital; I acquired it at school and at university, even though I did not read an arts subject. Today I get increasing pleasure from the 'high arts' and I want to see more people, especially those from similar social origins, having the same opportunities. I thus drew the opposite conclusion to that of my teacher friend and claimed that the school has a major responsibility for transmitting 'high art' to all pupils. My judgment is that to follow my teacher friend's proposal, and exclude 'high art' from the curriculum, would help to make Bourdieu's thesis become even more true than it now is; the way to undermine Bourdieu's thesis is to make 'high art' and its associated cultural capital more available to everyone. And this is not merely in the interest of redressing important social injustices: I believe the vast majority of people can have their lives enhanced by their initiation into at least some of the 'high arts'.

In saying this I hope I am not being misunderstood. We can, fortunately, only talk about the 'high arts' in a very loose way – though frequently people do not do so. There are highly diverse views among regular consumers of the 'high arts' – and among those responsible for the contents of galleries or concert hall programmes and the awarding of literary prizes – about what constitutes the 'best' painting, music or literature; and the fringes of the 'high arts' are extremely fuzzy, with no natural or uncontested boundaries. There is much room for dispute and personal preference. The teacher of the 'high arts' can, but certainly does not have to, *impose* an *arbitrary* set of works of art. If he or she is a good teacher, there will be made available to pupils a wide variety of what people consider to be good work, and whilst this selection will include the teacher's own preferences it would not be limited to them. Moreover, the consumer of the 'high arts' is not by any means necessarily committed to a contempt for the more 'popular' forms of arts and crafts. Many people, for instance, enjoy *both* the Western 'classical' tradition of music *and* folk music or music of the Afro-American tradition. It is surely a mark of the well educated person in the arts to display both breadth and open-mindedness. To be otherwise is not to be educated in the arts: it is to be a 'high culture' snob. We should not be distracted by the existence of such people. Nor does a commitment to the 'high arts' involve a necessary denigration of working-class cultural forms, which should also be celebrated in school, or of the wider functions of aesthetic education as a whole, which must educate pupils' perceptions of the whole of their environment, both natural and man-made.

When I began my own research I naturally tried to avoid clouding my perception of art lessons with my prejudice in favour of art appreciation. There is much more to art education than art appreciation. From my observations in comprehensive schools and from a reading of the relevant literature, I sought a more balanced picture of the aims of art education, and the inevitable contradictions within them. Out of this complexity[4] I compiled the following list of aims in art teaching.

1   Personal and Emotional Development

On this view, art (with other creative and expressive arts) makes a highly distinctive contribution to education, one which is neglected by the dominant academic/scientific emphasis of the secondary school curriculum. The artistic, aesthetic and affective domains have a special place in personal development and are realized through certain subjects. Without them, no pupil can achieve the balance and breadth of the educated person. This aim can be authorized by philosophers' treatment of the school curriculum: Phenix and Hirst can be invoked to justify aesthetics as a fundamental realm of meaning and the fine arts as a unique form of knowledge. Ross is a notable exemplar of this aim, when he tells us that in the arts the purpose of self-expression is 'the elaboration and development of our emotional life, of our capacity to make sense in feeling of the subjective world of feeling, our capacity to feel intelligently, to find our way among feelings by feeling.' This can be expressed more simply as 'education through art is education for emotional maturity' or as 'the long term aim of the arts curriculum is to further the healthy emotional development of the child by encouraging creative self-expression.'[5]

2   Visual Awareness

This aim of art education involves the improvement of perceptual skills and judgment, whether the objects of perception are natural or man-made. The range covers the whole of the human environment, both present and past, and can be taken to include the mass media in contemporary society. It is the aim of art education which relates closely to matters of design. In recent years, this aspect of art education has received considerable attention, not least from the Schools Council.

3 Skill Training

This aim of art education is concerned with helping pupils to acquire a wide range of technical skills in a wide range of media. Whilst it is recognized that such technical education can interfere with self-expression by pupils, and in that sense is seen by some to be subordinate to, or a means of expression for, more creative aims, skill training assumes great importance with those pupils who wish to specialize in art and to enter for public examinations at O- and A-level.

4 Compensation

A very large number of art teachers recognize that the art room can be a valuable sanctuary for difficult pupils who, whilst not necessarily showing unusual artistic talent, nevertheless enjoy art lessons, which allow considerable choice, autonomy and opportunity for self-expression. The art room acts as a relief from, and an important counter-weight to, the heavily academic and didactic curriculum that has induced a sense of failure and low self-esteem in many pupils. This use of the art room as a retreat complements the first of these listed aims. And I must add that I have been deeply impressed not merely by the willingness of art teachers to act in this way but also by the good conduct and hard work displayed in art by pupils who are found to be 'difficult' in other subjects.

5 Education for Leisure

School serves as a preparation for life. It is only a very small minority who will specialize in art, take art in higher education and then seek a career in which this art training is put to major use. For the majority, art education can make an important contribution to their leisure activities, either because they continue to be producers (for example, painting for pleasure, joining an art club, etc.) or as consumers (visiting art galleries, etc.).

6 Initiation in Our Cultural Heritage

One aim of art education is to give pupils access to the best of fine art over the ages and to the arts and crafts of other cultures. Just as the teacher of English literature familiarizes pupils with, and hopes to inculcate a love for, the work of Shakespeare, so the art teacher aims to introduce pupils to what are held to be the finest achievements of artists in the fields of painting, drawing, sculpture, architecture, etc., both in Europe and throughout the world. In former days this was often referred to as 'art appreciation'; nowadays it is more likely to be called (with a certain clinical coldness) 'critical studies' in art, and may include a substantial amount of art history.

These aims are not so discrete as a formal listing implies; in practice they overlap and interpenetrate. And since most teachers would subscribe to most of them, they are not so much alternative aims as different emphases within a broader over-arching aim. Yet these aims are not given equal emphasis in the day-to-day teaching of art in secondary schools; patently teachers see some aims as more important, or as requiring a greater time allocation, than others. Nor when I talk to art teachers do I find that they speak of their aims so neatly. Asking teachers about their aims is in any case a hazardous exercise, for it invites them to invent abstract aims or to indulge in a rhetoric which may not normally influence or reflect what they do. An alternative strategy which I have also adopted is to watch what teachers do and from these practices infer the aims that the teachers are seeking to realize. This is an equally risky venture, for there is no guarantee that my inferences would be an adequate or accurate account of what is in the teachers' minds. In general, however, I incline to put more reliance on what teachers observably do, rather than on what they – or books on art teaching – say they are or should be doing.

My general impression from witnessing some art teachers at work, however, is that the first three aims of my list appear to be very much more dominant than the last two. It is only very rarely indeed that I have heard art teachers referring to the notion that pupils should continue with their art for pleasure after they have left school. And only on unusual occasions have these teachers made use of established works of art, either as reproductions or as art objects on loan to the school, for teaching purposes; though of course normally the art room has a shelf of art books which pupils are encouraged to consult from time to time, mainly 'for ideas'. Lessons in 'art appreciation' are, according to my observations and to art education authorities,[6] rare events.

I have come to have a very clear expectation of what I shall see when I visit any particular art room for the first time; indeed, this expectation is now such a firm prediction that I am taken aback when it is not confirmed. Normally I see the pupils scattered around the room, all busily at work in planning or producing some kind of art work by practical activity. There is very little formal, public talk between teacher and the whole class, though there is usually a quiet hum of talk between pupils. Sometimes the teacher makes a short introductory talk, explaining what the pupils will do, perhaps offering a demonstration, perhaps organizing pupils into their preferred activities and distributing equipment. The major part of the lesson consists of the pupils working, sometimes all of them on a single activity, such as painting on one of a set of themes, and sometimes pupils choosing from a wide range of different activities in different parts of the art room – drawing, painting, batik, pottery, photography and so on. During this activity, the teacher wanders round the room, offering encouragement, help and advice and supplying materials, and usually spending at least a few moments with every pupil on more than one occasion.

The Teaching of Art and the Art of Teaching

If I come across a lesson in 'art appreciation' at all, it is normally a form of art history as required in public examinations for older pupils, and even then teachers tell me that part of their objective is to help pupils with their own creative work, by giving them insight into matters of composition, colour, technique and so on.

My work with one particular teacher, whom I shall call Keith, conforms closely to this general image of the art lesson. I do not want to call Keith a typical art teacher – there is no such creature, and in any event Keith seemed to me to be better than most teachers in the skill with which he managed to get his mainly working-class pupils to produce interesting and exciting work and in the sensitivity with which he encouraged them to overcome their adolescent fears of artistic incapacity. But Keith is typical in the general way he organizes his lessons, in his emphasis on practical work, and in his reluctance to conduct lessons in art appreciation. Keith would not for a moment deny that all pupils would benefit if they could be brought to enjoy visiting art galleries – indeed, that is why he organized occasional visits to galleries and exhibitions. Why, then, does Keith, like so many other art teachers, apparently avoid the sixth of my listed aims?

There are several possible explanations, the importance of which it is difficult to assess. There was relatively little 'art appreciation' in the formal art training Keith received during his own schooldays, his years at art college, or his teacher training. Like many artists, he thinks of himself more as a producer of art than as a consumer. Perhaps art appreciation, rightly or wrongly, is seen as inappropriate for the younger pupils, and with older pupils who opt for art the pressure of public examinations on practical work must clearly be given priority. Background training and active teaching experience conspire to push art appreciation to the periphery and give art teachers little opportunity – unless they positively choose to create such opportunities – to learn how to conduct art appreciation. Keith told me – and I think many other art teachers could cite similar experiences – that in the past he had tried showing film strips of famous paintings to a class, but they had soon become bored, restless and talkative. Pupils seemed to enjoy art lessons more, and his life was easier and more rewarding, if they were allowed to choose from a variety of practical activities of art making. I suspect that when teachers give complex reasons for ignoring art appreciation these are really rationalizations for not doing what they find pedagogically difficult rather than genuine explanations; but, for lack of evidence, this can be no more than a suspicion. So Keith, like many teachers, undertook art appreciation only incidentally in the course of ordinary lessons or when he had little choice, as in the art history periods with A-level candidates.

I then discovered, quite by accident, that Keith ran two art appreciation lessons for the fifth form. The fifth-year option scheme in this school was complicated, partly because the school was badly affected by falling rolls. Two of the fifth-form option groups had a 'spare' period; and they were assigned to Keith for this single lesson. He might, as did several of his colleagues faced with the same situation, have allowed the pupils to treat it as a 'free' period in which to get on with their own academic work or to prepare for the immediately following academic lesson. Instead, Keith decided to use this opportunity for some art education, not least because many of these pupils had opted against art in favour of other examination courses. Because it was a single period, there was too little time for them to engage in any serious practical work; so Keith decided on a lesson in art appreciation and the period was so labelled in the official timetable.

I asked if I could observe and record these lessons; Keith agreed, but with an unwonted reluctance, presenting a sharp contrast to his very willing consent that I should observe and record 'ordinary' art lessons, even with 'difficult' classes. Further conversation clarified matters: Keith's reservations sprang from his feelings that things were not going well, and he constantly indicated this to me by his apologetic tone when talking about these lessons and, rather unexpectedly, by his asking me for comments on the lessons. Naturally I understood his anxiety about my presence in lessons where he did not feel master of the situation or confidence in what he was achieving; and he continued to feel this even though in my view the lessons could not be legitimately regarded as a source of embarrassment to him, since the pupils were neither uncooperative nor disruptive and a clear minority seemed to enjoy them.

The key to Keith's sense of discomfort in these lessons lies, I believe, in an important difference between ordinary art lessons and those in art appreciation. This difference is not so much one of content but of the structure of teacher-pupil interaction. In ordinary, practical art lessons there was little public talk and most teacher-pupil interaction took place in small, intimate one-to-one 'consultations' as Keith moved about the class. In six practical art lessons I recorded and analyzed, these consultations occupied no less than 63 per cent of lesson time. For only 12 per cent of the time was Keith talking publicly to the whole class, with an additional 4 per cent for 'disciplinary' talk – telling the class to work more quietly or calling an individual pupil to account. In six art appreciation lessons I analyzed, by contrast, Keith's public talk accounted for almost two-thirds of the time. Further, this talk was across huge physical spaces. The tables in the art room were arranged end-to-end to form a large closed rectangle, the protected space in the middle being reserved for displays for object drawing. This arrangement worked well for practical lessons, the pupils all working side by side and Keith moving systematically round the rectangle for the individual consultations. In the art appreciation lessons the pupils sat round this same rectangle in positions which were hardly conducive to intimate discussion; as expected, public pupil-pupil talk was difficult and all communications tended to pass through Keith who stood at the centre point of one of the sides of the rectangle. Keith was, by the physical arrangements, forced into a central didactic role. This is common enough in ordinary classrooms, of course, but the role was one which Keith disliked and in which he felt strange.

Yet the way in which Keith sought to organize the discussion was in many ways exemplary. He would make a short introduction, showing the pupils some reproductions or slides, or reading short extracts from carefully chosen and provocative material, to stimulate thought and controversy. With considerable foresight, he repeatedly made it clear to the classes that the subject matter of each lesson was one on which various opinions were tenable and that there was no 'right' answer to any of the issues. He spent most of his time asking questions designed to elicit pupils' attitudes and opinions. A full third of his public talk consisted of questions and he asked a remarkable average of seventy-six questions per thirty-five minute lesson. On average almost half these question were 'open' ones, that is questions which require the pupil to express a judgment or opinion rather than to supply a predetermined correct answer. Such extensive use of 'open' questions is usually held to be a model of good practice. Yet at the end of every lesson Keith felt that *he* had done most of the work, perhaps a sound conclusion in view of the fact that pupil contributions accounted on average for no more than 16 per cent of the lesson time. Many of their answers were very short; indeed, many of the open questions received no answer at all. Why did the pupils have so little to say?

Part of the answer may be that Keith's questions, although open ones, were seen by pupils as difficult or unfamiliar. In contrast to English or religious education lessons which I also observed (after being told by the pupils that these two subjects included discussion sessions more often than any others), the pupils could not draw on textual material with which they were already familiar (English lessons in literature) or everyday moral problems (RE). Consider some of Keith's questions:

> What d'you think of that (picture)?
> Is that really art, d'you think?
> Do you like that?
> What makes a picture into art?
> Why should anyone bother to paint that?
> What d'you mean when you say it's religious?
> Is an artist different from ordinary people?
> How would you set about painting something as complicated as that?

Not only did the pupils seem to find these questions difficult, they also gave indications of their fears that an answer which expressed their true personal reaction to a painting would involve a degree of public exposure they were unhappy to risk. A few pupils learnt how to deflect questions by devising 'smart' answers which did not really answer the question at all. A small minority of pupils, who took a disproportionately large amount of the pupil talk, seemed sufficiently self-confident to take these risks. But in general most pupils lacked a backcloth of relevant experience on which to draw. They had little experience of looking at art objects in any serious way; they were not used to forming and then expressing judgments about them and were nervous of so doing; and most of all they lacked a working vocabulary in which to talk openly about their reactions beyond the level of 'I like that' or 'I don't like that'. Had they been given more lessons in art appreciation these difficulties might in time have been remedied. As it was, Keith became progressively dispirited and as the public examinations grew nearer he succumbed to the demands that lessons be used as a 'free' period for exam preparation.

Some might say that Keith ran the lesson badly, and that he had failed to give the pupils the extensive preparation that is needed for successful discussions of art objects. But that is a counsel of perfection and I think it rather unjust to accuse Keith of employing a poor teaching technique. A more telling point can be made against Keith, and it could be made by the fan of Bourdieu mentioned earlier. He could say that Keith's lesson in art appreciation with mainly working-class pupils was *predestined* to failure, for it could only succeed when pupils already possess the requisite cultural capital, which these pupils patently lack. He could then make two arguments. The first requires us to suppose that Keith could give the same lessons to some academically able, upper- and middle-class pupils, say in a famous English private ('public') school. Would not Keith feel much more successful here? He will still be unused to the role he adopts in art appreciation lessons, certainly, but the greater responsiveness of the pupils would ensure that this role discomfort could soon be forgotten. These pupils could readily draw upon relevant home experiences and upon the verbal skills they have acquired in related academic subjects, such as English literature. They would comment with considerable fluency on the pictures, making astute and witty remarks that betrayed a wealth of background familiarity so unselfconsciously accumulated over the years. They might even draw upon the vocabulary of the art critic. If this were so, it would be in line with Bourdieu's thesis, where cultural capital does not need to comprise – perhaps does not comprise – the aesthetic experience as such, but consists rather in the capacity to talk eloquently and with knowledge about art objects. This capacity *to talk culture* might even be a substitute for the aesthetic experience itself, and it could mislead Keith into believing that his art appreciation lesson had been a successful induction into aesthetic experience.

The second of the two arguments is this. Keith's problem is not merely that he cannot create an articulate discussion with his working-class pupils because they lack the appropriate cultural capital. His problem is much more acute than this: it is that he cannot, by struggling with a talk-dominated art appreciation lesson ever *generate* enough cultural capital (or do it quickly enough) to make a lesson rewarding for teacher and pupils. He is caught in a trap from which he cannot escape: in Keith's present situation, an art appreciation lesson is simply pointless.

There is surely some merit in the first of these arguments, though it remains a speculation rather than a tested hypothesis. And the second argument is reasonable, provided we make the crucial assumption that art appreciation lessons are primarily concerned with generating fluent talk about art objects. Here is the flaw. Of course, Keith might not have been so easily misled, as suggested in the first argument. He might soon realize when clear pupil talk was covering a lack of genuine aesthetic experience. Yet he wanted his own pupils to talk fluently about the pictures. At the same time, my observations of Keith's lessons suggest that he himself does not find it at all easy to express his aesthetic experience in words. This is commonly felt more strongly in relation to the visual arts than in relation to a play or a novel, where one has ready-made props in the form of plot or characterization on which to construct one's responses. It is not, I think, only the visual arts which are vulnerable to this severe difficulty: there is at least one other art form which poses a similar obstacle.

In a refreshingly frank article about the teaching of poetry in schools, Chris Woodhead notes that a competent English teacher can with relative ease set the scene for a public reading of a poem and arouse some preliminary pupil interest and attention.[7] The poem is then read with care and the pupils are caught up in its magic. What happens next? Well, if you enjoy reading poetry at home what do you do next?

> At home, if you read a poem to yourself or listen to a reading on the radio, and you are moved by what the poet is saying, then you probably sit for a while after the poem has ended to think about the words and images you can remember, and the effect that they have had on you. What happens in the school English lesson? Do teachers allow for this private and silent period of thought? Far from it: in my experience, we tend rather to open fire immediately with questions about the meaning of difficult bits. Or we will make platitudinous and/or coercive remarks about how 'powerful' or 'vivid' or 'immediate' the poem is. This at least is the kind of thing I used to do, and though I have visited many very different schools in the past four years, I have yet to find much evidence of a more intelligent practice.

The teacher of poetry has still much lesson time to fill and he or she begins to probe, through questions, for related experiences in the pupils' lives and then, steering the pupils back to the text, asks questions about difficult words and so on. These tend to be short, crisp and (most important) *closed* questions which call for a 'right' answer rather than the expression of a judgment. Woodhead argues that this process is essentially destructive of the original pleasure derived from the poem and these practices must take responsibility for creating in pupils a dislike of poetry.

This analysis throws considerable light on Keith's art appreciation lessons. Here, too, there was surprisingly little silence for the sheer act of *looking*. In Keith's lessons silent periods of looking accounted for less than a fifth of a lesson, and even when a long series of slides was shown less than a third of the time was devoted to silent looking. Keith, like our poetry teacher, felt impelled to pressure the pupils into talking about their response and towards the end of each lesson he greatly increased the rate with which he asked closed questions, many of which were of doubtful relevance to the purpose of the lesson. He was evidently 'spinning out' the lesson until, to his relief, the bell rang.

What lies behind this? Keith, like most teachers, is perhaps rather afraid of silences during lessons: talk is a means of keeping pupils busy and attentive and of preserving his own control. But there is more to teachers' addiction to talk than this. Perhaps teachers of art (and poetry) believe that pupils can be *talked into* an appreciation of art (or poetry), just as they can be talked into learning a scientific principle or a foreign language. From this it is but a short step to a further belief, that the pupils' demonstrated capacity to *talk about* art (or poetry) in a fluent manner is a valid index of the success with which they have been talked into an appreciation of the art form. Every teacher of the arts is aware that many pupils are on the 'outside' of an art form when they come to school and hopes that, by what happens in lessons, they can be brought onto the 'inside'. This seems reasonable, since the same transition from 'outside' to 'inside' occurs in learning science or a foreign language. In these subjects, however, the emphasis on talk is proper perhaps: when a pupil can explain a scientific principle verbally, or can speak freely in French, this surely justifies the preceding teacher and pupil talk by which the learning, the transition from 'outside' to 'inside', was accomplished. But does this model apply equally well to the appreciation of the arts? Is this the way that pupils are moved from 'outside' to 'inside' in relation to art forms? I doubt it. Herbert Read has put the issue succinctly:

> It should always be remembered that the appeal of art is not to the conscious perception at all, but to intuitive apprehension. A work of art is not present in thought, but in feeling; it is a symbol rather than a direct statement of truth. That is why a deliberate analysis of a work of art, such as I have been suggesting here only by way of explanation, *cannot in itself lead to the pleasure to be derived from that work of art.* Such pleasure is a direct communication from the work of art as a whole. A work of art always surprises us; it has worked its effect before we have become conscious of its presence.[8]

Keith, with his belief (shared widely among teachers) in the educative value of talk, ignored this point. He acted as if his pupils could be talked into art appreciation and was disheartened when they could not talk about art in a fluent way. He may have questioned his own teaching skills; he certainly questioned the value of continuing with his art appreciation lessons; but he never questioned his assumption about talk, perhaps because he could see no alternative. And if, as in our speculative example of the same lesson in a very different school, the pupils had talked fluently about the pictures, he might have been tempted to treat this as a confirmation of the belief that pupils can sometimes be talked into aesthetic experience, rather than (as Bourdieu might suggest) as a reflection of the pupils' pre-existing cultural capital. I think we should take Herbert Read's insight seriously, and I propose (to anticipate my later argument) that we cannot be talked into aesthetic experience and that the transition from 'outside' to 'inside' cannot be accomplished through talk. *Before* the transition, talk about art is a matter of cultural capital: *after* the transition, talk about art is very much more than a mere display of cultural capital.

To advance the argument we must examine more closely this widespread belief in the educative value of talk. It rests, I believe, upon a deeply held, common-sense theory of learning shared by most teachers (and perhaps by most people). I shall call this *the incremental theory of learning*. According to this view, learning, whether it be skill acquisition or the understanding of a principle, is a cumulative or additive process which succeeds as bit is built upon previous bit. The theory is most evident in the learning of mathematics or a foreign language: it is all a slow, systematic and progressive movement from the simple to the complex. This common-sense theory can ally itself to a behaviouristic psychology, the building up of S-R bonds or the reinforcement of responses, or with a Piagetian view, the movement from stage to stage. Talk is a basic method of fostering this incremental learning. Pupils must articulate where they are at any particular point and through their responding talk teachers reinforce the correct pupil behaviour or help the pupil to move from one stage to another.

I am not, let me hasten to add, trying to disparage this common-sense incremental learning theory. If it were not substantially sound the various forms of incremental theory in psychology would not for so long have debated among themselves the precise mechanisms of incrementalism. I am asserting not that incremental theory is mistaken, but that it is only part of the account of learning. And more, that the part which is neglected by incremental theory is of singular importance to aesthetic learning in matters which relate to appreciation as opposed to skill acquisition.

Although conventional psychological theories of learning are not easily applied to the aesthetic domain, we still tend to work on the assumption that when a more specific aesthetic learning theory is developed it will have essentially the same form as other incremental theories. This seems to be the view of the philosopher Richard Peters;[9] and the most important theory of aesthetic learning in recent years, that of Robert Witkin,[10] finds its inspiration in the work of Piaget. I do not wish to take issue with Witkin's theory – I do not understand it well enough to do that – nor do I wish for a moment to deny the importance of incrementalism for many aspects of aesthetic learning. But I do want to search for the aspects of aesthetic learning which incrementalism leaves out and consider their significance for art appreciation. Indeed, it is part of my argument that teachers often have trouble with art appreciation lessons (as did Keith) precisely because they mistakenly draw on incremental theories and talk when they should and could be drawing upon some alternative theory.

But how shall we uncover what I allege to be this neglected aspect of learning which I believe to be of such importance in the aesthetic domain? The classroom is not likely to help in this search, for I have argued as part of my case that it is neglected there. The strategy must be to stand back from classrooms for a moment and look at aesthetic learning from a wider perspective. To put the issue autobiographically, how have I come to learn aesthetically when I have had no lessons in art appreciation? It is immediately apparent that large numbers of people are in the same position. They have a deep interest in the arts, despite a lack of schooling in the appreciation of many of those arts and despite the lack of family cultural capital. Faced with this phenomenon the inclination of a social scientist like me, with an interest in symbolic interactionism and phenomenology, is obvious: one must, as an initial task, simply ask the relevant people to give an account of how they think they came to develop their deep interest in the arts. This is exactly what I have been doing as a complement to my school-based studies of art lessons. This is not the place to give an exhaustive account of those interviews, which are still far from complete. Instead, I want to present an outline of the theory which is emerging from these complex data, thus offering a preliminary sketch of an alternative theory of aesthetic learning. By 'alternative' here I do not mean a substitute for incremental theories, but rather a complementary theory; both are needed for an adequate theory of aesthetic learning as a whole. I shall call this complementary theory a *traumatic theory of aesthetic learning*.

One of the most immediate and striking features of my informants' accounts of how they came to be interested in an art form is the frequency with which they cite a particular event or experience, and sometimes even date that event with considerable precision.[11] Their experience was, to a greater or lesser degree, traumatic. Commonly we use this term with negative overtones: we use it in the original Greek sense of a 'wound', and the medical profession still so use it; or we draw upon the psychoanalytic sense of a disturbing experience which unbalances mental life. I am keen to retain something of this sense, because my informants remember their experience(s) as essentially *disturbing*. Indeed, it is because the experience was disturbing that it is remembered. (This is in contrast to psychoanalytic use in which the trauma is repressed and forgotten to the conscious mind because it was disturbing.) Some describe the experience as 'shattering'. It did indeed cause a kind of wound, one which injured or destroyed all their preconceptions about the art form, to which hitherto they were often hostile or indifferent. I want to give trauma both a positive and negative meaning, just as shattering can be applied to a distressing experience and to an unexpected but very pleasant surprise. In my use of trauma the two are combined into a single experience: preconceptions are destroyed by an unexpectedly pleasant experience.

This traumatic conception of learning is not entirely new: it has a precedent in William James's great masterpiece of psychological study, *The Varieties of Religious Experience*.[12] James was interested in the dynamics of religious conversion, but he did not explain this in terms of the incremental learning theories of his day. To explain the phenomenon he looked closely at the *nature* of religious conversion and then sought to tease out the *preconditions* which made it likely that, under the right circumstances, conversion would be experienced. I want to take a similar approach to aesthetic learning.

My informants report their aesthetic traumas and in some cases are so reminiscent of a religious conversion that a parallel or analogy between the two is in order. In both cases the initiating experience is sudden, dramatic, memorable and it is seen as the first step in a change of outlook with immensely important consequences. Of course, not all important aesthetic learning or religious conversions take this form, but we can begin with those that do. There is another parallel between a visit to a gallery, theatre or concert hall and a visit to an evangelical or revivalist meeting: in both cases the same 'objective' events can produce in some participants a conversion but in other participants an aversion. Just as a visit to, say, a Billy Graham meeting can put one off religion, a visit to, say, a Wagner opera can leave one with a distaste for Wagner (and perhaps opera) for life. The trauma can be aversive or conversive. I shall here ignore aversive traumas for the most part, and treat conversive trauma in greater depth. Conversive trauma's most notable characteristic is that it is a relatively sudden, dramatic and intensive process of initiation into an art form. The concept of initiation is nowadays a popular one in education, largely through Peters' justly celebrated essay on 'Education as initiation'.[13] I believe Peters and others have neglected the traumatic initiations with which I am here concerned and instead have tied initiation too closely to incremental learning theories.

I detect four elements in the conversive traumatic experience (or set of experiences). The first is the powerful *concentration of attention*. One is totally absorbed in or unexpectedly fascinated by the art object, caught up in it, even taken over by it. In a strong form of the trauma, one's sense of time and space is suspended and one loses consciousness of all extraneous matters. One is lost in the art object.

The second element is a *sense of revelation*.[14] One has a sense of new and important reality being opened up before one or of entering a new plane of existence which is somehow intensely real. It is not merely that one's senses are, in contrast to everyday living, heightened and accompanied by a profound emotional disturbance; there is also a feeling of discovery as if some already existing core of the self is suddenly being touched and brought to life for the first time, and yet inevitably so. The experience has cognitive or intellectual features certainly, but the emotional aspects are paramount.

The third element is *inarticulateness*: one feels unable to express what has happened in words, either to oneself or to others. For some there is no desire to communicate the experience to others; but when this urge is present it is usually impossible to achieve. The affective aspects can be so powerful that, as it were, feelings drown the words. People often mention how they were rendered inarticulate – 'I was struck dumb.' (This is in sharp contrast to the sudden 'insight' that can occur in intellectual matters: it is usually a test of the understanding of a scientific principle that it can be recounted in words.)

The fourth element is the *arousal of appetite*. One simply wants the experience to continue or to be repeated, and this can be felt with considerable urgency. In weaker versions of the trauma there is still a lingering fascination which leads people to say that they felt 'hooked' on the art object in some way.

I have purposely characterized the strong form of conversive trauma. Let me repeat that it is not always so dramatic and sometimes several experiences are required before the trauma is felt at its full force. My description is that of a simplified 'ideal type' of conversive trauma which is by no means always found in this pure form in the empirical world.

From an educational point of view it is the last element, the arousal of appetite, which is most significant: the motivation to continue or repeat the experience is an integral feature of the experience itself. This is in striking contrast to most incremental learning. Every teacher knows that the Achilles' heel of incremental learning theories is their failure to say very much about motivation. You do not have to be a teacher very long before you discover that your principal classroom problem is the one of pupil motivation. Even when pupils succeed in acquiring a skill or understanding a principle or mastering a body of knowledge, they do not automatically have the motivation to further their achievements. So often the teacher has to supply the pupils with some extra motivation or incentives from the outside. With conversive trauma there is always, at least immediately after the experience, strong internal motivation.

Conversive trauma, then, is always a first step in the process of initiation, but the one which drives the person forwards. One has moved, quite suddenly, from being on the 'outside' to being on the 'inside', but it is always recognized that one is only just on the 'inside': there is more to come and one rejoices in it. We can chart subsequent events in terms of four analytically distinct steps, though these should not be regarded as discrete stages which follow one another in any mechanical way. The first is that *conversive trauma leads to commitment*. This refers to the last element of the trauma of which motivation to further the initiating experience is an integral feature. The initial commitment is in some cases fairly weak, taking the form of curiosity or fascination, but normally the commitment is greatly strengthened in later steps. Then *commitment leads to exploration*. Initially one might, of course, simply seek a repetition of the original traumatizing experience where this is possible – think how during an exhibition one often returns to look at pictures which have moved one very deeply, or perhaps one buys gramaphone records of a work which has been overwhelming during a concert performance – but normally one is soon led to explore other works by the same *artist*. This soon leads to a more general exploration of the *art form*, often in a rather tentative and experimental way, by selecting works which are similar to the original traumatizing work. Thus one buys a book of other expressionist painters or one ventures from Beethoven's string quartets to those of Schubert. All this is accompanied by a sense of increasing discovery and exploration and a concomitant gain in motivation. Then *exploration leads to discrimination*. One learns to make qualitative judgments between aspects of the same work, between works of the same artist, or between artists. One's preferences begin to change, to become more subtle; and the pleasure one derives can be at its most intense in unexpected places. For instance, the third act of *La Bohème* is held to be finer music than the more popular and immediate first act; *Lear* is felt to be a more rewarding play than *Macbeth*; Turner's watercolours are thought to be greater than those of de Wint, and so on. One feature of this step is the revaluation of the art works associated with the original trauma. These are often held to be less good than one originally thought; since then one has 'advanced' in one's preferences, though there often remains an ineradicable fondness for the traumatizing work itself. The fourth step – and this does come rather late – is that *discrimination leads to the search for background knowledge*. Only after exploration and discrimination have been set in train is one motivated to seek out relevant background knowledge, such as a biography of the artist, critical appraisals of the art form, studies of the artist's particular techniques.

It is this last step which I believe has particular educational significance and is highly pertinent to the earlier discussion of classroom talk about art or poetry. The interest in acquiring relevant background information typically comes after – and often some time after – conversive trauma. One is not talked into trauma. At the pre-traumatic stage, as we saw in our earlier discussion of Bourdieu, middle-class pupils can draw on their cultural capital for impressive talk that is a substitute for aesthetic experience not a means of expressing it; whilst at the same pre-traumatic stage working-class pupils find such talk either difficult or tedious. Only after the trauma has done its work does have something to talk about and the motivation to use the cultural capital in a genuine and purposeful way, or (as with working-class pupils) the motivation to find a language in which to communicate one's feelings and acquire some cultural capital. In other words, only after traumatic initiation can aesthetic experience and cultural capital be truly conjoined. The conventional art appreciation lesson, so heavily saturated with talk, may be a poor means of achieving this conjunction as long as all or most of the pupils are at the pre-traumatic stage; and this can apply whatever the class background of the pupils.

This theory of traumatic learning in the aesthetic domain (and in other domains in which it may also operate) needs further refinement and testing. If the theory has any merit, it should guide us towards looking at the teaching of art (or of the arts more generally) in schools in a new way, for one of the main functions of theory is to provide an attractive prospective for, and a new perspective on, research. I think it likely, for example, that conversive trauma does sometimes occur in the classroom and we need to investigate if, when and how it arises. Research into aversive trauma in schools, which probably occurs more frequently, is equally important. Currently there are many good ideas for experimentation in schools with art history and art appreciation,[15] some schools are quietly developing their own relevant innovations,[16] and Rod Taylor's Schools Council project on critical studies in art, based in the Drumcroon Centre in Wigan, is clearly producing some exciting and highly relevant work.

It seems right to conclude with a tentative consideration of some of the educational implications of conversive trauma theory. If the theory is sound, then an important question is: can and do teachers stimulate or engineer conversive trauma? Few of my informants refer directly to classroom experiences. They would probably be highly sympathetic to Harry Rée's claim that schools are not places well suited to education in the arts.[17] Rée draws attention to the powerful impact on pupils of extracurricular activities in the arts, and my similar claim has led me to investigate this.[18] (I shall report on these findings in later publications.) It is difficult, and sometimes impossible, to simulate in the art room through reproductions or slides the impact of a gallery exhibition, just as the cinema film is in more than one sense diminished on the small television screen. An art appreciation lesson that is largely confined within the classroom will lose the terrible directness of art which seems to be essential to conversive trauma. In adapting to their classroom circumstances art teachers are in danger of forgetting this. Consider Peter Fuller's account of looking at Michaelangelo's *Moses* in San Pietro in Vincoli (and note how his comments support Herbert Read's comments above):

> That expression has been written about so much, subjected to layer upon layer of interpretation. And yet, as you stand there in the cool and gloom of the church, all those words seem irrelevant. You even forget the details and dates which you dutifully read up that morning in the guide-book which you are still holding in your hand. That stony face possesses a tremendous, urgent power. As you look upon it that power reaches you, touches you, and moves you directly.[19]

And later:

> ... I walked into the Holburne of Menstrie Museum in Bath and encountered (Natkin's) paintings for the first time. Characteristically, Natkins's exhibition spilled beyond the walls of the Museum to fill up the City's Festival Gallery as well. I had not heard of Natkin, let alone seen one of his paintings before that moment. I was, however, moved by what I saw. What do I mean by moved? I looked at these canvasses which were stretched around me like an ocean of light and I felt that feeling which I spoke about ... and I felt it to a marked degree: the feeling that these were *good*.[20]

If all this means that art teachers have to demand more time and opportunity to take pupils on out-of-school visits, so be it. These demands are more likely to be met if we can collect the evidence to justify such demands for an adequate art education.

Teachers already take pupils to galleries, rare though such visits may be. Always they face the problem of how much, and what type of, preparation should be given. Most teachers are reluctant to give no preparation, but to give too much of the wrong sort is to put the information cart before the traumatic horse and this may have aversive consequences. Here, then, is another important topic for future research. On some pupils the effect of a gallery visit is likely to be aversive, either strongly or mildly so. This aversion can easily be magnified if the follow-up involves additional work, for example, writing an essay about it. It would follow from the theory that after the visit aversive pupils should be left alone to recover in peace. But with the conversives, the evidence I have collected suggests that some of them will need some help and support. They will, as I have noted, develop some inherent motivation to advance. But, like religious converts, they may, if left alone, lapse as the effects of the trauma subside. Conversives may need to be put in touch with other conversives so that they can move to the exploratory phase together; after all, many of us prefer to take our aesthetic pleasures in sympathetic company.

Another important research topic is the elucidation of the preconditions which may be essential to conversive trauma. So far my research has not succeeded in uncovering these, relevant as they are to guiding teachers in the matter of preparation. It is possible that preconditions are best created by indirect means in which an openness to trauma is fostered by previous classroom experience. I wonder whether, for example, in place of the conventional art appreciation lesson of the type Keith conducted, pupils would be helped by selective self-exposure to art objects. In this method pupils are offered a range of reproductions or slides from which they make their *own* selection to look at and perhaps discuss in small self-selected groups.[21] It might avoid the aversive risk associated with the teacher choosing the exhibits and talking with the whole class. Another indirect means of preparation is available in collaboration between the art teacher and teachers of other subjects, rarely though this is done. An art teacher who is sympathetic to John Berger's approach[22] could easily present some relevant art in a variety of history lessons; and an English teacher who is teaching Blake's poems would surely be glad of the art teacher's help in showing the close association between Blake's poems and paintings. Again, help with the problem of talking about pictures might be given if pupils were encouraged to look at and make comments upon other pupils' art work, yet very rarely have I seen this done in an extensive or systematic way.

A final suggestion concerns what I shall call 'mini-traumas'. A feature of conversive trauma is the sense of surprise. There is no reason why teachers should not self-consciously plan surprise for pupils. Art rooms everywhere look remarkably alike: their walls are usually covered with pupils' work, and occasionally a reproduction or two can be found there. The trouble is, my observations suggest, the children so rarely look at the walls: the art work there is mostly treated as unimportant wall-paper. Encouragement to look at the walls could be fostered by planned surprise. For instance, one week the walls might be felt completely blank; another week just one picture exhibited; the next week pupils' work; then the week after some highly contrasting reproductions, and so on.

Art appreciation has been neglected by art teachers and no doubt they will continue to spend far more time on art production than art consumption. Authorities in art education have long insisted that in art education the relationship between production and consumption is one of mutual reinforcement.[23] The neglect of art appreciation may spring not from a rejection of this principle of complementarity between production and consumption but from the pedagogical problems of art appreciation lessons. I offer the theory of aesthetic learning by conversive trauma both to stimulate the further research into art teaching that is so desperately needed and to contribute to that movement which sees art appreciation as important in its own right. In the wise words of Herbert Read in 1936:

> Every man will, we hope, if he is not inhibited or deformed by his education, be able to express himself as an artist of some sort; but only a special kind of man can become a poet, painter, sculptor or musician of the special we call 'great' . . . If the number of those who are trained as painters, sculptors and 'creative' artists generally should be restricted, on the other hand the number of those to be trained in the appreciation of the arts should be vastly increased; indeed, no person would be exempt from such training except those hopelessly disqualified by stupidity or mental atrophy. For common sense as well as psychology tells us that the aesthetic impulses . . . are the normal possession of children . . . .[24]

Notes

1 HARGREAVES, D.H. (1982) *The Challenge for the Comprehensive School: Culture, Curriculum and Community*, London, Routledge and Kegan Paul.
2 The teacher was presumably drawing on the writings of Bourdieu such as: 'Systems of education and systems of thought', in YOUNG, M.F.D. (Ed.) (1972) *Knowledge and Control*, London, Collier-Macmillan; 'Cultural reproduction and social reproduction', in BROWN, R (Ed.) (1973) *Knowledge, Education and Cultural Change*, London, Tavistock; 'The school as a conservative force: Scholastic and cultural inequalities', in EGGLESTON, J. (Ed.) (1974) *Contemporary Research in the Sociology of Education* London, Methuen; and BOURDIEU, P. and PASSERON, J-C. (1977) *Reproduction in Education, Society and Culture*, London, Sage. A useful paper, is DI MAGGIO, P. and USEEM, M. (1982) 'The arts in class reproduction', in APPLE, M.W. (Ed.) *Cultural and Economic Reproduction in Education*, London, Routledge and Kegan Paul, pp. 181–201.
3 HALSEY, A.H., HEATH, A.F. and RIDGE, J.M. (1980) *Origins and Destinations*, Oxford, Clarendon Press; MUSGROVE, F. (1979) *School and the Social Order*, London, Wiley.
4 See, for example, BARRETT, M. (1979) *Art Education*, London, Heinemann; SMITH, F. (1980) 'Art', in STRAUGHAN, R. and WRIGLEY, J. (Eds) *Values and Evaluation in Education*, London, Harper and Row, pp. 143–68; FELDMAN, E.B. (1982) 'Varieties of art curriculum, in *Journal of Art and Design Education*, 1, 1 pp. 21–45; ALLISON, B. (1982) 'Identifying the core in art and design', *ibid.*, pp. 59–66.
5 ROSS, M. (1978) *The Creative Arts*, London, Heinemann, pp. 43, 63, 80.
6 FOR EXAMPLE, FIELD, D. (1970) *Change in Art Education*, London, Routledge and Kegan Paul; WITKIN, R.W. (1974) *The Intelligence of Feeling*, London, Heinemann; REID, L.A. (1980) 'Meaning in the arts', and SHAW, R. (1980) 'Education and the

arts', both in Ross, M (Ed.) *The Arts and Personal Growth*, Oxford, Pergamon.
7 WOODHEAD, C. (1980) 'Getting the proper attention,' in *The Times Educational Supplement*, 11 July.
8 READ, H. (1931) *The Meaning of Art*, London, Faber and Faber, pp. 66, 69. The present italics have been added and the original italics removed.
9 PETERS, R.S. (1972) 'The education of the emotions', in DEARDEN, R.F., HIRST, P.H. and PETERS, R.S. (Eds) *Education and the Development of Reason*, London, Routledge and Kegan Paul.
10 WITKIN, R.W. *op. cit.* A recent book, Ross, M. (Ed.) *The Development of Aesthetic Experience*, Oxford, Pergamon, contains two articles which review recent incremental theory in aesthetic education: REID, L.A. 'The concept of aesthetic development' and EVANS, D. 'Aesthetic development: A psychological viewpoint.'
11 All these informants are adults with experience of higher education.
12 JAMES, W. (1902) *The Varieties of Religious Experience*, London, Longman.
13 PETERS, R.S. (1959) *Authority, Responsibility and Education*, London, Allen and Unwin, pp. 81–107.
14 LOUIS ARNAUD REID takes up this question of revelation and aesthetic experience at some length in his book *Meaning in the Arts* (1969), London, Allen and Unwin. He naturally makes a link with religious experience and acknowledges his debt to the theologian H.D. LEWIS. I hereby acknowledge my debt to REID.
15 See, for example, DYSON, A. (1982) 'Art history in schools: A comprehensive strategy, in *Journal of Art and Design Education*, 1, 1, pp. 123–33.
16 I have been privileged to be aware of the important innovations being developed at Theale Green School, Berks, for instance.
17 REE, H. (1981) 'Education and the arts: Are schools the enemy?' in Ross, M. (Ed.) *The Aesthetic Imperative*, Oxford, Pergamon, pp. 90–9.
18 HARGREAVES, D.H., *op. cit.*, p. 152.
19 FULLER, P. (1980) *Art and Psychoanalysis*, London, Writers and Readers Publishing Cooperative, p. 49.
20 *Ibid.*, p. 180.
21 One of my colleagues at Oxford, Mr Peter Benton, is collecting some impressive evidence that pupils can discuss poetry in highly sophisticated ways in small groups without a teacher present.
22 BERGER, J. (1972) *Ways of Seeing*, London, BBC and Penguin Books. Such an approach to art appreciation in the classroom would display the radical and subversive character of much 'high art'. See MARCUSE, H. (1977) *The Aesthetic Dimension* London, Macmillan. This approach provides an important justification for art appreciation in the school curriculum and, though it can be treated further here, is a necessary part of the riposte against those who would exclude the 'high arts' in the alleged interests of working-class pupils.
23 Especially FIELD, D., *op. cit.* and REID, L.A., *op. cit.*
24 READ, H. (1936) *Art and Society*, London, Faber and Faber.

2
Gender and the Curriculum

7   Gender and Curriculum Choice: A Case Study

Teresa Grafton, Henry Miller, Lesley Smith, Martin Vegoda and Richard Whitfield

We are trying to build a cage around the children rather than putting the children into the cage.

This is a statement made by a deputy headteacher in a mixed comprehensive school about the process of curriculum construction and choice there. She was describing a situation which she saw as catering to the perceived needs and interests of pupils as opposed to imposing a rigid curriculum upon everyone. However, there is a paradox here, indicated by the metaphor of the cage. The constraints imposed by traditional assumptions, for example, concerning the nature of male and female social roles, may be just as real in a situation of open choice as they are in the context of a curriculum without choice.

During the past two decades the differentiation of educational experience according to sex has increasingly come to be regarded as unacceptable. In the mid-1970s equal opportunity legislation and the establishment of the Equal Opportunities Commission put an official seal of approval on attempts to eradicate discriminatory practices in the classroom, as elsewhere. And indeed attention has been given by researchers to gender based curricular differences for some time. Fifty per cent of the 587 secondary schools in Benn and Simon's (1972) sample had sex specific curricula in years 1 to 3 which limited later subject choices to those deemed appropriate for boys and for girls. In the Benn and Simon study, 'girls' subjects' most frequently mentioned by schools were catering, needlework, clothes design, dancing, human biology, jewellery and mothercraft. Boys' subjects were engineering, gardening, woodwork, metalwork, technical drawing, building, navigation, physics with chemistry, rural science, pottery and surveying. Options were usually not officially closed, but it was only occasionally that a member of the 'wrong' sex was admitted. The most common reason given for the exclusion of girls from 'boys' subjects' was that teachers refused to have girls in their class.

The DES Survey (1975) of curricular differences for boys and girls emphasized that exclusion from areas of the curriculum on the grounds of sex is unlawful in the light of the 1975 Sex Discrimination Act, and that no special application procedures should be necessary for pupils who wish to enrol for any subject. However, the report of the most recent secondary school survey made by HMI (DES, 1979) notes that:

> Most schools increasingly try to ensure that all fourth and fifth year courses are open to pupils of both sexes. Boys and girls seem reluctant

> to take full advantage of these opportunities and the traditional division between the sexes in technical and domestic craft subjects are still apparent... Similarly, the divisions in the sciences are still present.... (pp. 215–16)

This paper attempts to illustrate the relationship between gender and curriculum choice by focusing upon the processes involved within a curriculum which includes a subject centrally concerned with child care and the parental, specifically the maternal, role amongst the options available. Subjects such as this constitute the thinnest point in the ice for any claim that schools are offering a genuinely open and equal curriculum to girls and boys.

Curriculum options focusing on parenthood skills have grown out of home economics departments and been staffed for the most part by teachers (invariably women) with a background in domestic craft subjects. They occur as examination subjects in the curriculum for fourth- and fifth-year pupils. They have child care, child development, parental roles and family life as core themes and are becoming increasingly more academic, although primarily they attract pupils in the low to middle ability range. Such subjects may involve pupils in playgroup activities outside the school; other practical work is also undertaken in cookery, needlework, toy making as well as the physical aspects of child care. The theoretical component of these subjects may include human biology and child development, contraception and family planning as well as discussion of responsibility and commitment in relationships.

When Cox (1976) surveyed secondary schools in three counties he found that the curriculum of 51 per cent of schools contained subjects which aimed to educate pupils in aspects of parenthood and family life; these had developed during the previous five years. Of the twenty-six teachers involved in such courses who were selected by Cox for interview, the majority were doing so in the belief that they would influence the educational and personal development of the next generation. The reasons given for starting courses in the schools surveyed by Cox were to break the cycle of deprivation or to provide education relevant to pupils' lives, both currently and in the future.

One of the major influences on the development of these courses was the influential work of Bowlby (1951; 1953) on child development, with its emphasis on the significance of early child care and on the primary caring role of the mother. This became linked to the notion that maternal deprivation in childhood constituted a significant factor in relation to malfunction in adult life. This was an important concept in the 1970s when Sir Keith Joseph, discussing the consequences of inadequate or insufficient parental care, only partly attributable to external considerations such as poor housing and low income, suggested that intergenerational cycles of deprivation underlay persistent social problems and breakdown of the family. Following Joseph's initiative, consultation between government departments focused attention upon preparation for parenthood as a preventive measure. In 1974 the DHSS published two booklets entitled 'Preparation for Parenthood' and 'Dimensions of Parenthood', which included discussion of the role of the school curriculum in the area of personal life, a theme taken up in successive government Green and White Papers and Committee reports (for example, DES, 1977; DES, 1979; DHSS, 1978).

Concern about the impact on interpersonal relationships and family structure of an increased incidence of divorce, maternal depression, illegitimacy, latchkey children, non-accidental injury and delinquency, was a further influence on the development of parenthood-related subjects in the school curriculum. Pilling and Kellmer Pringle (1978) and Whitfield (1980) are amongst those who have written of apparent threats to the stability of family structures and to the security offered to young children. Education about parenthood in the curriculum, therefore, can be seen as arising out of concern for the quality of life that pupils will experience in relationships, as parents and in their social roles outside school. In addition, from the 1960s onwards education with a specific emphasis upon preparation for parenthood began to be viewed by many teachers as one way of avoiding what they saw as a transference of inadequate parent behaviour from one generation to another.

In the last twenty years there has been a mushrooming of subjects with an external examination in the areas of child care and development and parentcraft, both at CSE and GCE O-level. The vast majority of pupils who take these subjects are girls. We suggest, as does Scott (1980 pp. 106–7), that the existence in the school curriculum of subjects like these, specifically at examination level, constitutes a 'natural choice' for girls who 'select them voluntarily and opt out of the traditional boys' subjects'. This is likely to have significant consequences for future roles. Scott sees the school as playing a key part in relegating girls and women to a 'unique place in the family and a specific place in the workforce' (p. 100) for it furnishes women (and also men) with the requisite range of appropriate skills as well as the relevant level of consciousness. In her view, educational assumptions made about women are that: the main priority in girls' lives (particularly low ability girls) is to marry and raise a family; paid work will play a non-essential part in their adult lives; they will enter paid work only in limited fields; and the work they perform in the labour force is not important to society and only necessary to women as 'pin money'. In its emphasis on the link between girls and the roles of wife and mother, the presence of an option in child care reduces the possibility of girls being offered and selecting the same curriculum as boys. The teaching of preparation for parenthood through such an option can thus be seen as facilitating the movement of girls and boys into traditional roles within the family and labour market.

The Subject Choice Process

Ball (1981 p. 122) describes the process of subject choice as a 'crucial point in the school careers of pupils. Decisions made at this point by them, and their teachers and parents, clearly have implications for their future lives which reach far beyond the limits of schooling'. Ball and Woods (1979) have provided detailed analyses of the subject choice process. They note how the orientations of pupils and parents to the selection of curriculum options tends to vary by social class. In addition, they document the ways in which teachers channel the choices pupils make, cooling out or re-routing those who select courses which are judged to be 'inappropriate' for them. However, neither Ball nor Woods pays much attention to the way in which gender shapes the choices pupils make and teachers' conceptions of what courses are 'appropriate' to particular pupils. This issue is the focus of our paper. We look at two basic questions: *who* takes a subject dealing with preparation for parenthood and *why*?

The data on which our analysis is based come from a case study which took place in 1980 in a coeducational comprehensive school in south-west England. Its catchment area, though predominantly well-to-do and middle-class, included working-class districts containing a good deal of public housing and very few amenities. These districts were a distance from the school, on the edge of its catchment area. In the course of the research we carried out a detailed investigation of the fourth-year intake for a two-year family and child option.

Pupils made a choice of subjects at two points in their school career; at the end of the third year and then in the fifth year for those staying on into the sixth form. When pupils arrived in the school they were placed in one of three ability bands. Streaming by ability, therefore, began in the first year. This was done on the basis of a primary school assessment consisting of a verbal reasoning test score and recommendations made by headteachers and, in some cases, class teachers. During the early years the curriculum was as follows:

Year 1

English; maths; drama; French; art and pottery; religious education (RE); games; music; combined science; local studies; and a choice of either cookery/needlework or metalwork/woodwork.

Year 2

As year 1 with the exception that local studies was replaced by geography and history.

Year 3

As year 1 with the following changes:

(i) the more academic forms in the top band took a second language (German);
(ii) combined science developed into three science subjects for the top and middle band and into rural and physical science for the lower band.

While curriculum differentiation by ability only began in the third year, it occurred on the basis of sex from the beginning. Girls took two craft subjects, cookery and needlework, while boys took metalwork and woodwork. Some flexibility was technically possible although the practical facilities were said to limit numbers and in practice very few boys and girls took 'atypical' subjects. In one teacher's opinion, the extent to which this might occur depended upon the awareness of pupils or parents that there was any choice in the matter; however, in any such case special applications would have been required.

In February of the third year a lengthy process of option choice began, involving consultation at varying levels between school, parents and pupils (See Figure 1, which is the information sheet prepared and used by the school outlining the sequence of events involved).

As well as English and maths and various other compulsory subjects (such as games and RE), pupils studied five subjects chosen from an options scheme composed of seven 'lines', selecting one subject from each line:

Fourth-year Options 1980/81: The Choices

All pupils will take English (which includes Language for *all* pupils and Literature for those wishing and able to take this to O-level or CSE) and Mathematics in 'ability' sets. Choices must, however, be made between the alternatives listed below, one subject being chosen from each 'line'.

LINE 1 English
LINE 2 Mathematics
LINE 3 Biology ('O' and CSE), French ('O' and CSE), History ('O' and CSE), Religious Education ('O'/CSE), Citizenship (CSE), Rural Science (CSE)
LINE 4 Chemistry ('O' and CSE), French ('O' and CSE), Geography ('O' and CSE and possibly non-exam), German ('O')
LINE 5 Physics (Nuffield 'O' and CSE), Geography ('O' and CSE), History ('O' and CSE), Physical Science (CSE), Human Biology (CSE)
LINE 6 Biology ('O'/CSE), Woodwork ('O' and CSE), Metalwork ('O' and CSE), Cookery ('O' and CSE), Needlework ('O'/CSE), Art ('O'/CSE), Music ('O'/CSE), Commercial Skills (RSA/CSE)
LINE 7 Physics (Traditional 'O'), Chemistry (Nuffield 'O'), Technical Drawing ('O' and CSE), Motor Mech. (non-exam), Art ('O'), Cookery ('O'), Typing (CSE), Family and Child ('O' and CSE), Commerce ('O'/CSE)

T. Grafton, H. Miller, L. Smith, M. Vegoda and R. Whitfield

> *Note*: Periods for Games, PE, General Studies including RE, Careers, Education in Personal Relationships, etc., will be provided outside the options scheme.

On lines 3 to 7 subjects were arranged with the intention of allowing sufficient choice for as wide a variety of pupil needs as possible. Some subjects were available in more than one line, for example, geography, French, history, chemistry, art and biology, whereas others such as family and child and the practical subjects occurred only once. Therefore, needlework and commercial skills competed with woodwork and metalwork on line 6 and none of these subjects could be picked up from another line. On line 7 family and child, typing and commerce competed with motor mechanics and technical drawing; again, none of these occurred elsewhere. Cookery was available on two lines, 6 and 7, along with all the other craft subjects. It is interesting to note that line 7 also contained the more academic subjects of physics (traditional 'O') and chemistry (Nuffield 'O'). While these subjects were available on other lines they were not the same syllabi; physics (Nuffield 'O' and CSE) was available on line 5 and chemistry ('O' and CSE) on line 4. The significance of this lies in the fact that the Nuffield syllabus tended to be taken by the most able children.

Subjects were setted where possible to cater for a range of abilities. Each line contained an option geared to those pupils for whom it was felt that 'an external examination would be unsuitable'. Such options were citizenship, geography, physical science, human biology, art, motor mechanics, typing and family and child.

Course outlines were provided for third-year tutors in order that they could advise pupils and parents appropriately. Information was given as to which band – top, middle or lower – the subject would be likely to suit. Also pupils were advised that in the case of competition for a particular subject, the school's decision would be based upon its suitability in relation to a pupil's ability or intended career. The tutor was asked to consider the pupil's need for a broad general education; paradoxically this appeared to be waived in the case of 'high fliers' who might be directed towards more academic subjects. As one teacher at the school put it:

> We like them all, as far as possible, to do some sort of creative subject, but there are one or two who will miss out on that because, for instance, they choose three sciences; because we do make it possible for our better children to do three sciences and if you've got a humanity and you've got a language, you haven't really got any scope then for the creative subjects perhaps.

Finally, certain subjects, for example, woodwork, metalwork, cookery, technical drawing and family and child, were described as open to both sexes. However, tutor's guidelines requested 'prior discussion' in the case of boys who wanted to take the family and child option, while girls who wanted to take woodwork or metalwork had to 'show a sincere desire' to do so. (Perhaps not

Gender and Curriculum Choice: A Case Study

Figure 1
Fourth Form's Curriculum — Sequence of Subject Choice

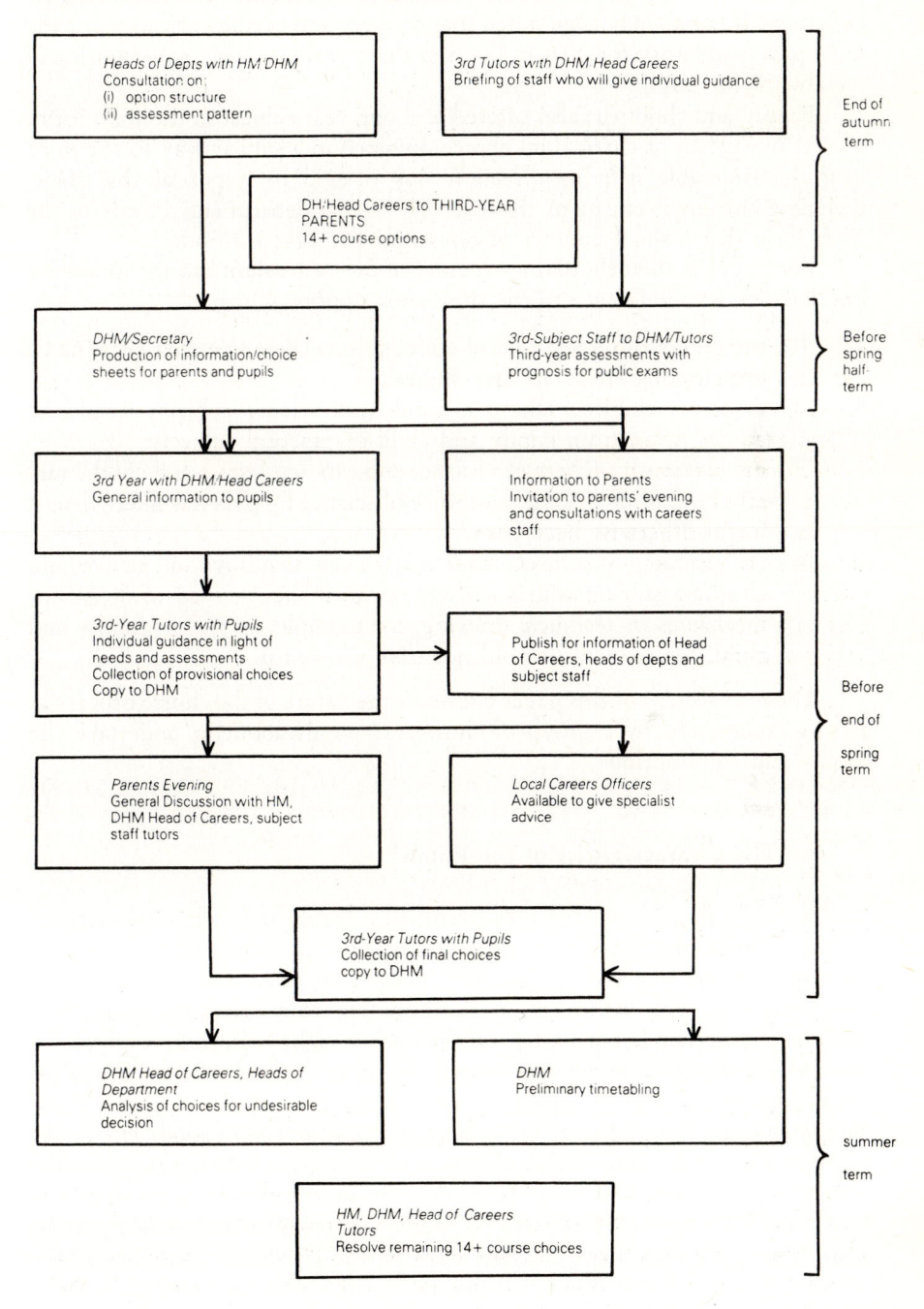

```
┌──────────────────────────────┐   ┌──────────────────────────────┐
│ Heads of Depts with HM/DHM   │   │ 3rd Tutors with DHM Head Careers │
│ Consultation on:             │   │ Briefing of staff who will give  │   End of
│ (i) option structure         │   │ individual guidance              │   autumn
│ (ii) assessment pattern      │   │                                  │   term
└──────────────────────────────┘   └──────────────────────────────┘
            │           ┌──────────────────────────────┐
            │           │ DH/Head Careers to THIRD-YEAR │
            │           │ PARENTS                       │
            │           │ 14+ course options            │
            │           └──────────────────────────────┘
            ▼                                   ▼
┌──────────────────────────────┐   ┌──────────────────────────────┐
│ DHM/Secretary                │   │ 3rd-Subject Staff to DHM/Tutors │   Before
│ Production of information/   │   │ Third-year assessments with     │   spring
│ choice sheets for parents    │   │ prognosis for public exams      │   half-
│ and pupils                   │   │                                 │   term
└──────────────────────────────┘   └──────────────────────────────┘
            ▼                                   ▼
┌──────────────────────────────┐   ┌──────────────────────────────┐
│ 3rd Year with DHM/Head       │   │ Information to Parents          │
│ Careers                      │   │ Invitation to parents' evening  │
│ General information to pupils│   │ and consultations with careers  │
│                              │   │ staff                           │
└──────────────────────────────┘   └──────────────────────────────┘
            ▼
┌──────────────────────────────┐   ┌──────────────────────────────┐
│ 3rd-Year Tutors with Pupils  │   │ Publish for information of Head │
│ Individual guidance in light │──▶│ of Careers, heads of depts and  │
│ of needs and assessments     │   │ subject staff                   │
│ Collection of provisional    │   │                                 │   Before
│ choices                      │   │                                 │   end of
│ Copy to DHM                  │   │                                 │   spring
└──────────────────────────────┘   └──────────────────────────────┘   term
            ▼
┌──────────────────────────────┐   ┌──────────────────────────────┐
│ Parents Evening              │   │ Local Careers Officers          │
│ General Discussion with HM,  │   │ Available to give specialist    │
│ DHM Head of Careers, subject │   │ advice                          │
│ staff tutors                 │   │                                 │
└──────────────────────────────┘   └──────────────────────────────┘
                    ▼         ▼
            ┌──────────────────────────────┐
            │ 3rd-Year Tutors with Pupils  │
            │ Collection of final choices  │
            │ copy to DHM                  │
            └──────────────────────────────┘
            ▼                                   ▼
┌──────────────────────────────┐   ┌──────────────────────────────┐
│ DHM Head of Careers, Heads of│   │ DHM                             │
│ Department                   │   │ Preliminary timetabling         │
│ Analysis of choices for      │   │                                 │
│ undesirable decision         │   │                                 │   summer
└──────────────────────────────┘   └──────────────────────────────┘   term
            ┌──────────────────────────────┐
            │ HM, DHM, Head of Careers     │
            │ Tutors                       │
            │ Resolve remaining 14+ course │
            │ choices                      │
            └──────────────────────────────┘
```

surprisingly, few boys and girls took up options traditionally associated with the other sex.) Needlework was described in the guidelines as being taken by girls only. It has already been noted that cookery and needlework were for the most part mandatory for girls in the first three years, as were woodwork and metalwork for boys.

Family and child was also offered as a one-year subject in the sixth form, where the system of curriculum choice operated in a similar way to the third year. Considerable help or direction was offered to pupils at this stage, including the involvement of the school's careers department. It was in the sixth form that a small number of boys opted to take the course.

For pupils at this school the structure of the curriculum had the following implications with reference to the third-year options scheme:

(i) the gender differentiation of craft subjects taken in earlier years had a pre-empting effect on later choice;
(ii) academic children taking a number of science subjects would be guided away from family and child or practical subjects;
(iii) the juxtaposition between science subjects and family and child could also be seen as making the choice of science by girls less likely than it might otherwise have been;
(iv) the grouping of subjects made it less likely that boys and girls would choose a subject which was untypical; if they wished to do motor mechanics or technical drawing, for example, as well as family and child, the structure would not have allowed it.

The next section of this paper considers the nature of the choice process as it was experienced by a group of third-year pupils about to undertake the family and child option.

The Characteristics of the Pupils

Twenty-eight pupils from the 1980 fourth-year family and child intake (out of a total of thirty-one) were interviewed in small groups of four or five. All were girls aged between 14 and 15. Virtually no boys took the course in the fourth and fifth years, with the exception of a very few from a remedial group who took part until they left at Easter. Of the twenty-eight girls, some were taking the O-level examination whereas others were to be entered for the CSE. Most would be doing one or other of the examinations and some would be double-entered. Pass rates for the subject in this school were good. The intake was initially divided into two classes or 'sets' for teaching purposes, according to teachers' assessment of the girls' ability. The ratio between the two sets was 13:15 (GCE O-level: CSE). Practical lessons were taught as mixed ability in the fourth year, whereas theory lessons were setted. There was flexibility in the setting, and girls might be moved up and down in the course of the year.

The course taken by each group was identical in most respects, and they were timetabled in parallel. Our discussions with pupils took place on the occasion of the first meeting of the class in September 1980. The girls were still together and had not been informed about their allocation to a particular set, although we were aware of who was going where. We were able to gather a certain amount of background information about the girls. All were white, reflecting the ethnic composition of the school as a whole. The family and child intake also reflected the nature of the school's catchment area, with a relatively small proportion (less than 25 per cent) coming from the working-class fringe. It was interesting to note, however, that when the twenty-eight were divided into the two ability based groupings around 50 per cent of the lower set came from this area as opposed to only 13 per cent of the higher group. Teachers also distinguished between pupils from the different areas, noting, for example, that most of the school's problems tended to be located in the fringe. These problems were defined by one teacher as comprising: '... "behaviour", low achievement, involvement with the police outside the school, emanating, as these things nearly always do, from family difficulties, separation, ineptitude on the part of the parents.'

As far as family background was concerned the picture that emerged was as follows. All but five of the girls were living with both parents. Eleven girls were living in families which contained more than two children and most did a fair amount of babysitting. Girls tended to know more about their mothers' educational background than their fathers', suggesting that mothers may constitute a more important reference in relation to their daughters' own plans. As far as parental occupations were concerned, most parents were currently in some form of paid employment – nineteen out of twenty-seven mothers; twenty-one out of twenty-six fathers. Most of the jobs listed were manual or routine non-manual (most of them relating to mothers), while three of the girls came from farming families.

Ability and Aspirations

In relation to their stated aspirations for the future, nineteen out of the twenty-eight were planning to leave school as soon as possible. Only three intended to go into the sixth form; these were all higher set girls. Most girls' immediate intentions focused on leaving school and not on further or higher education. However, their ideas about future jobs suggested that they might need some further education or training. Table 1 contains the girls' ideas about what they wanted to do on leaving school.

There was a lack of precision on this issue, though it should be remembered that these girls were only fourteen. Some girls gave more than one occupation as an alternative. The three who intended to stay on longest at school were thinking of careers with the police, secretarial work, nursing or work with children. There was a general vagueness typified by phrases like 'something to do with children' or 'work with horses or animals'. The girl who

Table 1 Girls' aspirations regarding post-school activities

Areas Mentioned	Frequency
Looking after/working with children	10
Working with animals	4
Catering (various aspects)	4
Secretarial/office work	3
Nursing	3
Policewoman/mounted policewoman	2
Something to do with needlework/art	2
Modelling	1
Beautician	1
Working with people	1
TOTAL	31

wanted to be a beautician was one of the few currently aiming at a particular career singlemindedly and knowing something definite about what it entailed.

These future career plans, when related to the reasons which the girls gave for their choice of family and child as an option, suggested that their choices did have a vocational aspect. Relatively few of the girls gave the probability that they would become parents themselves one day as the prime reason for undertaking the course. The most popular reason advanced was that they 'liked children'. However, when we asked the girls why they thought others in the group had chosen the subject, its utility in relation to future parenthood was often cited, for example: 'I think it's something everybody ought to know – how to look after children before you have them.' It was also very obvious that most of the girls had a great deal of experience already of looking after younger children, not only in their own families but also in those belonging to friends and neighbours. Curriculum subjects like this one would, therefore, appear to fit caring roles already adopted by many girls outside school.

There were virtually no differences between girls in the higher and lower ability groups in the matter of their future plans; yet in the options choices of the intake as a whole considerable differences could be seen between the subject profiles characteristic of the two ability sets (see Table 2).

Table 2 Options choices of higher and lower ability sets

Lines	Higher Ability Set	Lower Ability Set
1	Maths	Maths
2	English	English
3	Biology	* Citizenship or rural science
4	French	* Geography
5	History	* Human biology
6	Cookery or commercial skills	* Needlework or art
7	* Family and child	* Family and child

* these subjects could be taken without pupils taking an exam.

Gender and Curriculum Choice: A Case Study

How Choices Were Made

As has already been explained, the sequence of subject choice took place throughout most of the third year and involved all senior staff, third-year tutors, careers and subject teachers, as well as pupils and their parents. In his study of the subject choice process in a secondary modern school, Woods describes the relative roles of the three main parties concerned – that is, the school, parents and pupils themselves. These also seemed to be the main parties to the process of subject choice in the school we studied, though the influence on pupils of the experience of others who had taken the course previously, particularly sisters or friends, was also important, contradicting a finding of the recent Schools Council study of fourth-year options (Bardell, 1982).

Of all those potentially involved in the choice process a significant amount of influence would, not surprisingly, appear to have come from parents, particularly mothers:

> My parents did it. They chose which ones would be best for me, for my career. I want to be a chef and I need certain qualifications.
>
> I want to be a policewoman and my dad helped me. He said which subjects would be best.
>
> Mum says it is useful to know how to look after children; she said it's something good to have if you can get it.
>
> I just really want to do it and my mum wanted me to.

However, at least two girls had chosen the family and child option despite parental advice to the contrary:

> She [mother] said 'I don't see why you want to take it. If you ever need anything when you're older and you've got a family, you can ask me, so I don't see why you don't take needlework or something like that.' But I thought needlework – there's a lot of dressmaking. So I thought I can use these two lessons, they're something more interesting than needlework that will help me in my older life.

(This girl wanted to 'work with people' or do 'something with art'.) Another girl said: 'My friends who had taken it before had said it is a nice course to take so I thought "Well better than motor mechanics". My dad wanted me to take that.' Parental involvement was quoted more frequently by girls in the upper rather than lower ability set. Girls in the latter group tended to stress their own part in the matter: 'Well, my mum and dad just let me make up my own mind.' For the most part, tutors were not mentioned at all and, when questioned, pupils tended to deny they had been a major source of influence. In view of the emphasis placed upon the role of third-year tutors in the sequence of events as outlined by the school, their low profile is of interest. Here is one account of the process of interaction between home and school which shows the system operating 'by the book':

> I talked to my mum and my auntie and my tutor. My tutor discussed it with me.... She asked me how I was doing and then she got the ones she didn't think I'd get very far in. She got the teachers to say if they thought I was good enough. She got the reports back and gave them to me and sent a little letter to my mum and my mum said it was all right.

In relation to the role played by third-year tutors and by the school generally, we also asked the girls what information they had been given about the course at the time they were thinking about what to do. A group of pupils, all of whom had been allocated to the lower set for teaching purposes, were particularly emphatic that they had been given little or no previous information about the subject by teachers or tutors. On the other hand, another girl said that her 'old' tutor who also taught family and child used to bring in slides 'showing how accidents were caused in the home and prevention to stop them.' She would also answer any questions they had.

To summarize this account of how choices appear to have been made by these pupils, we noted with interest the primacy given to the opinions of parents, sisters and others with first-hand experience of the subject in question as opposed to official school-based advisers. We are, however, unable to assess the extent to which this may be an accurate reflection of what really took place.

Reasons and Expectations

Discussion with the girls helped to indicate some of the relevant factors which lay behind their selection of subjects. A consistent theme was the way future job aspirations influenced choice. Many girls also said they chose those subjects they liked best or were best at. Occasionally someone suggested she had not had an entirely free hand; for example, one girl seemed to think she had had to take geography on line 4, and another said of line 7: 'You either get typing or family and child', in spite of the fact that there were other choices she could have made. In general, however, responses to the question as to how the choice of options was made centred on the twin notions of utility and feasibility. One girl, when asked whether it was difficult or easy to make the decisions, said: 'It's easy if you know what you want, definitely know what jobs you want to do and what qualifications you've got to have.'

Reasons frequently given for choosing the family and child option were:

Because I like children
I (might) want to work with children
I thought it would be useful/interesting

Gender and Curriculum Choice: A Case Study

> It will help me when I have children of my own
> There was nothing else I could/wanted to do.

The order of these statements reflects the relative significance of each, with the first two often presented together. The emphasis was on the vocational motive. Relatively few of the girls gave the probability that they would become parents themselves one day as the *prime* reason for undertaking the course. One example, from the only girl in her discussion group who made this point, was:

> Well I don't really know. It's just something I think all mums should know, either learn it at school or go somewhere before they have a baby, how to look after children. I just thought it would be helpful if anyone got into difficulties when they're older.

Other reasons presented included:

> Just for fun
> I didn't want to do typing
> I wanted to be with my friends
> I chose child care because it's a different subject to before ...

The fact that there are some distinct differences between this and other subjects in the curriculum emerged strongly in the course of discussion with pupils about their expectations of it. Most expected themes like learning about babies and children; food, diet and cooking; making clothes and toys; looking after a home; visiting playgroups and dealing with problems. Comments ranged from the very vague: 'I don't know ... I suppose it'll be about children. I don't know' to:

> I think it will be about coping with the problems that you come across with them. The way they feel and think about things. You know, things they want to do and why they want to do them. Just really how to cope with their problems when they ask for anything. If they get into tantrums and that, learning what to do in that situation.

One or two girls mentioned the things they had heard others say about the course – especially its more sensational aspects: 'Well, when you're pregnant the things that go wrong, miscarriages and things like that. The things that make you miscarry. I think that puts you off.' When asked whether they did not also hear about the things that 'go right', one response was: 'Yes, but you tend to take more notice of the things that go wrong.' though 'Things like that just happen don't they. It's best to know about them.' Another girl, asked what she expected the course to be about, said:

> Well the safety in the home thing and that. My sister took it and she's got a baby now ... she was too young to have a baby really so she missed half the course through the baby. She didn't know that much, but she knew quite a bit.

The bit that she did take was, according to her sister, useful.

A number of the girls talked of the playgroup visits. This was a popular aspect of the course:

> Well, it's different, isn't it, nicer ... you're with them [children] as well. It's sort of different learning about them and you'll be with them, you can learn something real.

> You get to see babies and handicapped children and you get to handle them as well.

> Well my sister did it before and she enjoyed it because she went down to a playgroup just down the road from us and she helped and she made clothes for the children and she did cooking and she enjoyed it, so I thought well I'll take it as well.

> My friend said she didn't like the first part because it was just writing and things like that but the second part was good because you went on trips and got about.

Again the impression given was that the subject was considered to be 'different': 'I spoke to a girl in the 5th year who's doing it at the moment and she says you don't read from books, you learn from actual experience.'

This positive emphasis on the practical aspects of the family and child course and its relevance to 'real' things like children's day-to-day needs, presented a contrast to more negative attitudes towards school in general expressed particularly by some of the lower ability girls: 'You can't do nothing in school. It's boring – you're not allowed to do nothing'; 'It's like being in jail or something.'

Some indication of the way this subject was seen by the girls is also reflected in the following dialogue which occurred in a discussion group whose members had all been allocated to the higher ability teaching set:

> Some of the people skive.
> They just want to doss around.
> Some of them do, not all of them.

and

> If you want to actually get the O-level then you are going to have to work but it's a subject where people can mess about if they don't want to take the O-level.

It is interesting that for some pupils family and child appeared to have been chosen as an additional subject over and above the more 'academic' subjects which they saw themselves requiring for career purposes. These girls expected to experience this subject differently from the others they were taking. For example, one girl, when asked if she wished she could enjoy the other subjects in the way she expected to enjoy family and child, said:

Well, I don't know, I like work I like to be pushed but I like to have a muck about sometimes ... some people can't cope with it. They take the academic subjects and work for them and take this as a rest period. You don't get proper homework do you or anything like that?

Another girl said she regarded it:

as an easy subject – because I don't know what everybody else thinks but I find maths very difficult. I much prefer to do something quite easy and interesting for a relaxing afternoon or morning or whenever we have it. But you can't take that attitude in other subjects because you have to sit down and learn, but this is a subject I'd find easier to learn than maths or something like that.

The general view of the girls was that compared with subjects like maths, English and science, the school considered family and child 'a lower subject, an easier subject to take, and that the lower classes take it, the ones that aren't quite as bright as the top group.' Their own attitudes varied. Some did not agree with this view: 'You don't need to speak proper English, like posh or anything', and 'I do think that family and child care is more important ... because it does help you later on, maybe the other things do but that is more important in a way.'

However, the majority accepted the conventional status hierarchy of subjects, aware of the vocational implications of the relative status of these subjects in the curriculum:

Well, maths and English are most important – you need that for any job you want don't you?

If you're going for a job it's not really what they're asking for. They want the science and the academic subjects. They don't really consider this as one.

Well, if you go into a job, like you wanted to be an accountant and they said 'what O-levels or A-levels have you got?' and then you said family and child care – they wouldn't take much notice of that. But if you went into nursing and said you'd got family and child care they'd take notice of that and probably put you on the children's ward.

Girls' Subjects, Boys' Subjects

At this school the very few boys who took this subject were either in a remedial stream and not expected to take an examination, or they were taking it as a one-year extra O-level in the sixth form. The number of boys involved was very small. We were interested to know why boys did not choose this option. It was obvious that pupils had very definite notions about which subjects were taken by girls as opposed to boys. For example, during a general discussion about options available to them, one of the girls commented: 'They're the boys' ones, the metalwork and the woodwork.'

When it came to discussing boys' attitudes towards the family and child option, one girl said simply: 'It's not for boys, is it?', and when asked why not, said: 'Well I don't know, ask the boys.' We did ask a group of boys who were part of a small mixed group of pupils who had taken the subject as a one-year O-level in the sixth form for their opinions on this issue. The boys, whilst enjoying it, were aware of peer group reactions to their choice:

> It's always been thought of as a girls' subject and it's very risky, so to speak, I mean. I wouldn't have done it if it hadn't been for ... whatever you say you get a lot of ...

> Yes, people sort of laugh. When I was queuing for the exam people said 'what are you doing?' and when I said family and child they laughed.

The second boy went on to say that he would not have done the course if others of his friends had not been doing it as well. A similar theme was expressed by two of the girls in the group. According to one, 'I think boys think it's sissyish or babyish looking after children. They think it's girls' work or women's work.' The other said:

> Well, I think it's that as well really because if a boy said to his friend, 'I'm taking the child care course' I think he'd get a lot of teasing. I think half of it is because of that. I also think that I don't think it really interests them. I've never found a boy that really likes getting hold of his little brothers and sisters. You know, I do think they think it's for the women to do all that.

The way both groups of pupils saw the parental division of labour was, on the whole, very traditional. There was some acknowledgement that boys might in time become fathers and need to know something about bringing up a family, although it seemed to be assumed by both sexes that a man would only be called upon for this if his wife died, went into hospital, or left home for whatever reason. Otherwise he would be occupied outside the home earning the wherewithal to support his wife and family. So why did these boys decide to take this subject as part of their sixth form programme? Unlike the girls, no mention was made of any occupational motive associated with the decision. One boy who had taken science A-levels and already had a place at university commented that the fact that he had taken family and child gave him something to talk about in interviews. In general these boys gave the impression of filling in time, having already gained the more marketable qualifications. In this respect there were some similarities between them and the higher ability girls.

Conclusion

Despite the establishment of option choice systems, the traditional pattern of differential recruitment to subjects according to sex remains, with some courses still being regarded as 'girls' subjects, and in the main attracting only girls. Cookery is one of these subjects, though a few boys do opt for it. Cookery, however, has occupational significance; it leads into a variety of job areas entered by men. By contrast, a subject like family and child gives rise to a range of occupational and training opportunities none of which traditionally appeals to men. Moreover, a major focus of the subject is preparation for the parent role. This reinforces its status as a girls' subject since most pupils (and teachers?) still assume that women, as mothers, bear the major responsibility for care of children and the family. (One of the sixth-form boys we spoke to did, in fact, say that women were 'still the professional childbearers in our society'.)

The differences between girls and boys in the choice of options are clearly closely related to sexual divisions in the home and the labour market. Despite the efforts of the women's movement and some legal reform, women remain disadvantaged in the home and in the workforce (Deem, 1978). While the dynamics of gender relations are different within the family and the labour market, they are nevertheless interrelated. The traditional definition of women within the family, as housewives and mothers with prime responsibility for child-rearing, means that most women, whatever the realities of the situation, are seen as transient or second earners. Thus it is usual for them to be paid less than men. This not only finds its expression in the fact that they continue to receive lower pay for doing essentially similar work to that done by men, but perhaps more importantly in the relatively low rates paid for 'women's work', such as certain types of semi-skilled factory work, a variety of service occupations, like shop work, secretarial work and cleaning, and also the professions of nursing, social work and teaching where women fail to climb organizational ladders (DES, 1982). There is also widespread use of married women in part-time work; 40 per cent of women now work part-time (Breugal, 1979). This may fit domestic responsibilities, but wages are low, insurance costs and fringe benefits can be minimized and employment can be expanded or contracted with little resistance. The most insecure and worst paid section of the female labour force consists of the home workers where women who are usually paid a pittance for piece-work simultaneously bear triple responsibilities as worker, housewife and mother.

Conversely, women's disadvantaged position within the labour force may encourage them to seek personal satisfaction and social recognition within their roles as housewife and mother (Segal, 1983). In the most extreme case it has been argued recently that unemployed young women may seek recognition and some meaning to their lives by becoming pregnant and raising a child on their own.

It can be argued that to effect any real progress towards making opportunities for boys and girls equal, major changes in curriculum design would be required. For example, in Sweden's new comprehensive curriculum the traditional sex role pattern is being attacked in a deliberate way: home management, typing and technology are to be compulsory for both boys and girls at junior and senior level. Even so, it is arguable that without substantial changes affecting the socio-economic basis of the sexual division of labour such efforts on the part of schools are unlikely to achieve very much. As one teacher of family and child said on the issue of option choice:

> I think on the whole boys are not going to be going in for careers where they see child care as relevant as a subject. Until you get to a point where child care or education for parenthood is seen as something that is relevant to everybody then you're never going to get everybody educated in it.

Given this, ironically, the introduction of a subject intended to improve familial relations within a progressive and liberal option choice system may actually have the consequence of reinforcing traditional gender stereotypes.

References

BALL, S. (1981) *Beachside Comprehensive*, Cambridge, Cambridge University Press.
BARDELL, G. (1982) *Options for the Fourth*, London, Schools Council.
BENN, C. and SIMON, B. (1972) *Halfway There*, Maidenhead, McGraw Hill.
BOWLBY, J. (1951) *Maternal Care and Mental Health*, Geneva World Health Organization.
BOWLBY, J. (1953) *Child Care and the Growth of Love*, London, Pelican.
BREUGAL, I. (1979) 'Women as a reserve army of labour', in *Feminist Review* No. 3, London.
COX, M.H. (1976) *The Teaching of Child Development in Secondary Schools: A Preliminary Study*, unpublished master's thesis, University of Nottingham.
DEEM, R. (1978) *Women and Schooling*, London, Routledge and Kegan Paul.
DES (1975) *Curricular Differences for Boys and Girls*, Education Survey 21, London, HMSO.
DES (1977) *Education in Schools: A Consultative Document*, Cmnd. 6869, London, HMSO.
DES (1979) *Aspects of Secondary Education in England: A Survey by HM Inspectors of Schools*, London, HMSO.
DES (1982) The Secondary School Staffing Survey: Data on teachers' characteristics and deployment and on average class sizes in England and Wales, in *Statistical Bulletin* 5/82, March.
DHSS (1974) *The Family in Society: Dimensions of Parenthood*, London, HMSO.
DHSS (1974) *The Family in Society: Preparation for Parenthood*, London, HMSO.
DHSS (1977) *Prevention and Health: Reducing the Risk; Safer Pregnancy and Childbirth*, London, HMSO.
DHSS (1978) *Violence to Children: A Response to the First Report from the Select Committee on Violence in the Family* (Session 1976–77), Cmnd. 7123, London, HMSO.

PILLING, D. and KELLMER PRINGLE, M. (1978) *Controversial Issues in Child Development*, London, Paul Elek.
SCOTT, M. (1980) 'Teach her a lesson – the sexist curriculum in patriarchal education', in SPENDER, D. and SARAH. E. (Ed.) *Learning to Lose*, London, The Womens Press.
SEGAL, L. (1983) 'A question of choice,' in *Marxism Today*, Vol. 26, No. 1, January, London.
WHITFIELD, R.C. (1980) *Education for Family Life: Some New Policies for Child Care*, London, Hodder and Stoughton.
WOODS, P. (1979) *The Divided School*, London, Routledge and Kegan Paul.

8 Gender and the Sciences: Pupils' Gender-Based Conceptions of School Subjects

Lynda Measor

One of the most influential sets of factors which has an impact upon the curriculum is that of gender. Girls perceive and react to the curriculum differently from boys. In this chapter I shall document some of these gender-based differences in attitude and reaction in the physical and domestic science areas of the curriculum, and attempt to trace out some of their consequences. Data were drawn from interviews with and observations of first-year pupils at a large, urban comprehensive school during 1979 and 1980.

Girls and Physical Science: Current Explanations

For once, we know more about the girls, since girls' reactions to natural science have been the subject of official concern and HMI reports. The basic fact that girls do less well in science than boys and that fewer girls take the subject when the time comes for option choosing is now well known. Inevitably, as a result fewer girls get examination passes in the physical sciences. As HMI have recorded:

> Although the physical sciences and biology are normally available to both boys and girls at school, at the upper secondary level, one third of girls do no science at all, and over half do no physical science beyond the third year. (HMI, 1980, p. 1)[1]

There are also some important differences *within* the general science area: girls take biology more than chemistry, and chemistry more than physics. Thus, according to DES figures:

> 50 per cent of boys did physics in the 4th and 5th year while only 12 per cent of girls did. Conversely nearly half of all girls in the 4th and 5th years study biology while 28 per cent of all boys take this subject. (DES, 1975, p. 2)

In recent years, the issue has attracted a considerable amount of research attention (summarized in Kelly, 1981). At first, explanations concentrated on 'within school' factors. It was suggested that the problem lay in the poor provision of equipment and inadequate staffing of girls' schools. Renee Short, for example, argued in the House of Commons in 1955 that all would be well

171

when mixed schools replaced the single sex ones (Kelly, 1981 p. 99). Ironically, however, once mixed schools became widespread[2] it became clear that:

> Girls are more likely to choose a science in a single sex school than they are in a mixed school, although in a mixed school a higher percentage of pupils may be offered these subjects. (DES, 1975 p. 12)

The DES survey looked at other ways schools failed to provide equal opportunities for boys and girls and speculated upon their effects on girls' performance in science. Girls, it was argued, were often denied the opportunity of taking craft subjects, where the skills they learned could feed usefully into science. In addition to such curricular influences, teachers' attitudes, expectations and reactions were also said to have helped turn girls off science. Moreover, these expectations could well be reflected in the differential treatment given to boys and girls in science lessons (Galton, 1981). Lastly, given that the majority of science teachers, and especially senior teachers, are male, girls are often not provided with role models of scientifically competent females (Blackstone, 1976; Sharpe, 1976).

A second set of explanations involved ideas of differential abilities between boys and girls. J.A. Gray, for instance, argued that such sex differences have an inherent biological basis which cannot and should not be tampered with (Kelly, 1981, p. 43). Social learning theorists like Mischel (1966) and Bandura (1971) have suggested that early socialization, rather than biological inheritance, is responsible for these differences in ability. Early socialization lays down rules about and provides role models for sex appropriate behaviour and actions (Kelly, 1981; Saraga and Griffiths, 1981).

Recent research, including Kelly's own, confirms this view that achievement in science is an aspect of sex role learning. 'The characteristically low achievement of girls in science', she argues, 'is an aspect of the feminine sex role – that is learned behaviour which is appropriate for females in our society' (Kelly, 1981, p. 73). Kelly takes what she calls a 'cognitive approach' to sex role learning which 'conceives of the child as an active participant in structuring his or her experience and formulating sex role concepts' (Kelly, 1981, p. 74). Society is seen as presenting 'an image of feminine and masculine to the child' and the child 'puts together a cluster of the attributes that they label male or female, and they try to copy the appropriate cluster.' This approach moves away from the social learning theories which see society as crudely imposing sex role stereotypes upon the individual. The child is regarded as essentially self-socializing, first developing categories and then fitting him or herself into these categories. This is important for science, the argument runs, because science, or at least physics and chemistry, is conventionally seen as masculine (Haste, 1981).

As an HMI report noted, pupils saw science as 'leading to qualifications relevant to traditional male oriented occupations' (HMI, 1980, p. 9). It is not just that science is male dominated, but that in some way it is seen as 'masculine'. Consequently girls tend to reject physical science as part of their desire to become and be seen as 'feminine'. Science, then, like certain other areas of the school curriculum, has become invested with gender characteristics to which pupils react. These pupil perceptions are critical at puberty and in early adolescence, when individuals are consumed with a concern to establish themselves as feminine or masculine. As Kelly (1981) puts it:

> Each sex, when educated with the other, is at puberty almost driven by developmental changes to use subject preference and where possible subject choice as a means of ascribing its sex role. (p. 102)

If this argument is correct, the early adolescent years are crucial in the process of girls' disaffection from science, contrary to some assertions of HMI (1980, p. 22) that 'combined science courses ... with 11–13 year old pupils were generally successful in arousing the interest of the majority of pupils, both boys and girls.'

It seems that early adolescence is precisely the age and stage when girls are most likely to switch off from science, for it is during these years that sex role differentiation is most intense.

Science as a Resource in the Negotiation of Gender Identities

The research project from which this paper derives dealt specifically with the years 11–13, and involved an eighteen-month period of observation of pupils at 11+ to the end of their first secondary school year. In the area in which the research was carried out the age of transfer is 12+, so pupils were studied at both middle and upper school. The intensive character of the research allowed these issues and reactions to be documented in far greater depth than was possible for the HMI team. The science course the pupils followed was the integrated Nuffield science scheme, where all the sciences are combined. Its approach is a problem-solving one, with an emphasis on practical and experimental work.

Even while they were at middle school pupils showed a clear gender difference in reactions to the idea of doing science at the new school. They already knew something of the science curriculum at the upper school, through the latter's induction scheme for its new pupils. They had visited the school several times, and been shown around the remarkably well equipped labs where pupils were working. In addition, the science department had put on a display of its wares and the tricks of its trade in the school's lecture theatre, which was suitably darkened for the occasion, thus heightening the atmosphere. There were tug-of-war experiments which involved a vacuum cup and two teams of excited middle school children pulling each other's jerseys out of shape. Hamsters, rabbits and gerbils were produced, together with two goats, one of which ate the head of department's tie. The animals belonged to the school, and it was made clear that they were looked after entirely by the pupils. There were biological experiments which involved electric wiring of pupils, and rapid exercise which made light and heat meters react. Finally, the chemists put on a pyrotechnic display of flashes, sparks and explosions caused by chemicals, static electricity and batteries.

Most children thought the display, which closely resembled a successful Christmas pantomime, had been wonderful; though some of the girls had been rather afraid. The boys gave excited reports of the flashes and bangs.

> *Keith:* Gary put his hand up to spark off a flame with his finger with the help of a Van der Graph machine – he nearly burnt his finger off!
>
> *Pete:* I really liked that science lesson, we all stood up to see what happened.
>
> *Phillip:* Those experiments were great.
>
> *R.:* Which ones did you like best?
>
> *Phillip:* The hydrogen one or was it helium. He lit it in Bruce's hand. Great!

Bruce, the boy actually involved in the experiment, repeated with mingled pride and humour: 'As for that Chemistry man, he nearly blew my hand off on Monday.'

Such reactions to the experiments can be contrasted with those of the girls. As one of them remarked, 'I don't like fire, and my friend Anne, she don't like fire neither.' The girls displayed anxiety about their ability to cope with the new science subjects, which they saw as difficult. In the words of one girl, Sue, 'I am worried about their way of doing physics, and I am no good at it, the hard part.'

The boys, by contrast, were looking forward to the chance of working with the new and sophisticated equipment they had seen.

> *Keith:* Well, there is more of a chance to learn there, because in this school they haven't got the proper apparatus and that. Like in science, we have been told about these experiments, but we haven't been able to do them, there they have got science labs and everything.

As we might expect, given the statistics that more girls choose to do biology than boys, their response to this subject was different. Far from being fearful, the girls reacted very positively to the animals that had been brought in during the science department's 'show'. There had been appropriate 'Ooohs' and 'Aaahs', especially to the baby chicks, and the girls commented enthusiastically about the prospect of looking after those animals.

However, there was another aspect to their reactions to biology lessons which also demands attention. At middle school the girls had heard a story that in the secondary school science lessons they were required to dissect a rat later in the year. The responses of the boys and the girls to this prospect were very different. The boys said, 'Yes that's really good', and by and large gloried in the gory nature of the experiment, discussing eye-balls and lungs and other anatomical parts of childhood grotesquerie. The girls reacted differently, and judged it 'not very nice'. In a more detailed analysis of this data elsewhere we have already suggested that this differential response was an important element of sex role learning, and that it implied a gender code of behaviour (Measor and Woods, 1982). Clearly at this point in their anticipatory socialization, pupils displayed a gender-based difference in attitude.

These reactions and responses were maintained during the first term at secondary school, when the pupils found themselves in a Nuffield science scheme which involved them in doing experimental work each week. The girls did not enjoy or find themselves drawn to the activity. It is important to understand what their objections were. The girls protested about the smells that were produced in their science lessons. One project had involved making and mixing substances; the substances were then tested, and the testing included smelling them. Some of the substances had been particularly nasty. Jenny said, 'I felt sick', and insisted she really could not finish the work. Sally reported that the project had given her a headache; this was sufficiently bad for her to have to miss the disco that evening, which from her point of view was serious indeed! Others found the activities generally unappealing and even abhorrent.

> *Valerie:* In science we had that thermometer thing, when we had to stick it in our mouths.... That was horrible, I was sick that night.... I think I stuck it down me froat too far. It was 'orrible'.

The other dominant reported reaction was fear. The girls admitted that they felt some fear when confronted with the range of equipment and dangerous chemicals. Acids were especially threatening.

> *R.:* Do you find science difficult?
>
> *Clair:* Yes, because you have got all these acids, and you have got to remember which ones are harmful, and what they do to you. It is quite hard to do things, because I am scared of fire, and when I put on the bunsen burners I am really scared of them. I always think I am going to go up on fire.

This fear of fire and of the bunsen burners which had arisen in response to the induction scheme was a recurrent theme.

> *Amy:* I think Ros is scared of the Bunsen burner.
>
> *Rebecca:* She is, when I had her for a partner, I did everything, she was too scared to do anything.

There was one particular experiment where pupils had to heat, melt and manipulate glass rods. Many pupils did receive minor burns and the teacher cheerfully administered antiseptic cream, and encouraged them to continue. The girls remembered this with a particular sense of objection.

> *Sally:* I didn't like it when we had to burn down that glass.
>
> *Amy:* No I didn't like that, everyone burned themselves that day.

The girls contrasted their attitudes with those of the boys:

> *Sally:* The boys are a bit braver than girls.
>
> *Amy:* Yes, they will do anything, whereas girls won't all the time. I am not scared of the Bunsen burner ... but ... sometimes when we have to pick the Bunsen burner up, when it is alight, I get a bit ... once, we had to pick it up, and I nearly burned myself.

One day the experiment involved dropping water onto an alkali pellet, which then hissed and burned, and let off an unpleasant gas. Before they began the experiment the teacher explained in graphic detail the dangers of dealing carelessly with alkali, and cautioned care. The girls then stood at arms length, clearly displaying their fear. Again, in discussing this, the girls contrasted their own attitudes with those of the boys:

> *Sally:* With the boys it's 'You just do this'.
>
> *Rebecca:* When we boil water, I mean to say it is going to overflow, so I just get scared sometimes I am going to burn myself.

Another source of objection from the girls was that they got very dirty in these lessons. In one experiment pupils had to drop carbon into a solvent and it produced a black substance which got all over their hands. Again this led to protests:

> *Sally:* It made us all really dirty.

The others agreed with her, with expressions of real disgust on their faces.

> *Ros:* I was scared it was going to burn right through my fingers, like some awful acid or something.

Another afternoon the pupils were working with eye droppers and Indian ink. Ros spilt some on her hand. She inspected it anxiously complaining:

> *Ros:* Oh no, look what I've done.
>
> *Teacher:* That'll come off in a few days.

Ros was not in the least appeased, and explained to Amy, 'Tonight I have to serve sweets at this little bazaar my mum is running. This won't look very good to people will it?'

The girls also stated that they felt squeamish and disgusted by some of the things they saw in science lessons. The teacher showed the class a brain, preserved in a jar of formaldehyde. It was an example of teaching strategies which urge the teacher to bring concrete examples of lesson material into class. The girls displayed a really strong reaction to the brain, demonstrating once more their squeamish sense of what is 'not nice', though their reaction did reduce somewhat when it was explained that the brain was not from a human being.

The rat, which had a starring role in the stories told at middle school, was to make its appearance in the middle of the summer term. The myth had some of the details wrong, for it was a teacher who carefully did the dissection, not the pupils. Nevertheless, the gender messages and implications of the event were present. The girls displayed a squeamish sense of disgust and indignation at being asked to witness such impropriety:

> *Janet:* Just cutting up an egg, never mind a rat made me feel ill, because it is a cell, and I never knew that, and you see all the nucleus and the membrane, it's revolting. I haven't eaten an egg since.

Such activities are not only disgusting and objectionable to girls, they are labelled as specifically masculine, as things for men. Girls signal their differences:

> *Jane:* I think science is a boys subject, most of the science teachers are male aren't they. I think the reason why they are male teachers is because of cutting up rats. I don't think a woman could face that.

Indeed, science activities could serve as a resource in a positive way – to signal things girls did approve of doing and being. On one occasion the class had to look at the micro-organisms within pond water, under a microscope. Ros declared herself deeply revolted by them all, and by their wriggling movements. However, for other girls this experiment seemed to provoke more interest than many they had done, and the contrast is significant. Sylvia, for example, kept only one drop of water on her slide, and she declined to change it, although the instructions were to examine the whole range of creatures. Her slide had a particularly large and interesting being on it, which she called 'The Blodge'. Sylvia talked to her 'Blodge' and watched him attentively, and was very reluctant to return him to the common pool of water. She put him back very carefully, allowing all the drops to leave her slide to ensure he made it back safely.

Sylvia's reaction to this experiment, which involved looking after a creature, needs to be contrasted with the girls' reaction to dissecting and examining the rat. They displayed very different attitudes towards the two activities. One, the nurturing caring activity, is acceptable, the other, the clinical, 'cutting up' activity, is not appropriate. Again, some clear gender messages are being communicated about activities and attitudes that proper girls have and do.

In addition to this, girls commented on their differences in handling and controlling some of the scientific equipment, which was a problem they had anticipated. Ros, for example, could not cope with the microscope. She declared she found it impossible, repeatedly insisting, 'I don't understand this, I just don't.' She spent the entire lesson floating around the room, seeking aid and assistance; and incidentally ensuring that everyone knew she could not cope with this piece of equipment.

These data connect with the HMI view that 'girls had difficulties dealing with machinery, they were hesitant about experiments and practical work' (1980, p. 16). Yet it is important to point out that such hesitancy was not evident in all subjects. Domestic science provides an illuminating point of contrast. In needlework, it was Ros, despite her incompetence with microscopes, who was one of the first pupils to grasp the workings of the double needle electric sewing machine. She was in fact asked for help by others in the class, which is important, for it meant that everyone knew she was competent with this kind of a machine. Nor did any of the other girls seem to experience any great fear or difficulty in dealing with this machine. Similarly, there was no evidence of the fear of 'fire' and the bunsen burners that characterized physical science lessons when it came to lighting the gas in cookery lessons, or dealing with hot ovens and sizzling frying pans in domestic science lessons. It appears that girls only have difficulty with *some* machinery and are only hesitant about *some* practical work. The difficulties and hesitancies seem to be pronounced only in curricular areas which are perceived as masculine.

There was another point of objection too, which is important if we are to gain an accurate picture of the girls' perspective. The pupils had been told very firmly that they must wear safety goggles during the experiments they did. This rule had been heavily impressed upon them during their first weeks in secondary school. The defining characteristic of pupil response during this phase of what Stephen Ball has called 'initial encounters' (Ball, 1980) was a high level of conformity. Yet, despite the fact that this rule was insisted upon, some of the girls simply refused to wear the spectacles. The offending objects were large, plastic, unisize and unisex. One group of girls made an enormous fuss about wearing the spectacles, and made a range of silly jokes on the subject. One girl, Amy, stated that 'they really don't suit me', and decided she would not wear them; she was followed in this rebellion by a number of her friends. The context of this action should be emphasized. The girls were disobeying a very firm and strongly presented instruction given to them by their teacher, who happened to be the headmaster. The girls did this in the second week at their new school, in a situation where circumspect conformity to the demands of the teacher was the norm. The same behaviour was repeated the following week.

> *Rebecca:* I hate wearing these glasses they give me a headache, I had a headache until 4 o'clock yesterday.
>
> *Rosemary:* Yes it really does give you a headache.

The dislike of wearing the goggles emerged as a central element in Amy's definition of the subject. 'I don't like science, 'cos you have to tie your hair back and wear goggles.' Appearance is, of course, a central issue in the construction of a properly feminine image.

These views of natural science as essentially masculine, because of its awesome difficulty, its high technological complexity, its deafening noise, noisome smells and dirt, were central not only to the girls' perceptions of the subject, but to the boys' perceptions as well, as the following extract illustrates:

R.: Do you think girls work as hard as boys at school?

Bill: Well at what subjects?

R.: Any.

Bill: Well, it depends on the subject. I mean they're gonna work hard at something like needlework aren't they?

R.: Are they?

Bill: Well, they're gonna like it better than something like cutting rats up.

Ian: Boys know more about science than any of the girls in our class.

R.: Do they?

Ian: Girls are scared they might get burned or something. You know ... don't wanna get their hands dirty and things like that.

Mark: Yes girls have got better hands than boys ain't they.

The girls, then, had a strong reaction to their science lessons. They had a clear perspective that it involved things that they did not feel it was appropriate, or pleasant, or inviting to do. And the 'appropriateness' of that attitude was also recognized by the boys. Kelly's notion of a cluster of attributes that are conventionally labelled masculine or feminine becomes relevant in this context. The girls signalled their objection to the dirt and fumes and smells of science, and also to being asked to look less attractive. They displayed themselves as squeamish, frightened and weak, by their objections to science, and somewhat incompetent as well, especially in relation to certain kinds of complex machinery and technology. The activities in science contravened conventional views of what 'proper' girls should do, and therefore the girls resisted doing them. The pupils were reading sex related characteristics into activities and things, and responding to them as a result. This response goes to make their sex-based identity clear to those around them. My suggestion is that the girls actively used aspects of the school to construct their identity, in this case their feminine identity. They are not simply responding passively to school in terms of gender stereotypes. Science lessons provided an arena for the acting out of feminine susceptibilities in a public setting. They were a backdrop against which signals could be displayed about feminine identity.

This argument is strengthened by data gathered from interviews with the girls about possible careers or jobs. In these interviews the girls rejected any jobs connected with science since these were seen as essentially unfeminine.

> *R.:* Why do you think there aren't many girl scientists?
>
> *Ruth:* Just because they don't sort of go in for that job, because, say you are doing acid and that, they don't because they have got very delicate skin and that.
>
> *R.:* There aren't many girls in engineering either.
>
> *Jacqui:* No, because you sort of get all your hands greasy and that.
>
> *Ruth:* And lifting things a lot, and a noisy background.
>
> *Jacqui:* I want to be a secretary.
>
> *Ruth:* Yes or a telephonist.

The girls contrasted their own preferred identity, that of secretary or telephonist, with the noisy, dusty, dangerous, heavy, male jobs. Such contrasts, and the public signalling of which direction they personally had chosen, made clear statements about sex role identity.

The girls did have one example of a woman who had gone into an occupation based on science, since one of their own science teachers was a woman. But, as Kelly (1981, p. 34) has commented, women science teachers may not be an acceptable or appropriate role model for female pupils, and this certainly was the case here. Mrs Lines was unpopular with the girls. She was strongly disapproved of. The image of a woman who had gone into science, it seemed, was poor.

> *Amy:* Mrs Lines – she's too posh.
>
> *Ros:* Did you know, she's a judo expert Mrs Lines.
>
> *Rebecca:* Oh God, I didn't know that.
>
> *Ros:* That's why she must wear trousers, isn't it.
>
> *Amy:* Yes she's horrible.

There are class subjectivities in this perception, but additionally it was Mrs Lines' image of femininity which is commented upon. Her appearance was wrong, she wore 'trousers' not 'jeans' or even more acceptable 'straights'; and her activities, in particular 'judo', brought an exclamation of disapprobation since they were not regarded as proper feminine ones. This connects with Ebutt's (1974, p. 20) findings on the picture girls had of women scientists: 'Lots of thick glasses, flat shoes, big feet, judo types with muscular calves and sensible clothes.' It is the flat chested, flat heeled syndrome.

The girls' comments are an interesting example of the way a rationale is developed to cover a problem or a gap in the girls' view of the world. Science is seen as not feminine, not appropriate to women, not something women do. Yet there is a woman, Mrs Lines, who does it. A rationale is available to cover the problem: this woman cannot herself be very feminine, she is not a 'proper woman', after all she wears trousers and learns judo. There is no problem coming up with this rationale; it is an easily found explanation.

These data connect with other material on pupils, where the same mechanism was at work. The picture so far has suggested that all the girls disliked science. In fact, there were two important exceptions, cases which provide further insights. The two girls who admitted liking science were seen by the others in their class as being very conformist. They were described as 'goody-goodies'. The image and identity of these girls has been described in more detail elsewhere (Measor and Woods, forthcoming), but it can be stated that they were seen and defined as less feminine than the other girls. This recalls Willis' (1977) argument, that conformist pupils are often seen as less sexual, as having a less clear gender identity. The two girls were clearly regarded as less attractive: 'she wouldn't go out with a boy' and 'no one would go out with her'. The boys agreed with the view: 'Me – go out with HER!' (pronounced incredulously). The two girls involved found themselves friendless and isolated in their class. The other negative case was a boy, Geoffrey, who admitted that he did not much like science, and that he too was afraid of fire and the bunsen burners. He was, in turn, taunted about his sexuality, criticized for not being masculine enough. His diffident behaviour in science went together with other problems – he couldn't finish the cross-country run, was completely unable to fight and so on. A conformist to the extreme at school, he was liable to tell a teacher if he heard of deviant infringements on the part of other pupils. All of which earned him the title of 'poofter'; he was rewarded with a fairly miserable existence.

Bearing in mind both the general pattern and the significant exceptions, it seems that sex role learning plays a significant role in forming pupils' attitudes to science. Sex role differentiation it appears is centrally important in switching girls off physical science. If the latter's activities and qualities are seen as inappropriate for girls, then by refusing and rejecting them the girls have a useful device for signalling their own gender identity. The active nature of this process needs to be emphasized: girls come to evolve their own perspective on the 'cluster of attributes' they label as feminine, and they select and use aspects of the school context to throw their own feminine identity into clear relief. Science lessons are far from the only resource in this respect. Other areas of the curriculum, such as sport, are used for much the same purpose. But, given its association with educational and job opportunities, science is perhaps of particular concern.

In emphasizing the fact that girls take an active part in sex role differentiation, in the construction of a feminine identity, I would not want to imply that other pressures and constraints are unimportant. Much of the choice process is subject to strong social pressures. The girls are, after all, adopting a traditional and non-innovative set of attributes as feminine. Images of women and the social roles of women are currently in flux, but there is very little sign that newer ideas have permeated the lives of these girls, at least at this stage in their development.

Group processes also are involved, seeming to amplify the effects. As a girl rejects science, she puts pressure on others to do the same, to show that they too are feminine. Science is a useful resource for signalling identity, for signalling femininity, but it is simultaneously a constraint. Given peer group pressures, it is not possible to like physical science *and* be feminine; that constraint affects girls' academic careers and career opportunities. Science lessons are a fruitful resource, but ultimately they give girls an unhappy choice between expressing their sexual identity and making full use of their intellectual potential. There is an interesting body of research (Spender, 1981; Sharpe, 1976) which suggests that to succeed academically in any subject is to run the risk of being labelled unfeminine. In Spender's phrase, girls 'learn to lose'. Our research supports that suggestion, but the data on science enable us to make a further point. The curriculum is not viewed uniformly; different areas of it have different gender implications. Failing at science, we would suggest, is even more crucial than failing anywhere else. Girls might well work quite hard in needlework, maybe even in English, but physical science is a kind of boundary, around which no negotiation is possible, though biological science has partially escaped this labelling process, presumably because it is seen as nurturant and acceptable for girls (Kelly, 1981, p. 24).

Boys and Domestic Science

A number of the issues concerning girls and science can be usefully contrasted with boys' reactions when they were made to do something they did not regard as appropriately masculine. The argument is that sex role learning affects girls' attitudes to a particular area of the curriculum. It ought then to be possible to see boys reacting to the curriculum on gender grounds as well. For this reason, I selected the conventionally 'feminine' subject of domestic science for close scrutiny, a subject which was taught at the secondary school to all first-year pupils in mixed sex groups.

Even before the transfer to upper school, the boys had negative reactions to the idea of doing domestic science. They learned of their obligation to take the subject on their induction visit.

> A group of middle school pupils was taken into the needlework room. The boys eyed their surroundings uneasily and sneered at the dolls and furry toys on the display boards. The teacher explained the kinds of projects they would be doing at the school. The boys looked uninterested. The teacher asked for suggestions of objects the pupils would like to make. The suggestions all came from the girls. No boy put up his hand. (Field notes, June 1979)

Later the boys commented on the domestic science area of the curriculum, and elaborated their views in an interview:

R.: What do you think about doing Needlework and Cookery?

Phillip: Not a lot.

Keith: It's cissy.

David: Boys don't do Needlework.

Ian: Girls have got better hands.

David: It's not the sort of thing boys do is it?

Keith: I don't really like Needlework as much as other things like cutting up rats.

It is interesting that Keith chose the notorious and symbolic rat for his example of a 'properly' masculine phenomenon. The boys made clear prescriptive statements about domestic science; it was totally unacceptable to them. When boys were faced with activities that went against their sense of masculine convention they objected as strongly as the girls did to physical science, thereby displaying elements of their gender identity.

It is important to note, however, that cookery did not raise the same level of objections as needlework:

Keith: I don't mind cookery, I can cook.

Phillip: Oh cookery will be a laugh.

David: Loads of blokes are chefs.

R.: Loads of men are tailors too.

David: Yes ... but....

Nevertheless, it is significant that boys regarded cookery as a non-serious area of the curriculum; it was 'a laugh', unlike maths, for example, which was 'important, you need it for a job don't you?' It is not clear why there should be a gap in the way sewing and cooking are viewed in gender terms. The rationale the pupils used had something to do with adult occupations, and the fact that adult men made a living from the activity of cooking made it a not altogether inappropriate activity for them. A rationale of this kind seems to modify the 'intrinsic' quality of femininity in the activity.

It is additionally instructive to look in some detail at the ways the boys acted out their negative reactions to the subject area, and to compare these with the girls' reactions to science. There is an interesting body of research which suggests that the kind of resistance that girls employ in schools is different from that of boys (Llewellyn, 1980; Fuller, 1980). This research emphasizes the largely passive quality of the girls' strategies. The data in this study certainly support that conclusion, and perhaps point the way to some understanding of why that should be so. Most of the girls' resistance can perhaps best be termed 'work avoidance' strategies. Girls could quietly daydream and chat a lesson away, and in no way meet 'trouble' as a result; their resistance remained invisible to the teacher. The boys' tactics were more disruptive:

> One science lesson Valerie sat quietly drawing a very elaborate pattern, which she then carefully coloured in. Her 'front' of absorbed activity which also rendered her quiet enabled her to avoid any discipline message. (Field notes, February 1980)

Girls would be slightly late for science lessons, and they would try to edge a little time off the end of them, packing up their things early. They would wander around the room and chat to people. If challenged, they could claim that they were looking for equipment and again avoid trouble. Often a teacher would ask the rest of the class to help them in their search. In a quiet way, they tried to make time and space for their own interests within a lesson.

Girls could avoid answering questions, and keep out of class discussions if asked a question directly. They displayed a quality of shy quietness during verbal exchanges in class, especially in interactions between female pupils and male teachers. Girls could answer questions so quietly that they could barely be heard. On such occasions the teacher would usually sigh and pass on. The girls had answered after all. They had not been resistant and deviant, nor refused to meet a teacher's demand. They had only been shy and demure, and there is, after all, little objection to girls showing these qualities.[3] Girls repeatedly engaged in acts that were known to be deviant, albeit subtly and surreptitiously:

Pamela: We just suck polos in science lessons.

Sheila: We do, or the end of our pens – we all suck pens on our table, and don't take no notice.

Often the girls attempted to assert the priority of their informal concerns within the science lessons, chatting about clothes and shoes, for example. They would sit next to the windows so that they had a good view of the rest of the school; they could discuss the attractiveness of the older boys and the clothes of the older girls. Sometimes the girls would 'mess about' a bit, with Amy putting Tipp-Ex on Ros' nose and Rebecca tickling Valerie, for example. But these more overt forms of deviance never amounted to head-on disruptive confrontation as in the case of the boys.

To some extent the boys used similar tactics in domestic science. They avoided work and procrastinated on projects, so that these were never finished. One boy, Pete, an 'ace deviant' was able to boast, 'No, I ain't finished nothing all year, and I'm not bringing in my money to pay for it. I'm not robbing my mum of 75p for that rubbish.' Boys made time and space for themselves in the lessons, arriving late and attempting to pack up their things early. They would leave their work unattended, while discussing projects more dear to their heart. Ray and Matthew, for example, pored over racing tips for the Derby all one afternoon.

In addition to these tactics, the boys employed a further set, which were significantly more disruptive. They engaged in a lot of 'messing around', particularly in cookery which provided golden opportunities. There were ovens to turn off and on at inappropriate times, raisins to steal, cake mixture to put up other people's noses and in their hair, eggs to drop on the floor and so on. Needlework, too, had a range of equipment that could be put to good use. You could stick pins into each other, threaten to cut off ties, and worse, with the scissors, push over the ironing boards and throw material and kapok around the room.

In some cases the boys went further still, and made a series of challenges to the authority of the teacher. They asked silly questions to divert the paced progress of the lesson, they made jokes and engaged in repartee to create diversions. Such acts brought status to the perpetrator, especially if the joke had sexual connotations:

[Miss Blanche was attempting to teach macrame to a group of boys.]

T.: Make a knot in the end of that string.

Sean: How do you get knotted Miss?

[Sustained laughter from the rest of the class resulted in disruption.]

Sometimes the boys challenged their teacher directly, and more than once questioned, 'What do we 'ave to do this stuff for Miss?' All in all, this added up to a real problem for the teachers of these domestic science subjects. One probationary teacher of needlework freely admitted she found it difficult to control the boys and resented her training course for its neglect of the issue. The college course had made no suggestions for projects or curriculum material for boys. Two of the women who taught domestic science eventually refused the researcher permission to attend their classes, since discipline was proving so difficult for them, and they saw the researcher's presence as only making it harder. It is interesting that they were the only teachers in the school who did refuse entry to the researcher, so severe were their discipline problems.

In the case of both boys and girls, then, deviance is spread unevenly across the curriculum. While there are clearly factors which have a bearing on where the deviance is sited, the data discussed here strongly indicated that one of the most important of these influences is gender and gender codes. That is to say, both boys and girls used areas of the curriculum as a resource to signal their sexual identities.

This signalling was emphasized further by the differing styles and types of deviance that boys and girls respectively employed. The boys' strategies were more disruptive than those of the girls, being directed at the 'public arena' of the classroom, at the centre stage, to divert and control the flow and direction of the lesson. The girls, meanwhile, employed more passive forms of deviance, withdrawing unostentatiously from the lesson rather than challenging it publicly.

Lynn Davies (1979) has suggested that girls see themselves as quite as deviant as boys. This may well be true, but their deviance takes different forms. In eighteen months' research, only two examples of girls engaging in the public style of resistance were recorded. On both occasions the challenges met with strong sanctions, both from the teachers and from other pupils. The two girls involved were not popular and were labelled by other pupils as 'big mouths'.[4]

It seems, then, that certain classroom strategies are designated as male, and the girls avoid them. There are peer group pressures at work; it seems that socialization is not only or even mainly carried out by adults. This is only part of the explanation of the girls' passivity. For the presentation of a passive front was, paradoxically, an *active* statement in the construction of a properly feminine identity. Loud challenges to the teacher, public disruptions and jokes intended for a class-wide audience seemed to be exclusively a male preserve. So were the noisier forms of messing around. By their very nature they signified masculinity to those involved. Pupils could use their hostility to one of the science subjects – 'natural' or 'domestic' – to signal an interest in things masculine or feminine. At the same time pupils used strategies that were felt to be appropriate to their sex. This represented a strong, doubly loaded message about sex role differentiation and gender identity.

Teachers and the Sciences

Of course, I would not want to suggest that gender differentiation in schools is simply a pupil initiated phenomenon. Teachers no doubt also influence pupils, through their attitudes, expectations and interactions. In a sense they finish off and reinforce the messages that pupils have already learned through primary socialization. In our research there were examples of sex stereotyped messages, and teachers did sometimes communicate to the girls that they were less welcome, less interesting or less likely to do well in some subjects.

There were some clear examples of bias. The headmaster would welcome his class with, 'Come in my merry *men*.' One teacher, the head of the science department, always stood directly in front of the boys and talked to them almost exclusively. The class was divided on sex segregated lines, the girls occupying one half of the room, the boys the other. Pupils had themselves moved into this pattern early in their first term at the secondary school. This teacher would sometimes return to the desk in the centre of the room, but then rapidly go back to the boys' side. He gave out books to the boys first, and the whole direction of his talk and his eye contact was with the boys. The girls resented this kind of treatment.

Vivien: He always picks on the boys to do things.

Tina: He doesn't think the girls are capable.

The headmaster, who taught first-year science, found a need to issue a series of discipline messages to the girls. These specifically emphasized their gender.

> I don't want to hear anyone talking while I am – Girls!

> Girls, girls, come on, clear up over there, don't leave it for someone else to do. Don't sit around talking.

> Good Grief, get your books open. You're a family of fuss pots you girls.

On one occasion, when the girls were having difficulty with an experiment, his attitude was less than supportive: 'We seem to be dividing into two groups, those who can do it – and the girls.' This was to recur, as in his sarcastic remark, 'We've got the women's lib thing going on here, women saying we're dozy, we're female, help us.' The head was also willing to make jokes which improved his chances of a 'matey' relationship with 'the lads', but which were at the expense of the girls. When he was explaining electricity and conductivity, he warned, 'so the moral is, if you are wearing nylons, don't step on electric wire, because you'll get a nasty shock up your backside.' The girls certainly felt there was discrimination.

> *Margaret:* I think the boys get more help with the science really, because I think the teachers think it is a bit of a waste of time for girls. A lot of teachers have the type of idea, that the girls, they are going to be housewives and stay at home all the time.
>
> *R.:* All teachers?
>
> *Margaret:* The older ones might do, because they were brought up to it themselves.

There was very little attempt made to relate the physical sciences to girls' interests, a point made more generally by HMI (1980, p. 14). Examples used in science lessons tended to come from the 'male world' and were male-oriented, such as this example from a lesson on measurement:

> The teacher, in this case the Headmaster, was discussing measurement. He dealt with heat, measured by thermometers, with liquids measured in pints, like beer, and gallons, like petrol. The Head then went on to question whether any of the children had ever gone to France by car. This illustrated the difficulties caused by different forms of measurement; and the Head questioned how their *fathers* dealt with litres and kilometres. 'Have none of you got adventurous dads, that took the car to France?'

The social class models implied in this teacher's comment are interesting in themselves, but there are important gender implications too: of passive mothers who are taken places, if they are lucky. At one point the teacher did recognize the gap in his own teaching and curriculum illustration, and introduced material from the world conventionally defined as feminine: 'what are we measuring in Needlework.... And I suppose in our male chauvinist world, it is still girls who do Needlework, so I'll ask them for the answer.' As a teaching strategy this raises any number of issues, but the point is that this was the only occasion in eighteen months of observation of combined science where a specifically 'feminine' example was used.

The ways that domestic science teachers reacted to the boys and their strategies are also of interest. Unlike the natural science teachers and their treatment of girls, the female needlework teachers made specific provision for the boys. Indeed, the two teachers involved were acutely aware of the boys' feelings about domestic science, and they employed a range of strategies and devices to attempt to cope with, if not overcome, their resistance. They went so far as to change the name of their subject from Needlework to 'Fabrics'. The domestic sciences were administered by the craft department, and the latter purveyed the idea that in their first year pupils were learning craft skills and solving design problems upon a wide range of materials: paper, metal, wood, plastic, clay and fabrics. Within the subject, the teachers attempted to offer boys projects that had a 'masculine' feel to them. For example, the boys could design a football flag, or a banner or a bag to take fishing tackle. Teachers certainly did not insist that the boys shared the girls' project, which was to make a rag doll with a frilly Victorian pinafore. The teacher changed the setting of the room so that there were pictures on the walls of football teams with their slogans and mottoes, as well as girls' dress patterns. One teacher had offered a wide range of objects to make and design, which fell into categories, 'banners, bags and toys' being three of them. The teacher held up examples of objects from each category, but the only example of a toy she had was a doll:

T.: Or you could make a toy [holding up the Victorian-style rag doll in a Laura Ashley-style smock].

There was a visible sneer from the boys.

T.: OK, I know this is a doll, but you could make something else.

No criticism of the teacher's actions is intended; she was recognizing an attitude, derived from community culture and social pressures, which sex stereotypes a particular curriculum area and particular objects. She employed a range of strategies to break this down, and in some measure she succeeded. Whatever the outcome of her efforts though, it is interesting that there was no equivalent compensatory action for girls in the natural science lessons, no attempt to offer projects and examples of a more 'feminine' kind. Instead, as I have suggested, teachers sometimes did and said things that made matters worse. Science laboratories tend to be fairly austere places, except for those devoted to biology. They are not, for example, covered with posters about things that traditionally interest girls.

Perhaps the domestic science teachers were not committed non-sexist egalitarians, eager to 'switch boys on' to needlework. They probably only hoped to contain the situation, and remove some of the possibilities of disruption. As Elliot has pointed out,

> Boys are seen as the source of the fun and laughter, but also the confusion in the classroom. The dynamics of the classroom are radically affected by the presence of boys. Even a seasoned teacher can be dictated to by the dominant elements of the class. (Elliot in Spender, 1981, p. 105)

Thus the constraints operating on the domestic science teachers were largely those of maintaining discipline. In this sense the strategies used might be seen as belonging to Hargreaves' model of 'coping strategies' (Hargreaves, 1978; Pollard, 1980). For natural science teachers, however, the same constraint, the threat of disruption, does not exist to the same extent, since girls' disaffection is less threatening to teacher control. In addition, the fact that the girls switch off to physical sciences is a well known and accepted fact amongst the teachers interviewed. According to the headmaster, 'There's no sexual discrimination here, but at the end of the second year, when it comes to option choosing, all the girls get out of science.' The HMI (1980) and DES (1975) reports both acknowledged that teachers seemed to expect and accept this reaction amongst their female pupils. Some teachers lamented the fact but perceived it as socially acceptable; it did not contradict basic values and social reactions. These expectations may have constrained their attitudes, and in turn shaped the strategies they adopted with girls. Teachers' expectations and prejudices interact with those of pupils, as well as community attitudes, to make a very solid wall of resistance to any change.

Conclusion

In conclusion, the data from this research clearly support the view that sex role differentiation is an important factor in understanding pupil reactions to the curriculum. Particular school subjects do seem to act as one potent resource for pupils in their attempt to sort out and establish their gender identity at the early adolescent stage. Both boys and girls select curriculum areas to act as marker flags for their identities. Learning theory has tended to assume a gender-neutral pupil, but it does seem that gender needs to be put into the study of the curriculum.

There may be some policy implications to be derived from this analysis, about ways to 'switch girls on' to science. Certainly there is a case for removing what the HMI called 'the inadvertently discriminatory behaviour on the part of teachers' (HMI, 1980, p. 18). If we accept some of the speculations about girls' reluctance to engage in the 'public verbal arena' of the classroom, this has implications for teachers' tactics. Girls are not likely to be as willing as boys to join in open class discussion; they may go so far as to choose to withdraw from answering questions. There are teacher strategies to get round these problems, for example, girls could be asked questions directly, and addressed by name. Consideration must also be given to the notion of educating girls in single sex groups, for science at least.

The other major possibility of curriculum change involves trying to create what Allison Kelly has called a 'feminine science' (Kelly, 1981, p. 92), designing chemistry projects which show how nylon stockings are made, or doing experiments in which perfume is mixed, rather than carbon dioxide released in a mass of inky black vapour. However, this does raise some difficult issues. Such changes might keep girls more interested in the subject, though similar tactics were not markedly successful with the boys in needlework because of the strength of social pressures. Moreover, such a strategy does suggest that girls have a very restricted field of interests and activities, and that they are incapable of dealing with the 'larger things of life'. That was not, however, the reaction to the idea of introducing football banners for the boys in needlework: that seemed simply reasonable, a thoughtful attempt to accommodate the boys. The contrast raises some crucial questions about the nature and the status of different kinds of knowledge in our society. It seems clear that there is a 'sexual division of knowledge' and that it ties up with notions about gender-appropriate subjects for both boys and girls (Deem, 1980, p. 7). This means that we need to take account of gender in any work upon curriculum or curriculum innovation, and equally to attempt to grasp the very powerful forces which militate against change.

Acknowledgement

The author would like to acknowledge the financial support of the SSRC in the project from which this chapter derives.

Notes

1 HMI surveyed twenty-one schools, and fifteen of these were studied in more depth. They attempted to find schools which reprsented 'a social and geographical diversity' and visited the schools for three or more days, in parties of two or three Inspectors, one of whom was a woman. The schools were all fully comprehensive up to the age of 16, and had not been a girls' school in the previous decade.
2 Figures taken from 1975–76 DES Survey of all school leavers in England and Wales.
3 Girls occasionally produced what teachers regarded as 'insolent answers', but these usually stemmed from a teacher challenging girls' passive work avoidance strategies.
4 These data correspond with Mandy Llewellyn's (1980) picture of Sandy, a girl who was also seen as acting in ways inappropriate for 'proper girls', and who was labelled in exactly the same way.

References

BALL, S. (1980) '"Initial Encounters" in the classroom and the process of establishment', in WOODS, P. (Ed.) *Pupil Strategies*, London, Croom Helm.
DAVIES, L. (1978) 'The view from the girls', in *Educational Review*, 30, 2.
DEEM, R. (1980) *Schooling for Women's Work*, London, Routledge and Kegan Paul.
DEPARTMENT OF EDUCATION AND SCIENCE (1975) *Curricular Differences for Boys and Girls*, Education Survey, London, HMSO.
FULLER, M. (1979) *Dimensions of Gender in a School*, PhD thesis, University of Bristol.
HARGREAVES, A. (1978) 'Towards a theory of classroom coping strategies', in BARTON, L. and MEIGHAN, R. (Eds) *Sociological Interpretations of Schooling and Classrooms*, Driffield, Nafferton.
HASTE, HELEN WEINREICH (1981) 'The image of science', in KELLY (1981).
HMI (1980) *Girls and Science*, Matters for Discussion, No. 13, London, HMSO.
KELLY, A. (1981) *The Missing Half*, Manchester University Press.
LLEWELLYN, M. (1980) 'Studying girls at school: The implications of gender', in DEEM (1980).
MEASOR, L. and WOODS, P. (1983) 'The interpretation of pupil myths', in HAMMERSLEY, M. (Ed.) *The Ethnography of Schooling*, Driffield, Nafferton.
POLLARD, A. (1980) 'Towards a revised model of coping strategies', in *British Journal of the Sociology of Education*, 3, 2, 1982.
SHARPE, S. (1976) *Just Like a Girl*, Harmondsworth, Penguin.
SPENDER, D. (1980) *Learning to Lose*, London, Women's Press.
WILLIS, P. (1977) *Learning to Labour*, Saxon House.

3
Examinations, Accountability and Assessment

9 The Hidden Curriculum of Examinations

Glenn Turner

It has often been pointed out that schooling may carry messages and consequences by no means intended or foreseen by school personnel. Side by side with the manifest curriculum, the knowledge, skills and attitudes that schools are charged with teaching, there is a 'hidden curriculum' which may make as much if not more impact on pupils (Jackson, 1968; Snyder, 1971; Silberman, 1971). Examinations are an important element of secondary schooling and they seem to carry a hidden curriculum of their own. Whilst in principle they serve solely an assessment purpose, in practice they have numerous effects on pedagogy, on pupil work strategies and on the nature of teacher–pupil interaction itself.

Surprisingly little research has been done on secondary school pupils' perspectives on, and strategies for dealing with, exams. Yet success and failure in the school system are measured almost entirely in terms of examinations. While teachers and pupils are only too aware of this, sociologists have tended to ignore the effects of examinations, even when dealing with teacher-pupil interaction in examination groups.

We might expect that one of the strongest effects of examinations on pupils would be to stimulate conformity to teachers' demands. Indeed, it is plausible to suggest that it is those pupils committed to examination success who are most likely to conform to school requirements since their goals can only be achieved through such cooperation, since it is teachers who communicate the requirements of examination boards to pupils and prepare them to fulfil these. Pupils taking exams are, then, to a large extent dependent on the school. Moreover, since it is in the school's interests for pupils to be successful in external exams, there would seem to be no conflict of interests between the school and exam-oriented pupils. In theory, both pupils and teachers are working together to achieve the same objective. Here, in contrast to the case of the low stream or band two pupils given more attention in the literature, a consensus rather than a conflict model of classroom relations might be thought to be more appropriate.

However, while this reciprocity of interests would lead one to expect there to be an absence of deviance on the part of exam-oriented pupils, my observations of such pupils in lessons revealed that they quite frequently engaged in deviant activities and that there was indeed conflict with teachers (Turner, 1983). This clearly requires some explanation.

If pupils are committed to passing exams, deviance would appear to be contrary to their *own* interests as well as to those of the teacher. However, it is worth noting that passing examinations may not be the *only* concern these pupils have. Deviant acts might be motivated by alternative interests. Two plausible motives are:

(i) The attractions of deviance. Despite commitment to examination success, pupils may find certain deviant courses of action irresistible.
(ii) Peer-group pressures towards deviance. Exam-oriented pupils who wish to attain status in certain peer groups might have to be deviant on occasions in order to do so (Turner, 1983).

In that deviance motivated in this way is contrary to the academic goals of these pupils, teachers can appeal to such goals in attempts to enforce conformity. In examination classes teachers frequently made appeals of this kind:[1]

(1) *T.:* It's your O-level not mine and I'm not doing this for my own enjoyment. It's hard and it's boring but I can't help that.
(2) *T.:* Now look, if you want to do this O-level you've got to work. So books in on time otherwise I'll transfer you to CSE.
(3) *T.:* [Sets the class an essay] I wouldn't be asking you to do it unless it was going to come up in the mock exams or final exams. [pause] That is a hint.
(4) *T.:* Far too many people fail because they haven't done enough revision. I'll do my best, but unless you cooperate it's all useless.
(5) *T.:* [Tells the group that only about half of them are good enough to be entered for GCE.] It all depends on how hard you work.
(6) *T.:* If you will listen quietly I will tell you what you have to do. If you take notice of what I say now you will go into the exam fully prepared.

One aspect of the hidden curriculum of exams, evident in these extracts, is that with certain pupils appeal to exams can facilitate teacher control. The dependence of exam-oriented pupils on teachers gives these teachers considerable power over them. An obvious implication is that teachers have less ability to control those pupils who are not exam-motivated. Not surprisingly, perhaps, teachers sometimes tried to *make* pupils exam-motivated. Attempts were made to persuade low ability pupils that they could be successful in exams if they tried. This meant that some pupils were placed on CSE courses which teachers felt were really 'unsuitable' for them, and in which they were not expected to be successful:

(7) *Mr Cresswell* (Mathematics): I think on the whole most of my low ability teaching has been in examination situations, despite the fact that things like CSE really aren't suitable for them. Nonetheless you still try and do your best to try to get examination results for low ability groups – that is one of the

ways in which you avoid labelling people. It is no good saying at the beginning of the fourth year, 'Look you are not going to do exams', that would mean a serious deterioration in their response. So it's a case of trying to find a syllabus which in fact suits their needs and at the same time which gives them something which they can be interested in.

(8) *Mr Bradshaw* (Geography): I think that you have got to remember that all these people are put into CSE classes, Mode 1, designed for those pupils under O-level. You have got the top 25 per cent doing O-level, then the next 40 per cent CSE and it wasn't meant to cater for that 40 per cent of the less able children. They were put into classes and that course was unsuitable for them, and they weren't going to pass it anyway, and it is sad that they had to do it, but they had to be put somewhere.

So CSE comes to the rescue in the battle to control lower ability pupils, even when they are not likely to pass it. Indeed, Woods (1977) goes so far as to suggest that CSE is 'the biggest aid to teacher survival introduced into schools since the war' (p. 279). Because the main problem was to find a course which would give pupils the kind of work they could do, as well as to provide the possibility of taking an exam at the end of it, in some subjects CSE Mode 3 was introduced:

(9) *Mr Bradshaw:* We have just started, I have introduced a Mode 3 CSE which, once again, they might not pass, but I think is more suitable for them. They can do different types of work, they haven't got to do the syllabus as it is, country after country, area after area.

If one aspect of the hidden curriculum of exams is the facilitation of teacher control, another is 'instrumentalism' on the part of pupils (Hargreaves, 1982). That is, the examination itself is perceived as the sole purpose of school. Official goals which are unrelated to exams are dismissed. Moreover, the pupils set out to learn not the official syllabus, but only what is needed in order to pass the exam. One pupil who had adopted this instrumental attitude felt that if you were not taking exams at all school would be a complete waste of time:

(10) *John:* If your ambition was to be an agricultural labourer or something you would find it [school] just a waste of time probably.

Similar views on the part of pupils are reported by Fuller (1980). She argues that some of the black girls she studied in a London comprehensive school adopted the goal of academic success without identifying with other goals which would bind them to the school. They conformed to the stereotype of the 'good' pupil only insofar as they worked conscientiously at the work they were given. Often they engaged in deviance. Moreover, they came to judge for themselves what did and did not count in the pursuit of academic qualifications.

Such assessments were also made by many pupils at Stone Grove, the school in which I carried out my research. Even when pupils were specifically given work to do in preparation for exams, some of them were still anxious to estimate its instrumental value, and would ask teachers how far the work was in fact exam-related:

(11) *Raymond:* Is it compulsory to do a question on West Africa?
(12) *T.:* I'm a bit worried about what we've done on Africa.
Ian: Will there be a question on Africa?

For such pupils, work had to be exam-related. They were well aware that work could be given for reasons irrelevant to exams, to keep them quiet, for example:

(13) *Diane:* Half the time he [Mr Maxwell] gives us work just because we talk, like he did with that politics.
Susan: Yes he gives us things like politics and knows nobody understands anything about politics....
Diane: He gives it to us because we are talking.

Similarly, there is evidence that pupils tried to adopt 'short cuts' of the kind described by Becker *et al.* (1961, 1968) in their work on university students. If a topic is not compulsory in the exam it can be treated as non-essential. Similarly, if a certain topic is unlikely to come up in the exam there are good grounds for dismissing it as unimportant. Of course, at university level, because the lecturers set the questions and mark the papers, students tend to be sensitive to cues about what is likely to be on the exam paper. Indeed, Miller and Parlett (1974) show that some students actively seek this information. Becker *et al.* (1968) also note that some students try to find out what the faculty thinks is important and revise only those topics. However, in schools, because exams are external, teachers can be no more than 'cue conscious' themselves. So, for school pupils, finding out what the teacher thinks is important may be of no help whatsoever since the examiners' favourite topics and those of individual teachers are unlikely to correspond. The teacher may engage in 'question spotting' and can base his or her guesses on considerable knowledge of previous exam papers. One teacher, for example, said to his history class, 'It's almost as though, gazing into my crystal ball, I can see something coming up in the O-level and CSE exams about agriculture in the twentieth century.' Nevertheless, it is up to the pupils themselves to decide whether the teacher's guesswork is likely to be any better than their own.

As well as 'question spotting', some teachers were prepared to provide pupils with 'tips' on how to pass exams and to go along with the instrumental attitude, accepting that it was not the subject that was being learned but how to pass the exam. Teachers were sometimes quite explicit about this:

(14) *T.:* I regret doing West Africa, I'll say that. If I had my way we wouldn't do this. It's just a load of information. I think the stuff on Europe is more relevant. Its only because this is on the syllabus that we're doing it.

(15) *T.:* This syllabus is out of date, but are you here to do Geography or to do an exam?

(16) The teacher gives out last year's Biology paper 1, section 1, consisting of multiple choice questions. He tells them that the purpose of the exercise is to assist them in getting through the exam rather than to improve their Biology – that could be done in Mr A's and Mr B's lessons.

He says: 'When you have done a question, don't change your mind. Nearly always those who change their minds change from a right to a wrong answer. Also do all the ones you can and then any left go through with a B (or A, C or D). This gives 25 per cent chance of success. Answers are evenly spread so put the letter that has least occurred in the answers.' Taking the first question on section 1 he says, 'first eliminate the wrong ones'. D was wrong because it was 'nonsense disguised with jargon which is often put in to put you off'. He warns them to beware of that. Then using their knowledge of Biology he narrows it down to C.

As far as pupils are concerned, such 'tips' may well comprise the most important things to learn on any exam course. There is certainly evidence that pupils do take note of such advice:

(17) *Researcher:* Do you have a good idea of what they are looking for in exams – what to ignore and what to put in ...

John: We are told most of that. We are told 'don't waste time writing down unnecessary things, get down to the facts.' We have had loads of exams as it is. Every half year we have an exam.

R.: When you get a paper do you look at the questions and think, 'I know all about that' and start writing or just spend some time thinking about it?

John: No, I'm told to spend about a quarter of an hour reading the paper.

R.: And do you?

John: Yes it's much more sensible.

Through their experience of exams and the 'tips' given by certain teachers pupils appear to arrive at their own assessments of what constitutes good preparation for exams. These assessments can then be used as criteria for evaluating whether work given is exam-related or not.

In the pupils' eyes some teachers provided inadequate preparation for exams either because of their inability to do so, or because they did not attach enough importance to them:

(18) *R.:* Are there cases where you don't think teachers are preparing you adequately for the exam?
Stephen: Yeah there are – I mean a lot of teachers just give you past papers and say 'do those'. I don't think that's preparing you at all. You sort of get bogged down with those and panic and think, 'If this is what the exam's gonna be like I'm going to fail that as well as this paper now.' A lot of teachers do that – just give you past papers to work on.

(19) *Tony:* Mr Jackson, I don't like him ... he can't explain things, he just don't know his stuff.
R.: How do you know that?
Tony: A number of times people have asked him things, about things he wasn't prepared to talk about, you know.

(20) *John:* The English teacher's pretty hopeless – that's why we're all doing CSE.

Another reason for conflict between exam-oriented pupils and their teachers, then, is that they differ over what they consider to be important or legitimate work activities. Not only does such conflict reflect different attitudes regarding what constitutes adequate exam preparation but it also arises from differences in the degree of emphasis pupils and teachers place on exams. As far as some teachers were concerned, exams were not their main concern. They viewed exam work as uninteresting, and exam classes as relatively unrewarding to teach:

(21) *Mr Maxwell:* I get most out of teaching my lower ability fifth year and my seconds and third than I do out of teaching my O-level kids, simply by way of the fact that they seem to have more to offer, they have got more personality, they are more of a challenge to me.

While many of the teachers clearly did attach significance to exams, few approached the degree of exclusive interest characteristic of instrumental pupils. In their overall evaluation of what constitutes an 'ideal' pupil, teachers seemed to regard the 'right attitude' as more important than ability or pupils' willingness to take exams. Thus when asked about their perceptions of the 'ideal' pupil, many teachers said little about exams. The dominant theme of their responses was the importance of 'behaviour' and 'attitude':

(22) I think that what I look for and hope for in every pupil – and I am therefore bound to be disappointed obviously – is a pupil who is ... has the basic attributes of a civilized human being: they are courteous, polite, considerate of other people, this kind of thing, in minor little ways, without having to make a great

The Hidden Curriculum of Examinations

effort to do it because somebody is watching or anything like that. I think that I would like all pupils to have a proper respect for authority and I don't mean by that a slavish acceptance of it, but a proper understanding that it is necessary for the good ordering of society and all that it stands for. That there shall be those in authority and that they shall be obeyed – providing that their authority is properly used and not over-used.

I think that I would hope that every pupil will seek to get out of school, in every sense, everything that it has to offer them, whatever their talents and inclinations are. And that at the same time, and the two things I don't think can be separated, that the pupil should be seeking – perhaps not consciously – to put back into the school whatever talent that pupil has. (Headmaster)

(23) I would rate very highly a cooperative attitude; a desire to receive from the school the maximum benefit and to contribute to the maximum in school life. That is to say, I rate motivation very highly. (Head of Social Studies)

(24) [Talking about one of the lower ability pupils] He is a very hard working lad; the sort you could trust and would always do his best, and they are the ones I really feel sorry for with a course like that, which they are not going to get anything out of, and we should be saying at the end of it that he has done a course, he has worked hard, he should get a really good reference for his attitude. (Head of Geography)

These extracts suggest that exam-oriented pupils are not necessarily those thought most highly of by the teachers. Indeed, some teachers spoke out against the instrumental attitude of many pupils. The head, for example, referred to them as a 'take all-give nothing' group. One teacher even expressed the nature of the difference between himself and such pupils:

(25) I find I work better in a friendly situation – a tatty atmosphere, and I find that the kids, as long as they know where to draw the line, work better in that atmosphere. Of course with certain individuals it doesn't work.... I think you are on a bit of a sticky wicket with this friendly sort of chit chat relationship with somebody who is very conscientious and is only interested in the academic side; whereas I am interested in not only the academic but the social side as well. (Mr Maxwell)

The pupils committed to exam success showed little interest in the broad school goals of a social or personal kind that were so central for some teachers. Not only was their commitment to school almost entirely instrumental, but they were also quite willing to engage in deviance when circumstances permitted. An ironic implication of the contrast in attitude between such pupils and the staff is that for exam-oriented pupils school is perceived to be acting at least some of the time *against* their interests. While many pupils simply want to pass exams, the school places most stress on having the 'right attitudes'.

A further basis for conflict exists if such pupils reject these attitudes and resist the school's attempts to make them amenable to discipline. If pupils consider that teachers are more concerned with enforcing conformity to rules than they are with exams, they are likely to be suspicious of teacher appeals for conformity in the name of exam goals:

(26) Geography Lesson: teacher enters and distributes reprographed sheets on which is printed the following:

Exams this year

December – Mock exams
If you do well then you can probably try O-level. But this may, in Geography, *need to be a high mark* such as 60%. The mark will be decided later.

Your work is vital. The teacher is not doing the exam *you* are. You need to learn all you are taught. You need to practise drawing maps and sketches to help your answers. You need to work hard in class.

You will get the chance to practise in class, make the most of this. You have about 55 lessons left before CSE/GCE (GCE a few more) do not waste a single one; you may be ill later and miss more.

Remember, we are working together to help you do well.

Teacher leaves room and re-enters with a film projector. Pupil asks, 'Are we having a film'? Teacher says later in the lesson. Stephen shouts out, 'How are we going to get 60% through having a film?'

(27) A-level Geography: several pupils ask teacher what is the point of having a mock exam. Teacher says they've got the wrong attitude.
Heather: You keep giving us homework.
T.: Well other years managed in the past.
Rosemary: Last year didn't though.
T.: One year worked hard, did the mocks and did pass. Only those skivers last year didn't do the mocks and failed.

Not only is there conflict over the utility of work given but (as is evident in extract 27) over the amount considered necessary, or more precisely, the amount teachers think pupils ought to do in order to pass an exam and the amount pupils are actually prepared to do. Thus, whilst pupils sought short

The Hidden Curriculum of Examinations

cuts, teachers frequently tried to persuade pupils to do more work. Even teachers who gave pupils 'tips' on how to pass the exam tended to disagree with their pupils over what was an acceptable level of output. The following extract is from the biology teacher in extract 16:

> (28) The teacher has been commenting on the poor quality of their essays. He says that he knows a boy who attends a different school who takes two evenings over his essays and produces about sixteen sides. 'He will pass A-level.'

Pupils, on the other hand, are inclined to question the validity of lengthy essays as the best kind of exam preparation since they contain far more than can be remembered or used in any exam:

> (29) *John:* [On the subject of a pupil who does 6000-word essays] It won't be of any good when you get to the exam because he isn't going to remember his old essays when he gets in there, he is just going to be on his own, and if he took seven hours to write that he is going to have to do it in two hours, which is the exam time.

As we have seen, teachers, aware of the 'instrumental attitude' of pupils, often emphasize the relevance of the work they set to the examination. They also sometimes try to persuade pupils to do more work by suggesting what they think pupils will take as an acceptable minimum. Pupils are asked to do more but not a great deal more:

> (30) *T.:* Most of your stuff in the [mock] exams was from my notes. Some people say you should read more. Don't do all that much. Don't get bogged down but add odd little bits. Important things, not too much detail.

Although pupils might disagree with teachers over exam preparation it must be remembered that they are very dependent on teachers in this respect. The pupil who feels that the teacher is not providing adequate preparation has little choice but to accept the situation as it is. Of course, a pupil may try to 'go it alone' – that is, to more or less discount what the teacher asks them to do and make his/her own preparations. However, this course of action is problematic for at least three reasons:

> (i) The resources required to prepare for exams are almost exclusively in the hands of teachers, and pupils are likely to encounter problems in trying to acquire these resources independently.
> (ii) Perceptions of exam requirements are not developed independently from teachers. Teachers cannot be *totally* ignored since pupils cannot be sure that their own assessments of exam requirements are realistic.
> (iii) Teachers have control over exam entry and can use this power to force pupils into compliance.

The pupil who tries to 'go it alone' is faced with the inequality of the teacher-pupil relationship.

There are few means by which pupils can counter the power teachers have over them. However, some pupils do find ways round the obstacles facing them. Support from parents can be effective especially in terms of (i), since the resources needed can often be acquired from a parent who is willing to pay.[2] The power of teachers may also be eroded by some of the policies of the school as a whole. With regard to exam entry, at Stone Grove pupils not entered for O-level could still take the exam if they paid the fee themselves. Because of this policy individual teachers could not stand in the way of a pupil actually taking an exam. Consequently, in spite of the refusal of two teachers to enter him for O-level in their subject, John in fact took O-level exams in geography and English. The professional judgments of certain teachers were not necessarily accepted by particular pupils and parents. Moreover, the outcome of the exam could be taken as 'proof' of 'who was right'. John did in fact pass O-level in both geography and English – geography with a grade B!

Teacher refusal to enter pupils for exams was rarely effective as a means of controlling pupils. In any case, pupils knew that once they had been put in for an exam they were unlikely to be withdrawn from it:

(31) *Pupil:* What happens if we don't do very well in the mocks?
T.: If you don't do well you'll fail. You don't *have* to be put in for it.
Pupil: They've gone in already.

Despite conflict over preparation for exams and output, it is notable that pupils did not seem to challenge the mode of teaching prevalent in exam courses. Thus one aspect of the hidden curriculum of exams which seemed to be accepted by both pupils and teachers was the utilization of formal instruction and dictation as the best way to cover the material on the exam syllabus. Obviously, teaching style was to some extent dictated by the subject. In maths, for example, formal instruction tended to be predominant in exam classes. In geography nearly every lesson at sixth-form level consisted of dictation. Indeed, the teacher only had to begin speaking and pupils would begin writing down what he said!

In non-exam classes, however, especially with the less able, this mode of teaching was almost entirely absent and the teaching was very activity-based; the reason for this was that such pupils were expected to find more formal methods too difficult and uninteresting. With those doing exams, material had to be taught in what was assumed to be the most efficient way – interesting or not. Teachers did not see it as part of their role to *have* to motivate exam pupils.[3] Such pupils were expected to be self-motivated:

(32) When they get into the fifth year, the idea is that if they are in an O-level group and they have been selected for O-level and they have elected for O-level, they are old enough and ugly enough to

want to learn, and my theory or my basis of teaching is that I am teaching pupils who are interested in getting on, as well as in the subject, and want to know. (English teacher)

Conclusion

I have considered some of the effects of external examinations on those pupils for whom passing exams is an important goal. The implication of much existing work on pupil orientations is that these pupils would be expected to adopt a 'conformist' orientation to school and that teacher and pupil relations would be characterized by consensus. However, this does not seem to be the case, suggesting the need for a deeper exploration of the reasons for deviance on the part of exam-oriented pupils.

What emerges is a difference between such pupils and their teachers over the centrality of exams. Although all deviance cannot be accounted for in this way, some of it appears to result from disagreements among pupils and teachers over the priority of exam preparation. Whereas teachers give considerable emphasis to the social side of school, many of the most 'able' pupils adopt an instrumental attitude, rejecting what does not help to prepare them for exams. They are not willing simply to conform to all institutional requirements. Indeed, they exercise their own judgment even over what kinds of school work will and will not help them to pass their exams. As a result, pupils we might have expected to share the values of the school and to conform to its demands come into conflict with their teachers, and over an issue on which one might have expected there to be consensus – over helping them to pass examinations!

Notes

1 The data used in this paper are from observation and interviews with pupils and teachers in a comprehensive school in the English Midlands which I have called Stone Grove. The pupils were mostly in band one of the fifth form, and I focused on those who had adopted examination success as a major goal. For more details on these pupils and the methods adopted, see Turner (1983).
2 These resources include books and equipment and, if necessary, private tutoring. One pupil was placed in a private school because of his poor academic performance at Stone Grove.
3 Although, as I have said, they did try to do this on many occasions.

References

BECKER, H.S., GEER, B., HUGHES, E.C. and STRAUSS, A.L. (1961) *Boys in White: Student Culture in Medical School*, University of Chicago Press.
BECKER, H.S., GEER, B. and HUGHES, E.C. (1968) *Making the Grade: The Academic Side of College Life*, Wiley.

FULLER, M. (1980) 'Black girls in a London comprehensive', in DEEM, R. *Schooling for Women's Work*, London, Routledge and Kegan Paul.
HARGREAVES, D.H. (1982) *The Challenge for the Comprehensive School*, London, Routledge and Kegan Paul.
JACKSON, P.W. (1968) *Life in Classrooms*, New York, Holt, Rinehart and Winston.
MILLER, C.M.L. and PARLETT, M. (1974) *Up to the Mark: A Study of the Examination Game*, Society for Research into Higher Education, Monograph No. 1.
SILBERMAN, M.L. (Ed.) (1971) *The Experience of Schooling*, New York, Holt, Rinehart and Winston.
SNYDER, B. (1971) *The Hidden Curriculum*, Cambridge, Mass., MIT Press.
TURNER, G. (1983) *The Social World of the Comprehensive School: How Pupils Adapt*, London, Croom Helm.
WOODS, P. (1977) 'Teaching for survival', in WOODS, P. and HAMMERSLEY, M., *School Experience*, London, Croom Helm.
WOODS, P. (1978) 'Relating to schoolwork', in *Educational Review*, 30, 2.

10   Teachers' School-Based Experiences of Examining

John Scarth

Since the mid-1960s there has been a rapid increase in the number of pupils entered for, and passing, public examinations. In 1965 entries for external examinations totalled approximately 650,000, with almost 1,500,000 passes at GCE and CSE.[1] By 1979 this had increased threefold to 1,700,000 exam entries and 4,500,000 passes.[2]

The involvement of increased numbers of pupils in public examinations, brought about largely through the introduction of the Certificate of Secondary Education (CSE) in 1963, has also meant an increase in examination work for teachers. It is against this background that examinations are often viewed as a major 'constraint' on teachers' practice. There are at least two aspects to this conception of constraint: *first*, that the administration of public as well as internal examinations restricts the amount of time teachers can devote to carrying out other aspects of their work. Hilsum and Strong (1978, Ch. 12), for example, report that public examinations are an all-year-round feature of schooling, taking up an increasingly large proportion of the teacher's day. More specifically, this study suggests that teachers may spend, on average, at least twenty minutes a day on the invigilation and administration of external examinations. Furthermore, this figure should be seen as a minimum. Teachers also participate in the examining process on subject panels, moderating boards, external exam marking, etc. and, additionally, spend time on the preparation and marking of internal exams.

The *second* conception of exams as a 'constraint' is that the scope for introducing relevant but tangential subject matter is greatly restricted and, relatedly, that pedagogy becomes characterized by sustained teacher exposition and excessive pupil note-taking. For example, in their recent Report, *Aspects of Secondary Education in England* (DES, 1979b), HMI claim that 'in at least one fifth of the schools [inspected] the demands of public examinations appeared to be an important factor in the impoverishment of reading, with the least able pupils suffering most' (p. 248). They further suggest that in mathematics and science, also as a result of external exams, there is a tendency to emphasize standard routines and concepts which are unrelated to pupils' everyday experiences.[3] Similarly, Broadfoot (Two volume) claims that 'assessment procedures act as one of the greatest constraints on classroom practice'. Indeed, Whitty (1978) argues that even where teachers are nominally given some control over the examination, in Mode 3 exams, 'examinations [are] a mechanism of curriculum control *within* the school' (p. 134). This constraining function of exams, Whitty argues, is manifest in the imposition by examination boards of what is to count both in terms of the syllabus and assessment.

However, while there is a considerable literature on both these effects of examinations,[4] there has been little or no research on teachers' own perceptions of and orientations to examinations or on the strategies they employ to deal with them. Using data collected in a case study of an 11–16 comprehensive school (hereafter called 'Brookview') this paper seeks to explore the fine-grain of teachers responses to the requirements of examinations.[5]

Functions of Examinations: Pupil-Centred and Teacher-Centred

Teachers at Brookview by no means regarded exams or examination boards simply as a constraint on their practice. Whilst acknowledging that examining created some problems, they also believed that examinations performed important positive functions in school. From the teachers' perspective, there were two main types of functions: those which concerned pupils and those which were more directly related to their own practice.

Pupil-Centred Functions

Teachers at Brookview recognized that pupils on leaving school needed qualifications to obtain employment. Thus by preparing pupils for examinations they were, in their view, performing an 'essential service' (Ginsburg *et al.*, 1980). Typical of these teachers' comments were the following:

> the kids who go for jobs need to go with maths qualifications and people want maths qualifications ... it's my job as a teacher to make sure then that the kids do as well as they can, that's my job.... (Head of Mathematics Department, in conversation)[6]

> We do have a responsibility to the kids to get them as good a grade as we can because when they go for an interview for a job that's the first thing an employer will look for. (Scale 1, history, interview)

GCE and CSE exams were, of course, interpreted as catering for pupils of different abilities who had to be properly identified and entered for the right exam so that their chances of success could be maximized:

> there is an emphasis on exam attainment there's no doubt but at the end of the day whether we like it or not in the 5th year it's exams they are going to be taking whether CSE or O-level and one wants to enter them for the exam that they are most likely to gain success in.... (Scale 2, mathematics, in conversation)

This identification process was closely linked to the school's internal organization, on the basis of which pupils were grouped into three ability bands. Each of these bands was identified as requiring different examination courses: the top band should take GCE; the middle band should be entered for CSE; and the bottom band should be allocated to a combination of CSE and non-exam courses. Internal examinations played an effective role in maintaining the continuity of these organization arrangements through their use as indicators of pupil ability. As one senior house tutor put it (during interview), 'we want to get people into the course group which their achievement level and their ability level merits; hopefully the two will be one but obviously it isn't always, which puts the onus on the [internal] exam.'

Thus the function of examining as an 'essential service' involved not only the improvement of pupils employment prospects via the public examination system, but also the provision of an important aid to the identification of pupils' abilities and, thereafter, the right external exam for which they should be entered.[7]

The second pupil-centred function of examinations noted by Brookview teachers was that they enabled the assessment of pupils, a practice which many teachers regarded as a central facet of their work: 'I think at the end of the day that our job basically, yes, is to assess the pupils . . . we have to educate them I know, but the assessment part is perhaps the most important (Scale 2, history, interview). Moreover, in relation to pupils' assessment at 16, teachers argued that if an assessment was indeed necessary then the external exam was particularly appropriate for two reasons. *First*, that external exam assessments were accepted nationally:

> if it was left to individual schools to assess pupils there would be a large subjective element; but also nobody would know what each school's standard was . . . every school would have different ways of marking and assessing kids . . . at least with the present system everybody knows what an O-level means and what a CSE grade means. . . . (Head of Department, Humanities interview)

Similarly, for the headmaster, external assessments avoided the creation of 'meaningless' grades: 'If every school devised their own grades for their pupils it would be hopeless. Nobody would have a clue what they meant, they would be utterly meaningless.' (Headmaster, interview).

Second, by being external to the school, favouritism was avoided and thus, teachers contended, all pupils had a fair chance of success:[8]

> certainly for me one of the benefits of exams is that the lads are treated equally by the examiners . . . they don't know who Johnny Smith is or Sara B . . . the assessment is simply on their performance in the test. . . . (Scale 2, English, in conversation)

Relatedly, the growth of multiple choice questions on examination papers may partly reflect teachers' desires for an objective assessment of pupils:

one of the things I like about the multiple choice is that it is totally objective all they've got to do is put one letter they don't lose marks for handwriting or spelling or anything like that, it gives some of them a chance to pick up a few more marks.... (Scale 1, history, in conversation)

Teacher-Centred Functions

Both the essential service and the assessment functions are concerned with the *product* of exams. However, the first teacher-centred function relates to the *process* of examining. Some teachers argued that one of the most important functions of exams was that they provided an additional means of classroom control (see Turner, this volume).

now come on 3N we've got a lot to do today you'll never get through the exam if you carry on like this.... (Scale 1, geography, in class)

Now listen! I'm all right, I've passed my exams I don't need them anymore so if you want to waste your time, and we've not long left now, that's entirely up to you.... (Scale 2, French, in class)

Similarly, one of the benefits of internal examining was that the process of taking exams itself created a sense of discipline and control throughout the school. Comments made by teachers during the Christmas examination period, are illustrative of this: 'you've never seen this lot working so hard ... I look forward to these bits of quiet' (Head of Department, Humanities in conversation); 'isn't it lovely and quiet.... I wish it was like this all the time' (Scale 1, mathematics, in conversation).

However, examinations also aided classroom control by enhancing pupil motivation through providing a highly specific goal, namely passing the examination. The head of the French department explained this succinctly: 'The pupils know what they've got to do to pass the exam and as exams get closer you can visibly see the class try harder.' That pupils know 'what they've got to do' to pass exams aids the teacher in classroom control. Moreover, in this case, rather than the control being imposed on the pupils by the teacher, the proximity of the exam is itself sufficient to increase pupils' self-control in the classroom.

Just as examinations made specific demands on pupils that they had to meet if they were to pass, by the same token examinations provided teachers with specific work schedules in the form of syllabi. The syllabus provides teachers with a detailed course content from which a selection of material is covered. Furthermore, in many cases, textbooks are also available which mesh closely with the requirements of the syllabus. Such an arrangement greatly reduces the amount of work teachers would otherwise have to do:

With the Social and Economic course, we follow the text more or less completely ... it gives them a useful reference book and of course it certainly cuts down on the number of work sheets I've got to prepare. (Scale 1, history, in conversation)[9]

Indeed, one of the key practical considerations acting against the development of Mode 3 courses would seem to be that the expected gain does not match the costs involved in the changes in practice required (House, 1974). As one teacher engaged in Mode 3 work expressed it:

> Ask how many teachers have opted for Mode 3 CSE. I think it'll be a surprise to you that so many of them are prepared to accept Mode 1. Why? It's easier, they don't have to submit a syllabus to the Board they don't have to go before the panel of the Board, it's easier just to take a Mode 1 syllabus.... (Head of Subject, biology, interview)

While changes in the mode of examination were not popular, somewhat more common were changes in examination board registration (although this still involved only a small number of teachers). In this case the 'cost' involved – in terms of time spent on administration – is balanced by the perceived gains from the new syllabus. A case in point was the English department, where the head of department opted for a new syllabus which '... gives my teachers the maximum flexibility in the classroom and gives them a fair chance of doing as best they possibly can.' In this case, a change of exam board had the function of facilitating preferred classroom practices.[10]

The third teacher-centred function of examinations was their use in the process of teachers' self-evaluation. It is perhaps a seldom acknowledged feature of teaching that there are few indicators by which teachers can assess their own performance. Lortie (1975), for example, argues that teachers' experience of insecurity is heightened through the lack of a measure by which they can assess their own effectiveness. Examinations may provide precisely this kind of information. For teachers at Brookview this evaluative function had two dimensions, corresponding to external and internal examinations.

External exams were used by teachers as a public expression of a teacher's or pupil's *success*. These results were 'public' insofar as a detailed list of all exam passes, by pupil and department, was displayed on the staff noticeboard early in September. Moreover, there was a further breakdown of these results by subject, indicating the number of pupils achieving each grade at O-level (*not* CSE).

By so tabulating the results, comparisons between departments relating to their relative 'success' in the exams inevitably arose:

> Well, we weren't as successful as last year but I see we've done better than biology this time. (Head of Subject, geography, in conversation)

> I always check to see where we are. We're not too far down the list so I think that'll be OK. (Scale 1, French, in conversation)

> Maths are always top and that's how I like it I must admit..... I

wouldn't let anyone in this school beat us I couldn't, my pride's involved, my professional pride. (Head of Department, Mathematics, in conversation)

However, the nature of teachers' evaluation of external exam results appears complex. On the one hand, the majority of teachers seemed convinced that achieving a large number of grade 'A' passes at O-level was, at least in part, a reflection of the teachers' good work. As the head of the English department put it (in conversation): 'to get grade 'A's obviously the kids have to be bright but I also think that if a teacher gets quite a few as Harry did in Chemistry then he must be doing something right.' On the other hand, however, there appeared to be little criticism of teachers, or departments, who achieved relatively few grade 'A' passes. Indeed, some of the teachers who had the 'worst' exam success rate were congratulated by several of their colleagues. As one teacher said when annotating the results table for the researcher:

I wouldn't go too much by these results [pointing at the bottom subject] it may not look particularly good but believe you me Stuart [the teacher] has had probably the roughest group in the school for the last two years, he's done really well to get that out of them. (Head of Subject, music, in conversation)

It is an interesting feature of external exams that the very process of examining itself allows different interpretations of the final result. That is, due to the numerous variables which may affect pupil success in examinations, there is a marked leeway for teachers' interpretation of the results.

If external exams were a public measure of success, then internal exams were essentially 'private' indicators of a teacher's or pupil's *progress*. They were private insofar as they were not available for 'public' scrutiny within the school, the results were either kept separately by heads of subject or collectively by a deputy headmaster. In either case, no teacher outside the senior management team saw a full list of internal exam results for each subject. Furthermore, these results were indicators of 'progress', rather than being a statement of 'success', inasmuch as they provided teachers with an instrument by which to judge whether interim aims and objectives were being achieved and if adjustments would be necessary. For example, with reference to the first-year chemistry exam paper, the head of subject said:

I think any exam the purpose of it should be to evaluate whether you are achieving the aims and objectives that you laid down ... if I found one particular concept which had been examined had been answered badly by everybody there would be two main inferences I could draw. Either the concept is being presented too early or I didn't teach it very well. (Head of Subject, chemistry, interview)

Similarly, illustrating the manner in which teachers interpreted exam results as an indication of their, or pupils', performance, a maths teacher, referring to the first-year exam at Christmas, commented: I find these exams useful really, they give you a guide as to how the class are settling down, if you're going too quick or if some things are difficult to grasp ... (Scale 2, mathematics, in conversation).

Such orientations illustrate that internal exams should not be interpreted simply as a training for external exams. Undoubtedly, this was a feature of their design at Brookview,[11] but they were also used by teachers as an *aid* to their teaching.[12]

The final teacher-centred function of examining I shall mention is that they provide a framework within which time is coordinated (Jackson, 1973, p. 2). That is, exams provide a focus for the work of teachers, they synchronize time and activity throughout the school year:

> One thing with the exams, you know where you are. When we come back in September the whole year ahead of us is already carefully planned and arranged so that what we do fits in with when the exams fall. (Head of Subject, geography, in conversation)

> This school is geared to exams, I should say, but then I suppose they all are ... exams give us a framework, if you like, in which to coordinate work not only each year but also between years. (Head of Department, Mathematics interview)

One of the unacknowledged benefits of examining may be that, through this synchronization of time and practice, a *sense of order* is achieved. Thus examinations are not perceived by teachers as simply a constraint, for they are central to the practice of teaching itself and, as such, teachers approach them in the same way as they do other aspects of their work. There is a growing number of studies (for example, Bossert, 1979; Denscombe, 1980; Doyle and Ponder, 1977; Hargreaves, 1978; Pollard, 1980) which suggest that teachers' orientation to their work is characterized by a 'practicality ethic' (Doyle and Ponder, 1977).

Teachers' 'Practical' Approach to Examining

One of the key characteristics of teachers' responses to examining was a concern with *time*. More specifically, this was with 'finding time' in the school day in which to meet the requirements that participation in examinations involved, and with the 'timing' of the exam in the school year.

Teachers at Brookview found time for examination work through a variety of strategies. For some it involved 'balancing' (Pollard, 1980) their time between normal duties and exam preparation:

> it's always the same at this time of year either you spend your time working and doing the usual things or you get on with the exam work, you can't really do both.... (Scale 1, history, interview)

> I'm going to set revision as homework this week ... I might be able to get on with the exams then. (Scale 1, French, interview)

> writing exams if you do it properly is a really time-consuming business I certainly don't try to keep up with all my other business as well. (Head of Department, Humanities interview)

The significant remark, 'if you do it properly', suggests a commitment to a particular set of predispositions and practices related to examining, the implementation of which may be in conflict with other classroom-based teaching activities.

Relatedly, an important element of teachers' responses to examining requirements is that a large proportion of the necessary activities is conducted in teachers' *own* time, there being little time set aside in the timetable for examination work. Thus, for some teachers 'finding time' involved accomplishing the task in a manner which, whilst professionally acceptable, was economically and administratively feasible:

> one of the first things I work out when I'm writing an exam is, 'how long will it take to mark?' There's no point writing an exam which is going to take ages to mark.... (Scale 1, history, interview)

> when you examine everyone in the school at the same time 1st to 5th year that's a heck of a lot of marking. If *you've* got to set it and *you've* got to mark it, then it comes down to the problem of I've got to set something that I can mark easily because I don't want to be marking all Christmas (Scale 2, English, interview)

In this case the teacher designs the examination on the practical criterion that the test should be easy to mark. Other teachers saved time by using the previous year's exam paper: 'I always use last year's exam it saves me the time of having to write a new one each year ...' (Head of Subject, geography in conversation). The 'saving of time' by the re-use of exam papers reflects a situation in which teachers had competing demands made on their time, not only by extracurricular activities but also by the regular administrative duties involved in teaching (registration, reports, requisitions and so forth).

Hilsum and Strong (1978) noted that there are considerable variations in the length of the teacher's working day. Specifically, they found that for their sample teachers worked on average less than seven hours a day on forty days and for more than nine hours a day on sixty days in the year. Similarly, the study by Lyons (1976) of the work of head and senior teachers indicates 'troughs' and 'peaks' of activity in the school year and that the content of the task varies according to the time of the year, forming a distinctive pattern of activity for each school. A recent study of curriculum reappraisal in secondary schools (North West Education Management Centre, 1981) suggests that from these workload patterns, distinctive 'time-pressure-profiles' for schools can be constructed. Examinations are a key aspect of these profiles, representing significant periods of increased workload.

The *timing* of internal examinations within the time-pressure profile may also be important. For example, one teacher particularly concerned with the timing of the Christmas examination as it was very close to the end of term, said:

> I think I don't get out of the exams what I would like because it is held in the next to the last week of term ... the next time you see them is the last week of the Christmas Term obviously Christmas pantomime going on; going out to see old people obviously there's a lot going on they're in a carol concert you really don't see them together long enough to make it worthwhile going over the exam.... (Head of Subject, chemistry, interview)

Here the 'timing' of the Christmas exam impinges on the teacher's strategy for using the examination as a means of evaluation. Implicit in this is a recognition that, in terms of time allocated, there is an unequal emphasis between the setting and taking of the exam and the marking and feedback. More particularly, there is a lack of structured time, of time in the exam timetable, in which teachers may either prepare for, or evaluate the exam.

In other cases, an important practical consideration when setting an exam was making sure that the pupils could do it:

> *Teacher:* When setting an exam an important criterion is making sure they can do it it's no good setting an exam if after 15 minutes they sit back and can't do any more....
>
> *J.S.:* Do you write the exam each year or do you look back to last year's and use that?
>
> *Teacher*: Well yes I do use last year's, there is a certain amount of that if it was successful.
>
> *J.S.*: What do you mean by successful?
>
> *Teacher:* Well really if it keeps them occupied for the full time; often with the lower ability bands I will revise an exam before they get it so that they can do it. (Head of Department, Humanities interview)

Keeping pupils occupied[13] during the examination was part of a rationale for ensuring that the pupils were able to complete the exam. Teachers were also concerned that their class would not cause any difficulty for the invigilator. Disturbances of this kind might reflect badly on their capacities as a teacher and also on their ability to set examinations. Following a noisy incident in a third-year examination, a teacher remarked:

> really whilst I do accept that the classroom was stuffy and the children had been doing exams all day ... there is no excuse for that kind of

behavour ... some of them finished their exam in less than an hour which is ridiculous (Deputy Head, in conversation)

In this case, the teacher who had set the exam could well have been judged by the 'performance' of the class. By revising what is in the exam a teacher assures that the pupils are able to do the test and thus remain occupied for its full duration.

Examining as Habit and Routine

Clearly then, the process of examining at Brookview is viewed by teachers as a normal part of their work. It does create problems; in particular, it adds considerably to the pressure on teachers' time at certain periods in the year. But then other aspects of their work lead to problems too, and those arising from examinations are approached by the teacher in the same way as all the others: pragmatically. Practical solutions are found and, moreover, if these 'work' they become 'routinized' (Berger and Luckman, 1966). In other words, if they succeed in resolving the problems for all practical purposes, they become synonymous with examining itself. Setting end-of-term exams frequently reflects the routinized nature of the response of some teachers to the requirements of examining:

> *J.S.*: Are you also setting exams at the moment?
>
> *Teacher:* Setting exams? What do you mean? We've got one that was written a few years ago and that seems to work so we use that. (Scale 2, mathematics, in conversation)

Whilst the exam 'works' it is accepted as *the* exam and the form remains unquestioned. This reflects another important characteristic of habitualized action, namely, the consideration of alternative forms of practice is reduced: 'I haven't had to set one because it's set, it's the same one every year' (Scale 1, geography, interview). Through the process of habitualization it becomes unnecessary for those involved to redefine their activity anew in each situation. For example, on one occasion a teacher new to the school approached his head of department to find out what he should be doing about the exams:

> *Teacher*: I've been worried about the exams ... what do I have to do? Shouldn't I be doing something?
>
> *H. of D.*: No not yet there's plenty of time I wouldn't worry about it....
>
> *Teacher*: When do I start then?
>
> *H. of D.*: Well, what classes do you have?

Teacher: ... 1G, 1L, 2O and 2G....

H. of D.: Oh well you should be all right then, I wrote exams for most of those a few years ago, I'll give them to you later so you can get them run off ... (Scale 1 teacher Head of Department, Geography in conversation)

By using existing examinations the head of department both allays the anxiety of the new member of staff and also provides an exemplar for future practice. In like fashion, a science teacher explained the setting of the first year exam: 'if you want the honest truth it's last year's exam. In fact it usually is ...' (Head of Subject, biology, interview).

Thus a key feature of the teachers' orientations towards examinations was that they were a normal and natural feature of schooling. As teachers interviewed at Brookview remarked:

Teacher 1: Exams are just part of the usual routine of the school ... (Head of Department, Art interview)

J.S.: Why are you having these exams now?

Teacher 2: Well we always have exams at Christmas I suppose it's a bit like the annual cross-country race or staff soccer match.... (Scale 1, geography, interview)

J.S.: Why are you having exams?

Teacher 3: Why? Because we always do, we've got to have some way of sorting out the children.... (Head of Subject, physics, interview)

Innovative Practices and Examining

While most teachers at Brookview treated examining as a matter of normal routine, some did try to innovate in both internal and external exams. These teachers were very much in the minority. Of the forty-six teachers in the school, only six had introduced any innovation in the preceding three years and, of these, four were still actively engaged in innovation during the period of fieldwork. Moreover, many of their innovations were purely administrative in nature, focusing on increasing the efficiency of the test, rather than involving any modification of the *form* of the examination.

At the simplest, innovation in *external* examining arrangements involved transferring registration to another examination board, one which offered a different and in some way 'better' syllabus. For example, soon after his arrival, the head of chemistry switched examination boards. Explaining his reasons for the change (in interview), he said: 'I wasn't very happy, when I first arrived,

with the course. I wanted to make it much more skill-based.... I switched to this Exam Board because I feel they give us much more scope to do that....'
Thus changes of exam board could facilitate the introduction of learning activities which, in their own right, staff members interpreted as providing a better 'service' for pupils.

A more complex and demanding innovation relating to external examinations was to change the *mode* of exam. Some teachers who were discontent with Mode 1 examinations, the dominant mode of external examining at Brookview, changed to Mode 3 examinations, wherein there was an element of teacher participation, both in the construction and assessment of the course (Torrance, 1982a). Indeed, the introduction of these courses was heralded as an opportunity for teachers to have more control in the examining process (Whitty, 1978; Torrance, 1982b). At Brookview an environmental science course had been developed involving continuous assessment and a Mode 3 exam. The teacher with responsibilities for the course commented: 'I have never been in favour of formal exams and so I opted for Mode 3, it'll be a much better way to evaluate these kids in Environmental Science ...' (Head of Subject, biology, interview). The guiding rationale, then, for these innovators is that a Mode 3 examination would be a better or fairer test for pupils. Furthermore, changing the mode of examination gave these teachers sufficient scope to introduce the pedagogic practices they preferred (that is, 'pupil-centred' rather than 'teacher-centred'; a greater emphasis on project work or a redefinition of what counts as assessment).

Most changes in *internal* examinations were essentially administrative in nature, designed to improve examining arrangements by making them more efficient. 'Administrative' innovations included the introduction of improved marking techniques; more efficient ways of organizing revision timetables; making clearer the vocabulary used in examinations or 'updating' exam content to more accurately reflect course design. This form of innovation does not involve much change in teachers' practices relating to the preparation, taking and marking of exams. For example, an art teacher explaining a new 'objective' marking scheme said: 'I was aware that my mood might significantly affect the marks so what I have done this year is to make a mark scheme in three parts: design, technique and my own subjective feeling.... I suppose it's to try to make the marking a little more objective ... (Head of Subject, Art, interview). Whilst improving the efficiency of the existing examining arrangements (by enabling a more comprehensive evaluation of pupils' abilities than previously possible, although using the same test), such administrative innovations involved no changes to the *form* of the exam itself. Accordingly, teachers' practices relating to the setting and taking of exams were not significantly affected. By the same token, classroom-based activities relating to examining (for example, revision and course design) remained unchanged.

There were, however, some more 'substantial' innovations in internal examining, making changes to both the *form* and *content* of the examination, which involved teachers and pupils changing classroom practices. For example, testing acquired skills rather than memory or book-knowledge in examinations reduces the need for specific periods of classroom-based revision activities. Similarly, designing a test during which pupils may talk and ask questions produces a different teacher-pupil relationship which may reduce pupil anxiety and tension. Furthermore, in this type of innovation different sets of teacher practices are associated with the preparation, taking and marking of exams which have an influence on the type of classroom-based activities available to the teacher.

One such innovation was in the English department, where a new second-year exam was designed to test the pupils' understanding of the concept of 'sequencing', a skill which previously had not been evaluated in the school. The test involved giving each pupil a set of nine numbered paragraphs which had to be arranged in the correct sequence during the exam. The head of department explained why he regarded this as innovatory practice:

> it was a genuine innovation because (a) it highlighted awareness of a reading skill which hadn't been tested before; (b) we had to devise the material, select the passage, we had the manual business of chopping it all up and numbering it all (Head of Department, English meeting)

Furthermore, unlike other examinations the invigilator took an *active* part in the exam: '[the invigilator] will actually have to do a fair bit of work with the kids. We wrote instructions "there's nothing wrong with talking to the kids during the exam"' (Head of Department, English meeting). This represents a radical innovation, breaking with the traditional form of examining which emphasizes recall of knowledge and reflects the dominant curriculum practices of classrooms.

Of course, examining is enshrined in a set of institutional practices linking exam room to the classroom, as, for example, in the encroachment into 'teaching time' of practices like revision, associated with, and necessary to, the participation in examining. By innovating with the *form* of examining, the teacher was doing more than simply changing the examination paper. Without an emphasis on memorizing, book-learning or revision, teachers were able to pursue different topics in the classroom and in different ways. As one teacher put it: 'I've only just realized it actually I hadn't thought about it before but I've no real revision to do this year; they can't. So I'm carrying on with what I want to do till the actual exam ...' (Scale 2, English, interview).

However, even among teachers engaged in radical innovation of this kind, which involved changes not only to the process of examining but also to other aspects of teaching, examinations were not regarded as something external, as a constraint on their teaching. Exam work was *part* of their teaching and they sought changes in it which more closely matched their ideals as well as allowing them to teach in ways they felt to be more appropriate. Moreover, the process of innovation was very much governed by, and legitimated in terms of, the practicality ethic.

Conclusion

There has been considerable debate about the effects of public examinations on secondary schools. In particular, it has been suggested that such exams represent a major constraint on innovation among teachers. Thus, for example, Whitty challenges Eggleston's (1975, p. 8) claim that the major obstacle to innovation comes 'not so much from curriculum development agencies and examination boards but rather from the teachers' own consciousness'. Drawing on a study of teachers engaged in developing Mode 3 exams, both GCE Mode 3 CSE and GCE, Whitty (1978, p. 136) claims that

> teachers have not in fact themselves been able to make radical innovations in many cases, since the various aspects of the boards' regulations and procedures tend to impose conventional notions of syllabus and assessment procedures upon them.

Whitty argues that while Eggleston may have been substantially correct at the time he was writing, in the early 1970s, later in that decade examination boards began to place greater restrictions on Mode 3 assessment (Bowe and Whitty, this volume).

I have documented in some detail the orientations to examinations of teachers in one school. From one point of view, this evidence may be regarded as throwing doubt on Whitty's claims. While the teachers at Brookview did find examinations a major source of problems in several important respects, they did not experience examinations as set apart from teaching, acting as an external constraint upon it. Brookview teachers viewed examinations, both internal and external, as serving several important positive functions: for example, providing an 'essential service' for pupils, giving teachers a basis for self-evaluation and setting up a framework for teaching, in terms of the knowledge to be presented, its ordering and timing. For many of the teachers, despite the fact that it sometimes caused problems, examining was a normal and natural part of their work and was approached in a highly pragmatic and routinized manner. Their attitudes to examinations were embedded in a network of practices tailored to meet the demands made on them and to suit the conditions in which they worked.

There were, of course, some Brookview teachers who developed innovations in assessment practice, in relation to both internal and external examinations. However, most of these innovations were administrative, involving no change in the form of assessment and having only minor consequences for pedagogy. Moreover, even those few teachers in the school who were engaged in substantial innovations in examining practice did not seem to find the regulations and procedures of the examination boards a hindrance.

However, while this evidence suggests that exam board regulations and procedures do not represent the constraint Whitty suggests they do, it must be remembered that Whitty was particularly concerned with that 'persistent minority' of teachers who regard 'the subversion of prevailing curriculum content and methods of teaching and assessment, and the substitution of more radical alternatives, as an important political tactic' (Whitty, 1978, p. 135). From this point of view there may be no real conflict between the views of Eggleston and Whitty. Eggleston may be quite correct in the case of the majority of teachers. On this view, it might be argued among Brookview teachers the major obstacle to innovation is not material but ideological constraint. They do not find exam boards a source of constraint because their conceptions of curriculum and pedagogy are 'hegemonically determined'. Hargreaves (1981, pp. 305–6) summarizes this argument as claiming that:

> while teachers hold a range of views about education and exhibit a diversity of patterns of thought in this area, *they do so within very definite and unquestioned limits*. Beyond these limits lie a set of educational and social practices which would be viewed by most people as potentially threatening to the existing order of capitalism and the broad social and political assumptions which help sustain it. Existing practices (what passes for normal teaching and education under capitalism, that is), therefore become not one version of reality among many, but the only conceivable one; standing at the deepest levels of teachers' consciousness as the only normal, natural and reasonable ways of proceeding....

One way of understanding the orientations of Brookview teachers towards examinations is to see them as under the influence of liberal or social democratic ideology (Bowles and Gintis, 1976;, CCCS, 1981), and also perhaps of common-sense knowledge deriving from their experience as teachers. As a result, they see no contradiction between the requirements placed on them by examination boards and the task of educating their pupils. Indeed, these requirements are not even experienced as external; they have been internalized and have shaped the teachers' whole conception of education.

However, before accepting such an argument, we should note how in moving from Whitty's account of 'radical' teachers facing material constraints to Hargreaves' explanation for the relative absence of radicalism among the teachers he studied (see also Hargreaves, 1978), the concept of 'constraint' has undergone a subtle transformation. In the first case, 'constraint' referred to the teachers' experience of not being able to engage in the kind of teaching which they felt to be appropriate. In the second case, that of teachers such as those at Brookview, there is no such experience. Paradoxically, constraint, albeit of an ideological or hegemonic variety, is offered as an explanation *for why they do not have* such an experience. This argument has a curious theoretical substructure. It assumes that were it not for the influence of hegemony teachers such as those at Brookview would become similar in orientation to that 'persistent minority' of radical teachers with which Whitty was concerned. In other words, were it not for the effects of society, these teachers would 'naturally' engage in 'radical innovation'.

The origins of this view are to be found within 'the new sociology of education' (Young, 1971; Gorbutt, 1972; Karabel and Halsey, 1977), though it is probably most clearly expressed in Dawe's (1970) well-known article, 'The Two Sociologies' (p. 214):

> The key notion of [the sociology of social action] is that of autonomous man, able to realize his full potential and to create a truly human social order only when freed from external constraint.

Underlying theories of ideological and hegemonic constraint, as currently expressed, is the notion of individuals as truly human and autonomous beings, separate from and somehow prior to society, who are struggling, or should be struggling, to free themselves from the shackles placed on them by society. In some ways this is an appealing notion, but it is simplistic. It was a major target of criticism for both Marx and Durkheim. Despite their other differences, both argued that social structures produce and are reproduced by individuals; they are, as Giddens (1979) observes, both the medium and the outcome of people's actions.

We must ask on what grounds it is assumed that some teachers are merely ideological dopes who have been effectively indoctrinated, while the practices of those teachers which the analyst regards as 'radical' are founded upon 'penetrations' to the truth, however partial (Giddens, 1979; see also Willis, 1977). Where is the evidence for the assumptions about the validity of different forms of teaching that underlie such accounts? This mode of explanation trades upon implicit values and policy assumptions which should not be taken as given, especially not by those who claim to be challenging 'taken-for-granted assumptions'.

Moreover, these assumptions determine the kind of explanations developed to account for the behaviour of different actors. Indeed, the importance of the differences between teachers highlighted by this theoretical approach is premissed upon the assumed validity of those implicit policy prescriptions. As a result, the latter represent a significant source of political bias and pose a serious threat to our understanding of the activities of teachers.

My argument is not that the theories proposed by Whitty, Eggleston and Hargreaves are incorrect. The explanatory factors they appeal to in accounting for teacher behaviour are undoubtedly important ones: teaching is shaped by both ideological and material factors. The point is, rather, that these different explanations must not be applied selectively on the grounds of the analyst's values. The behaviour of actors with whom he or she shares ideals and policies must not be explained in ways which imply that commitment to those ideals and policies does not require sociological explanation, while the beliefs of other actors are accounted for in such a manner as to dismiss them as simply false and misguided (Hammersley, 1981).

The forms of teaching one finds in schools are historically developed patterns shaped by the goals pursued by teachers, the demands made on them and the conditions in which they work; as well as by changes over time in each of these. Of course, one finds teachers adopting different approaches to teaching, but the appropriate contrast is not between coping strategies on the one hand, and transformative strategies on the other (Hargreaves, 1978). All forms of teaching to be found in schools are 'adaptive' to some degree, otherwise they and their practitioners would not survive (Woods, 1979 and 1981). Indeed any strategy for change must be well adapted to its circumstances if it is to be successful.

Moreover, all forms of teaching, even the most 'radical', are both socially facilitated and constrained. Variation arises not simply from differences in the power of constraints, as, for example, with primary school teachers being freed to practise truly progressive teaching by the abolition of the 11+,[14] but also from changes in the goals of teachers, in the demands made upon them and in the opportunities open to them. Rather than trading on an implicit ideal regarding how teaching ought to be, measuring extant practice against it and setting out to find the constraints which prevent its realization, our aim should initially be to describe and explain the forms of teaching we find in secondary schools. We should not *assume* that those educational ideals or forms of pedagogy of which we disapprove require different forms of explanation to those of which we approve.[15] Otherwise, we run the risk of misunderstanding the nature of curriculum and pedagogy as they occur in schools through the influence of our own values. From this point of view, external examinations enter the theoretical account not only as a possible source of material constraint but also as an important component of many teachers' goals, as well as of the demands made upon them by others. And whether they represent goals or are experienced as constraints, they are open to the same kinds of sociological explanation. The nature of the problems to which examinations sometimes gave rise at Brookview, and the ways in which the teachers there resolved them, can only be properly understood in this theoretical context.

Acknowledgment

I am grateful to Martyn Hammersley (The Open University), David Halpin and Murray Saunders (University of Lancaster) for reading and commenting on an earlier draft of this paper.

Notes

1 1965 was the first year of CSE entries. The total entries (derived from DES, 1979a) for GCE and CSE were: CSE 64,863; GCE 587,339. The respective numbers of passes were: CSE 216,339; GCE 1,257,683. A 'pass' at CSE is defined as being above grade 5.
2 This figure does not include Wales. The total number of pupils entered for GCE and CSE in this year were markedly different: CSE 654,445; GCE 1,092,076. Whilst GCE entries had doubled, CSE entries had risen over tenfold. The passes were also significantly different: CSE 2,741,802; GCE 1,685,380.

3 Furthermore, examinations have been the focus of a not inconsiderable number of other reports and research investigations. Most of these have also been critical, stressing one or more of the following:

  (i) that exams, as presently constituted, are an unreliable measure of learning achievement (see, for example, Hartog and Rhodes, 1935);
  (ii) that exams have a negative effect on the curriculum and teaching (see, for example, the Spens Report, 1938; the Norwood Report, 1943; and HMI Secondary School Survey, 1979);
  (iii) that exam success is strongly correlated with social class and occupational attainment (see, for example, Halsey et al. 1980);
  (iv) that exams play a key role in selective assessment for cultural reproduction (see, for example, Bourdieu, 1971; Broadfoot, 1979).

  For an interesting account of how one examinations syndicate addresses these questions, see University of Cambridge, 1976.
4 In addition to the sources mentioned above (see note 3), see Board of Education, 1911; Norwood, 1929; Kelly, 1971; Schools Council, 1975; Stones, 1975; Mortimer, 1980.
5 The researcher was involved with Brookview school from September 1980 to July 1981. The methodology was, broadly, ethnographic. The study focused on teachers' practices, and a key area of the research was examinations. This involved not only the formal examinations, GCE and CSE, but also those sets of practices directly related to examinations: end-of-term assessment, reports, subject choice procedures in the third year, the construction of the timetable. Although semi-structured interviews were used at the start of the fieldwork, the majority of the data were collected either by recorded conversations with teachers or by informal interview. The status, department of the teacher and the context of the extract is shown in the text.
6 The relevance to employers of examinations in traditional knowledge areas is a matter of controversy. The famous Ruskin College speech by the then Prime Minister, James Callaghan, and the Great Debate which followed, posed questions about the preparation for industry and work that schools were giving to pupils. However, recent evidence given to a Parliamentary Committee by the CBI (House of Commons, 1981) suggests that the form of examinations, at least, is acceptable to that body; they state that they have 'strong support for a sound and impartial public examination system' and that 'the GCE system has been valued particularly for its dedication to intellectual application' (p. 118).
7 Generally, teachers at Brookview were convinced of the importance of their professional role as an improver of pupils' employment prospects via the public examination system. However, a significant minority were sceptical of the value of 'low-grade' exam success, that is, in relation to the task of securing work. As one teacher put it:

  what's the use of the exam? How can you tell a kid 'come on work for your CSE you'll get a grade 5 and it'll get you a job' when they know that the bloke who's got 5 O-levels hasn't had a job for 2 years so why all this hassle about exams? (Scale 2, English, interview)

8 That 'fairness' is an important element in external examining is graphically illustrated by the recent correspondence between discontented teachers and officials of the AEB with regard to the English Literature O-level of July 1982 (see *The Times Educational Supplement*, 1982, Nos. 3463 and 3465). Staff members' concern was that the Exam Board did not appear to be marking pupils' scripts fairly and, consequent upon the board's unwillingness to meet their requests for the scripts to be seen by the teachers concerned, they resolved to register their pupils with a

different exam board. However, notwithstanding the AEB's reaction in this case, generally exam boards also recognize the importance of being fair, and being seen to be fair. The University of Cambridge Local Examinations Syndicate, for example, in their review of the function of school exams, stress that 'examinations have to be scrupulously honest and impartial and seen to be so' (University of Cambridge, 1979, p. 8).

9 The reliance on text books was thrown into stark relief in the minority of cases where there was not a sufficient number of textbooks for the whole group. One such case was the O-level group in the geography department. Rather than change his practice of working from textbooks, the teacher accommodated the shortage, as he explained:

> generally it doesn't make that much difference in class, one can normally share or have one between a group, the real problem is setting homework ... what I do now is to set work for only half of them at a time which seems to work OK. (Head of Subject, geography, in conversation)

10 By the same token, the change in exam board not only affected exam course teaching but also the teaching in other year groups. For example, with reference to recent changes in the French O-level examination, the head of department said: 'it's not just 4th and 5th year teaching which is affected by the existence of a form of examining but throughout the school teaching is affected by what is coming' (Head of Subject, French, meeting).

11 The headmaster clearly indicated that internal exams were intended as a training for external exams, when he said at a meeting:

> When I first came here there was one exam a year which was at the end of the summer term and I said 'it's not enough', particularly when people are judged on their exam performance at the end of the day. They must have practice in exam technique so we must have two exams a year. (Headmaster, meeting)

12 Moreover, the extent and nature of teachers' self-evaluation based on internal exams was, in practice, varied. Only a minority of staff actively engaged in any detailed analysis of pupils' performance on the test or of the suitability of the test to assess the pupils. For the greater number of teachers self-evaluation was based simply on the raw scores and rank placings of their pupils. Apart from a lack of specialist knowledge that may be necessary to analyze exam papers, two important factors contributed to teachers unwillingness to engage in a more systematic form of evaluation. *Firstly*, that the structured time available to staff members (that is, the exam timetable) did not incorporate specific periods of time *after* the examination for reflection and reappraisal (indeed the 'timing' of the exam at the end of term was a major factor which contributed to the unwillingness of teachers to engage in an immediate evaluation of the course), and *secondly*, that a literate bias in the examination *form* (that is, that exam papers should involve written questions requiring a written answer) prevented the practical and science subjects from testing much of what had been taught (and this negated any self-evaluation). Reflecting on these arrangements and with reference to the first-year science course which was essentially practical in nature, a science teacher remarked:

> the trouble with the first year exam is we can't have a practical exam and any evaluation of practical ability which as I see it is a major part of the course ... we can't give them any form of practical exam where they are working on their own.... (Head of Subject, chemistry, interview)

13 See, for example, SHARP and GREEN (1975), who suggest that the concept 'busyness' is an important consideration in the teacher's day.

14 There is, of course, little evidence that primary teachers do pursue, let alone approximate, the progressive ideal even under these circumstances (SHARP and GREEN, 1975; GALTON, SIMON and CROLL, 1980). Their behaviour has more complex origins (BERLAK and BERLAK, 1981).
15 For a somewhat similar argument in the area of deviance, see MATZA (1969).

References

BERGER, P.L. and LUCKMAN, T. (1966) *The Social Construction of Reality*, Harmondsworth, Penguin Books.
BERLAK, A and BERLAK, H. (1981) *Dilemmas of Schooling*, Methuen.
BOARD OF EDUCATION (1911) *Report of the Consultative Committee on the Secondary School*, London, HMSO.
BOSSERT, S.T. (1979) *Tasks and Social Relationships in Classrooms*, Cambridge University Press.
BOURDIEU, P. and PASSERON, J. (1971) *Reproduction in Education, Society and Culture*, Sage Publications.
BOWLES, S. and GINTIS, H. (1976) *Schooling in Capitalist America*, Routledge and Kegau Paul.
BROADFOOT, P. (1979) *Assessment, Schools and Society*, Methuen.
BROADFOOT, P. (1983) 'Assessment constraints on curriculum practice: A comparative study', Chapter 12, this volume.
CENTRE FOR CONTEMPORARY CULTURAL STUDIES (1981) *Unpopular Education*, Hutchinson.
CONSULTATIVE COMMITTEE ON EDUCATION (1938) *Secondary Education* (The Spens Report), London, HMSO.
DAWE, A. (1970) 'The two sociologies' in *British Journal of Sociology*, 21, 2.
DENSCOMBE, M. (1980) 'Keeping 'em quiet! The Significance of noise for the practical activity of teaching', in WOODS, P. (Ed.) *Teacher Strategies*, Croom Helm.
DES (1979a) *Statistics of Education*, Vol. 2, School Leavers, London, HMSO.
DES (1979b) *Aspects of Secondary Education in England, A Survey by HM Inspectors of Schools*, London, HMSO.
DOYLE, W. and PONDER, G.A. (1977) 'The practicality ethic in teacher decision making', in *Interchange*, 8, 3, pp. 1–12.
EGGLESTON, J. (1975) 'Conflicting curriculum decisions', in *Educational Studies*, 1, 1, March, pp. 3–8.
GALTON, M., SIMON, B. and CROLL, P. (1980) *Inside the Primary Classroom*, Routledge and Kegan Paul.
GIDDENS, A. (1979) *Central Problems in Social Theory*, Macmillan.
GIDDENS, A. (1981) *A Contemporary Critique of Historical Materialism*, Macmillan.
GINSBURG, M. et al. (1980) 'Teachers conceptions of professionalism and trades unionism: An ideological analysis', in WOODS, P. (Ed.) *op. cit.*
GORBUTT, D. (1972) 'The new sociology of education', in *Education for Teaching*, 89, autumn.
HALSEY, A.H. et al. (1980) *Origins and Destinations*, Oxford University Press.
HAMMERSLEY, M. (1981) 'Ideology in the Staffroom? A cintique of false consciousness', in BARTON, L. and WALKER, S., (Ed,) *Schools Teachers and Teaching*, Lawes, Falmer, Press.
HARGREAVES, A. (1978) 'The significance of classroom coping strategies', in BARTON, L. and MEIGHAN, R. (Eds) *Sociological Interpretations of Schooling and Classrooms*, Nafferton.

HARGREAVES, A. (1981) 'Contrastive rhetoric and extremist talk: Teachers, hegemony and the educationist context' in BARTON, L. and WALKER, S. (Eds) *Schools, Teachers and Teaching*, Lewes, Falmer Press.
HARTOG, SIR P. and RHODES, E.C. (1935) *An Examination of Examinations*, Macmillan.
HILSUM, S. and STRONG, F.R. (1978) *The Secondary Teacher's Day*, Windsor, NFER.
HOUSE, E.R. (1974) *The Politics of Educational Innovations*, McCutchan.
HOUSE OF COMMONS, 1981 *Education, Science and Arts Committee, The Secondary School Curriculum and Examinations*, Minutes of Evidence Wednesday 11 March 1981, London, HMSO.
JACKSON, R. (1973) 'Old questions asked at exam time', in *The Times Higher Education Supplement*, 95, p. 2.
KARABEL, J. and HALSEY, A.H. (1977) *Power and Ideology in Education*, Oxford University Press.
KELLY, P.J. (1971) 'Re-appraisal of examinations', in *Journal of Curriculum Studies*, 3, 2, pp. 119–27.
LORTIE, D. (1975) *School Teacher: A Sociological Study*, University of Chicago Press.
LYONS, G. (1976) *The Administrative Tasks of Head and Senior Teachers in Large Secondary Schools*, University of Bristol.
MATZA, D. (1969) *Becoming Deviant*, Prentice Hall.
MORTIMER, P. (1980) 'Time to re-examine the system', in *The Guardian*, 24 June 1980.
NORTH WEST EDUCATIONAL MANAGEMENT CENTER (1981) 'A Study of the Process of Curriculum Re-Appraisal in a Group of Secondary Schools in one Local Education Authority', mimeo report.
NORWOOD, C. (1929) *The English Traditions of Education*, Murray.
POLLARD, A. (1980) 'Teacher interests and changing situations of survival threat in primary school classrooms', in WOODS, P. (Ed.), *op. cit.*
SCHOOLS COUNCIL (1975) *The Whole Curriculum, 13–16*, Working Paper 53, Evans/Methuen.
SECONDARY SCHOOLS EXAMINATION COUNCIL (1943) *Curriculum and Exams in Schools* (The Norwood Report), London, HMSO.
SHARP R. and GREEN, T. (1975) *Education and Social Control: A Study in Progressive Primary Education*, Routledge and Kegan Paul.
STONES, E. (1975) 'Black light on exams', in *British Journal of Teacher Education*, 1, 3, pp. 299–303.
TIMES EDUCATIONAL SUPPLEMENT, THE (1982) 'Exam dispute prompts boycott', No. 3463, 12 November, p. 2, and 'Upset over bizarre O-level grade', No. 3465, 26 November, p. 17.
TORRANCE, H. (1982a) 'School-based examining in England: A focus for school-based curriculum development and accountability', paper presented to the Annual Meeting of the American Educational Research Association, 19–23 March 1982, New York.
TORRANCE, H. (1982b) *Mode 3 Examining: Six Case Studies*, Longmans.
TURNER, G. (1983) 'The Hidden Curriculum of Examinations', Chapter 9, this volume.
UNIVERSITY OF CAMBRIDGE (1976) *School Examinations and their Function*, University of Cambridge Local Examinations Syndicate.
WHITTY, G. (1978) 'School examinations and the politics of school knowledge', in BARTON, L. and MEIGHAN, R. (Eds), *op. cit.*
WILLIS, P. (1977) *Learning to Labour*, Saxon House.
WOODS, P. (1979) *The Divided School*, Routledge and Kegan Paul.
WOODS, P. (1981) 'Strategies commitment and identity: Making and breaking the teacher', in BARTON, L. and WALKER, S. *Schools, Teachers and Teaching*, Barcombe, Falmer, Press.
YOUNG, M.F.D. (1971) *Knowledge and Control: New Directions for the Sociology of Education*, Collier-Macmillan.

11   A Question of Content and Control: Recent
     Conflicts over the Nature of School Examinations
     at 16+*

Richard Bowe and Geoff Whitty

This paper draws upon two overlapping pieces of research carried out in England and Wales between 1973 and 1982. One concerned the relationships between teachers and examining boards and the other explored those between the examining boards and the wider society (see Whitty, 1976 and 1978). Although the initial focus of the research was on the extent of teacher autonomy within the existing GCE and CSE examination systems, the developing controversy over the proposed common system of examining at 16+ became increasingly significant to it.[1] Therefore, it became increasingly concerned with interrelationships between the existing system of examining and the proposals for a new system intended to replace it. It seemed that developments within the existing system were affecting proposals for the new one and *vice versa*. In particular, the experiences of the various boards within the existing system appeared to influence the stances they took up in relation to the proposed changes, while their jockeying for position within the new system seemed in turn to affect the ways in which the boards operated the existing one. The most noticeable trend within both contexts during the period of our research, and the one upon which teachers remarked most often, was a reversion by the boards towards traditional approaches to examining and a consequent questioning of the ideology of direct teacher involvement in public examinations which had received some currency during the 1960s and early 1970s. There was thus something of a retreat from the concept of teacher control of assessment and the belief that examinations should reflect the needs of the curriculum, the very ideals that had informed the Beloe Report (SSEC, 1960) and led to the establishment of the CSE boards. Although these ideals were never fully translated into practice even by most of the CSE boards, there is little doubt that what developments there had been in this direction have suffered some serious reversals in recent years.

There has, in particular, been an increasing tendency on the part of the boards to favour placing restrictions upon those teachers who wish to utilize the Mode 3 regulations whereby classroom teachers can be directly involved in designing and assessing examination courses for their own pupils. Much of this paper focuses upon the fate of these Mode 3, or school-based, schemes of

---

* This chapter is based on a paper delivered at St Hilda's College, Oxford on 22 September 1981; it has been revised to take account of developments up to November 1982.

examination because they represent, and are publicly seen to represent, the fullest devolution of assessment powers to classroom teachers that has been attempted in English school-leaving examinations to date. Indeed, in the view of some observers, they provide opportunities for pupils themselves to be involved in the negotiation of curricula and assessment procedures (Murdock, 1974). For this reason, Mode 3 examinations provide a critical case for analyzing changes in approaches to examining over the past two decades or so, along with the determinants of those changes. However, even the less extreme ideology of professional teacher control of the committee structures of curriculum agencies and examination boards (which does not in itself imply any greater involvement of classroom teachers in the assessment of their own pupils) has also suffered challenges to its legitimacy during the same period.[2]

The research reported here was carried out through observation and interviewing in schools, examining boards and other relevant organizations and interest groups. It also involved scrutiny of the minutes of some of the examining boards and the regulations and circulars they issued to schools during the period of the research. The authors were themselves involved in 16+ examining for much of the period, but this experience was used only to provide background knowledge and access to key personnel rather than as a direct source of data for the research. As the research became increasingly concerned with the controversy over the proposed new system of examining, additional sources of data were sought in official pronouncements about the proposals, the various responses to those pronouncements and the press coverage of the ongoing debate. Part of our concern was to understand the effects of such developments on the practices of the examination boards and to explore their implications for teachers and pupils within schools. At the same time, we wanted to consider how far changes in policy and practice in school examining were congruent with other contemporary developments in and around education, such as the pressures for greater public accountability by schools and for a closer relationship between the curriculum and the professed needs of a modern industrial society. All this led us to examine the usefulness of various sociological theories for making sense of the developments we were studying and to assess the implications of our conclusions for future policies.

Mode 3 in the CSE and GCE System

In themselves, Mode 3 examinations, which permit teachers to set their own syllabuses and assess their own candidates (subject to moderation of syllabuses, assessment instruments and standards by the various CSE and GCE boards), are a relatively marginal aspect of the English examination system. The dominant method of examining English school leavers, as epitomized by the School Certificate and Mode 1 GCE examinations,[3] has entailed the use of externally devised syllabuses and unseen examination papers set and marked by examiners who have had no part in teaching the candidates. Even the CSE examinations have been dominated in most parts of the country by modified versions of this Mode 1 style of examining. Nevertheless, the period 1969–78 saw a steady rise in the proportion of CSE and GCE examinations being conducted under the alternative Mode 3 regulations. The proportion of CSE subject entries under this mode increased from just over 12 per cent in 1969 to just over 26 per cent in 1978. However, that year seems to have represented the peak of their influence and the 1979 and 1980 examinations have both witnessed small but perceptible decreases in the proportion of Mode 3 subject entries.[4] In the GCE examinations, where the proportion of entries under the equivalent specially approved syllabus regulations has always been considerably smaller, it is possible to detect a similar pattern of an increasing use of these regulations in the early 1970s and a relative decline in their use towards the end of the decade. Although many Mode 3 syllabuses continue in operation, they are being placed under increasing pressure. Indeed, there are many who argue that school-based assessment is inappropriate in the context of public examinations (UCLES, 1976) and some have gone so far as to suggest that it is dangerously subversive of both educational and political order (Cox, 1980). Whether or not such charges are valid, it seems that it is becoming increasingly difficult to get Mode 3 schemes of examination accepted by the boards and that those which are entirely school-based may become something of a rarity in the years to come.

Yet, even at the peak of their popularity, Mode 3s cannot be said to have destroyed the effectiveness of the external examination system as 'almost all that remains of the "public" aspect of the school curriculum' (Maclure, 1975). Even in the CSE, most entries have continued to be made under the Mode 1 regulations and standards in the other modes have been defined by reference to them. Those few regions, such as TWYLREB,[5] which adopted radically different structures and procedures, have generally been regarded as anomalies by most other boards. Many of the actual Mode 3 syllabuses that are in operation are relatively conventional in the nature of their content and the assessment techniques they employ, and many of those that can be seen as innovative are designed to bring into the curriculum practical or vocationally-related subjects excluded from the Mode 1 schemes offered by the boards. In many schools, we found that the major motivation for introducing Mode 3s had been to extend the public examination system beyond the top 60 per cent of pupils, not as a means of undermining that system's legitimacy, but as a way of solving motivational and social control problems within the school. In view of this, it is tempting to agree with Donald that 'it remains puzzling that Mode 3s should be regarded as subversive' (Donald, 1978) and it is, therefore, necessary to explore in some detail how and why the growth in Mode 3 examinations had been effectively checked by the end of the 1970s.

It is evident from a study by Smith (1976) that, as early as 1973, the boards were growing increasingly uneasy about certain aspects of Mode 3s, and by 1976 many boards were either implementing or contemplating greater controls over Mode 3 schemes. Though not even all the GCE boards shared the extreme views of the Cambridge syndicate (UCLES, 1976), most operated increasingly stringent criteria for the acceptance of Mode 3 schemes by the mid-1970s. In his 1974 survey, Smith found that generally 'GCE boards accept only those Mode III proposals which they are confident are fully comparable with their own Mode I syllabus'; he goes on to say that some GCE boards accept them only from schools they consider, from past experience, to be of 'good standing' (Smith, 1976, p. 22). Even the originally more open non-university-linked GCE board began to make it increasingly difficult for new schemes to be accepted from the mid-1970s onwards and, at the same time, demanded major modifications to existing ones, though not always making clear precisely what the new criteria of acceptability actually were.[6] Another strategy favoured by GCE boards was to defuse pressure from teachers for Mode 3 examinations by absorbing some of their demands into their main Mode 1 structures. This approach is summarized in, for example, a memorandum issued by the JMB Examinations Council in October 1975, entitled *Notes on the Submission of Applications for Specially Approved Syllabuses*, which instructed its subject committees as follows:

> Subject Committees are therefore instructed to follow a specific policy of guiding centres which submit proposals for specially approved syllabuses towards:
> 1. adopting syllabuses and schemes of assessment which make use of part of the published syllabuses and examinations,
> 2. co-operating with other centres to produce common schemes for special approval,
> 3. co-operating with the Subject Committee to produce syllabuses which could be included in the JMB schedule as available to all centres. (JMB, 1975)

At the same time, those new schemes which did continue to be accepted by GCE boards were required to be more closely linked to the nature of Mode 1 syllabuses. For example, the University of London Schools Examination Board included for the first time in its 1977 revision of *Specially Approved Syllabuses (Modes 2 and 3): Notes for the Guidance of Centres* the following statement:

> Mode 2 and Mode 3 proposals in certain subjects must ... satisfy specific subject criteria. Details of the subject criteria are available on request. Criteria for Integrated and Interdisciplinary subjects are also available: these criteria include guidance on naming. (ULSED, 1977)

While a look at these subject criteria indicates variations in the degree to which they restricted teachers' freedom in the choice of subject matter and assessment procedures, elements of Mode 1 content were quite clearly laid down in some of the criteria produced.

There seems to be a hint of worries about political extremism in a new instruction from one GCE board to its moderators in 1975 to ensure:

that material used in the course and the content of examination papers presents a balanced view, and, in particular, avoids a one-sided and tendentious presentation of social, political, religious and other controversial questions....[7]

However, this does not initially seem to have been the major issue. Rather, our discussions with board officials indicate that the boards' manifest reasons for making the changes described above, and thus applying a brake to the growth of school-based syllabuses from the mid-1970s onwards,[8] were the result of the bureaucratic difficulties these syllabuses created for the boards as organizations. This was quite clearly the case with the GCE boards, where the continued expansion of Mode 3 was seen as causing considerable problems of cost and administrative load. One GCE board official, interviewed in December 1976, put the case as follows:

> this is why perhaps as a board we have tended to see Mode 3 as a means of going towards a Mode 1 examination, and perhaps not geared ourselves generally to a system of Mode 3 examinations. I mean historically we were set up for Mode 1.[9]

Similar difficulties were referred to in another GCE board's internal research committee paper, discussing links between examinations and school curricula:

> The ambiguities are emphasised by its dual role (of examining body and matriculating authority) and by the structure of the committee system and the strategy which results from that structure for making decisions. The board seems to be well organized for producing Mode 1 examinations but is less well-equipped for the consideration of specific proposals from individual schools.[10]

Thus the GCE boards found that elements of their structures and their historic role made it administratively difficult to deal with Mode 3s.

Constitutionally, the CSE boards had more difficulty in controlling the growth and nature of Mode 3 schemes, since strictly speaking they could only reject a submission if it was incapable of being assessed or if its title did not correctly reflect its content. Therefore, they tended to employ administrative devices as a way of restricting the burgeoning growth of new and disparate Mode 3 schemes. These included the listing of approved titles, the lengthening and tightening of their submission procedures and requesting considerably more detail about aims, objectives, course content and assessment procedures than had hitherto been the case and, indeed, sometimes going far beyond that which was required for new Mode 1 syllabuses. Changes were also made to moderation procedures. Meanwhile, some of the boards began to consider more drastic measures such as the development of subject criteria and the insistence on the inclusion within all Mode 3 schemes of a core paper from a relevant Mode 1 examination, despite the fact that the constitutional legitimacy of such measures was open to question.

Even though the CSE boards did not adopt identical approaches to the GCE boards, there were thus considerable similarities in their attempts to increase control over school-based syllabuses and assessment procedures. It is clear that these measures made definite inroads into teacher autonomy within the CSE system and, indeed, by 1982 one board official commented that: 'quite frankly there are some [CSE] boards that in my view have gone really to a GCE stance in the control of syllabuses.'[11] Thus, although the CSE boards were set up specifically to cater for all modes of examination,[12] many of them expressed similar concerns to the GCE boards and, with only TWYLREB as a total exception,[13] their approaches to Mode 3 schemes have increasingly come to resemble those of the GCE boards. Established with centralized administrative structures (though to varying degrees) and run on a committee basis, many of the CSE boards also became alarmed at the costs and administrative load created by Mode 3s. Indeed, given the far greater demand for Mode 3 schemes in the CSE system, these boards often found it necessary to rationalize their submission procedures to an even greater extent than the GCE boards, some of which were able to maintain individual relationships with trusted schools. The rationalization of procedures in the CSE boards tended to draw control into an anonymous central adminsitrative machinery, producing the perception on the part of many teachers that power was being taken away from the grassroots teacher and that the relationship of mutual trust between fellow professionals was being destroyed. Such a development was recently confirmed to us by a CSE board official in the following terms:

> I think there has been a shift in what I would call the power balance between, from the original teacher, I mean the actual grassroots teacher who was marking scripts within the consortium to in fact, if you like, the institutionalized teacher within the board structure and in some senses also the LEAs and the heads have played a bigger part in the maintenance and organization of the system and the board staff have also.[14]

The increasing centralization and alienation experienced by teachers thus reflected a growth in the power of CSE board officials and the 'institutionalized teachers' who dominated the boards' committee structures and whose professional concerns sometimes became more closely identified with the organizational needs of their boards than with the educational requirements of their colleagues on the classroom floor.[15]

However, it would be misleading to assert that the nature and demands of the boards' administrative structures were alone responsible for the increasing controls over Mode 3s. There were also doubts about the quality and comparability of many Mode 3 schemes in relation to Mode 1s. Smith's (1976) study reported worries about mode comparability and public confidence in Mode 3 standards, while many of the board officials we spoke to during 1976 and 1977 expressed concern about the public image of Mode 3. Most felt that this supposedly poor public image was misplaced, at least in respect of their own boards' schemes, but, nevertheless, they argued that it had to be taken into account. For board officials 'public confidence' requires showing that an examination is objectively assessed and that standards are consistent from year to year and from examination to examination. In part this requirement was translated into technical considerations of validity, reliability and comparability. One particularly sensitive issue for the boards was the charge that it was easier for pupils to gain high grades on Mode 3 examinations but, at least in terms of the crude index of how many pupils gain Grade I passes in CSE Modes 1 and 3 respectively, the massive discrepancies that had existed in the early years had already disappeared by 1974.[16] In other words, this particular cause of public anxiety had already been eradicated prior to the major tightening up on Mode 3 submissions and moderation procedures that we have noted here. Nevertheless, it seems that at least as important in the notion of 'public confidence' as any technical considerations of this sort is a concern that assessment should be independently conducted by an outside person or agency. That in some respects this concern could override all other considerations is evident in the following remarks of one of the CSE board officials that we interviewed:

> At the moment, well, the whole history of CSE has shown an ever-increasing growth of this internally assessed component, and at some stage I think that one must look at this and determine how far it can grow without destroying the validity of the examination and undermining public confidence.... Rightly or wrongly, probably indeed wrongly in many respects ... the public's view is that they set great store by externality which they associate with impartiality and the idea, to many people, that the teacher is in fact responsible for examining his own candidate is abhorrent.[17]

There was, then, in the eyes of board officials, a tension between the growth of internal assessment and the traditional ideology of examinations, the latter being associated in most people's minds with the GCE boards' external assessment procedures. This traditional ideology has a long history, as is clear from an observation in the Dyke-Acland Report of 1911 which provided the basis for the School Certificate system. Referring to the university-based examining boards, it stated:

> They possessed an academic standing and an impartiality which were above question, and they achieved a right of entry into schools where any attempt at State interference at that time would have been hotly resented....[18]

A very similar view was expressed to us by the secretary of one of the university boards in 1977:

> Now you can't give teachers complete, absolute freedom, and in this country we've restricted teachers' freedom by making the examination

system the controlling element in the end.... I think our system ... is infinitely preferable to some dictation from on high.... In the wrong person's hands this could be dangerous.[19]

His view that the university boards were 'completely independent and impartial' agencies is widely held and the existence of such an external system, independently constituted, is frequently held to be the only proper guarantee of objectivity in assessment. A concern to prevent devaluation of their certificates led the boards to question the degree of internal assessment they should allow if they were to retain public confidence. Such concerns, together with the administrative considerations already referred to, justified the GCE boards' resistance to an extension of school-based assessment and led the CSE boards to revert towards conventional GCE-style procedures and structures, despite the fact that this sometimes conflicted with their original *raison d'être* and even, on occasions, their own assessment of what was educationally desirable.

However, the problems and doubts being experienced within the boards might well have been resolved differently had the issue of school-based assessment not become bound up in the late 1970s with the effects of public expenditure cuts, the 16+ reform controversy and the Great Debate. Even if the root problem had been a lack of teacher skill in syllabus construction and assessment, which clearly was very far from the whole story, the solution in a period of economic expansion might have been a massive programme of in-service training in this respect. In the context of education cuts and the general suspicion of professional autonomy generated during the Great Debate, this did not prove to be the preferred solution. Yet, interestingly, some elements of the Great Debate came to influence the controversy over the reform of 16+ examinations more than others. While the theme that the teaching profession should be made more accountable to those outside it clearly influenced the development of the examination reform proposals, the refrain that declining standards were at the heart of the problems facing Britain gradually took precedence over the other great concern, expressed particularly by industrialists and government ministers at the start of the Great Debate, that the school curriculum was largely irrelevant to the needs of contemporary society. Increasingly, the view of the *Black Paper* contributors, and their supporters in the Conservative Party, that what was needed was a return to rigorous academic standards and the curbing of the influence of trendy left-wing teachers superseded the corporatist concerns of industrialists and Labour ministers with modernizing the curriculum and enticing the 'best brains' into industry to foster economic growth. This development within the public and political arena permitted the university lobby and the GCE boards to win some quite striking victories in the negotiations over the future of 16+ examining in the late 1970s and early 1980s, thus reinforcing the trend towards traditional approaches to the practice and control of school examinations that, we have suggested, was already under way.

Recent Conflicts over the Nature of School Examinations at 16+

The 16+ Controversy

The Schools Council's recommendations for the future of examining at 16+ were published in September 1975 (JESC, 1975). In view of the fact that these proposals included the retention of opportunities for school-based assessment in the new common system of examining, and predicted that the proportion of candidates entered under other than Mode 1 arrangements would continue to grow, it is not surprising that they featured in the growing education debate.[20] The newspapers over this period were continually peppered with attacks upon schools and their falling standards and on progressive and radical teachers who had 'let our children down' (CCCS, 1981). The concentration upon standards fostered by the *Black Papers* seems to have been further extended by a concern about teacher assessment and, indeed, the two issues became fused together both within the 16+ controversy and within the Great Debate. Although by no means all the critics of the 16+ proposals accepted the claim made by *Black Paper* editor Cox that 'a main aim of the reformers is that CSE Mode 3 (teacher assessed) exams will become the norm' or even shared his own suspicions about their 'underlying ideological purpose' (Cox, 1980), the possibility that teacher-assessed work would be a significant part of any new examination arrangements did seem to provide a major source of concern for many of those commenting upon the Schools Council recommendations. Conservative politicians, some industrialists, senior university academics, as well as the more traditional GCE examining boards, joined in a massive onslaught on the initial proposals. During 1975 and 1976 the press contained numerous letters, articles and reports of speeches attacking CSE standards and the Mode 3 option and trying to ensure that such models did not come to dominate the new examination, upon whose credibility the legitimation of access to high status occupations might depend. Norman St John Stevas, Lord Belstead, Lord Annan, the CBI, the CVCP and the London and Cambridge examination boards were amongst those who publicly attacked the 16+ proposals by citing the problems of teacher-assessed elements or teacher control of the system.[21] It is hardly surprising that, in the face of this sort of opposition, Shirley Williams, the then Labour Secretary of State for Education, chose, in October 1976, to delay the implementation of the Schools Council's proposals and to submit them instead to a further round of deliberations by the Waddell Committee.

It was at this very time that, in response to the growing 'moral panic' about education, the Great Debate was being launched with the preparation of the Government's Yellow Book, and the now-famous speech by Prime Minister Callaghan at Ruskin College on 18 October 1976. Indeed, Hopkins has suggested that it was 'partly because of the Schools Council's injudicious exam proposals', which 'seemed to imply the most radical extension of teacher-power, with a heavy reliance on the Mode 3 principle', that 'teacher power was one of the main targets the Yellow Paper shot at' and hence one of the central issues in the subsequent Great Debate (Hopkins, 1978). Thus, if the William Tyndale affair was to provide the major pretext for the reining in of teacher autonomy (Dale, 1981), Mode 3 and the issue of teacher control of examinations also played its part. An article by Christopher Rowlands (1977) in the *Daily Mail* in April 1977 helped to keep the issue before the public view, while the statement by Tom Howarth to a meeting at the House of Commons that 'we cannot afford to become a CSE Mode 3 nation'[22] implied there was a link between teacher power and national decline and thus helped to legitimate attempts to restrict or abolish Mode 3s and to modify those parts of the Schools Council's proposals that pointed in the direction of teacher control. Yet the groups involved in this attack on the 16+ proposals were far from homogeneous. They had differing motives in arguing for the abandonment or modification of the proposals, and what now seems to be emerging will almost certainly be of more satisfaction to some of those groups than to others.

Thus, as the general political climate moved against the concept of teacher autonomy that had developed to some extent during the 1960s, it was the universities which were quick to reassert their traditional role as definers of school knowledge and external arbiters of standards, even though in the early stages of the Great Debate they had been deemed almost as culpable as school teachers for Britain's economic decline through their maintenance of elitist and overacademic curricula. Despite the fact that their own internal examination arrangements themselves constituted an extreme example of Mode 3-type procedures, the universities led the way in questioning the extent to which this would be an appropriate style of examining for the new 16+ examination. As already indicated, the university-based GCE boards modified their existing procedures for dealing with special syllabuses to accord with the changing climate and most CSE boards followed suit. In a situation where the various boards were competing for influence in the proposed new system, and given the prevailing ideological and political climate, the CSE boards would have been reluctant to support too great an emphasis on school-based assessment, even if the internal pressures we noted earlier had not been present.

Particularly significant in the discussions amongst the CSE boards outside the Midlands region was a fear that high status schools would defect to any new examining group that included the Oxbridge boards and thus create a hierarchy within the system. They felt it essential to appear totally respectable in terms of the traditional criteria upon which any such hierarchy would be based. This problem was exacerbated by the formation of a strong traditionalist GCE pressure group, COSSEC, consisting of the three Oxbridge boards and the SUJB, and was only partially alleviated by the eventual withdrawal of the Oxford Delegacy from this grouping.[23] For a crucial period, the activities and pronouncements of COSSEC severely restricted the willingness of other boards and groupings of boards to consider large-scale devolution of assessment powers to grassroots teachers under the new system. Although the more extreme position of the COSSEC grouping was not always accepted by the more liberal of the GCE boards (Doe, 1982), the debate was effectively located very firmly on terrain defined by the GCE rather than the CSE boards. When it came to defining subject criteria for the new examination, the GCE boards established 'shadow' committees to ensure that their own interests and traditions were not being sacrificed in the official joint bodies that were developing the criteria.

This reassertion of the role of the universities and the GCE examining boards also appeared to receive an increasing amount of official encouragement as the 16+ proposals went through their successive modifications. The Waddell proposals (DES, 1978a), in granting the universities a status different from mere 'users' of examination certificates (such as employers and non-university further and higher education) in its proposed regional supervisory bodies, seemed to legitimate their traditional role in defining knowledge and standards for schools. Furthermore, the GCE boards themselves seemed to be the key factor in the official acceptability of the various consortia of boards being considered. Although it is clear that they had already won some significant victories in the 16+ controversy well before the Conservative Party returned to power in May 1979 (DES, 1978b), these boards' traditional preference for external modes of assessment resonated particularly strongly with the views of leading Conservative politicians. Thus, when Mark Carlisle eventually announced his decision to proceed with a modified version of the common examination system, it was one in which the GCE boards were to be given an effective veto over the standards and assessment methods to be applied to the award of the top three grades in the new system (Fairhall, 1980). More recently, Sir Keith Joseph has been reported to be under pressure to preserve the GCE system in its entirety (Shaw, 1982) and seems at least to be considering confining non-traditional modes of examining, including teacher assessment, practical work and project work, to schemes eligible only for the award of the lower grades of the new system (Stevens, 1982).

The consequences of this increasing official encouragement for the traditions and practices of the universities and their examining boards are of considerable interest in view of the sorts of criticisms being made of schools during the Great Debate. They seem to legitimate something of a resurgence of traditional O-level styles of examining at the expense of some of the innovations developed within the CSE system during the 1960s and early 1970s (Doe, 1981b). These conventional modes of assessment are associated with the traditional high status curriculum, characterized by Michael F.D. Young as embodying literate, abstract, differentiated and uncommon sense knowledge (Young, 1971). This is not the knowledge demanded by corporate industry, but rather that very knowledge of the liberal academy that industrialists such as Weinstock (1976) and politicians such as Callaghan (1976) argued in 1976 was less than appropriate to contemporary needs. That this irony within the outcome of the 16+ controversy is recognized within the government and the DES is hinted at in the following report from *The Times Educational Supplement* in July 1981:

> Lady Young one of the Junior Education Ministers refuses to be drawn on whether the commitment to maintain 'standards' rules out the

opportunities to change the exams to fit what some see as the real demands of adult and working life. But DES officials make it clear that the priority is to get the new exam off the ground rather than introduce all the reforms that might be considered desirable. (Doe, 1981a)

It seems, then, that the universities and the GCE examining boards have been able to take advantage of broader attacks on teacher autonomy to regain some of the influence over the school curriculum that they ceded to the teaching profession in the 1960s. They have been able to do this, in the context of the 16+ reforms, by a selective utilization of the rhetoric of the Great Debate in which they exploited the previously-mentioned tension between the concept of 'standards' and the concept of 'relevance'. Furthermore, in reasserting their role as upholders of standards, they have reimposed a conformity to conceptions of school knowledge that had increasingly come under challenge in the preceding period, not only from progressive and radical teachers, but also from those concerned to make the curriculum serve the needs of industry. In granting part of what was demanded in the broader, but uncoordinated, attack on schools and teachers, the university lobby appears to have stolen something of a march on some of its early allies in that attack. Not only has the growth of Mode 3 assessment in the present systems been halted, and probably reversed, it now appears that the GCE boards will continue to dominate any new system of examining that takes us into the 1990s and, in some senses, with increased rather than diminished power. Part of the reason for this no doubt lies in the emergence of Cox's coeditor of the *Black Papers*, Rhodes Boyson, as an education spokesman for the Conservative Party and in the particular balance of forces that constitutes that party at the present time. Yet it also derives from the fact that the university lobby had a relatively clear view of the alternative to teacher assessment that it offered. Meanwhile, the industrial lobby was much less clear or united about its own preferred alternative and the organized teaching profession felt obliged to adopt a largely defensive posture in the face of what it perceived as a betrayal partly initiated by its erstwhile allies in the 1974–9 Labour government.

Analysis

We have seen that in recent years there has been something of a delegitimation of school-based assessment even within those parts of the examination system in which it had apparently been gaining increasing acceptability in the earlier period. This can be seen as partly an effect of the particular bureaucratic structures employed by the boards, but it was also influenced by an accelerating public concern about a perceived lack of objectivity and externality in assessment at 16+. Particularly in the context of the controversy over the proposed common examination system, this led even those boards established on the basis of teacher representation and control to limit the degree of classroom teacher participation in the actual process of assessment. Although some of the changes that we have outlined might be interpreted as expressions of the sort of technical rationality that is often seen as serving the developing needs of corporate capitalism, others involve a reassertion of traditionalist values and approaches to examining and seem rather less easily explicable in such terms.

In view of the apparent complexity of the origins and of the effects of these changes in examining at 16+, it is necessary to raise some questions about the ways in which developments in examination policy have been discussed by various neo-Marxist commentators on education. Some of these authors have attempted to explain examination reform, like other recent developments in education, in terms of a general set of requirements derived from the economic and political needs of capitalism in a period of crisis. Thus, for instance, Donald (1978) has drawn upon the work of Holloway and Picciotto (1977) to suggest that, as part of the functionalization of the state for the accumulation of capital, one would expect to find 'examinations being made more "efficient" in terms of what they test, how the testing is done, and how the system is controlled' (Donald, 1978, p. 5). In broad terms, he regards this as the thrust of the changes that have taken place in school examinations in recent years, though later in the article he does recognize that a wide range of determinations has contributed to them. More concretely, Hurford has argued that the 16+ reform proposals

> represent a way in which the 'space' that education once had within society is being eroded, as the ruling class seeks a more direct and effective control over education than can be achieved through the Teacher Establishment....
>
> The CSE Boards have not been as dominated by the higher education interests as the GCE and have therefore been a less effective means of curriculum control. The new GCE [sic] boards will correct this and ensure more proper representation from 'industry'.
>
> Put in these terms it is easier to see how the 16+ will fit the new scenario where on the one hand education is more clearly seen to serve the interests of the nation/industry and on the other appear to give equality of opportunity in the shrinking job market. (Hurford, 1979, p. 7)

Yet, while the effects of an accumulation crisis can be seen as influences on the developments discussed here, particularly through the impact of public expenditure cuts on educational priorities and in the demands of industrialists and Labour ministers that education should serve the needs of industry, the situation seems much less straightforward than Hurford and even Donald imply. Our own account suggests that both their analyses tend to overestimate the homogeneity of the state and the ruling class and underemphasize the extent to which outcomes, while influenced by the requirements of capital, are also contingent upon a variety of concrete historical struggles and may potentially be at variance with those requirements.

Put at its simplest, it seems clear that the outcomes of the examinations controversy are out of step with the views of capital's requirements articulated by large sections of the industrial lobby, even if this lobby is somewhat unclear about the precise requirements it has of the examination system and about where control of the system should lie. While the influential article by Weinstock (1976) that presaged the Great Debate was entitled 'I blame the teachers', it had also attacked the Platonic traditions of English academic life out of which the GCE examination system had developed. Our own interviews with employers even pointed to a rather more ambivalent orientation towards Mode 3 examinations than we had anticipated. Where they were reasonably well understood, concern about the difficulties of maintaining comparability was often balanced by more favourable comments about the ways in which Mode 3 courses were sometimes of greater industrial and vocational relevance than the typical range of Mode 1 syllabuses offered by the boards.[24] It is also pertinent to note that the Rubber and Plastics Industry Training Board was making an extremely favourable appraisal of the local relevance of many Mode 3 schemes at the very time that the Confederation of British Industry was arguing at national level that school-based assessment threatened standards in the new 16+ examination (Jackson, 1976). These tensions contributed to the failure of the industrial lobby to organize as effectively as the universities and the GCE examination boards, a failure marked by the fact that the only concessions made by these boards to the industrial lobby have been largely cosmetic ones, such as the co-option of industrialists onto committees that have no direct involvement in syllabus development.[25] In these circumstances, it is scarcely surprising that there is little in the current proposals for the new 16+ examination which suggests that they have been influenced significantly by the agreed, if vague, demand of the industrial lobby that examination courses be made more relevant to the needs of industry.

However, to show that the industrial lobby has little direct influence over school examinations, or that recent developments are not in accord with its overt demands, does not, of course, establish that such developments fail to function effectively for capital. It is necessary to give consideration to the more sophisticated argument that the exercise of control on behalf of capital is carried out largely behind our backs. Thus, for example, Bourdieu and Passeron (1977) have pointed to the way in which the apparent autonomy of the traditional academic curriculum, and its associated assessment procedures, from direct capitalist control has produced a systematic misrecognition of the vital role of the school in the reproduction of capitalist social relations. Yet, whatever the historic role of the academic curriculum, it seems questionable whether the approaches of university traditionalists and industrialists would be equally functional for capital at the present time. Indeed, the reassertion of university influence in the current conjuncture in Britain can be seen as, in some respects, an attempt to resist a reorientation of the education system towards a model more in accordance with the requirements of a new phase of capitalist development.

Nevertheless, Apple (1980) has suggested that, rather more important than the fate of any direct attempts by industry to influence the nature of the curriculum, has been the introduction into schools of the sort of technical modes of control over the workforce that are increasingly dominant within the capitalist labour process. While Apple's own examples are based upon the large-scale introduction of teaching packages into American schools, the systematic tightening of control over British teachers via changes in technical procedures within examination boards would also seem to lend support to his thesis. This is particularly so in the case of those examining boards that introduced tight statistical moderation procedures to counter charges of a lack of reliability and comparability in the assessment of Mode 3 components. In view of the fact that these changes were partly a response to DES pressures for greater standardization and accountability, they would seem to offer credibility to the notion of the state functionalizing education for capital. There are problems with this argument too, however. For, even assuming that such developments within education operate in the interests of capital, it has not usually been those boards most advanced in developing moderation techniques approximating to Apple's conception of technical control that have been at the forefront of the developments described in this paper. Furthermore, the technical efficacy of the traditional Mode 1 GCE styles of examining which are experiencing something of a resurgence is highly questionable in relation to some of the newer styles of assessment developed by the CSE boards.

The contradictory nature of this evidence suggests that the relationships between capitalism, the state and education are rather more complex than some neo-Marxist analyses have implied. Such analyses can have the effect of deflecting our attention from aspects of recent developments that could have important implications for the future policy and practice of those who wish to contest those developments. Our account suggests that it is inappropriate to view recent developments in and around examinations purely in terms of the requirements of capital accumulation. Further, it is important not only to chronicle the fact of the subjection of teachers to greater external control, but also to detail the struggles over how that control is to be exercised and to identify the nature and goals of the various parties involved. These struggles can usefully be viewed as taking place between the industrial trainers, the old humanists and the public educators, the three groups which Williams (1961) has argued have traditionally been involved in defining the nature of the English school curriculum.

In broad terms, the contemporary industrial lobby corresponds to Williams' industrial trainers and is centrally concerned that schools should teach the knowledge, skills and particularly the attitudes that are relevant to, and promote a positive image of, industry. Its lack of precise prescriptions in the examinations field has, however, already been alluded to. The universities and their associated examination boards correspond to the old humanists and support a broad liberal education based upon the traditional academic disciplines. They are particularly concerned with the maintenance of standards amongst that section of the population deemed capable of undertaking academic studies and with the preservation of 'high' culture. Although it would be misleading to treat contemporary universities as a monolithic 'old humanist' lobby, we would argue that, even today, the activities of British universities remain far less fully integrated with those of corporate capitalism than, say, their North American counterparts. What Weinstock (1976) terms the 'respectable' version of the anti-industry lobby, has remained strong and, for reasons outlined by Wiener (1981), this apparently residual set of cultural values has remained remarkably resilient within British society and its universities well into the late twentieth century. In the examinations controversy, the universities and the GCE boards have had the advantage of a clear curriculum model, while defence of traditional values has appealed to the sort of 'golden age' mentality engendered by the current crisis and encouraged by some leading Conservative politicians.

The third group, the public educators, is made up of the teaching profession and the labour movement, and its central aim has been to extend the right to education to all groups in society. Its main curriculum concerns have been to avoid anything too narrowly vocational or anything that would place restrictions upon the professional judgments of teachers. In the particular conflict under consideration here, this lobby was severely handicapped by the fact that a Labour government had been at the forefront of the attack on teacher autonomy and, in the aftermath of the recriminations caused by this, it lacked both the unity and common purpose necessary for the development of a more progressive alternative appropriate to the changing context. Salter and Tapper (1981) have argued that a fourth group, the educational bureaucrats, has become influential in the development of curriculum policy in recent years, but in this case its influence seems to have been confined to the early days of the Great Debate and it has certainly declined rapidly since the change of political control at Westminster.

In this situation, the university and GCE board initiatives have been able to ensure the maintenance of a more significant place for old humanist conceptions of a liberal secondary education than might have been predicted from the sorts of attacks on the traditional school curriculum that emanated from representatives of government and industry in those early stages of the Great Debate – or, indeed, from the cruder versions of neo-Marxist theory that have been used to explain them. Though there has not been a complete reversion to the tight curricular control ensured by the School Certificate system prior to the 1950s, the old humanist lobby appears to have secured a considerable influence over the committee structures, syllabus content and assessment procedures for an examination system intended to serve a much larger proportion of the population than was ever the target for the School Certificate or GCE systems.

Implications

In terms of future policy, our own interest lies in the development of a viable strategy for curricula and examinations on the part of the public educators, and, in particular, one that is in keeping with the broader political objectives of the labour movement. We propose, therefore, to conclude with a fuller consideration of the role of the public education lobby in the 16+ controversy to date and of its potential role in the future. In retrospect, it is apparent that the public educators have, through their overriding concern to secure a common system of examining almost regardless of its nature, permitted key questions about the content and control of that system to be decided by the other parties involved. In practice, this has meant that, with the relative decline of the CSE model of school examining, the teaching profession itself has effectively lost some of the control over examinations which it has been exercising in recent years. Meanwhile its traditional allies in the public education lobby, the Left and the labour movement, have become increasingly divided over the best way to proceed. Initially, their stance in the 16+ debate paralleled their involvement in the development of comprehensive education itself, with the major emphasis being placed upon the achievement of a common organizational structure and the presumption that teachers should decide on the content of that structure. When the Labour government signalled its abandonment of the position that the nature of the school curriculum was an issue legitimately left to the professional judgment of teachers and seemed to place its weight behind the industrial lobby (Callaghan, 1976), the Left and the labour movement found themselves without a clear position. Some continued to back the traditional policy of professional autonomy, others backed the parliamentary leadership, whilst still others seemed to favour the old humanist position as offering space within which socialist teachers could resist corporate encroachments into education. What was not in evidence was any attempt to develop and insert into the debates on curricula and examinations a distinctively socialist position around which to mobilize. As it became clear that conventional notions of teacher autonomy were no longer able to command widespread support, this absence was a crucial one and it allowed the issues to be contested between the old humanists and the industrial trainers, neither of whose approaches was primarily egalitarian or democratic in orientation.

It is tempting, and perhaps even consoling, for those on the left to argue that a distinctively socialist policy on curricula and examinations would either be an irrelevance or doomed to failure in the face of capital's need to restructure the education system in its interests. Yet our study suggests that, although the genesis of many recent state initiatives may have been related to an attempt to secure the conditions of existence for a new phase of capitalism, the outcomes have not in any straightforward sense been a determined effect of capitalist economic imperatives. Outcomes are achieved through ideological discourse and political struggle and there is considerable scope for resisting such imperatives, as the old humanist lobby appears to have done in this particular instance. The Left has a propensity to fall victim to its own theories, so that theories of tendency too often and too easily become statements of necessity which effectively obscure possibilities for contesting the terrain upon which tendencies become real outcomes. This is not to suggest that socialist alternatives can readily be established within an educational system of a capitalist society, but mobilization around such alternatives can produce different compromises, some of which are more likely to provide secure bases for future struggles than others. Thus, it should not be assumed that a more positive intervention by the Left in the examination controversy, based upon a programme distinct from that of either the old humanists or the industrial trainers, and superseding a blind commitment to professional autonomy, would have been without significant effects. Just as the actual compromise now achieved by the intervention of the supposedly residual old humanist elements within British society is decidedly different from that which might have been read off from the more economistic theories that have been used to account for recent developments in education, so a rather more progressive outcome might also have been attainable. Although any settlement likely to have emerged would have been well within the limits of what Kellner (1978) terms hegemonic ideology, a more concerted intervention by the Left might have led to a compromise with more potential for future counter-hegemonic struggles than this one. The extent to which any settlement would or would not be in the long-term interests of the Left would, however, be highly dependent upon its relationship to the outcomes of other struggles in and around the state. There is, therefore, every reason for the Left to develop a position on curricula and examinations as part of the broader political strategy of the labour movement.

Indeed, the development of such a position can be seen to be a matter of some urgency when it is recognized just how fragile the emergent settlement discussed here actually is. We have already pointed to a number of tensions in the foregoing debates, and particularly that between 'standards' and 'relevance'. It seems likely that these will re-emerge as the industrial lobby comes to recognize just how little impact it has had on that part of the educational system that so often defines its prevailing ethos. The proposed abolition of the Schools Council and its replacement with separate councils for curricula and examinations represents a further blow to the professional wing of the public education lobby, but also makes representation of other interests on the examinations council entirely a matter of patronage by the Secretary of State.[26] The continuing prevarications of the present Secretary of State, Sir Keith Joseph, about whether the common examination at 16+ will actually go ahead both adds to the uncertainty and leaves open the possibility of new initiatives. In these circumstances proposals for a more genuinely democratic and responsive system of school assessment could exploit some of these tensions and gain support from some of the groups excluded from the current settlement. Much could be learnt from the more devolved approaches to examining, such as those developed by TWYLREB in the 1960s, but devolution would need to be conceived not just as devolution to the grassroots teacher, but to a wide range of community interests as well. By responding to criticisms of professional control, while resisting the narrow or elitist alternatives offered by the industrial trainers and the old humanists, the labour movement might thus begin to build an alternative that could command widespread support and contribute to the realization of its political objectives.

Notes

1 This chapter is concerned particularly with school examinations at 16+. The General Certificate of Education (GCE) Ordinary Level examinations (which superseded the old School Certificate system in 1951) are intended for the top 20 per cent of the age cohort and are administered by examination boards which, in all but one case, have strong university links. The Certificate of Secondary Education (CSE), administered by regional boards dominated by teacher and local authority interests, are intended for the next 40 per cent of the age group, but in practice have been extended somewhat beyond this. The as yet unnamed proposed common examination at 16+ is to be administered by regional consortia of existing boards and is intended to cater for 60 per cent of the age group. Provision for the remaining 40 per cent is not discussed here and may well be subject to different influences from those identified. However, there is recent evidence of the GCE boards attempting to operate in this sector through the development of graded tests (see *The Times Educational Supplement*, 5 and 12 November 1982) though it also seems likely that the recent Manpower Services Commission initiatives in the school sector are more likely to influence the curriculum of this 40 per cent than that of those taking conventional public examinations (see *The Times Higher Education Supplement*, 19 November 1982).

2 The shift away from teacher control, and even teacher representation via clearly defined constituencies, is symbolized by Sir Keith Joseph's decision to make the new Examinations Council, which is to take over the examinations functions of the Schools Council, an appointed rather than a representative body. The model of teacher control associated with the CSE boards and the original Schools Council appears to be less acceptable in the present climate than the GCE board approach where the basis of representation is often less clear-cut and varies at different levels within the boards. It is impossible to do justice to the complexity of the constitutions of the various boards in a brief chapter of this nature. Some of the GCE boards have gone further in involving teachers than others, but in most boards the modes of appointment to the various committees make them even less clearly representative of practising teachers than the CSE boards. The relationship of the GCE boards to the universities is also complex but, although only the London board remains fully incorporated within its parent university, the appointment procedures that are employed by all the university-based GCE boards effectively ensure that they retain a university-oriented ethos.

3 In Mode 1, the board provides the syllabus, sets the examination and carries out the assessment, in Mode 2 the school provides the syllabus but the board carries out all the assessment procedures, while in Mode 3 the school provides the syllabus and carries out its own assessment procedures subject to moderation by the board. Although the terms Mode 1, 2 and 3 derive from the regulations governing the Certificate of Secondary Education (CSE), they have subsequently been applied generically to the long-standing Special Syllabus procedures in the General Certificate of Education (GCE) examinations. In some CSE boards, Mode 1 papers are initially marked by candidates' own teachers, while some Mode 1 schemes contain a teacher-assessed element, though these schemes are perhaps better considered 'mixed

mode examinations', especially where the school has freedom of choice over the content of that element. Methods of assessment are not restricted to particular modes of examination, but in practice traditional unseen examination papers remain the standard method of assessment in the vast majority of Mode 1 syllabuses, whilst continuous assessment and coursework assessment procedures are often favoured within Mode 3 schemes, though usually in combination with formal examination papers.

4 Department of Education and Science, *Statistics of Education*, Vol. 2 for each of the years 1969–80. These were published by HMSO for the years 1969–79 and are available from the DES for 1980. Recently available figures for 1981 confirm this downward trend. In addition, these findings were broadly confirmed by a Schools Council-sponsored study by H. Torrance entitled *Mode III Examining: Six Case Studies*, available from Longmans Resources Unit, York.

5 The West Yorkshire and Lindsey Regional Examining Board had the most fully devolved system of examining of all the CSE boards and the highest proportion of subject entries under the Mode 3 regulations, these entries accounting for over 68 per cent of all entries in 1974. Smith (1976) notes that because 'TWYLREB's administrative arrangements, *from the outset*, have been designed to encourage positively the development of Mode III ... Mode III schemes are no more expensive to operate than Mode I' [our emphasis]. However, it remains to be seen how far the traditions of TWYLREB are maintained when it merges with a neighbouring board, as a TWYLREB official claimed to us in an interview that his board 'was really the *only* one of the boards that can claim itself to be truly teacher-controlled' (fieldwork interview, 4 March 1977).

6 Many of the teachers interviewed commented that they were in the dark about what was required by the board in the way of evidence that would justify the retention of their Mode 3 schemes. One teacher, who was also a Mode 1 chief examiner, made the revealing remark, 'I wouldn't know a lot about the criteria on the O-Level, but for the fact that, since I'm involved as an examiner outside the Mode 3 procedures, I as a chief examiner was called to a series of meetings in London ...' (fieldwork interview, 13 January 1978).

7 From the document outlining the duties of Mode 3 moderators issued to its moderators by one of the GCE boards in 1975.

8 Because of the time involved in submission and resubmission procedures, this did not affect subject entries until the late 1970s.

9 Fieldwork interview, 16 December 1976.

10 GCE board internal research paper, 1975.

11 Fieldwork interview, 19 May 1982.

12 All the CSE boards were required to include in their constitutions, under the section entitled 'Duties and Powers of the Board', a statement accepting their duty to provide for all modes of examination.

13 See note 5 above.

14 Fieldwork interview, 19 May 1982.

15 On this aspect of the development of the CSE, the recent comments of P. Reynolds, a member of the Cockcroft Committee, are of interest. In a letter to *The Times Educational Supplement* on 30 July 1982, he claimed that 'teacher control of CSE boards is no longer a reality. The boards appear to be self-perpetuating bodies, more concerned with financial security and maintaining existing systems.... The wonderful ideal of examinations to suit the needs of pupils has become a farce.' Many of the teachers in our research expressed similar views about their local CSE boards.

16 Department of Education and Science, *Statistics of Education*, Vol. 2, 1969–79, London, HMSO, 1971–81.

17 Fieldwork interview, 5 November 1976.

18 *Parliamentary Papers*, No. XVI, 1911.

19 Fieldwork interview, 16 December 1976.
20 Opponents of 16+ reform chose to exaggerate the extent to which the Joint Examinations Sub-committee actually advocated a radical extension of school-based assessment.
21 See, for example, *The Guardian*, 24 November 1975, *The Times Educational Supplement*, 9 January, 16 January, 27 February, 19 March, 9 April and 28 May 1976.
22 Reported in *The Times Educational Supplement*, 20 May 1977.
23 COSSEC, the Cambridge, Oxford and Southern Schools Examining Consortium, originally consisted of the University of Cambridge Local Examinations Syndicate, the Oxford and Cambridge Schools Examination Board, the Oxford Delegacy of Local Examinations and the Southern Universities Joint Board.
24 For example, the training officer of a heavy engineering firm interviewed during our fieldwork remarked that he was 'delighted to hear the chap who was talking about this Technology Mode 3 course' because the teacher concerned had tried to involve local industrialists in its planning to ensure that it was 'a course that *had* a relevance to local industry'. He also stated that he would 'buy Mode 3 Maths because a man can cut out a lot of old-fashioned things and keep in a lot of things that somebody feels are old-fashioned and damn well aren't, like imperial measure' (fieldwork interview, 14 October 1977). See also a recent publication by Jamieson and Lightfoot (1982) which suggests that the sort of liaison fostered at local level by the Schools Council Industry Project sometimes led to an increase in school-based examining methods in the project areas.
25 This was a strategy for coping with the Great Debate described by an official of one of the GCE boards in an interview on 22 June 1977. The perception of such arrangements by industrialists is typified by the response of an industrial training officer to a question about his own contact with school examination boards during our interview on 14 October 1977. He replied, 'No contact at all ... I would think that somewhere somehow at some odd committee our Engineering Employers' Federation ... would have some contact, but whether it's fruitful, I would doubt....' See also the recent comments by the Director-General of the National Economic Development Office about the 'effective autonomy [of examination boards] from influences outside the education sector', quoted in *The Guardian*, 10 November 1982.
26 In Cockcroft, Sir Keith Joseph's appointee as Chairman of the Examinations Council (*The Times Educational Supplement*, 26 November 1982), the government has at least appointed someone with rather more credibility with a range of interests than would have been the case if the earlier rumours of the appointment of Brian Cox had been substantiated. Nevertheless, the basis of representation on the new body remains unacceptable to many groups and, at the time of going to press, the National Union of Teachers had resolved to boycott its deliberations.

References

APPLE, M.W. (1980) 'Curricular form and the logic of technical control', in BARTON, L., MEIGHAN, R. and WALKER, S. (Eds), *Schooling Ideology and the Curriculum*, Lewes, Falmer Press.
BOURDIEU, P. and PASSERON, J.-C. (1977) *Reproduction in Education, Society and Culture*, London, Sage Publication.
CALLAGHAN, J. (1976) 'Towards a national debate', in *Education*, 22 October.
CCCS (1981) *Unpopular Education*, London, Hutchinson.
COX, B. (1980) 'How education fails Britain's children', in *Now*, 52.
DALE, R. (1981) 'Control, accountability and William Tyndale', in DALE, R., ESLAND,

G., FERGUSSON, R., and MACDONALD, M. (Eds), *Schooling and the National Interest*, Lewes, Falmer Press.
DES (1978a) *School Examinations*, Parts 1 and 2, London, HMSO.
DES (1978b) *Secondary School Examinations: A Single System at 16 Plus*, London, HMSO.
DOE, B. (1981a) 'Fears grow on eve of 16 plus exam preview', in *The Times Educational Supplement*, 3 July.
DOE, B. (1981b) 'Alarm spreads over proposals for new 16+ exams', in *The Times Educational Supplement*, 20 November.
DOE, B. (1982) 'Cambridge plan for 16 plus rejected by GCE boards', in *The Times Educational Supplement*, 5 March.
DONALD, J. (1978) 'Examinations and strategies', in *Screen Education*, 26.
FAIRHALL, J. (1980) 'Single exam system to replace O-level, CSE', in *The Guardian*, 20 February.
HOLLOWAY, J. and PICCIOTTO, S. (1977), 'Capital, crisis and the state', in *Capital and Class*, 2.
HOPKINS, A. (1978) *The School Debate*, Harmondsworth, Penguin Books.
HURFORD, J. (1979) 'Testing times', in *Rank and File Teacher*, 64.
JACKSON, M. (1976) 'Sniped at now from all sides', in *The Times Educational Supplement*, 3 December.
JAMIESON, I. and LIGHTFOOT, M. (1982) *Schools and Industry*, London, Methuen.
JESC (1975) *Examinations at 16+: Proposals for the Future*, London, Schools Council.
JMB (1975) *Notes on the Submission of Specially Approved Syllabuses*, Manchester, Joint Matriculation Board.
KELLNER, D. (1978) 'Ideology, Marxism and advanced capitalism', in *Socialist Review*, 42.
MACLURE, S. (1975) 'The Schools Council and examinations' in BELL, R. and PRESCOTT, W. (Eds), *The Schools Council: A Second Look?* London, Ward Lock.
MURDOCK, G. (1974) 'The politics of culture', in HOLLY, D. (Ed.), *Education or Domination?* London, Arrow Books.
ROWLANDS, C. (1977) 'How the teaching cheats brand our children', in *Daily Mail*, 5 April.
SALTER, B. and TAPPER, T. (1981) *Education, Politics and the State*, London, Grant McIntyre.
SSEC (1960) *Secondary School Examinations Other Than the GCE*, London, HMSO.
SHAW, D. (1982) 'Forget single 16 plus exam, says MP', in *The Standard*, 4 February.
SMITH, C.H. (1976) *Mode III Examinations in the CSE and GCE* (Schools Council Examinations Bulletin 34), London, Evans/Methuen.
STEVENS, A. (1982) 'O-levels face a test', in *The Observer*, 14 February.
UCLES (1976) *School Examinations and their Function*, Cambridge, University of Cambridge Local Examinations Syndicate.
ULSED (1977) *Specially Approved Syllabuses (Modes 2 & 3): Notes for the Guidance of Centres*, London, University of London School Examinations Department.
WEINSTOCK, A. (1976) 'I blame the teachers', in *The Times Educational Supplement*, 23 January.
WHITTY, G. (1976) 'Teachers and examiners' in WHITTY, G. and YOUNG, M. (Eds) *Explorations in the Politics of School Knowledge*, Driffield, Nafferton Books.
WHITTY, G. (1978) 'School examinations and the politics of school knowledge', in BARTON, L. and MEIGHAN, R. (Eds), *Sociological Interpretations of Schooling and Classrooms*, Driffield, Nafferton Books.
WIENER, M.J. (1981) *English Culture and the Decline of the Industrial Spirit, 1850–1980*, Cambridge, Cambridge University Press.
WILLIAMS, R. (1961) *The Long Revolution*, London, Chatto and Windus.
YOUNG, M.F.D. (1971) *Knowledge and Control: New Directions for the Sociology of Education*, London, Collier-Macmillan.

12 Assessment Constraints on Curriculum Practice: A Comparative Study

Patricia Broadfoot

There is a long-standing assumption that in 'centralized' education systems such as those of France and Sweden, teachers' practice is more closely controlled than in 'decentralized' systems such as that of England or the United States.[1] This paper sets out to show that such an equation of strong control with a high degree of centralization is misleading for it fails to take into account less obvious and generally much more powerful sources of control and constraint.

In particular, I want to propose that a more useful way of identifying differences in the control of teachers' curriculum practice in different types of education systems is in terms of the different assessment procedures employed within those systems, since in any sort of mass education system assessment procedures act as one of the greatest constraints on classroom practice. In this sense, much of the variation between systems in terms of their dominant patterns of control can best be understood in terms of the particular *form* that control by assessment takes in each case. Such differences in control, I must stress again, cannot be reduced simply to differences between centralized and decentralized systems. Assessment procedures vary on grounds other than this. They may, for instance, be informal or formal, school-based or external. This does not mean that the importance of assessment factors makes the centralization issue irrelevant to the study of control over teachers' practice. Indeed, a centralized, government-controlled external assessment apparatus possesses great power to enforce the pursuit of a centrally determined curriculum. But the distinctions between different forms of assessment are much more subtle than this: more than a dichotomy between school-based (decentralized) and external (centralized) procedures of assessment. For, where a number of more or less independent institutions like the English examination boards and the Schools Council provide for external assessment, control can be both tight *and* uncentralized.

It is, therefore, important to distinguish between the *degree* of assessment control on curriculum practice on the one hand (strong or weak) and the *source* of that control (central or local) on the other. This distinction is crucial, for the tendency to conflate *strong* control with *central* control within the concept of centralization has led to an overpreoccupation with administrative variables in the study of differences between educational systems and a consequent disregard for how that control is actually mediated and ultimately experienced by teachers in the schools.

In this chapter, I compare two education systems – those of France and England – since they are often taken to be classic instances of centralized and decentralized systems respectively (Archer, 1979). Despite initial appearances, I suggest, the two systems are characterized by a remarkably similar *degree* of control over teachers' practice. Much more significant, I propose, are the differences between the systems in the *form* that control through assessment takes and in *where* power over those assessment procedures is located. In the so-called centralized system of France there has traditionally been a great emphasis on assessment by 'process evaluation', by the exertion of control through the bureaucratic relationships of accountability to which teachers are subject. This is essentially the control of inspection of the quality of the educational process itself. By contrast, within the very strong traditions of curricular freedom and professional autonomy which have characterized the English decentralized system, control over teachers' behaviour and the basis of their accountability has, in the main, been via 'product evaluation' – by evaluation of educational products as expressed in various forms of measurable pupil achievement.[2]

On the question of *where* power over assessment procedures is located, this too is associated with the form of evaluative control – process or product. In process evaluation, power over assessment procedures resides in that part of the education system which controls inspection – usually central but to some extent also local government. In the case of product evaluation, power is located more within those institutions which control the design and administration of assessment procedures – usually in central government together with local government authorities to whom some limited power has been devolved, and also, in decentralized systems, in a large number of other non-statutory bodies such as examination boards and their clients (notably parents, pupils, employers and, of course, teachers themselves).

Thus, a consideration of the nature and amount of control over their practice experienced by teachers in terms of assessment procedures demands a more complex conceptualization than the traditional centralized/decentralized dichotomy. In particular, it requires a theoretical model which is based on the way in which the education system actually works rather than on its formal administrative arrangements alone (Zeldin, 1979). Only such a model, which takes the form and location of assessment procedures as determining criteria, can explain the increasing convergence in the form of control between the two societies at the present time, a convergence which, as the following section sets out, cannot be explained simply in terms of movements along the continuum between centralization and decentralization.

Control by Assessment: A Model

It is widely accepted that education systems in advanced industrial societies are becoming increasingly similar in their organization and objectives.

Assessment Constraints on Curriculum Practice: A Comparative Study

It is possible to wonder, today, whether a certain degree of centralization is not required for the efficient running of education systems given the nature of their objectives. At a time when we are rightly asking ourselves in France about the advantages of a greater degree of freedom and thus of a greater degree of deconcentration other countries with different traditions look with interest towards a more centralized model better adapted to the achievement of equality in education. The decade which is now beginning could be marked by a greater homogeneity of structures within education systems....[3]

The reason for this increasing similarity, it is usually suggested, is that the central governments of countries like England are exerting ever more centralized control over a whole range of educational provision, most notably on curriculum, assessment and finance,[4] while countries such as France are moving in the opposite direction towards decentralization (*déconcentration*) in finance and administration (see Figure 1).[5]

Figure 1. Model of control over the education systems of England and France

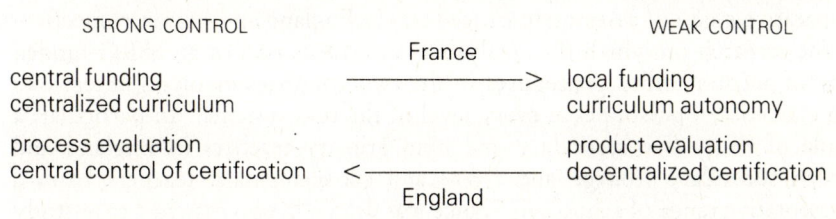

```
        STRONG CONTROL                                    WEAK CONTROL
                              France
central funding              ─────────────>    local funding
centralized curriculum                          curriculum autonomy

process evaluation                              product evaluation
central control of certification  <─────────    decentralized certification
                             England
```

This model of two systems which are the polar opposites of one another gravitating towards a mid-point of similarity is misleading, however. For, in many respects, the systems are not polar opposites at all. In reality, the movement of the French and English systems respectively towards a common pattern of centrally directed control by product evaluation, has, in each case, commenced from very different starting points which cannot be identified simply on a centralized-decentralized continuum. As I pointed out earlier, the traditional associations between decentralization and product evaluation on the one hand, and central control and process evaluation on the other misrepresent what tends to occur in practice. Thus, while England is maintaining its traditional emphasis on product evaluation, it is doing so within a context of increasingly centralized control. France, by contrast, is changing its traditional pattern of assessment towards an English-style emphasis on product evaluation, but is doing so without lessening its central grip upon the education system (see Figure 2).

As Figure 2 shows, it is no longer sufficient to conceptualize control over education in terms of its strength or weakness (as in Figure 1) because control cannot be equated with centralization. Rather, what appears to be important in determining patterns of educational control is the relationship between the two

Figure 2
Representation of changing patterns of assessment control in France and England

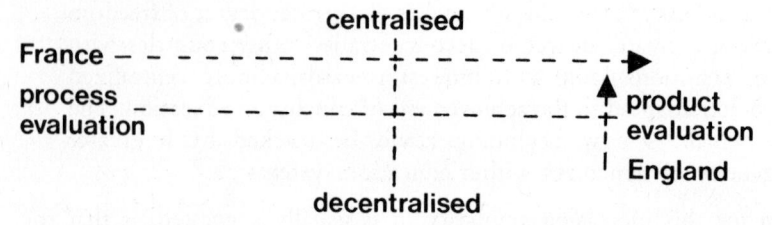

```
                      centralised
France — — — — — — — — —+— — — — — — — — —▶
process                  |              ▲ product
evaluation — — — — — — —+— — — — — — —+  evaluation
                         |             |  England
                      decentralised
```

variables mentioned earlier – *the form of assessment control*, and *the location of power over assessment procedures*.[6] Thus, it is not the gravitation of centralized France and decentralized England towards some educational mid-point that has produced the convergence between the two education systems, but the particular way in which these two variables, the *form* and the *location* of assessment control, intersect in the two countries.

In order to substantiate this argument, I turn now to a more detailed comparative study of assessment procedures in England and France respectively. The research on which this analysis is based was part of an SSRC-funded study of accountability procedures in the two countries involving interviews with educational personnel at every level of the two systems.[7] In particular, a sample of thirty-five secondary and nine primary teachers in England and thirteen secondary (*collège* and *lycée*) and six elementary teachers from a representative range of schools in France was drawn in two matched case-study local authorities. In the course of an extended, semi-structured interview, teachers in both countries were asked to identify what they understood by the term accountability, to whom they felt themselves to be accountable (in order of priority), what constraints they experienced in their classroom practice and any significant changes in respect of any of these questions in recent years. Their answers, which can only be referred to briefly here, nevertheless illustrate well the significance of assessment procedures of one kind or another as a source of constraint on teachers in both countries, and also the different and changing focus of this control in England and France.

Assessment in England

The tradition of 'disjointed incrementalism' (Fowler, 1981) characteristic of English provision is a reflection of an 'anarchic ideology of teacher autonomy' and strong local authorities which have been united in their opposition to central government interference as 'a monstrous entity to be resisted at all costs' (Neave, 1979). The kind of centralized prescriptions not only familiar to French teachers but also typically welcomed by them as the basis for equality of provision and protection from the pressure of local interests would be an anathema to English teachers. Nevertheless, for all its lack of centralization, the amount of control in the English system is still very considerable, its most manifest form being the 'product evaluation' of teachers by results. At times in English educational history, such control has been explicit, as in the nineteenth-century Revised Code 'Payment by Results' system,[8] or in contemporary local authority testing. Sometimes it is more implicit, as, for example, in the control exerted by public examinations. The statement by Selby-Biggs on behalf of the Board of Education in 1927, 'we must look to examinations rather than inspection to check, test and secure the efficiency of public education' (Silver, 1979 p. 7), sums up the English attitude well. While the degree of devolution over this source of control may vary with the prevailing economic climate, the importance of assessment in regulating educational practice does not. Thus the 'democratization' (that is, a downward trend of the vertical arrow in Figure 2) of examinations which took place in the sixties with the institution of CSE (particularly Mode 3), together with the demise of the old Secondary Schools Examination Council in favour of the teacher-dominated Schools Council, can be said to have strained the traditional methods of system control in England to the limit.

The 1970s and 1980s have seen, by contrast, a marked decline in teacher responsibility for product assessment. Among the manifestations of this has been the end of teacher control in the reconstituted Schools Council and, more recently, the Secretary of State's 1982 proposal to abolish the Council altogether in favour of a revived Examinations Council and a smaller (and weaker) Curriculum Council. In addition, the Council has also received a major snub in relation to its long-standing research and development work on the proposed 16+ examination – further evidence that central government intends to keep a tight rein on the future form and content of new 'product-evaluation' procedures (Broadfoot, 1980). The apparent growth in central government initiative and control in English education in recent years has already aroused a good deal of public speculation and disquiet.

However, these contemporary developments in England are not only an initiative on the part of central government to gain *more* control over the provision and practice of education as a whole (Salter and Tapper, 1981) but, more importantly, they also constitute an attempt to change the *power bases* of that control. This, so it seems, is to be achieved by central government intervening more directly in 'product assessment' so as to tighten the constraining effect of assessment procedures over the content of schooling. Thus, while recent attempts by central government to exert more control over the curriculum have been widespread and explicit – as in, for example, Mr Callaghan's Ruskin College speech in 1976, the 1977 DES Yellow Book and the subsequent Green Paper, 'Education in Schools', the 1980 DES paper 'A Framework for the School Curriculum', and the 1981 'The School Curriculum' – it is only when these attempts are linked to evaluation initiatives that they become more than mere rhetoric. This is well illustrated by the interesting example of Circular 14/77 which required local authorities to report to central government on their curriculum provision. This initiative represented a quite novel attempt at 'process evaluation' and arguably had little effect since it was not explicitly linked with any product evaluation procedure. More typically, attempts at curriculum control have been given teeth by the recourse to various kinds of product evaluation such as, from 1982, the legal requirement on schools to make available past public examination results as a result of the 1980 Education Act.[9]

Perhaps the most significant initiative, however, is the 'ringmaster' role currently being played by the DES in the merging of GCE exam boards into three or four different groups for the purposes of the new 16+. Plans for the new 16+ itself reveal an increasingly interventionist stance on the part of central government, a stance which was made explicit in the 1978 White Paper: 'The Government agree ... that there will be a need for stronger central co-ordination of the new single examination system....' Nuttall (1979, p. 10) speculates whether 'the Government's real motive in accepting the proposals for a common system at 16+ was not to secure the undoubted pedagogic, educational and administrative advantages of the common system, but to obtain much firmer central control of the activities of the examination boards and hence, of the curriculum.' The requirement on the boards to produce national criteria in each subject is particularly significant in the control this is likely to exert over the secondary school curriculum in future years. It has long been tacitly accepted that public exams are the major control over teachers' practice in the secondary school, 'the price we pay for no central control'.[10] The difference in this respect is that this source of influence will pass to a considerable extent from the partially autonomous boards to the Department of Education and Science itself.[11] This is likely to mean a considerable reduction in the freedom of the various examination bodies to play a determining role in curriculum content as well as its assessment. Yet for English teachers the effect of this gradual transfer of power over their activities from one external authority to another within the dominant control paradigm of 'product evaluation' is unlikely to be experienced as an increase in either the amount of constraint on their practice or a significant change in its form.

Evidence from this study indicates that in England teachers already identify assessment procedures – particularly public examinations – as the main control over their practice. The teacher is 'behind closed walls' (S11),[12] the attitude being 'we don't know what's going on in there, but it gets the results at the end, so we might as well leave it alone' (S12). The effect in many teachers' eyes is that 'exams rule the school' (S11) and that there is 'a tendency to concentrate on that which can be measured' (S. DH 10).

> I'm also responsible for what I teach, getting my pupils through exams. I think there's quite a heavy pressure, knowing at the end of your teaching there's this outside exam which is a bit of an unknown quantity and yet you're supposed to be teaching towards it (S24).

Other teachers commented: 'apart from the exams, I have total autonomy' (S36); 'you accept what the [Exam] Board offers even if you don't like or approve of what it is' (S30). Many teachers identify an increasing pressure on examinations because of the need for qualifications in a context of widespread unemployment combined with a competition between schools as cutbacks and falling rolls threaten many schools' very existence.[13]

This emphasis on 'product evaluation' through examination results is a source of control which secondary teachers in the main seem both to recognize and accept despite its many undesirable effects including the inhibition of curriculum development and an excessive emphasis on exam preparation. This seems to be because it meshes with their concept of accountability as being principally to 'clients' (that is, parents and pupils) and the headteacher (Elliott et al., 1982). French experience, however, suggests that teachers may well resent constraints which emanate from 'non-professional' bureaucrats rather than bodies such as the examination boards or the inspectorate which are made up of recognized experts in their field. This argument has already been borne out to some extent by teachers' reactions to the rapid growth in external demands for school accountability (Becher and Maclure, 1977). Typical of central government initiatives in this respect is the DES-based Assessment of Performance Unit set up in 1975 to establish the incidence of underachievement in the nation's schools on a 'product-evaluation' basis (DES, 1978). Although carefully designed to avoid the identification of the results of particular schools and teachers, there has been a significant reaction on the part of teachers against accountability based only on central or local government initiated procedures for product evaluation (McCormick, 1982). This reaction has taken the form of a quite novel concern with 'process evaluation' through institutional and personal self-review. Although this movement has arguably been of great significance in helping to improve the quality of education at a time of dwindling resources and morale, and of helping to foster a stronger bond between schools, local authorities and parents, it has yet to offer a serious challenge to the more traditional control exerted by 'product evaluation' procedures and thus to the trend identified in Figure 2.

The pattern for primary teachers has been rather different. In the era of 11+ selection, their subjugation to external assessment procedures resulted in a very similar pattern of control to that still experienced in secondary schools: 'It was very much the class teacher and the class, and as long as the results came out right in the end, the way in which we did things was left to the individual ...' (P5). Now that most primary schools have not been constrained by a formal examination for a decade or more and, at the same time, the dominant ideology of the 1960s and early 1970s has been eroded to a considerable extent by a backlash of utilitarianism, 'product evaluation' is increasingly evident in the form of internal testing and monitoring (Wood and Gipps, 1982). The William Tyndale case (Gretton and Jackson, 1976) provides clear testimony to the fact that despite a period of very few external product controls, concern with standards is never far away as a constraint in most schools.

Thus, to sum up the English position, the strong ideological tradition of grassroots autonomy in educational practice which historically is both a product of, and in turn has reinforced, a structure of local and institutional autonomy, has led to England being regarded as something of an 'ideal type' of decentralized mass educational provision. Control of this devolved structure (necessitated by its large call on the public purse and the close relationship between education and the occupational structure) has been more or less overt at different times, but has always centred on a 'product evaluation' approach involving various kinds of educational assessment. A combination of economic and political forces has both prompted and allowed central government to take a more explicitly directive role with regard to this control at the present time, rather than leaving it traditionally to the universities and more recently also to market forces (since the exam boards at least are business enterprises) to bring about much the same effect indirectly. In involving itself in new examination initiatives, the DES is now seeking the independent power not simply to control the schools but to be able, where necessary, to challenge traditional definitions of curriculum content as laid down by the universities. Herein lies the answer to the puzzle posed by 'the similarity between schools in a situation where the legal framework gives you the theoretical possibility of infinite variety'.[14] As two percipient teachers in the English sample noted,

> ... it is not a direct order but the message is very clear and you'd be very silly if you didn't listen to it. (S, H 18)

> ... these things [constraints] are not really defined securely in British education but it would be difficult to step outside what one feels are acceptable bands, you couldn't suddenly change your policy radically.... (S, DH 10)[15]

It is interesting that the effect of recent developments in England is likely to be very similar to those taking place in France. In both countries there has been a rapid growth in the use of corporate management strategies for educational control. Whereas in the past reliance on 'product evaluation' took relatively little account of curriculum content as such, recent years have seen an explicit effort on the part of central government to build curricular norms into the system, notably through the insistence on common subject criteria for the new 16+ examination. Another way in which this is being achieved is by the encouragement, through local authorities, of curriculum review and school self-evaluation where the norms for such evaluations are centrally prescribed.[16] Less obvious but not insignificant developments in this respect have been made possible by financial stringencies. As suggested earlier, there is likely to be greater central control of funding for education in the future, centrally prescribed staffing policies and a generally closer monitoring of educational arrangements and processes through corporate management procedures and through inspection. Thus the increasing English emphasis on 'process evaluation' means that England is moving correspondingly closer to the traditional

Assessment in France

The hierarchic, bureaucratic and centralized organization of French educational provision is a direct legacy of the French Revolution and the Napoleonic era.[17] The system is organized in terms of two hierarchies of control – administration and content – with only the Minister of Education having jurisdiction over both. In practice this has meant the control of budget, staffing, provision and organization on the one hand, and that of the more explicitly professional concerns of pedagogy, curriculum and evaluation on the other.[18] Thus, traditionally, local authorities in France had little discretion over the size and allocation of the budget, or the size and composition of the teaching force – two of the cherished bastions of local authority independence in England. At the institutional level, too, neither the school nor individual teachers had any formal discretion over syllabus, pedagogy or examinations, all three being centrally prescribed and enforced by a system of national inspection given teeth by its role in the promotion of teachers. This is a classic picture of what may be termed "*a priori*", 'central' or indeed 'bureaucratic' control. It is control of teaching rather than of learning, of teachers rather than of pupils, of process rather than of product. The result was a system which has traditionally prided itself on being so closely ordered that it used to be the boast of Ministry officials that any hour of the school day they could say with confidence which page of which textbook any pupil of a given age would be on.

In fact, 'there's a theory that the system is so centralized, it doesn't control things very well';[19] this emphasizes the point made earlier that it is a mistake to equate centralization with effective control. It has been said that 'French central planning can influence everything except teachers',[20] and this is a recognized problem.[21] Despite the fact that the 18+ *Baccalauréat* exam allows for considerable central control at this level,[22] that the French *Ministère de l'Education* can and does set detailed syllabuses and performance criteria of the expected outcomes of schooling at each stage,[23] that teachers' promotion depends on the results of individual inspection (Dulck, 1977), that there is close control of educational publishing and textbooks (Becher and Maclure, 1978), and that there is a range of official manuals on appropriate pedagogies, it is probable that in practice the French classroom teacher has more autonomy than her English counterpart – if much less inclination to use it. 'There's a gap between theory and practice, and centralization is the culprit.'[24]

The reasons why centralization does not actually lead to more effective control of teachers is because in practice it results in teachers being insulated from both 'top down' and 'bottom up' demands. Central government control is vitiated in a number of ways. Even with a bad *nôte* (grading) teachers will still eventually progress – albeit at a slower pace – to the top of the salary scale,[25] and even this now greatly reduced power of the inspector to affect promotion is further weakened by the requirement for teachers to be notified of an inspection and by its comparative rarity – often less than once in five years.

This inability of central government to 'police' curriculum provision and pedagogy adequately with inspection methods devised to control state educational provision in the Napoleonic era is compounded by the equally traditional weakness of local government. *Départemental* and *Académie* authorities have, until recently at least, had very little discretion over either budgetary priorities or staffing ratios. Far from this comparative vacuum being exploited at school level, headteachers and senior staff have very little more formal power than their most junior (tenured) colleagues in a way that is hard for those accustomed to English traditions to understand. The reality is, however, quite simple. Teachers regard themselves as professionally accountable to their employer and professional superior – to the inspector, that is – who is both a subject expert and representative of the employer – central government. They do not regard themselves as accountable to institutional or local authorities as English teachers would.[26] Thus, if the inspector is not an effective presence, 'top down' control becomes merely nominal. Unlike their English colleagues, however, the enduring bureaucratic structures and ideology of central control protect French teachers very effectively from 'bottom up' pressure from the community and parents. Despite the newly instituted rights of parents to a degree of consultation in bodies like the *Conseil d'Administration* and the *Conseil d'École* created since 1968,[27] these bodies are still largely 'talking shops', crucial professional decisions being taken by the teachers themselves in their own committees.[28]

Thus, despite efforts at 'democratization', teachers' formal position as civil servants continues to allow them to recognize only the authority of a central government from whose effective control they are defended by layers of bureaucracy and whose sheer size prevents the ready implementation and supervision of activity in the schools. For this reason too, the most recent moves towards a greater democratic voice in the education system via the decentralization and deconcentration of authority (the expediting of which is an explicit policy of the current socialist Minister of Education, Alain Savary) are likely to have quite the opposite effect. By cutting through some of the inevitable inefficiencies and red tape of these layers of bureaucracy and by giving more power to the local representatives of central budgetary authorities, he is likely to increase 'top down' rather than 'bottom up' control.[29] This policy of deconcentration is producing another unlooked for effect in that the apparent weakening of central control under the rhetoric of democratization without giving teachers any more formal decision-making power has led many to feel they are being used as scapegoats for contemporary social problems as' the public associate this apparent weakening of central control with increasing problems among young people. Devoid as they still are of the means or the right to work together creatively in the pursuit of relevant local educational strategies and, at the same time, remote from central sources of professional support and legitimation, this kind of attitude has been one of the contributory factors to the very low levels of morale in the teaching profession in recent years (Isambert-Jamati, 1970).

The emergence of an explicit policy of 'deconcentration' in France is also closely tied up with the enormous central power of the teacher unions and the internecine and explicitly political strife between these unions and central government. This power has also been significant in helping to protect teachers by creating a situation in which, provided the teacher abides by certain rules of overt behaviour such as punctuality and dress, she has considerable freedom in the classroom.

The reality is readily recognized by the teachers themselves: 'Everybody teachs what he is in the final analysis'.[30] The result: 'situations vary a great deal from one *collège* to another and what goes on here does not necessarily go on elsewhere'.[31] In the words of one French commentator, 'we are no longer in the country of Descartes, we are nearer the pragmatism of the English' (Latourte, 1961, p. 228). It is this growing recognition of the limitations of central control in practice that helps to explain the emergence in France of assessment procedures which combine elements of both English and French traditions.

If French teachers are in practice able to ignore to a very considerable extent the traditional, 'process evaluation' machinery of the central government bureaucracy, they are largely immune from 'product evaluation' also. Although it has always been true, in France as elsewhere, that 'a school is judged by its exam results',[32] individual teachers and schools who are assumed to be closely following central curriculum and pedagogic objectives, are not held accountable for these results in the way that they are in a system, such as the English, where there is almost total statutory freedom for schools themselves to determine what and how to teach.

A consequence of this relative insignificance of external 'product evaluation' procedures has been the possibility of progressively abolishing much of the elaborate traditional pupil assessment apparatus. Where once a pupil's life was dominated by regular tests and yearly hurdles to be passed in order to move up into the next class, they are now largely free of any formal assessment of this kind until the 18+ *Baccalauréat* stage if they stay at school or until they reach the final stages of other kinds of technical and vocational training. As the importance of formal assessment for *selection* purposes has declined with 'qualification inflation' (Broadfoot, 1979), so there has been an increasing emphasis on teacher-based, continuous assessment. Thus the *Brevet d'Etudes Secondaires* – the French equivalent to the 16+ – is now based on an average of class marks and is achieved by the majority of pupils (Dundas-Grant, 1975). For those few pupils and parents who dispute the teachers' verdict, there is still provision for an examination.

The extent of this decline in the importance of formal examinations is reflected in the plans, now well advanced, to allow open access to the hitherto highly selective, post-16+ *lycée* stage. Even the prestigious *Baccalauréat* is now being diversified to an extent that, although it continues to exert a degree of 'product evaluation' control over the last two years of schooling uncharacteristic in French education, it no longer holds the significance it once did as matriculation and hence as the automatic passport to university entrance. The major selection procedures now take place within the universities themselves on the basis of the type of *Baccalauréat* achieved along with their own examinations.[33]

The reasons why responsibility for assessment has been progressively handed over to teachers themselves in recent years, are well summarized by Fraser (1971, p. 167) who describes the strains in

> a system that depends upon impersonal assessment of achievement, that has only recently introduced more personal and continuous evaluation, that needs to 'mark' precisely and that must therefore set a syllabus and questions that can be reduced to measurable data. The curriculum is taught abstractly, verbally, precisely. The machinery of examinations needs constant maintenance and minor adjustment, but seems not to be able to cope with the pressure of large numbers of aspiring, articulate students, conscious of their power.

What has been evolved to try to meet the dual need for more relevant curriculum content and for some means of controlling 'bottom up' pressure from the inevitable disaffection caused by too many aspiring students is an assessment procedure which provides for a very gradual 'cooling out' kind of selection (Clark, 1962). This return to what is essentially an updated version of the traditional sponsored mobility (Turner, 1960) approach provided for by selective schooling is clearly highly significant for pupils but it is also significant in substantially adding to teachers' power. As one teacher has suggested, 'French education is centred on the syllabus whereas the English is centred on exams. Assessment is an integral part of the French system but the English works better ... we are now trying to make the French more informal....'[34] The form this increasingly 'informal' assessment is taking is that of *orientation* procedures instituted as part of the 'Haby' reforms of 1975.

This *orientation* procedure requires that throughout a pupil's school life vocational guidance is to be based on continuous observation by his or her teachers, recorded in a cumulative *dossier*. Regular meetings are to be held between the teachers, a guidance counsellor (*conseiller d'orientation*), a school doctor and psychologist, and representatives of parents. Such meetings are to be held every year, with two major ones taking place at the end of the second and last years at *collège*, when decisions must be made on the basis of the *dossier* as to the type of studies the pupil will subsequently undertake.

During the spring term before these meetings, the parents are invited to express their wishes concerning the guidance of the child; taking account of these wishes, the council draws up and submits to the parents a proposed programme of future studies or training for their child. The parents' final views are considered by the guidance council which sits during the summer term; it includes the head and several other teachers, one of whom is the child's class teacher, a doctor, school social welfare officer and guidance counsellor.

When the parents feel the decision of the guidance council is unacceptable, an appeal committee, including the *inspecteur d'académie*, examines the case. If their advice still differs from the parents' wishes, an examination is set for the child and the results assessed by a committee external to the *collège*. By contrast to the traditional 'sieving out' approach to selection, the principle of *orientation* is positive guidance in which no educational path represents failure, the paths rather being equal but different:

> what must be avoided at all costs is orientation by failure.... There is no job which corresponds with failure but there are jobs which correspond with diverse dispositions.... Orientation cannot moreover, be done by the school alone. It must be the result of a collaboration between children – the most closely affected, parents who are responsible for them and the school. (M. Beullac (Prime Minister) in *Le Monde de l'Education*)[35]

Despite the rhetoric of partnership, however, in reality it is teachers who play the determining role in pupil orientation through their classwork assessments and in the decisions of the *Conseil de Classe*. But if this development has increased teachers' professional responsibility, it also potentially makes them a great deal more vulnerable to 'bottom up' pressure from parents and pupils to whom they must be able to justify or account for their decisions. That this has yet to become a problem is very much the result of the concurrent growth in corporate management procedures in which the arbitrary power of the individual teacher is replaced by the benign and scientific efficiency of an impersonal norm which is operated by teachers.[36]

Berger suggests that in French education 'control' – assessment based on impersonal norms – is replacing 'evaluation' – the personal assessment of an individual's value.[37] Furthermore, he suggests that the growth of *orientation* as the dominant vehicle of that 'control' is part of a more general movement towards 'corporate management' in education in which the traditional, personal authority of local officials, inspectors and teachers is being replaced by the impersonal regulation of statutory obligations and mechanized administration.

Crucial to this development is a computer-based facility for collecting and coordinating a whole range of information about the functioning of the education system on a national basis.[38] Thus, if *orientation* is part of a policy of 'democratization', it is also, and more significantly, closely connected with this 'rationalization' of educational administration and hence control.

'Orientation leads almost inevitably to computer-based administration'.[39] If continuous assessment in relation to detailed, nationally prescribed norms of performance eliminates the injustices of the caprice of an individual teacher and the variations in the exam papers set by the various *Départements*, it is by the same token more irresistible. Moreover, it is also a means of making a practical reality of the tradition of imposing curricular and pedagogic norms which was hitherto the responsibility of the inspector and thus represents a shift from process to product evaluation.

Thus, the assessment *dossier* – the elaborate profile which follows a pupil throughout his or her school career – combined with a series of *orientation* decisions taken by a pupil's teachers in the periodic meetings of the *Conseil de Classe* carries into the classroom the same assumptions of scientific rationality which characterize all aspects of corporate management. That is to say that the norms of performance chosen are taken to be in some sense absolute and are given the pseudo-legitimacy of science and not the values of a particular group and time. As authority within the education system is thereby dispersed, control becomes a composite and increasingly impersonal phenomenon, impossible to pin down and hence to resist. If what is to be taught to whom, when, how and why, can only be answered by reference to particular values, disguising such pedagogical and curricular decisions under the cloak of an apparently objective, scientific assessment is perhaps the most effective form of educational (and thus social?) control yet developed.[40] Thus where traditionally assessment represented the personal and possibly arbitrary judgment of an individual, it now tends to disguise both these under an appearance of conformity with rational norms. When the then Minister of Education, M. Haby, instituted the computerization of pupils' *dossiers* as part of his major reform of the education system in 1975, there was sufficient public outcry for this practice to be abolished shortly afterwards. But although there was public disquiet at this very obvious step towards '*l'informatisation*', the potential significance of the power of continuous cumulative group assessment to provide for both 'process evaluation'-based control of curriculum and pedagogy (by the central prescription of objectives) *and* the 'product evaluation' of pupil performance is not yet generally perceived. This itself further enhances that potential.

Thus the *orientation* procedure neatly solves several problems at once. First, it provides a means of selection and of controlling pupil and parent frustration at a time when public opinion is still strongly egalitarian and democratic. Secondly, it provides for greater 'product evaluation' control of teachers by clearing away some of the traditional assessment bureaucracy and making teachers directly and visibly responsible for their actions. Thirdly, it allows for a more technocratic, depersonalized approach to educational administration and more efficient 'process evaluation'. Fourthly, it provides for the most effective sort of assessment control of teachers – a combination of 'process' and 'product' evaluation in which the central prescription of curriculum norms is linked to the formal processes of pupil assessment.

For teachers, the effect of these four closely interrelated processes which nominally increase their power is likely to be the removal of much of the traditional impotency of central government whilst giving them a quite new vulnerability to consumer pressure. Teachers in France are thus likely to find themselves moving steadily nearer the top of the vertical axis in Figure 2, becoming increasingly more like their English colleagues than hitherto.

Assessment Constraints on Curriculum Practice: A Comparative Study

Summary

Where does all this leave the teacher? This chapter has described some of the limitations on the autonomy of the teacher in two ostensibly very different education systems. It has been particularly concerned with the way in which that autonomy is regulated by assessment procedures. I have suggested that teachers in both systems are closely controlled by the prevailing assessment procedures although these have traditionally taken and continue to take different forms in the two countries. In England there has been something of an oscillation between a more 'free market', decentralized approach to assessment control mediated by the semi-autonomous exam boards and the links they in turn have with the universities at times of plenty, and more directive, centralized strategies based on the tighter control of public examining and institutional accountability when economic and social problems dictate a more utilitarian direction for educational activity. In France, by contrast, the development has been from what was, in fact, the relative freedom of a highly centralized system in which assessment control was vested in national, government-run selective examinations and personal teacher inspection. This has been replaced by a nominally more decentralized, positive control based on a reflexive relationship between teacher-conducted continuous assessment according to nationally prescribed norms, and an increasingly corporate management approach to educational administration, provision and control. The information thereby generated provides an increasingly powerful means of both directing the careers of individual pupils and the education system as a whole. By the same token, the institution of continuous assessment based on national norms now not only exhorts teachers – as the system has always done – but makes that exhortation effective as these norms relate directly to the assessment of pupil progress and simultaneously provide for the national statistical monitoring of educational standards within the system.

Typically, the trends in England are less clear-cut. The activities of the Assessment of Performance Unit are similar to some aspects of the French initiative. The search for national norms as assessment criteria at the present time in England is also a comparable development. A currently less developed but potentially very significant trend in England is the increasing government as well as popular support for the idea of 'profiles' based on continuous assessment and culminating in a 'positive' statement or certificate for all pupils. Whilst this initiative, like that in France, has much to recommend it educationally, it has the potential to provide for the very effective imposition of centrally-determined curricular norms and pedagogic directives. If in some ways such a development can be seen as a step towards greater equality of educational provision, it is much more significantly a step towards much greater control of teachers' aims and practice. In the past English teachers' autonomy was safeguarded by the lack of central curricular prescriptions which meant that, despite the very powerful control exerted by the emphasis on 'product evaluation', there was considerable room for individual teachers, pressure groups and semi-autonomous bodies such as the exam boards to influence the *content* of that control. In the same way, in the past, French teachers' autonomy was safeguarded by the relatively minor role of 'product evaluation' despite their location within a highly centralized, bureaucratic education system in which every aspect of pedagogic activity, and especially curricular objectives, was tightly controlled. The increasing similarity of the two systems reflects the fact that each is tending to institute the aspect hitherto lacking to ensure effective control.

Perhaps even more important than this increasingly effective control, however, is the growing association of educational administration in both countries with a corporate management approach. Such an approach is likely to disguise the essentially political nature of educational goals – in an ideology of scientific rationality. In this event, value judgments appear as merely *administrative* decisions dictated by rationality and the goal of maximizing efficiency. It seems probable that effective educational control implies the existence of a social order ready to concur in educational goals – the way in which assessment procedures help to bring this about will perhaps prove ultimately more significant than their role in imposing such goals.

Notes

1 See, for example, Unit 15 of course E222, *The Control of Education in Britain*, The Open University, 1979, or, for the layman's view, TURPIE, L. (1978) *Report on Strathclyde Regional Council Study Tour of French Educational Establishments*, mimeo.
2 This argument is made in more detail in my paper, 'Assessment curriculum and control in the changing pattern of centre-local relations', in *Local Government Studies*, November 1980. Throughout this paper accountability and control are taken to be virtually synonymous since the giving of an account is only significant when linked with the possibility of reactive sanctions or ongoing control.
3   On peut aujourd'hui se demander si un certain degré de centralisation n'est pas réquis par le souci de l'efficacité et la nature des objectifs que se donnent les systèmes d'éducation. Au moment où nous nous interrogeons légitimement en France sur les avantages d'une plus grande souplesse et donc d'une plus grande déconcentration, d'autres pays de traditions différentes regardent avec intérêt vers un modèle plus centralisé et, partant, mieux adapté à la réalisation de l'égalité devant l'education. La décennie qui s'ouvre pourrait être marquée par une plus grande homogénéité des structures des systèmes éducatifs....

P. GARRIGUE, Chef du Service des Affaires Internationales, Ministère de l'Education, Paris, *Etude comparative des Systèmes éducatifs*, ministerial paper, October 1980, p. 3. It is not clear, however, whether the explanation for this tendency is the common experience of economic recession, or a more inevitable progression towards some optimum arrangement in keeping with the economic realities of technological competition in advanced industrial societies *per se*.
4 Evidence of this intention with regard to curriculum is manifest in most recent

government publications on education since the Great Debate of 1977, notably the 1977 Green Paper, *Education in Schools*, the 1980 response to the 1977–9 review of local authority arrangements for the curriculum (report published 1979) namely, *A Framework for the School Curriculum*. With regard to assessment, see, for example, VICKERMAN, C. (1982) 'The organization and structure of the new examining groups', in *Secondary Education Journal*, 12, 1 and the 1982 DES booklet on the new Certificate of Pre-Vocational Education, *17+: A New Examination*, which illustrate similar intentions. The direction towards increased financial control is expressed in the revised procedures for the allocation of the Rate Support Grant and in hints that government may be exploring the possibility of an education 'block' grant (see, for example, Annex B of the Green Paper, *Alternatives to Domestic Rates*, para.7).

5 See, for example, SAPIN, C. (1980) *Déconcentration et Modernisation de la Gestion au Ministère de l'Education*, Paris, Ministère de l'Education.

6 It would be misleading, however, to regard the trends depicted in Figure 2 as anything more than general tendencies and to ignore the many examples of resistance on the part of educational practitioners and consumers to such changes which may be identified and the associated pattern of negotiation between politicians, administrators, teachers and the public which this has made necessary.

7 Support from the SSRC Accountability in Education Panel for this research is gratefully acknowledged. A full account of the methodology and results of this research can be found in the final report of the project to SSRC and is available from the author.

8 This mode of assessment, instituted by Robert Lowe in 1862 as part of his 'revised code' meant that teachers' pay depended on the progress of their pupils as measured by an inspector (see, for example, MIDWINTER, E. (1970) *Nineteenth-Century Education*, Seminar Studies in History, London, Longman). It was thus a particularly interesting form of 'product evaluation' incorporating many features of 'process evaluation' (such as inspection) and being quite exceptional in English terms for the amount of central curricular norms it allowed to be imposed. It provides an interesting parallel with contemporary developments in England and France described in the final section of this chapter.

9 The 1980 Education Act requires schools from 1982 to provide detailed information for parents about their arrangements and to make available past public examination results.

10 J. Mann, Secretary, The Schools Council.

11 Central government control over public examinations is not a complete novelty. GCE certificates require a signature from the DES, for example. The Schools Council, even in its old format, was dominated in financial terms by central government representatives. Perhaps a further qualification in the argument is necessary here, that control is not simply becoming more centralized but more *visibly* centralized.

12 Teachers are referred to by number, by school level (S = secondary; P = primary) and by promoted post (for example, DH = deputy head) where applicable.

13 The Government White Paper on school closures published in June 1981 explicitly increases this pressure.

14 Interview with V. Botterill, Secretary, National Union of Teachers, Exeter.

15 The case of the William Tyndale School provides a good example of this.

16 See, for example, the schemes developed by London, Solihull and Oxfordshire LEAs.

17 In fact a centralist approach may be traced back in France to Richelieu, Louis XIV and before.

18 A confidential report from the Directeur Générale de la Programmation et de la Coordination at the Ministère de l'Education in France identifies three sorts of

potential autonomy – of pedagogy, of (financial) means, and of administration (for example, staffing).
19 An Inspecteur Départemental, Calvados, France.
20 An Inspecteur Générale, Paris.
21 Mlle Navarro, Institut National de Recherche Pédagogique, Paris.
22 The *Baccalauréat* is set regionally (by *Département*) and there is considerable variation in standards. Despite this, as with so much else in French education, the fact that it is nominally at least a national qualification blinds people to such variations and tends rather to reinforce the impression of central control.
23 See, for example, *Le Courrier de l'Education*, 11 April 1977 and 25 April 1977. Detailed booklets are provided for each age group and regularly revised.
24 An Inspecteur Départemental, Calvados, France.
25 Interview with M Lucien Géminard, Doyen de l'Inspection National.
26 In the above study, priorities in accountability were identified by teachers in England, both primary and secondary, as first to the head of department or school and second to the pupils themselves.
27 For example, *Le Conseil d'Administration* includes representatives of the Ministry of Education, usually the *inspecteur d'académie*, elected representatives of the teaching and administrative staff, parents, pupils, and local authorities; subjects cover moral, financial and material matters. Also important is the *Conseil de Classe*, consisting of the head, the guidance counsellor, school doctor and welfare officer, the teachers and two elected representatives each of parents and pupils of the class in question. The Council deals with the progress of the class and has a key role to play in the 'orientation' process.
28 *Le Monde de l'Education*, March 1981.
29 Monsieur Buzet, Chef de Budget, Ministère de l'Education, Paris and Dr G. Neave, Maître de Recherche, Fondation Européenne de la Culture, Université de Paris IX-Dauphine.
30 Instituteur (1), junior school teacher, Calvados, France.
31 *Le Courrier*, 16 October 1978.
32 Headteacher (11), Collège (11–16 School), Calvados, France.
33 BOURDIEU, P. and PASSSERON, J.C. (1976) *La Réproduction*, Sage, provides a good illustration of the important distinctions between different 'bacs' and, in particular, the paramouncy of the '*bac*' 'C' on maths and science. It is interesting that the key points of selection are the '*propédentique*' exam taken after the first year of university study and the entrance examinations taken one or two years after the *Baccalauréat*, for the '*Grandes Ecoles*'.
34 Instituteur (2), Calvados, France.
35 Interview, 'L'orientation doît faire partie de l'enseignement', in *Le Monde de l'Education*, March 1981, (p. 1.)
36 As CICOUREL, A. and KITSUSE, J. (1968) suggest in 'The social organization of the high school and deviant adolescent careers', in RUBINGTON, E. and WEINBERG, M. (Eds) *Deviance: The Interactionist Perspective*, New York, Macmillan, the choice process in guidance and counselling of this type is not nearly as open and voluntarist as this description suggests. See also ROSENBAUM, J.E. (1976) *Making Inequality: The Hidden Curriculum of High School Track*, New York, Wiley.
37 DR G. BERGER, Département des Sciences de l'Education, Université de Paris-Vincennes.
38 Service de Statistique et de Sondage, Ministère de l'Education, Paris.
39 Mme T. Catz-Trévenin, Université de Paris-Vincennes.
40 Jurgen Habermas, in *Legitimation Crisis* (Beacon Press, Boston, 1975), disputes this argument in maintaining the central importance of voluntary agency in social life.

References

ARCHER, M. (1979) *The Social Origins of Educational Systems*, London, Sage.
BECHER, T. and MACLURE, S. (1977) *Accountability in Education*, Slough, NFER.
BECHER, T. and MACLURE, S. (1978) *The Politics of Curriculum Change*, London, Hutchinson.
BROADFOOT, P.M. (1979) *Assessment, Schools and Society*, London, Methuen.
BROADFOOT, P.M. (1980) 'Assessment, curriculum and control in the changing pattern of centre-local relations', in *Local Government Studies*, November.
BROADFOOT, P.M. (1982) 'Towards a sociology of assessment', in BARTON, L. and WALKER, S. (Eds) *Schools, Teachers and Teaching*, Lewes, Falmer Press.
CLARK, B. (1962) *Educating the Expert Society*, San Francisco, Calif. Chandler Publishing Corporation.
DEPARTMENT OF EDUCATION AND SCIENCE (1978) Report on Education, *Assessing the Performance of Pupils*, London, HMSO.
DULCK, J.A. (1977) 'Decision-making and the curriculum in France', in GLATTER, R. (Ed.) *Control of the Curriculum*, London, University of London Institute of Education.
DUNDAS-GRANT, V. (1975) 'Attainment at 16+: The French perspective', in *Comparative Education II*, 1, March, pp. 13–22.
ELLIOTT, J., BRIDGES, D., EBBUTT, D., GIBSON, R. and NIAS, J. (1982) *School Accountability: The SSRC Cambridge Accountability Project*, London, Grant McIntyre.
FOWLER, G. (1981) 'The changing nature of educational politics in the 1970s', in BROADFOOT, P. et al. (Eds) (1981) *Politics and Educational Change*, London, Croom Helm.
FRASER, W.R. (1971) *Reforms and Restraints in Modern French Education*, London, Routledge and Kegan Paul.
GRETTON, J. and JACKSON, M. (1976) *William Tyndale: Collapse of a School or a System?* London, Allen and Unwin.
HM GOVERNMENT WHITE PAPER, *Secondary School Examinations: A Single System at 16+*, Cmnd 7368, London, HMSO.
LATOURTE, M. (1961) 'Economic planning in France', in *PEP*, 27, 454, London.
MCCORMICK, R. (Ed.) (1982) *Calling Education to Account*, London, Heinemann.
NEAVE, G. (1979) 'Statements at 16+. A European perspective', in BURGESS, T. and ADAMS, E. (Eds) *Outcomes of Education*, London, Macmillan.
NUTTALL, D. (1979) 'A review of accountability in the area of examinations', paper to the SSRC Panel on Accountability in Education.
PARKES, D. (1977) 'Response', in GLATTER, R. (Ed.), *op. cit.*
SALTER, B. and TAPPER, T. (1981) *Education Politics and the State*, London, Grant McIntyre.
SILVER, H. (1979) 'Acountability in education: Towards a history of some English features', paper for SSRC Panel on Accountability in Education.
TURNER, R. (1960) 'Sponsored and contest mobility and the school system', in *American Sociological Review*, 25 October, pp. 855–67.
WOOD, R. and GIPPS, C. (1982) 'An enquiry into the use of test results for accountability purposes', in MCCORMICK, R. (Ed.), *op. cit.*
ZELDIN, T. (1979) *France 1848–1945: Politics and Anger*, Oxford, Oxford University Press.

Contributors

Stephen BALL	Lecturer, Education Area, University of Sussex
Dorothy BARNES	Research Fellow, School of Education, University of Leeds
Douglas BARNES	Senior Lecturer, School of Education, University of Leeds
Richard BOWE	Research Student, School of Education, Open University
Patricia BROADFOOT	Lecturer, School of Education, University of Bristol
Teresa GRAFTON	Projects Coordinator, Development Education Centre, Birmingham (formerly Researcher, Department of Educational Enquiry, University of Aston in Birmingham)
Ivor GOODSON	Director of Schools Unit, European Research Centre, University of Sussex
David H. HARGREAVES	Reader, Department of Educational Studies, University of Oxford
Lynda MEASOR	Research Assistant, School of Education, Open University
Henry MILLER	Lecturer, Faculty of Management and Policy Sciences, University of Aston in Birmingham (formerly Lecturer, Department of Educational Enquiry, University of Aston in Birmingham)
John SCARTH	Research Assistant, School of Education, Open University
Lesley SMITH	Lecturer in Community Education, Centre for Continuing Education, Open University (formerly Research Fellow, Department of Educational Enquiry, University of Aston in Birmingham)
Caroline ST. JOHN-BROOKS	Education Correspondent, New Society
Les TICKLE	Lecturer, School of Education, University of East Anglia

Contributors

Glenn TURNER	Research Fellow, School of Education, Open University
Martin VEGODA	Development Officer, Southmead Family Unit, Bristol (formerly Senior Research Fellow, Department of Educational Enquiry, University of Aston in Birmingham)
Richard WHITFIELD	Director of Child Care, Save the Children Fund (formerly Professor of Education and Head of Department, Department of Educational Enquiry, University of Aston in Birmingham)
Geoff WHITTY	Lecturer in Urban Education, Faculty of Education, King's College, London

Author Index

Abbs, P., 73, 87
Acker, S., 9, 12
Adams, A.
  see Burgess and Adams
Allison, B., 146 n4
Anyon, J., 7, 12
Apple, M.W., 7, 12, 146, n2, 243, 249
Archer, M.S., 61, 62–3, 64, 78, 87, 252, 269
Archer, R.L., 71–3, 75–6, 87
Arnold, R., 36

Ball, S.J., 1, 7, 8, 12, 18, 36, 38, 41, 42, 57, n2, 58, 61–88, 153, 154, 168
Ball, S.J. and Lacey, C., 7, 12, 18, 36, 37, 41, 57, n8, 58, 79, 87, 178, 191
Bandura, 172
Bardell, G., 161, 168
Barnes, D., 7, 13, 57 n7, 58
Barnes, Dorothy, 8, 17–36
Barnes, Douglas, 8, 17–36
Barrett, M. *et al.*, 58, 146 n4
Barton, L. and Meighan, R., 14, 125, 191, 226, 227, 250
Barton, L. and Walker, S., 59, 226, 227, 269
Barton, L. *set al.*, 249
Becher, T. and Maclure, S., 257, 259, 269
Becker, H.S. *et al.*, 198, 205
Bell, R. and Prescott, W., 250
Beloe Report
  see SSEC
Benn, C. and Simon, B., 151, 168
Bennett, N., 108, 125
Berger, J., 145, 147 n22, 263
Berger, P.L. and Luckman, T., 216, 226
Berlak, A. and Berlak, H., 109, 125, 226
Berlak, H.
  see Berlak and Berlak
Bernstein, B., 3, 5, 13, 35 n3, 37, 40, 42, 47, 57 n10, 58
Beullac, M., 263
Blackstone, 172

Bloom, B.S. *et al.*, 5, 13
Board of Education, 10, 13, 14, 66, 67–8, 79, 87, 105, 224 n4, 226
Boas, F.S., 66, 74, 75, 77
Boissevain, J., 87
Bossert, S.T., 213, 226
Bourdieu, P., 5, 6, 13, 37, 54, 55, 56, 58, 128–9, 136, 138, 143, 146 n2, 224 n3, 268 n33
Bourdieu, P. and Passeron, J.–C., 146 n2, 226, 242, 249
Bowe, R. and Whitty, G., 11–12, 229–50
Bowlby, J., 152, 168
Bowles, S. and Gintis, H., 34, 36, 107, 108, 125, 221, 226
Boydell, D., 108, 113, 125
Boyson, R.
  see Cox and Boyson
Brecht, B., 50–1, 53
Breugal, I., 167, 168
Britton, J., 83
Broadfoot, P., 12, 207, 224 n3, 226, 251–69
Broadfoot, P. *et al.*, 269
Brown, R., 13, 146 n2
Bruce, Assistant Commissioner, 68–9
Bryan, P.W., 97
Bucher, R. and Strauss, A., 63–4, 67, 71, 76, 78, 83, 84, 87
Burgess, T. and Adams, E., 269
Byrne, E.M., 104, 105

Callaghan, J., 2, 13, 39, 224 n6, 237, 239, 245, 249, 255
Carey, W.M., 93, 105
Carson, S., 98–9, 104
CCCS (Centre for Contemporary Cultural Studies), 2, 13, 221, 226, 237, 249
Central Advisory Council for Education, 13
Channon, C., 95, 105

273

Author Index

Cicourel, A. and Kitsuse, J., 268 n36
Clark, B., 262, 269
Collins, R., 38, 58
Consultative Committee on Education, 226
Cooper, B., 84, 87
Corin, B.R. et al., 58
COSSEC (Cambridge, Oxford and Southern Schools Examining Consortium), 238, 249
Council of the Geographical Association, 105
Cox, B., 231, 237, 240, 249
Cox, C.B. and Boyson, R., 2, 13
Cox, C.B. and Dyson, A.E., 2, 13
Cox, M.H., 152, 168
Currie, W.B., 80, 87

Dale, R., 237–8, 249
Dale, R. et al., 249–50
Davies, L., 186, 191
Dawe, A., 222, 226
Dearden, R.F. et al., 147 n9
Deem, R., 167, 168, 190, 191, 206
Denscombe, M., 213, 226
DES (Department of Education and Science), 2, 11, 13, 86 n4, 98, 105, 151–2, 153, 167, 168, 171–2, 189, 190 n2, 191, 207, 223 n1, 226, 239, 248 n4 and n16, 250, 255, 257, 267 n4, 269
DHSS (Department of Health and Social Services), 152–3, 168
Di Maggio, P. and Useem, M., 146 n2
Doe, B., 238, 239–40, 250
Donald, J., 231, 241, 250
Dore, R., 38–9, 58
Doyle, W. and Ponder, G.A., 213, 226
Dulck, J.A., 259, 269
Dundas-Grant, V., 261, 269
Dyhouse, C., 77, 87
Dyke-Acland Report, 235
Dyson, A.E., 147 n15
  see also Cox and Dyson
Ebutt, 180
Eggleston, S.J., 58, 61, 62, 65, 78, 87, 146 n2, 220, 221, 222, 226
Elliot, 189
Elliott, J. et al., 257, 269
Esland, G., 6, 13, 37, 58, 61, 87
Evans, D., 147 n10

Fairhall, J., 239, 250
Feldman, E.B., 146 n4
Fereday, E.L., 95, 105

Field, D., 108, 124, 125, 146 n6 147 n23
Fisher, C.A., 96–7, 105
Ford, J. et al., 55, 58
Fowler, G., 254, 269
Fowler, J.H., 81
Fraser, W.R., 262, 269
Fuller, M., 183, 191, 197, 206
Fuller, P., 144, 147 n19 and n20
Fyson, A.
  see Ward and Fyson

Galton, M., 172
Galton, M. et al., 108, 125, 226
Garnett, J., 102–3, 105
Garrigue, P., 226 n3
Geographical Association, 105
Giddens, A., 222, 226
Gilson, E., 44, 58
Ginsbury, M. et. al., 208, 226
Gintis, H.
  see Bowles and Gintis
Gipps, C.
  see Wood and Gipps
Giroux, H., 7, 13
Glatter, R., 269
Gleeson, D. and Mardle, G., 36
Goodson, I., 8–9, 61, 62, 87, 89–106
Gorbutt, D., 4, 13, 221–2, 226
Grace, G., 57 n2, 58
Grafton, T. et al., 151–69
Gray, J.A., 172
Green, A.
  see Sharp and Green
Gretton, J. and Jackson, M., 257, 269
Griffiths
  see Saraga and Griffiths
Griffiths, B.C. and Mullins, N.C., 87
Guardian, The, 249 n21 and n25, 250
Gurrey, P., 83

Habermas, J., 268 n40
Hadow Report, 90, 105
  see also Board of Education
Halsey, A.H., 224 n3, 226
  see also Karabel and Halsey
Halsey, A.H. et al., 128, 146 n3
Hamilton, D. et al., 3, 13
Hammersley, M., 7, 13, 110, 118, 125, 191, 222, 226
  see also Woods and Hammersley
Happold, F.C., 93–4, 105
Hargreaves, A., 3, 7, 9, 13, 125, 189, 191, 213, 221, 222, 223, 226, 227
Hargreaves, D.H., 57 n4, 58, 113, 125,

127–47, 197, 206
Hartog, Sir Philip, 82–3, 87 n8
Hartog, Sir Philip and Rhodes, E.C., 224 n3, 227
Haste, H.W., 172, 191
Hilsum, S. and Strong, F.R., 207, 214, 227
Hirst, P.H., 3, 4, 13, 61, 62, 87, 88, 130
HMI (Her Majesty's Inspectorate), 85, 171–3, 178, 187, 189, 190, 191, 207, 224 n3
Hodgson, J.D., 44, 54, 58, 69, 71, 87
Holloway, J. and Picciotto, S., 241, 250
Holt, J., 53, 58
Honeybone, R.C., 91, 95–6, 105
Hopkins, A., 237, 250
Hotchings, G.E.
   see Wooldridge and Hotchings
House, E.R., 211, 227
House of Commons, 224 n6, 227
Howarth, T., 238
Hulme, T.E., 57 n1
Hurford, J., 241, 250

Illich, I., 108, 125
Incorporated Association of Assistant Masters, 81
Isambert-Jamati, 261

Jackson, M., 242, 250
   see also Gretton and Jackson
Jackson, P.W., 195, 206
Jackson, R., 213, 227
James, W., 140–1, 147 n12
Jamieson, I. and Lightfoot, M., 249 n24, 250
JESC, 237, 250
JMB (Joint Matriculation Board) 232, 250
Johnson, R., 57 n11, 58

Karabel, J. and Halsey, A.H., 4, 13, 221–2, 227
Keddie, N., 6, 7, 58
Kellmer Pringle, M.
   see Pilling and Kellmer Pringle
Kellner, D., 246, 250
Kelly, A., 171–3, 179, 180, 182, 190, 191
Kelly, P.J., 224 n4, 227
Kerr, J.F., 13, 88
Kirk, W., 91, 105
Kitsuse, J.
   see Cicourel and Kitsuse
Krishnamurti, 107, 125

Kuhn, T.S., 80, 88

Lacey, C.
   see Ball and Lacey
Lander, G., 27, 36
Latourte, M., 261, 269
Lawrence, D.H., 46, 52–3
Lawton, D., 3, 13
Layton, D., 89–90, 105
Leavis, F.R., 86 n7
Lee, Sir Sydney, 66, 70, 77
Lewis, H.D., 147 n14
Lightfoot, M.
   see Jamieson and Lightfoot
Llewellyn, M., 183, 190 n4, 191
Lortie, D., 211, 227
Luckmann, T.
   see Berger and Luckmann
Lyons, G., 214, 227

McCormick, R., 257, 269
MacKinder, H.J., 89, 90, 91, 92–3, 100, 105
Maclure, S., 231, 250
   see also Becher and Maclure
McNeil, L., 7, 13
Mansell, T. and Silver, H., 84, 88
Marcuse, H., 39, 58, 147 n22
Mardle, G.
   see Gleeson and Mardle
Matza, D., 226 n15, 227
Measor, L., 10, 171–91
Measor, L. and Woods, P., 175, 181, 191
Meighan, R.
   see Barton and Meighan
Midwinter, E., 267 n8
Miller, C.M.L. and Parlett, M., 198, 206
Mills, C.W., 88
Millward, R., 97, 105
Milroy, L., 88
Ministry of Education, 94, 105
Mischel, 172
Mortimer, P., 224 n4, 227
Mortimore, P., 11, 13
Mullins, N.C.
   see Griffiths and Mullins
Murdock, G., 230, 250
Musgrove, F., 3, 5, 13, 61, 62, 88, 128, 146 n3

Neave, G., 254, 269
Newbolt Report, 77–9
Newsom Report, 3, 13
   see also Central Advisory Council for

Author Index

Education
Nicholls, A.D. 99–104, 105
Nixon, J., 3, 13
North West Education Management Centre, 214–15, 227
Norwood, C., 244 n4, 227
Norwood Report, 10, 14, 98, 224 n3, 227
 see also Secondary Schools Examination Council
Nuttall, D., 256, 269

Parkes, D., 269
Parlett, M.
 see Miller and Parlett
Pegis, A., 58
Peters, R.S., 61, 139, 141, 147 n9 and n12
Phenix, P.H., 4, 14, 61, 130
Piaget, J., 139
Picciotto, S.
 see Holloway and Picciotto
Pilling, D. and Kellmer Pringle, M., 153, 169
Pollard, A., 125, 191, 213, 227
Ponder, G.A.
 see Doyle and Ponder
Prescott, W.
 see Bell and Prescott

Quiller-Couch, A., 73

Read, H., 108, 124, 125, 138, 144, 146, 147 n8 and n24
Rée, H., 144, 147 n17
Reeve, J.M.
 see Shaw and Reeve
Reid, L.A. 146 n7, 147 n10, n14 and n23
Reynolds, P., 248 n15
Rhodes, E.C.
 see Hartog and Rhodes
Rosenbaum, J.E., 268 n36
Ross, M., 130, 146 n5, 147 n6, n10 and n17
Rowlands, C., 238, 250
Royal Geographical Society, 94–6, 105
Rubington, E. and Weinberg, M., 268 n36
Rudduck, J., 67, 86 n4, 88

St John-Brooks, C., 8, 9, 37–59
Salter, B. and Tapper, T., 244, 250, 255, 269
Sampson, G., 73
Sapin, C., 267 n5
Sarage and Griffiths, 172

Scarfe, N.V., 106
Scarth, J., 11, 207–27
Schiff, H., 77, 88
Schools Council, 11, 14, 38, 58, 104, 107, 108, 109, 124, 125, 130, 224 n2, 227, 237, 238
Schutz, A., 58
Scott, M., 153, 169
Segal, L., 167, 169
Selby-Biggs, 85, 255
Shakespeare, W., 47–8, 131
Sharp, R. and Green, A., 9, 14, 58, 108, 113–15, 123, 125, 225 n13, 226 n14, 227
Sharpe, S., 172, 182, 191
Shaw, D., 239, 250
Shaw, D.M. and Reeve, J.M., 108, 124, 125
Shaw, R., 146–7 n6
Shayer, D., 65, 77, 78, 79, 81, 88
Silbermann, M.L., 195, 206
Silver, H., 255, 269
 see also Mansell and Silver
Simon, B.
 see Benn and Simon
Simon, B. and Willcocks, J., 108
Simpson, P., 68–9
Smith, C.H., 231–2, 234, 248 n5
Smith, F., 146 n4
Smith, L.E.W., 88
Smith, N., 71
Snyder, B., 195, 206
Spalding, 93
Spender, D., 182, 189, 191
Spens Report, 224 n3, 226
 see also Consultative Committee on Education
SSEC (Secondary Schools Examination Council), 227, 229, 250
Stenhouse, L., 3, 14
Stevens, A., 239, 250
Stones, E., 224 n4, 227
Straughan, R. and Wrigley, J., 146 n4
Strauss, A.
 see Bucher and Strauss
Stray, C., 73, 80, 88
Strong, F.R.
 see Hilsum and Strong
Sutcliff, R., 49

Tapper, T.
 see Salter and Tapper
Taylor, C., 40, 58
Taylor, R., 143

Thomas, P.R., 97, 100, 106
Thompson, D., 86 n7
Tickle, L., 9, 107–25
Times Educational Supplement, The,
   70–1, 81–2, 224 n8, 227, 239–40, 247
   n1, 248 n15, 249 n21, n22 and n26, 250
*Times Higher Education Supplement,
   The*, 247 n1
Torrance, H., 218, 227, 248 n4
Torrance, P., 107, 125
Turner, G., 11, 195–206, 227
Turner, R., 262, 269
Turpie, L., 266 n1
TWYLREB, 231, 234, 246, 248 n5
Tyler, R.W., 4, 14
Tyndale, W., 267 n15

UCLES (University of Cambridge Local
   Examinations Syllabus), 231, 232, 250
ULSED (University of London School
   Examinations Department), 232, 250
University of Cambridge, 224 n3, 225
   n8, 227
University of London, 106
Unstead, J.F., 93, 100, 106
Useem, M.
   see Di Maggio and Useem

Vickerman, C., 267 n4

Walker, S.
   see Barton and Walker
Ward, C. and Fyson, A., 99–100, 106
Waring, M., 63, 88
Weber, M., 38–9, 58, 61
Weinberg, M.
   see Rubington and Weinberg
Weinstock, A., 239, 242, 244, 250
Wheeler, K.S., 100, 106
White, J., 85, 86 n6, 88
Whitfield, R.C., 153, 169
Whitty, G., 6, 7, 14, 207–8, 218, 220–1,
   222, 227, 250
   see also Bowe and Whitty
Whitty, G. and Young, M.F.D.,14
Wiener, M.J., 244, 250
Willcocks, J.
   see Simon and Willcocks
Williams, M., 91, 92, 106
Williams, R., 1, 14, 57 n1, 58, 243, 250
Willis, P., 55, 181, 191, 222, 227
Wise, M.J., 96, 106
Witkin, R.W., 139, 146 n6, 147 n10
Wolff, J., 109, 125
Wood, R. and Gipps, C., 257, 269
Woodhead, C., 137, 147 n7
Woods, P., 12, 36, 38, 57 n9, 58, 87, 154,
   169, 197, 206, 223, 227
   see also Measor and Woods
Woods, P. and Hammersley, M., 206
Wooldridge, S.W. and Hotchings, G.E.,
   96, 106
Wrigley, J.
   see Straughan and Wrigley

Young, M.F.D., 3, 4, 5, 6, 14, 37, 58, 59,
   61, 87, 88, 146 n2, 221–2, 227, 239,
   250
   see also Whitty and Young

Zeldin, T., 252, 269

Subject Index

accountability, 7, 10–12, 195–269
aesthetic learning, 127–47
APU (Assessment of Performance Unit), 2, 85, 257, 265
art appreciation, 127–47
art and design education, 9, 107–25, 127–47
art teaching
  see art and design education
assessment, 2, 7, 10–12, 195–269
  see also examinations

Baccalauréat, 259, 261–2, 268 n22 and n33
BEC (Business Education Council) courses, 17–36
Black Papers, 2, 13, 236, 237, 240
Board of Education, 64, 72–80, 83, 84, 85, 86 n6, 255
Boyson, Rhodes, 240
Bullock Committee, 82
bureaucratization, 38–9
  see also centralization
business departments and English teaching, 17–36

Carlisle, Mark, 239
centralization, 2, 12, 234, 251–69
  see also bureaucratization; decentralization
child care teaching, 10, 151–69
City and Guilds courses, 17–36
Cockcroft Committee, 248 n15, 249 n26
communications curricula, 17–36
comprehensive schools, 1–2, 4, 8, 10, 11, 37–59, 98, 127, 130, 154–69, 171–91, 195–206, 207–27
corporate management and educational administration, 251–69
creativity
  and art and design education, 106–25
CSE (Certificate of Secondary Education) examinations, 1, 11, 42, 57 n5, 86 n5 and n6, 153, 156–8, 196–202, 207–27, 229–50, 255
  see also examinations; GCE examinations
cultural capital, 6–7, 8, 9, 12, 37–59, 128, 136–7
curriculum, *passim*
  and assessment, 251–69
  evaluation 2, 3
  and examinations, 1, 2, 6, 7, 10–12, 17–36, 39, 73–80, 158, 195–206, 207–27, 229–50, 251–69
  and gender, 7, 9–10, 151–91
  'hidden', 7, 11, 195–206
  innovation and the, 6, 11, 217–23
  and labour movement, 245–7
  and personal development, 107–25
  and social interaction, 61–88
  see also school subjects; [and entries under individual subjects]
Curriculum Council, 255

decentralization
  and assessment, 12, 251–69
  see also centralization

DES (Department of Education and Science), 2, 39, 64, 85, 102, 243, 256, 257, 258, 267 n11
design education
  see art and design education
deviant activities, 11, 178–9, 184–6, 195–6, 198, 205, 215–16
domestic science, 10, 171–91

education, *passim*
  see also curriculum
England
  curriculum in, *passim*
  education system in, 12, 251–69
English Association, 64, 66–73, 74–80, 83, 84, 85, 86 n4
English teaching, 8, 9, 17–36, 37–59,

278

Subject Index

61–88, 131, 137, 219 history of, 61–88
environmental studies, 8, 89–106
Equal Opportunities Commission, 151
evaluation
see curriculum, evaluation of; process evaluation; product evaluation
examinations, 1, 2, 6, 7, 10–12, 17–36, 39, 73–80, 158, 195–269
and innovation, 217–19
see also assessment
Examinations Council, 2, 255

feminism
see gender
Ford Teaching Project, 3
France
education system in, 12, 251–69
further education, 8, 17–36

GCE (General Certificate of Education), 1, 11, 17, 20, 22, 86 n5, 104, 153, 156–8, 207–27, 229–50, 267 n11
see also CSE; examinations
gender
and the curriculum, 7, 9–10, 47, 76–7, 86 n5, 151–91
Geographical Association, 89, 92, 93, 99, 101
geography teaching, 8–9, 89–106
Great Debate, 2, 39, 224 n6, 236, 237–40, 242, 244, 249 n25, 267 n4

Haby, M., 262, 264
HMI (Her Majesty's Inspectorate), 2, 98, 151, 171–3, 190 n1
Humanities Curriculum Project, 2

integrated studies, 2, 8–9, 89–106

Joseph, Sir Keith, 152, 239, 246, 247 n2, 249 n26

Keele Integrated Studies Project, 2

learning
theories of, 139–46, 172
LEAs (local education authorities), 2, 234, 255–6, 267 n16
life skills, 8, 30–2, 33, 34
see also skills

methods
of teaching
see teaching styles
Ministère de l'Education, 259, 260, 264
Mode 1 examinations, 197, 218, 230, 231, 232, 233, 234, 237, 243, 247–8 n3
Mode 2 examinations, 247 n3
Mode 3 examinations, 11–12, 197, 211, 218, 220, 229–50, 255
Modern Languages Association, 74–5
MSC (Manpower Services Commission), 39, 247 n1

neo-Marxism, 241–3
'new, maths', 1
Newbolt Committee, 80, 84
North America, 3
Nuffield Science Project, 1, 63, 173, 175

options
choice of, 10, 151–69
orientation, 262–4

personal development
and English teaching, 37–59
physical science, 10, 171–91
see also science teaching
process evaluation, 251–69
see also curriculum, evaluation of
product evaluation, 251–69
see also curriculum, evaluation of
pupils' attitudes
and examination preparation, 195–206
and gender, 151–91

rationalism, 8, 38–59
romanticism, 8, 38–59
RSA (Royal Society of Arts) courses, 17–36

SAFARI, 3
school subjects, 5, 7–9, 17–147, 151–69, 171–91 and examinations, 195–206, 207–27, 229–50
see also (entries under individual subjects)
school-based examination work, 207–27, 229–50, 251–69
Schools Council, 2, 84, 103, 143, 161, 246, 247 n2, 251, 255, 267 n11
Schools Council Industry Project, 249 n24
science teaching, 1, 10, 63, 171–91
Sex Discrimination Act, 151
sex roles, 151–69, 171–191

Subject Index

see also gender
16+
  examinations at, 229–50, 255, 256, 258, 261
skills
  and education, 37–59
  teaching of, 107–25, 131
  see also life skills
social class, 8, 9, 55–6, 154, 159
social interaction model
  of curriculum change, 61–88
social studies, 89–106
sociology
  and the curriculum, 3–7, 61–88
  of education, 3–7, 11, 61–88, 221–3, 230, 245–7
SSRC (Social Science Research Council), 8, 35 n1, 254, 267 n7
subject sub-cultures, 37–59
subjects
  in the curriculum
  see school subjects

Sweden
  curriculum in, 168

teachers
  and examinations, 195–269
  and school subjects, 17–147
  and self-evaluation, 211–12, 220, 225 n12
teaching styles, 8, 17–36, 37–59, 107–25, 132–47, 186–9, 195–206, 210–16, 220–3
TEC (Technician Education Council) courses, 17–36
technical departments
  and English teaching, 17–36
Tyndale, William, 237–8

universities
  and examinations, 229–50, 258
Versions of English Project, 8, 17–36
vocational courses
  and English teaching, 17–36